A Southern Underground Railroad

CARL & SALLY GABLE FUND
for Southern Colonial American History

EARLY
AMERICAN
PLACES

A Southern
Underground Railroad

*Black Georgians and
the Promise of Spanish Florida
and Indian Country*

PAUL M. PRESSLY

The University of Georgia Press
ATHENS

© 2024 by the University of Georgia Press
Athens, Georgia 30602
www.ugapress.org
All rights reserved

Set in 10.5/13.5 Adobe Calson Pro Regular
by Kaelin Chappell Broaddus

Most University of Georgia Press titles are
available from popular e-book vendors.

Printed digitally

Library of Congress Cataloging-in-Publication Data

Names: Pressly, Paul M., author.
Title: A Southern Underground Railroad : Black Georgians and the promise of
Spanish Florida and Indian country / Paul M. Pressly.
Other titles: Black Georgians and the promise
of Spanish Florida and Indian country
Description: Athens : The University of Georgia Press, [2024] |
Series: Early American places |
Includes bibliographical references and index.
Identifiers: LCCN 2023057782 | ISBN 9780820366326 (hardback) |
ISBN 9780820366852 (paperback) | ISBN 9780820366869 (epub) |
ISBN 9780820366876 (pdf)
Subjects: LCSH: Fugitive slaves—Georgia—History. |
Fugitive slaves—Florida—History. | African Americans—Relations with Indians. |
Seminole Indians—Florida. | Creek Indians—Georgia. |
Florida—History—Spanish colony, 1784-1821. |
Georgia—History—1775-1865.
Classification: LCC E450 .P75 2024 | DDC 306.3/6209758—dc23/eng/20240404
LC record available at https://lccn.loc.gov/2023057782

For Jane

And for John C. Inscoe,
devoted teacher and passionate scholar
of Southern history

CONTENTS

ILLUSTRATIONS

Maps

Figures

ACKNOWLEDGMENTS

The long journey in creating this book began with my role in mounting a symposium on African American life and culture on the Georgia coast and in assisting Philip D. Morgan in editing the resulting material for a book. This grand enterprise gave me the chance to work with historians Jacqueline Jones, Michael Gomez, Erskine Clarke, Betty Wood, and Vincent Carretta. In a subsequent symposium on the environmental history of coastal Georgia, Paul Sutter gave me an incomparable lesson in editing the papers for yet another book. One participant, Tiya Miles, offered her encouragement and direction in how to approach the question of Black resistance.

The research for my book *On the Rim of the Caribbean: Colonial Georgia and the British Atlantic World* (University of Georgia Press, 2013) brought to the surface ample material for studying the topic of Black resistance from a Black perspective. It was another matter to piece together the bits and pieces of information found in multiple archives, primarily in the Georgia Archives in Morrow, the Hargrett Library at the University of Georgia, the Georgia Historical Society, and the extensive East Florida Papers left by the Spanish government, now in the Library of Congress. A windfall came in December 2021 when the 65,000 documents constituting the East Florida Papers were placed online. The person to whom I am most indebted is Jane Landers, whose voluminous studies of Black society in Spanish Florida have long set a standard for those looking at the Spanish Caribbean. Her work provided a constant source of inspiration while her review of my writing kept me focused on the main thesis. In addition, Jim Cusick, curator of the P. K. Yonge Library of Florida history at the University of Florida, provided timely advice.

The turning point in the final stages of putting together the manuscript came with my participation in a "Coffee House" in the spring of 2021, a creative idea of the Omohundro Institute in response to the pandemic. Twelve scholars met via Zoom under the direction of Simon Newman, professor emeritus of the University of Glasgow. The discussions forced me to rethink my approach to the motivation of freedom seekers, the reality of archival silence, and the limits to the use of historical imagination.

I owe a special debt of gratitude to Kevin Kokomoor of East Carolina College who read my chapter on the Creek war captives.

I thank the staff of the Georgia Historical Society, especially Todd Groce, president, and Stan Deaton, senior historian, for their constant support over a lengthy period. At the same time, the staff at a long list of institutions enabled the research to unfold in relatively smooth fashion, the pandemic not withstanding: the Georgia Archives in Morrow; the Hargrett Rare Book and Manuscript Library, University of Georgia Libraries; the George A. Smathers Libraries at the University of Florida; the Historical Society of Pennsylvania; the William L. Clements Library, University of Michigan; the Library of Congress at College Park; and the National Archives and Records Administration in Washington and Atlanta.

Elizabeth DuBose, executive director of The Ossabaw Island Foundation, and Robin Gunn, project coordinator, were instrumental in helping me delineate the role of the island as a seedbed of freedom seekers in the late eighteenth century. As director of the Ossabaw Island Education Alliance (a consortium of the Georgia Board of Regents, Department of Natural Resources, and the foundation), I spent time researching the life of African Americans from their arrival on the island in the 1760s to their creation of a descendant community at Pinpoint, five miles away on the mainland, in the 1890s.

I owe special thanks to the staff of the University of Georgia Press, with whom I have worked for over fifteen years. Lisa Bayer, the director, has set the press onto a firm path of balanced growth while playing a major role in the world of academic presses nationally. Nathaniel Holly, my editor, was instrumental in raising pertinent questions and honing the text.

My debt extends to historians Erskine Clarke and John Inscoe for their continuing advice and unfailing graciousness. John has been influential at every turn in my work as an independent scholar since the 1990s. It is with gratitude that I dedicate this book to him.

FOREWORD

Flights to freedom are among the most compelling stories in American history. From Hannah Dunston's 1697 self-liberation to the Abenaki to David Ogden's escape from the Iroquois in 1781; from Harriet Tubman's trek to freedom to *Afromexicanos* who took shelter in independent Mexico; even from Yaqui fugitives escaping Mexican extermination among kindred in Arizona to Dull Knife's Cheyenne Outbreak of 1874, we sense the universality of a desire to command one's own life story.

Yet seldom do we hear tales of enslavement and emancipation that combine American Indians and African Americans in the same pages. Looking to the Deep South during the Revolutionary and Early Republic eras, Paul Pressly brings us the fascinating story of a multi-faceted Southern Underground Railroad that destabilizes simpler narratives about the institution of racial slavery in the Old South. Opening with the surreptitious journey of a fugitive-packed twenty-foot yawl that slipped away from Ossabaw Island in 1781, and extending as far west as Indian Territory, Pressly's little-known Southern variant of routes to freedom offers a vivid new narrative on the universal human urge to self-determination. Dr. Pressly, of course, is the ideal writer to bring us this story. Long-time director of the Ossabaw Island Education Alliance and award-winning historian who is deeply immersed in the landscape, cultures, and archives of the early South, his skill for enlivening critical turning points and characters is evident on every page.

Pressly's keen eye for the telling detail makes clear the protean nature of a colonial society where, we might assume, incorrectly, that race was one of the more stable categories. In early Savannah's cobblestone streets and signature squares, premised on the prohibition of enslavement, a visitor might see free people of color, enslaved Black people, even enslaved Indians under the power of Native trading elites like Coweta-born Mary Musgrove. From its very inception, the anti-slavery colony of Georgia, with founding Governor Oglethorpe's explicit endorsement, engaged in the Indian slave trade as the big bills of exchange for a reciprocating market in gunpowder, lead, muskets, rum, and the finely tanned deer skins to produce the butter-soft riding pants prized by English Gentry. The Caribbean export trade in Indian slaves, however, once the engine of wealth production in early Carolina, dwindled as importation of African slaves was approved by the Trustees in 1750.

From the opening days of the Seven Year's War (1756–63) to the American war for independence, through the rise and fall of the William Bowles and his strikingly multi-racial United Nations of the Creeks and Cherokees (1799–1803) into the era of Indian expulsions (1814–38) that followed the Creek War, Pressly shares the complexities of relations between self-emancipating enslaved folks from the coastal rice and henequen plantations and expanding cotton frontier, and the Creek and Seminole peoples to the west and south. Freedom-seeking Black people from the Sea Islands might head for British-held Florida (1763–83), which offered them independence in return for military service, an extension of Spain's earlier strategy of employing fugitive Black escapees as frontier militia to counter British designs on Castillo San Augustine.

Or they might also head for Indian Country, where divergent cultural developments would shape their lives. In northeast Florida, Indigenous peoples reconstituted from tribes shattered in colonial wars were coalescing in the stronghold of Alachua Prairie as the Seminole Nation, receptive in its own multi-ethnic diversity to the incorporation of Black people as affines and kinfolk. The emergence, however, of Native creoles or mestizos, often the mixed-descent offspring of British, Spanish, or French traders married into Lower Creek matrilines, cultivated as class-allies by American agents like Henry Knox and Benjamin Hawkins, would solidify the primacy of a Euro-Indigenous Planter Class under the leadership of elite men like Sam Moniac, Lachlan McGilvray, and William McIntosh. From these latter would evolve the White Stick opposition to Tecumseh's revolutionary movement to unite the Indian tribes of the cis-Mississippi frontier.

The Creek War ended in 1814 at Tohopeka, or Horseshoe Bend, with Andrew Jackson's annihilation of Menawa's Red Stick coalition, and the long era of contingency, in which Black people and Indians alike experimented with freedom and alliance, ended. Territorial status opened the floodgates to settlers and land speculators alike, while Creeks, Choctaws, and Chickasaws suffered deportation (the wealthy among them marching their enslaved with them as capital-on-foot). The Plantation Era celebrated by films like *Gone with the Wind* would last a mere generation, yet in the deeps of Florida's multi-racial maroon communities, in the Gullah communities of the Sea Islands, and in Indian Territory, the complex legacy of the Black and Indigenous drive for independence survived to take new forms. Paul Pressly has re-envisioned both the birthplace and the early foundations of freedom-and-justice seeking in the United States, and we are the beneficiaries.

James Brooks

A Southern
Underground Railroad

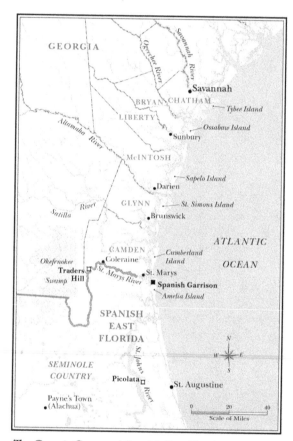

The Georgia Coast and Spanish East Florida, circa 1795

INTRODUCTION

On a humid evening in 1781, nine people gathered at a dock on Ossabaw Island, twenty miles south of Savannah, to peer at a twenty-foot yawl recently covered with pitch, and dream a dream that a husband and wife had long entertained. The five adults proposed to put their four children and themselves into the small vessel and set out for St. Augustine, the tiny capital of British East Florida, one hundred miles away. They were leaving behind over one hundred acquaintances on three plantations, enslaved people who cultivated indigo, raised cattle, grew provisions for Savannah, and cut live oaks to build transatlantic ships on this seemingly isolated barrier island. If the British invasion of Georgia two years earlier had brought a mass exodus of slaves from their settlements in and around Savannah, the people on these Morel plantations had remained in place and continued life much as they had since the island was settled twenty years before.[1]

Betty and Hercules, one born in South Carolina, the other in Angola, had been laying plans to escape with their sons, Prince and Winter, for several months.[2] Far from allowing themselves to be frustrated by an earlier failed attempt, the two began thinking more boldly and brought into their plot another family, Jupiter and Auba and their two children, as well as Jack, a single person in his forties, also from Angola. They chose the only accessible vessel, a yawl with four oars and one small sail that Hercules had helped build for the Morels, three brothers whose father had purchased the island and left each with a plantation. The idea of going well over a hundred miles in a twenty-foot yawl, designed for short distances, overloaded with nine people, spoke to the strength of their beliefs.[3] It was a leap of faith.

In a remarkable feat of seamanship, Hercules piloted the boat to East Florida without incident. Once there, the squat, strongly built man placed himself and his family under the protection of one of the most powerful and capable British officers in the province, Col. Thomas Brown, commander of the King's Rangers during the Siege of Savannah in 1779.[4] Jupiter, Auba, and Jack chose another route. According to a notice placed in the *Gazette of Georgia* in 1785, "[They went up] among the Indians from St. Augustine and have not been heard of since." Jupiter and family knowingly chose to carve out a life for themselves among the Seminoles and to live in a society where they would enjoy relative autonomy and a measure of respect in return for an annual tribute from their crops.[5]

The choices facing Georgia and Carolina slaves in the East Florida capital were limited. During the remaining years of the eighteenth century, at least thirty-one other enslaved people from the Morel holdings or nearby plantations made for the St. Marys River, the boundary between the state and the Spanish colony, in the hopes of securing their freedom.[6] They had good reason. At the end of the Revolution, Spain had regained sovereignty over its old colony of Florida, founded in 1565 and lost to the British in 1763. The Crown did not hesitate to resume its former policy of offering asylum to fugitives from English-speaking territories who converted to Catholicism. Rooted in medieval and Roman law, the Spanish judicial system recognized a legal personality in enslaved people as well as freemen, while Spanish society showed a sensibility in matters of race and freedom that was radically different from that of Anglo Americans.

Those Morel plantation–based slaves were not following an idiosyncratic path. In prerevolutionary times, Carolina freedom seekers had sought out St. Augustine and been a staunch ally of the Spanish. The movement all but stopped when the British seized East Florida but resumed with the outbreak of the War of Independence. From the beginning of the American Revolution to the eve of the First Seminole War in 1817, hundreds and eventually thousands of Africans and African Americans in Georgia, and to a lesser extent South Carolina, crossed the borders and boundaries that separated the Lowcountry from the British and Spanish in coastal Florida and from the Seminole and Creek people in the vast interior of the Southeast. Even in times of relative peace, there remained a steady flow of individuals moving south and southwest, reflecting the aspirations of a captive people.

In recent years, scholars have been reconceptualizing the geography of freedom in America during the time of slavery. Perhaps no period has received greater attention than the Age of Revolutions, when thousands of Black people crossed borders, boundaries, and frontiers in North America, Hispaniola, and the British and French Caribbean, with many heading to Canada, England, continental Europe, and Africa in the quest for liberty.[7] The renewal of scholarship on the Underground Railroad and the Fugitive Slave Law has likewise extended attention to areas beyond the United States, first and foremost Canada but increasingly Mexico, the British Caribbean, and Indian lands to the west. By the 1830s, crossing the borders of the United States offered the possibility of formal freedom recognized in law as opposed to the semiformal freedoms that fugitives gained in northern towns where their status remained ambiguous or in the informal freedoms found in southern towns where it was possible, but highly risky, to pass oneself off as a free Black person.[8] In this outpouring of work, one area has been neglected: the movement of freedom seekers in the Southeast from the Revolution to the end of the First Seminole War.

Throughout this period, movement was an essential characteristic of life along the coast, a precursor of the phenomenon known as the Underground Railroad. The actual numbers did not approach the volume of people leaving the Upper South between 1830 and 1860, estimated at somewhere between one thousand and five thousand per year in a population that approached four million in 1860.[9] But the American Revolution in Georgia had opened vistas to people of color who discovered something of the geography of the coast, whether through escaping, at least for a time, or being rudely dislocated from their plantations as patriots and loyalists fought over them as the spoils of war. The creation of a fictive state by a British-backed adventurer in Seminole country in 1800 and the multiple conflicts associated with the War of 1812 provided additional opportunities. Between these major events, there was a steady flow of freedom seekers attracted to Spanish Florida even after the official policy of sanctuary ended in 1790. The tolerance for fugitive slaves combined with a short-handed government to create a relatively welcoming space.

Nor were fugitive slaves the only Black people crossing the borders, a reality that makes the Southeast unlike any other region of the United States. The various movements included all those who were not part of the quest for freedom: war captives whom Creeks and Seminoles seized during the Revolution or in sporadic raids in the years thereafter; Black people purchased directly by Natives, never a large number but still part of the diversity of people of African descent who found themselves in Lower Creek or Seminole towns; those who were kidnapped by outlaws on both sides of the St. Marys River to be sold in another polity; those who were carried across boundaries by enslavers at the end of the Revolution; and those brought by planters escaping debt in Georgia in 1791–1793, a surprising one thousand people. Nor can one neglect the significant flow of Black people into Georgia during the early 1780s, when loyalist planters sold their enslaved people to gain liquidity for their move to another colony of the empire, while others decided to return to the new state as the best of all the options. Several captives fled to become members of one of the largest and longest-lived maroon communities in the history of the United States; others escaped back to Florida, contributing to the rich mosaic of crossings.[10]

Too often, coastal Georgia is seen as a backwater region where enslaved people existed in a deeply isolated space on barrier islands or coastal plantations, a world that was overwhelmingly Black and where customs and traditions brought from Africa were preserved until the mid-twentieth century. Indeed, the Gullah Geechee people evolved a unique culture with deep African retentions that are clearly visible in their distinctive language, arts, crafts, foodways, and music. The image, however, needs considerable amending. The Africans and African Americans on the coast of Georgia resisted slavery with all their might, and hundreds and eventually thousands took the chance and made their way to other lands. Far from being cut off and ignorant of the flow of events and ideas in the Atlantic world, they became participants in the great struggle over who would prevail in the Southeast, leaving traces that were picked up and mirrored several decades later in the Underground Railroad.[11] Although no network of hardy "conductors" existed, and individuals or groups crossed borders on their own initiative, the commitment of these freedom seekers to self-emancipation was every bit as significant.

Who were these people willing to risk leaving behind family and friends and make a break for distant lands where the outcomes were uncertain? Most fugitives originated in the small number of counties bordering the Georgia coast, a strip of land already integrated into the Atlantic world through the rice and deerskin trade with Britain and the timber and livestock trade with the Caribbean. The Treaty of Paris in 1783 had created an anomalous situation when, by the terms of the treaty, it paired the state of Georgia, whose population was growing at a rapid rate, with Spanish East Florida, whose population was many times smaller and relatively static, a modest military colony little more than a northern outpost of a struggling Spanish Empire.

Few captives on coastal plantations decided to escape alone. The odds of making it by water or overland through wetlands or along the few paths or roads were long. Most escaped in groups, often in families, with women frequently present. They faced daunting odds. Crossing boundaries required a plan, indeed a sophisticated plan to navigate the challenges. For much of the period, boats or canoes had to be secured; supplies had to be accumulated, including water, food, clothing, and sometimes a gun; a waterman needed to be part of the escaping party; and tides and ocean currents had to be calculated. If one headed to Seminole or Creek territory, one had to discover Indian trails and paths and be ready to confront Indigenous people whose reception might be less than friendly.

Most succeeded in escaping by crossing the St. Marys River or Cumberland Sound at the entrance to the Atlantic Ocean. Only a few hundred yards wide at its widest point, the modest river separated the two polities and became an international border of consequence. The boundary between Florida and Georgia mirrored the deep political, religious, and cultural divides in this multicultural region and the many cross-currents that regularly swept through it. The river extended to the Okefenokee Swamp, turned south, and then looped northward, offering an ideal terrain for horse and cattle thieves, adventurers, men seeking to escape their debts, Black people in search of freedom, and Creeks and Seminoles who on occasion rode down the river systems of both territories to raid for cattle and slaves.[12]

Indeed, the area from the Altamaha River to the St. Johns River in Florida, a seventy-mile stretch of wetlands, savannas, grasslands, and pine forests, represented a borderland characterized by a disconcerting vacuum of power. Neither the Americans nor the Spanish were in full control of an of a lightly populated area on both sides of the border that attracted people looking to take advantage of the relative absence of state power. Native Americans continued to assert their undeniable claims to sovereignty. Over the decades, this region represented as much a process as a place, one where African Americans found a constantly changing set of circumstances.

Escaping across these borders demanded a substantially different set of calculations than the flight into the swamp and woods surrounding coastal plantations that others undertook, whether to see family, seek a time-out from a harsh work routine, or become a maroon seeking autonomy in a hidden landscape. The planning more nearly foreshadowed the planning involved in finding boats and watermen to cross the Ohio River or using the railroad system from Maryland to Pennsylvania during the 1840s and 1850s. Scholars have now broadened our understanding of the Underground Railroad to free it from the romanticized tale of conductors operating an inter-connected system full of codes, tunnels, and hidden messages in which al-lies, white and Black, guided the process. The role of white abolitionists and free Blacks must be understood in more modest terms as scholars bring forward the determination and risk-taking of the fugitives themselves. The bravery, fearlessness, and willingness to face daunting odds were found in both periods.

However, the similarities in the motives and roles of fugitives between the two periods can take us only so far. The stories of the lives of fugitives from the Georgia Lowcountry illustrate a larger and more fundamental truth. The movement of people of color across borders and boundaries over a long pe-riod of time was an integral part of the sustained struggle for dominance in the Southeast, not only among the Great Powers but also among the many different groups of people that inhabited the region and contended for power. Prominent were the Creeks of the Upper and Lower Towns, the Ala-chua and Mikasuki Seminoles, Spanish colonists, British imperialists, ad-venturers and freebooters of all nationalities, expansion-minded American settlers, Africans, and African Americans. Through this diverse mixture of communities, the Atlantic world laid special claim to this part of the North American mainland, a claim that lost none of its force through the 1810s.

Historian Elijah Gould reminds us that no European power posed a greater threat to the new American Republic or cast in sharper relief the post-independence vulnerability to foreign powers than Spain.[13] Its empire on the North American continent stretched from Upper California to the Florida Keys and enabled the Spanish during the later 1780s and early 1790s to intervene in the affairs of the United States in multiple ways: providing sanctuary to escaped slaves in Florida, refusing to allow Anglo-American farms to ship goods through New Orleans, and encouraging secessionist talk among disaffected settlers in Kentucky and Tennessee. Even after it ended the policy of offering sanctuary to escaped slaves in 1790 and opened the Mississippi to American trade, Spanish America still remained important to the story of people of African descent.

Over a long and productive career, historian Jane Landers has pulled from obscurity the vitality and richness of Black life during the Second Spanish Period (1784–1821) and re-created a lost world where Black women could be litigants in court, Black entrepreneurs carved a niche for themselves in St. Augustine, Black couples married in the Catholic church, and a Black mi-litia evolved into the most reliable pillar of defense outside St. Augustine. The "Atlantic creole," that African who crossed many countries and kingdoms in a lifetime, spoke several languages, and was willing to take great risks to achieve a measure of freedom, thrived in this setting that eventually pitted Black Georgians fighting white Georgians.[14] Fugitives from Georgia and South Carolina formed the backbone of the Free Black militia that became an essential prop of the Spanish government and hence a key player in the balance of power in the Southeast. White Georgians raged at "the vilest species of troops" on their doorsteps and the example being set for their own captives.[15]

When Spain repealed its policy of sanctuary in 1790, benefits still accrued to Black residents of East Florida, and the colony remained a destination for fugitives. But a growing number headed for the towns of the Seminole Indians on the Alachua Prairie in the east or to the Mikasukis near the Apalachicola River in the northwest of Florida. The Seminoles had coalesced into a society that remained open and inclusive, capable of absorbing a range of people that included Ochese Creeks from what later became central Georgia, Mikasuki speakers from among the Lower Creeks, Upper Creek refugees expelled from their towns for various misdeeds, Yuchis, and "Spanish Indians," Natives who had intermarried with Cubans and worked on fishing boats along the Gulf Coast. Drawing on earlier notions of captivity, we can see a remarkably pluralistic society in which African Americans found a place that offered more freedom, respect, and opportunities than in any other society in North America at that time. In this unique setting, Black freedom seekers became an even more significant factor in the constantly shifting balance of power in the Southeast. They evolved from cultural brokers and interpreters to occasional fighters alongside bands of warriors to Black Seminoles fighting together as a unit.[16]

The Creek Nation had a more problematic relationship with Black people on the Georgia coast because of the infusion of war captives and those purchased during the Revolution and immediately afterward. The Creeks in the Lower and Upper Towns held most African Americans in some form of captivity that ranged from absolute servitude to required light labor to the possibility of achieving freedom through incorporation into a clan or family. Although many were war captives taken by raiding parties, Black people still made their own way to the Indian towns along the Chattahoochee and Flint Rivers. That decision posed a more equivocal choice than heading to East Florida, where a white man's culture held sway and the markers were easier to understand. To go from a coastal plantation to a Native town was to face a radically different culture, different expectations, different ways of communicating, and unknown outcomes.[17] Whether as captives or as free actors, Black people played a minor but distinct role in confronting white settlers pushing the boundaries of Georgia beyond the Oconee and Altamaha Rivers.

A study of this scale and covering this length of time requires choices. The first is focusing on the lives of a handful of people whose careers throw light on the geopolitical landscape as well as on how individual decisions were made. The narratives of individuals like Titus and Nelly, John Peter, Mahomet, Hercules and Betty, Nancy, and Ned Simmons allow the reader to dive beneath the surface and explore the many dimensions in making an escape and in understanding the types of power arrayed against these freedom seekers. The story of Black Georgians in Indian country poses a special challenge for scholars given the paucity of sources. The claims for compensation for "war captives" by coastal planters provide a valuable and underused resource. The career of a Scots-Indian named John Kinnard on Kinchafoonee Creek offers an exceptional window for assessing the collective experience of men and women like Pompey and Betsy—who were captured, purchased, and maybe escaped—and how they influenced relations between the United States and the Creek confederacy.

This epic story constitutes a powerful counter-narrative to American history, a tale of how Black people found freedom and human dignity not in Jefferson's Empire of Liberty but outside the expanding boundaries of the United States. The rise and fall in the numbers of freedom seekers between the Revolution and the First Seminole War serves as a potent reminder of the strength of Black resistance in the postrevolutionary South, a remarkable gauge of the depth of feeling and commitment that existed among all African Americans. Their constant movement across boundaries and borders, whether through flight or as unwilling captives, marked the closing act of a chaotic eighteenth century in which empires struggled for position and Native peoples resisted the relentless advance of empires and nations bent on eroding their lands and freedom. It is a powerful reminder that Africans and African Americans in the Georgia Lowcountry were far from an isolated people stuck on coastal plantations and cut off from the flow of news and ideas in the Atlantic world.

For the eighteenth century and the first fifteen years of the nineteenth, the enslaved population of coastal Georgia could nourish a realistic hope for a life beyond the chains of an enslaved existence. Much like those gaining freedom during the period of the Underground Railroad, the freedom seekers heading south were primary actors who emancipated themselves or failed by a hair's breadth in feats that showed an indomitable courage, a willingness to take high-level risks, and a dogged perseverance. In contrast to those in the Underground Railroad, enslaved people on the Georgia coast sought out the competing visions for the region's future offered by the many racial, ethnic, and religious groups in the Southeast and played a distinctive role in tilting the balance of power in the region, if only for a moment of time.[18] It is a little-known story that highlights the role of Black Georgians in knowing how to take advantage of the patchwork of identities and cultures in the Southeast to pursue their own aims and coincidentally stiffen resistance to the expansion of the United States.

CHAPTER 1

Black Sailors, Oglethorpe's Georgia, and Spanish Florida

Although poor, Savannah was a distinctive town in British North America. Only six years old in 1739, the settlement could boast a distinctive architectural grid with over six hundred inhabitants living in 140 houses placed around six spacious squares, with a guardhouse, a courthouse, a jail, a wharf, and a set of bailiffs, constables, and wardens to maintain order.[1] Within that time it had established itself as a significant urban center planted on the southernmost tip of the British Empire, a frontier settlement facing the Spanish in Florida, Native Americans in the interior, and the French advancing inland from New Orleans. The inhabitants were men and women of modest origins, artisans, "mechaniks" or skilled laborers, minor officials, a small number of shopkeepers, indentured servants, charity settlers, and a few "adventurers" who sensed opportunity. All major decisions about the life of the colony of Georgia were made in London by a trust of twenty-one men, typically philanthropists, "men of good birth," and Members of Parliament, or by James Oglethorpe, a wealthy visionary and the one trustee who came to the colony and acted as its virtual governor for the first decade of its life. Most distinctive was the prohibition of slavery in Georgia by executive fiat, then by an act of Parliament in 1735, making Georgia the only province in British North America or the Caribbean where this was so.[2]

Situated next to South Carolina, where Black people outnumbered whites by a two to one margin and where rice plantations dominated the economy, Savannah's mix of people seemed odd. No slave ships docked at the single wharf. No auctioning of human beings on the wharf or in back

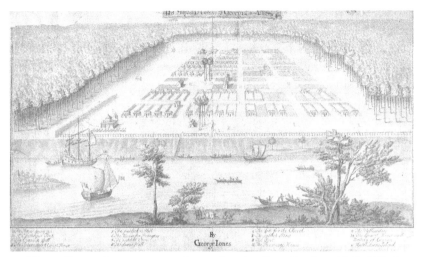

View of Savannah, 1734, an engraving attributed to Peter Gordon, chief bailiff of
the town. This image of the one-year-old settlement shows a grid of streets and
squares carefully planned out by James Oglethorpe. A set of stairs leads up to the
steep bluff from the river to four trees under which Oglethorpe's tent rests. Courtesy
of Hargrett Rare Book and Manuscript Library, University of Georgia Libraries.

streets took place. No slaves handled the heavy lifting required for the life of
the town. No Black women tended households. No barrels of rice stood on
the dock, and little agricultural produce was visible. For anyone coming from
across the Savannah River, it was a strange sight to step from a slave society where Black slaves outnumbered whites to a place that seemed like the
poorer quarters of an English town. For most observers, the story was an improbable one.[3] Driven by a philanthropic vision, Oglethorpe, John Perceval
(the first Earl of Egmont), and the other trustees had determined to create a
colony for the "middling poor" of England, a place for "decayed tradesmen,
or supernumerary workmen . . . who cannot put their hands to country affairs or are too proud to do it."[4] Slavery, the trustees believed, would depress
wages, stigmatize labor, and promote idleness among the very people they
intended to redeem, a choice dictated by practical considerations, not as a
matter of principle.[5] For the first nine years, the prohibition seems to have
remained in force, at least in and around Savannah.[6]

Creolization, or the merging of habits and practices from different European cultures to create something new, was much in evidence in Savannah during the 1730s.[7] By the end of the decade, the town was an extension
of the original vision of the "worthy poor," with a population of predominantly English-born people, middle-aged, characterized by a relatively flat

profile: laborers, carpenters, a former wigmaker, mariners, taverners, "victuallers," and artisans. But not entirely so. A significant Jewish group, mostly Sephardic, had arrived in several boatloads and by the end of the decade boasted twenty families.[8] Comparatively wealthy Lowland Scots came over determined to make a significant investment in agriculture and, when their indentured labor proved unreliable, moved to town and began lobbying for the removal of the ban on slavery. Italian families worked the Trustees' experimental garden; Germans operated the crane on the Savannah River; and Swiss settlers helped keep the cows across the river on Hutchinson Island.[9] Out of the cultural interactions across social class and ethnicity, a hybrid society was emerging, but it seemed to lack Africans.

Notwithstanding the clearly enunciated policy against slavery, people of African descent were never absent from a town catching its first breath and dependent on many forms of labor. A small number were always to be found around the single, crudely built wharf below the forty-foot bluff, handling the merchandise and supplies brought from Charles Town or Beaufort to keep the colony alive. Even if present for a short time, these sailors, both free and enslaved, brought attitudes and habits shaped by their roles in trading with the enemy at St. Augustine as well as their sailing throughout the British Caribbean into this tiny space, providing a window into the intercultural frontiers of the Southeast. Far from passive individuals, they were well aware of the geopolitical and social landscape, and the enslaved were ready to seize the moment when the time seemed ripe to make a break for the freedom offered by Spanish Florida to fugitives from British colonies.[10]

Despite the exclusion of enslaved Black people, local authorities could never seal off the town with its population of several hundred residents from contact with all Africans and African Americans. In the course of a year, dozens of small schooners and sloops eased in and out of the wharf, transporting supplies purchased with subsidies provided by Parliament. Most of the sailors were enslaved or free Black men skilled in maneuvering through coastal waters, carrying crops and timber from plantations along the Carolina coast to Charles Town and manufactured goods and supplies back again.[11] Seasoned veterans, they were a relatively closed community proud of their special standing, carriers of stories and news. As the century progressed, all-slave crews increasingly manned the river-going and coastal boats of South Carolina.[12]

The secretary of the Trustees, William Stephens, described for the Trustees how the challenge of Black sailors in an all-white community was met.

"Whenever any Vessel arrives here with Negroes," he explained, "during their Stay, the Slaves are permitted to come ashore on the Strand by the Water-Side, to boil their Kettle; but in case they come up into Town, they are liable to be seized."[13] Most seamen stayed under the bluff toward the eastern end where they carved out a place for themselves to eat and sleep, talk and share stories, and create their own temporary home. Surprisingly, perhaps, a Black man in Savannah was treated with more suspicion and contempt than in Charles Town.

Stephens's comment that they were likely to be seized should be treated with a degree of skepticism. A number made it into town for purchases or even socializing. The secretary went out of his way to assure London of the enforcement of the informal prohibition. He reported that a mariner named Peter Shepherd brought one of his slaves into his lodgings in town, tied him up, and whipped the man for "a Piece of Thievery on board . . ., which occasioned a great uproar among the Neighborhood."[14] Shepherd was instructed to take him back to South Carolina. Stephens mentioned another "Negro Slave" that belonged to a Mr. Dyson who died in Savannah. Dyson traveled back and forth between the two colonies and presumably allowed the sailor to stay in or around his living quarters. The magistrates took the Black man into custody until Oglethorpe could pronounce on the case. Without hesitation, the general ordered the sailor to be sold. Stephens opted for a public auction. Of the several bids received, the highest came from sea captain William Thompson, who sailed regularly to London. And so the man passed from one sea captain to another for £25, a competitive rate for enslaved sailors.[15]

Another type of boatmen congregated under the bluff. They were the hardy souls who rowed flat-bottomed periaguas filled with valuable deerskin from Augusta to Charles Town and then returned with British goods. Savannah was a stopping point for them, a way station for rest and nothing more. On the journey, a white patroon stood at the rudder while the rowers, typically four, performed their backbreaking labor facing the stern. Coming down the river may have taken a few days but going back against the current required four to five weeks. The crew slept along the banks in abandoned Indian villages or in the woods, living a rough-and-tumble existence in which isolation was a distinguishing feature.

The movement of Black people along the coast and on the rivers nourished a complex web of communication, as sailors and rowers exchanged information with the local population as well as each other. Black watermen carried news throughout the region. They were privy to the latest talk about the trade with Creeks and Cherokees. They were apprised of developments in both the white and Black communities in Charles Town. They picked up on happenings in this peculiar colony where people of African descent were kept to a minimum. Part of that conversation turned on stories about boatmen who escaped or tried to escape to Spanish Florida, whose government promised freedom and a better life. Sailors and rowers were critical to the spreading of news up and down the coast and into the interior.[16]

Black sailors may have drawn contempt when climbing up the bluff to gain access to town, but Savannah was too young a society, too raw, and too subject to sudden death and displacement to maintain the ties that undergirded a deferential social order. Self-interest dictated acceptance. That logic may explain why a mixed-race person could become the manager of the principal store offering trading goods from the West Indies. Capt. Caleb Davis was a sometime trader, privateer, and occasional pirate who operated from his base in Beaufort, South Carolina, kept a two-story house in St. Augustine where he regularly sold goods, and established the one store in Savannah that offered access to goods otherwise absent in this frontier community.[17]

In recognition of the military and political intelligence that the captain provided from his voyages to Florida, James Oglethorpe paid Davis the ultimate compliment of awarding him one of the best lots on the strand on top of the bluff overlooking the Savannah River below. The mariner built a store operated by his consort, a mixed-race enslaved person whom William Stephens described as having "an exceeding fine Shape and, setting aside her swarthy Countenance, might compare with [a] *European*." Here in a town where slavery was banned, Davis kept a Black consort for all to see and set her up as a shopkeeper selling goods brought from the Caribbean, her presence a testimony to the fluidity of social boundaries in a place of casual borders and blurred lines of authority. Echoing the ethos that prevailed in the Caribbean, Stephens dismissed Davis's relationship with this "mulatto Servant (or Slave)" as his most visible foible.[18]

There were good reasons for Davis's "mulatto Servant (or Slave)" to feel relatively secure in the context of Trusteeship Georgia. Women were little more than a third of the immigrants recorded between 1733 and 1741. Most came in family groups; death was ever-present; marriages often ended quickly; and cohabitation outside wedlock was a frequent occurrence. Tolerance for relationships that fell outside the European norm was high, creating opportunities for low-status women to marry above their rank in the Old World. Yet marriages were, in the words of historian Ben Marsh, irregular, distorted, and unconventional. Families became diffuse, ethnically mixed, and fragmentary. If a woman could not find a mate, she was exposed to the harsh economic realities of the time.[19]

Davis's confidence in his mistress confounded the discomforted secretary. The captain had taught her how to keep his books. "More astonishing," Stephens mused, "was that . . . he suffered almost every Thing to pass through her Hands, having such Confidence in her, that she had the Custody of all his Cash, as well as Books; and whenever he ordered any Parcel of Silver to be weighted out for any Use, whether it were two or three hundred ounces, more or less, in Dollars, she had the doing of it." The secretary could not refrain from speculating that the "Life of such Slavery was not a heavy burden upon her," the easy assumption of an Englishman who never tried to pierce the veil that hung over enslavement.[20] Yet he had a point. At least for a short while, the mistress was the access point for most Savannahians in obtaining goods from the Caribbean.

Nor was this unnamed woman a simple object of convenience for the captain. William Stephens, Cambridge-educated and once a member of Parliament, referred to her as "this Damsel" and "Madam," willing to accord her a certain standing. "She had Art enough," he judged, "to shew, [that] all Persons who had any Business with Captain Davis, were expected not to treat her with Contempt." A shipwright failed that test. Mr. Pope, whom Stephens described as a "rough Tar," built vessels at Beaufort and sailed with Davis when not otherwise occupied. When Pope walked into the store and let fly a volley of insults, she fired back with a stream of expletives all her own that outdid his. Taken aback, he hit her in the face and stormed out. When Davis heard of the affair, presumably from his consort, he discharged Pope as master of the vessel being loaded in the river for a destination in the Caribbean. Pope rallied a portion of the crew and took the vessel down the Savannah River for the open sea, but Davis declared them pirates and used his influence with Oglethorpe to have the vessel seized. Although the matter ended up before the colony's magistrates, the unnamed mistress continued to hold forth and received her due in a town where function and utility rather than skin color prevailed when access to basic commodities was at stake.[21]

The unnamed "Damsel" was a self-confident entrepreneur who came out of the Black sailing community of Beaufort, South Carolina, a village founded in 1712 that had become the center of a newly created plantation economy forty-five miles northeast of Savannah. The small port sheltered mariners from the Caribbean and the freewheeling world of Bermuda and the Bahamas where privateering had long been another form of business and mixed-race crews a necessity. The most important of these captains, Caleb Davis, "a shrewd, cunning Fellow" in Stephens's judgment, fit the model of the master who sailed in search of profit and occasional plunder and traded across imperial boundaries with a multiracial crew changing loyalties as needed.[22] For much of the 1730s, Captain Davis lived in Beaufort and St. Augustine at the same time, comfortable in the ferociously anti-Spanish world of South Carolina and the Hispanic world anchored by the Castillo de San Marcos, with its community of freed slaves. The tiny port of Savannah, hardly more than a single wharf with a crane to lift cargo, now joined the exchange of goods between towns that were enemies in all but trade.

As Spain and Great Britain drifted toward a war, Caleb Davis was engaged in an increasingly risky enterprise, as one of only a handful of merchants who ran vessels to Florida, a lucrative venture despite the odds. Three successive governors purchased thirteen thousand pesos' worth of goods for the garrison between them and many thousands more for foodstuffs, wine, rum, and other spirits.[23] Writing from the Tower of London where he was imprisoned for debt at the end of a colorful career, Davis claimed with considerable truth, "At this time in life, I lived in a good deal of splendor and in friendship with the Spaniards by which means I supplied all South Carolina and Georgia with all the Silver as these Provincials and Colonials had to traffick with among themselves."[24]

Established as a military outpost in 1565, the small town of St. Augustine had begun as a vital part of Spain's Caribbean defenses, evolved into the anchor of a Franciscan mission system that spread Spanish influence among Native Americans, and maintained a viable Hispanic presence on the North American continent.[25] Florida's peninsular configuration offered Spain ports on both the Gulf and Atlantic coasts and proximity to critical ports in New Spain (Mexico), Hispaniola, and Cuba. In the 1730s, the colony retained its character as an outpost of strategic importance characterized by exceptional ethnic diversity as well as a cosmopolitan outlook. Spanish soldiers took Native American wives. Numerous officials had enslaved African domestics while free Blacks and mulattoes occupied the lower ranks of the Spanish community and became Spanish in language use and faith. The Portuguese, some of whom were Jewish, figured prominently among the colony's ship captains, pilots, and merchants, their vessels combing the coast for cargoes from wrecked ships and castaways. Florida's importance was strategic rather than economic, and the colony never developed an agricultural infrastructure beyond cattle ranching on the Alachua and Diego Plains.[26]

The founding of Charles Town in 1670 marked the beginnings of a bitter rivalry for territory and influence, a mirror of the larger contest between Spain and England in the Americas. Early on, Carolina merchants pushed aside the Spanish in the deerskin trade throughout the region and won the loyalty of increasing numbers of Indians until their rapacious business dealings and selling of thousands of Natives as slaves in the Caribbean produced a stunning counter-reaction. The Yamassee Indians led a confederacy of aggrieved tribes in a surprise attack that killed ninety traders on a spring day in 1715 and eventually hundreds of white and Black men, women, and children.[27] If South Carolina received a stunning setback in the Yamassee War, the ultimate goals of the British never changed. Imperialists in London saw the newly created town of Savannah as part of a chain of defensive settlements, a step in expanding British influence over the "debatable lands" between the Savannah and St. Johns Rivers, one more step in driving the Spanish from the Southeast.[28]

When Oglethorpe returned to England in 1735, he convinced Parliament to make two momentous decisions. Responding to his urgent request, it granted £26,000 for the creation of two fortified towns, one at the mouth of the Altamaha that became Darien, the other on St. Simons and given the name Frederica.[29] Then, more consequentially, Parliament passed an act that prohibited "the Importation and use of Black Slaves or Negroes" in Georgia, citing the danger of exposing its white population to the "Insurrections Tumults and Rebellion of such Slaves & negroes."[30] Of the twenty-two colonies in British America in 1740—thirteen in North America and nine in the Caribbean, Georgia became the only one ever to repudiate plantation slavery, a radical departure from imperial policy but undertaken as a practical matter rather than one of antislavery principles, which thus far had found few roots in English society.[31] In 1739, the Highland Scots of Darien, Georgia, called out the danger of succumbing to the lure of enslaved black labor: "The Nearness of the Spaniards, who have proclaimed Freedom to all Slaves, who run away from their Masters, makes it impossible for us to keep them, without more Labour in guarding them, than what we would be at to do their Work."[32] It was an argument that most Georgians and Carolinians understood.

The illegal selling of commodities and British dry goods by Caleb Davis and other mariners brought desperately needed silver currency into the cash-starved economies of the southern colonies and helped underwrite the exchange of goods between British North America and Great Britain while providing a lifeline for the Spanish colony, always desperate for provisions and supplies.[33] As a resident of St. Augustine, Captain Davis was living a double life, an especially delicate matter as tensions heightened between the English colonies and Spanish Florida. It seemed not to faze him that a governor could dispatch a party of four dozen Yamasees northward and offer one hundred pieces-of-eight "for every live Negro they should bring."[34] Nor did two edicts issued in 1733 by the Spanish king, prohibiting the sale of fugitives and offering freedom conditional on four years of service to the Crown. Black freedom seekers continued to petition for their freedom rather than being condemned to indentured servitude under widely varying terms.[35] In an ironic turn of events, Davis had unintentionally converted his Black sailors into serving as the lynchpin of two radically opposed economies in the Southeast, with silver coinage the connecting link. He encouraged the governor and other officials, military as well as civilian, to run up debts for goods purchased, confident that his vital role would keep him in a protected space.[36]

Throughout these comings and goings, his sailors were cognizant of the stakes. On March 15, 1738, they and the captain were standing on the plaza of St. Augustine where a crowd had assembled to hear a proclamation made by the new governor, Manuel de Montiano, a veteran army officer with long experience in North Africa and Central America.[37] He had arrived a year earlier when Oglethorpe's combative moves translated into unmistakable signs of a forthcoming invasion. Together with the military engineer who accompanied him, the governor undertook aggressive steps to improve the dilapidated defenses of the town. Perhaps reflecting his service in North Africa, he showed a keen understanding of the racial dynamics of the region. According to a report submitted to the South Carolina Commons House of Assembly, the proclamation was announced "by Beat of Drum round the Town of St. Augustine (where many Negroes belonging to English Vessels that carried thither Supplies of Provisions etc. had the Opportunity of hearing it) promising Liberty and Protection to all Slaves that should desert thither from any of the English colonies but more especially from this (one)."[38] Mindful of the psychological dimensions of warfare, Montiano was making clear that the policy of sanctuary extended to every freedom seeker from the British colonies. Nor was Caleb Davis slow in grasping the consequences. A returning captain of an English coasting vessel, presumably Davis, testified before the House that "he heard a Proclamation made at St. Augustine, that all Negroes, who did, or should thereafter, run away from the English should be made free."[39]

Montiano was refining a tactic used by Madrid since the late 1600s to threaten the stability of the plantation economy in the Lowcountry and encourage ever-growing fears among planters of slave insurrection. In the last decade of the seventeenth century, freedom seekers from South Carolina commandeered canoes and other watercraft that they steered across more than 150 nautical miles of open water and began appearing in the port, pleading for their freedom. On November 7, 1693, Charles II, the last Hapsburg ruler of Spain, responded by issuing an official proclamation that fugitives be granted their freedom if they converted to Catholicism and accepted the "True Faith," "the men as well as the women . . . so that by their example and by my liberality others will do the same."[40]

The effect was profound. Freedom seekers appeared in increasing numbers.[41] In 1726, planters near Stono River demanded government action after fourteen of their enslaved people fled to St. Augustine. That same year, the Spanish carried off four slaves from Port Royal, and a vessel manned by Spaniards and Carolina runaways entered the North Edisto River, where its crew struck the Ferguson plantation and carried off seven "Negroes." The government sent a raiding party to the vicinity of the Spanish capital, burned a few houses, but was unable to inflict serious damage to the massive Castillo de San Marcos, where the town's population gathered. In June 1728, Acting Governor Arthur Middleton sent a formal complaint to authorities in London: "[The Spanish are] receiving and harbouring all our Ruanway Negreos . . . [and] have found out a new way of sending our own slaves against us to Rob and Plunder us." He fumed, "They are continually fitting out Partys of Indians from St. A to Murder our White People, Rob our Plantations and carry off our slaves soe that We are not only at a vast expence in Guarding our Southern Frontiers but the Inhabitants are continually alarmed, and have noe leisure to looke after theire Crops." He added for good measure, "The Indians they send against us are in small Partys . . . and sometimes joined wth Negroes, and all the Mischiefe they doe, is on a sudden and by surprise."[42]

Although the appearance of freedom seekers in St. Augustine was episodic and their fate subject to the outlook of the particular Spanish governor, the frequency of escapes continued to grow. The demographics of the Lowcountry contributed to an increasingly tense situation. By the end of the 1730s, the enslaved population was two-thirds of the total population along the coast; and, when only rural parishes are considered, the ratio of Black people to whites was more nearly four or five to one. More than half were less than ten years removed from Africa, and a much larger proportion had been born in Africa.[43]

In this hothouse atmosphere, Davis's sailors listened with special attention to Montiano's announcement in his March proclamation that he was

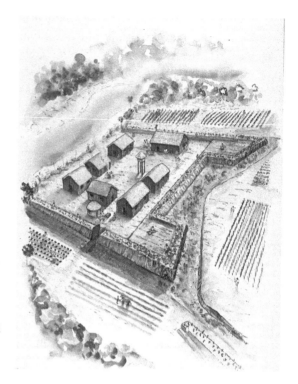

"A Sketch of the Second Fort Mose." A drawing of the free Black village of Gracia Réal de Santa Teresa de Mose, about two miles north of St. Augustine. The first Fort Mose was destroyed during the War of Jenkins' Ear and subsequently rebuilt. Courtesy of the Florida Museum of Natural History, Historical Archaeology Collections.

establishing a fortified town, Gracia Réal de Santa Teresa de Mose, for all former fugitive slaves two miles north of the capital. The governor's actions were hardly revolutionary in terms of Spanish America. Throughout the empire, imperial officials had increasingly turned to free people of African origin as a means of countering repeated assaults from Natives, home-grown rebels, and Europeans.[44] In arming a Black militia, Spanish Florida was following long-established Caribbean precedents in helping the Crown to populate and hold territory threatened by foreign encroachment. Moreover, officials had long legitimized free Black towns as a way of defusing racial animosity and removing the need for curfews and pass systems. This initiative carried a double meaning. The colony became the first to host a community of free Black people in North America, a high percentage from its bitterest enemy South Carolina.[45]

Most of Mose's residents began their lives in West Africa, survived the Middle Passage, labored on Carolina plantations, and displayed considerable skill in escaping over hundreds of miles of land and water. They were risk takers willing to remake their identities in a Spanish world that offered a legal and moral personality denied them elsewhere. They personified the Atlantic Creole that historian Ira Berlin first described, a black or mixed-race person who had the linguistic skills, social malleability, and cultural flexibility to adapt in successive locations around the rim of the Atlantic world, a concept that Jane Landers applied so effectively in bringing the story of Fort Mose to life.[46] Combining military and humanitarian aims to best effect, the governor well understood that the Blacks of Fort Mose would be "the most cruel Enemies of the English," preferring death to being taken back into slavery.[47] Almost one hundred individuals began constructing what became the Pueblo de Gracia Réal de Santa Teresa de Mose, a modest affair with a stone wall banked with earth and surrounded by a ditch and thatched huts and a well inside. The fields lay outside.

As Davis feared, his crew became carriers of a powerful story that transformed the landscape of the Carolina Lowcountry. On returning to Beaufort, the sailors spread the news among their community and began plotting their own escape. Six months after the dramatic proclamation in November 1738, nineteen people—including men, women, and children—boarded a launch and headed out into the open sea.[48] According to a report submitted to the Commons House of Assembly of South Carolina, "fifty other Slaves belonging to other Persons inhabiting about Port Royal ran away to the Castle of St. Augustine." Although that number seems an exaggeration, other small vessels were rowed down the Inland Passage past the silent guns of Fort Frederica.[49] The exasperated Davis eventually submitted a claim for twenty-seven of his slaves "detained" by the governor, whom he valued at seventy-six hundred pesos, for the boat in which they escaped and for the supplies that they had taken.[50]

From a larger perspective, the escape benefited from the maritime culture that Marcus Rediker describes in his studies of seafaring life: a society of men populated chiefly by the poor, bonding in the face of frequent danger on the high seas; a severe shipboard regimen of despotic authority, discipline, and control; and a spirit of rebellion characterized by frequent mutinies.[51] Well before they heard the Proclamation of 1738, those on Davis's schooners were motivated by shipboard standards of egalitarianism that spawned an oppositional culture in the face of the autocratic authority exercised by the captain. The role of sailors on the high seas and in numerous ports gave them an opportunity to take charge of their lives. If Rediker sees an early indication of class conflict, the spirit of rebellion born in the hothouse atmosphere of a ship's hold took on a different meaning when Black sailors became seekers of freedom. As the War of Jenkins' Ear approached, those with Captain Davis learned how to use the various tactics of resistance and forms of organizing oneself to the fullest.

Confident of his standing in Florida, Captain Davis hurried to St. Augustine to recover his slaves, his case made all the stronger since the governor, royal officials, military officers and other notables were indebted to him for goods purchased.[52] The captain of Fort Mose, Francisco Menendez, and at least one other at Mose had an open account with the mariner, an anomaly that suggests English merchants were indirectly subsidizing the creation of Gracia Réal de Santa Teresa de Mose.[53] When he disembarked, Davis encountered a radically changed setting. At ease on the landing in the port, his former bondsmen hailed him in a mocking way. When he ordered them to board his vessel, he was shocked at their sarcastic laughter. He proceeded angrily to the governor's residence to enlist his expected support. Montiano cut him short, holding up a copy of the edict issued by Charles III more than forty years before, waving it in his face.[54] Twenty-three Carolina slaves, including Davis's nineteen, were sent to Fort Mose to begin a new life under the command of Capt. Francisco Menendez.[55] Furious, Davis sailed to Savannah and met with a sympathetic Oglethorpe, who, despite a looming war, sent a trusted officer to St. Augustine to negotiate with Montiano on the captain's behalf, a testimony to their close relationship. This too failed.[56]

The very man to whom Davis had extended credit embodied the subversive values that these sailors now sought to embrace. The captain of the Black militia, Francisco Menendez, was a Mandinga probably from the Gambia River region, captured by other Africans, sold to slave traders, and brought to Charles Town in the early 1700s. Seeing his chance for freedom, he had joined the Yamasee Indians in the hard-fought Yamasee War and fought valiantly with the Yamasee chief, Jorge, for three years. Escaping to St. Augustine at the war's end in 1717, he came into possession of another warrior, Yfallaquisca, who traded him to the then-governor as a Crown slave. In turn, the governor sold him to Don Francisco Menendez Marques, a royal official and landowner who became his patron, leading him to take his master's name and embrace the Catholic Church. Within the space of little more than a decade, Francisco Menendez had been enslaved by Africans, Englishmen, Yamasees, and Spaniards, a prime example of the Atlantic Creole whose survival depended on considerable linguistic skills, an ability to adapt to different cultures, and being socially adept. Valued for his military skills, he was made captain of the Black militia and earned a special place when he led his men in repulsing a surprise raid by Carolinians and Creeks that burned part of St. Augustine in 1726. His petition for full freedom was denied until Montiano appeared as governor.[57]

Events in South Carolina changed the landscape radically. In September 1739, ten months after Davis's sailors fled for Spanish Florida, the Stono Rebellion took place, one of the bloodiest uprisings in American history. The widely known flight of Davis's sailors may have provided a critical spark to Africans well aware of the Spanish offer of freedom. In the face of a lack of evidence, scholars have been cautious about linking the motive for a massive slave revolt to a desire to flee to Spanish Florida. They describe the event as a violent but abortive blow for liberation, the only full-scale slave rebellion to erupt in the British colonies in North America.[58] However, flight to Florida and the idea of insurrection are not mutually exclusive phenomena. The enslaved people of the Carolina Lowcountry were well aware of the preparations for war with Spanish Florida and recognized that any challenge of the Spanish to English mastery in the region was all to their advantage.

On September 9, 1739, two dozen Africans on the Stono River not far from Charles Town attacked a local storehouse to obtain weapons, killed twenty or more whites, and then began moving southward, perhaps toward St. Augustine, with drums beating and at least one flag flying. The casualties are not known, but the rebellion was without precedent for its total surprise, ruthless killing, considerable property damage, armed engagements, and protracted aftermath stretching over eight days. The rebellion also marked an unprecedented escalation in Black resistance to slavery and sent shockwaves across the whole of British North America.[59] Receiving an account from the lieutenant governor of South Carolina, Oglethorpe ordered a troop of rangers to fan out across Georgia, placed men at the most likely crossing of the Savannah River, and issued a proclamation ordering the constables of Georgia "to pursue and seize all Negroes" headed to the Spaniards.[60]

Caleb Davis, caught in a quagmire of his own making, survived the revelations of his Janus-like behavior only because of the intervention of Oglethorpe. When the captain sailed into Savannah a few weeks before the declaration of the War of Jenkins' Ear in October 1739, a mob grabbed him for allegedly selling four hundreds stands of arms to the Spanish and threw him into the ill-kept jail. Oglethorpe intervened to restore his one-time spy.[61] In a mismanaged invasion, Oglethorpe led an army of nearly two thousand men into Spanish Florida, swept past the settlement of Fort Mose, and then stumbled into a futile siege of St. Augustine, where the thick walls of the Castillo de San Marcos repelled bombardment by a small contingent of the Royal Navy. In a well-planned counterattack, three hundred

Spanish soldiers, Natives allied to the Spanish, and the still-intact Black militia, including perhaps some of Davis's former slaves, rushed a party of 142
English and Scots encamped at Mose, catching them still asleep and killing 75, mostly Scotsmen from Darien.[62] Once back at Fort Frederica on St.
Simons, Oglethorpe waited for the expected counterattack. By then, he had
conscripted the vessels of Capt. Caleb Davis and used them in both defensive and offensive operations during a two-year interlude before the next
battle. It is more than likely that Davis's crews continued to reflect a significant African presence despite the earlier experience because of the scarcity
of white sailors, a common complaint of sea captains.

In the spring of 1742, Governor Manuel de Montiano dramatically appeared off St. Simons on the Georgia coast with a flotilla of thirty vessels
and a multiracial army of two to three thousand men, led by Black as well as
white officers. Unrealistic thinking, bad weather, poor leadership by officers,
and lack of knowledge of the terrain doomed the expedition. The Battle of
Bloody Marsh at the southern end of the island ended as little more than a
minor engagement. Advancing along a narrow path toward Fort Frederica,
Spanish troops were ambushed by the English, became disoriented and con-
fused in the smoke-filled swamp, and lost their bearings. About fifty men,
mostly Spanish, were killed.[63] The expedition marked an inglorious end to
the last major offensive mounted in Georgia. Although neither side considered matters settled and conducted raids to probe defenses, a stalemate ensued. For the rest of the 1740s, the Spanish kept a low profile in recognition
of their lack of resources and the defeat of Spanish arms elsewhere.[64]

Throughout the War of Jenkins' Ear on the southern frontier, the Trustees
were simultaneously conducting a debilitating battle with a tight-knit group
of mostly well-to-do Savannahians, dubbed the "Malcontents." The origins
of the war had much to do with attempts by British merchants to break into
the closed markets of South and Central America. Commercial expansion
of the British Empire was an underlying motive that gave the Malcontents
of Georgia running room to make their case that the colony was far from realizing its potential.

A small group of Savannahians advocated slavery for a colony that, as
they pointed out, produced no agricultural surplus and ran a deficit sustained
only by the grace of parliamentary grants. Between 1738 and 1742, a war of
words took place in stridently phrased pamphlets circulated in North America and England that sapped support for the humanitarian enterprise.[65] Despite clever rhetorical thrusts that bore something of the image of a modern
advertising campaign, the dissidents failed to budge the Trustees. Although

the intense lobbying was over by the end of the war and the leaders had departed the colony, it was a bitter victory for the Georgia Trust. Skepticism about the viability of the colony spread, and the humanitarian impulse behind the project weakened. In 1746, a minor official who remained loyal to the Trustees noted in disgust, "My Lord(s), they are stark Mad after Negroes" and pointed to artisans and formerly indentured servants as well as wealthier people.[66] In reality, the single most important factor in undermining the Trustees' labor policy was not the emotionally draining war of words but rather Oglethorpe's victory at Bloody Marsh and his return to England. With the waning of the Spanish threat, the antislavery argument lost much of its force.[67]

In the final years of the Trusteeship, the integrity of the Georgia Plan was tested by the emergence of the town of Frederica on St. Simons Island as a poorly hidden slave market. Built in the shadow of a fort that held nearly six hundred soldiers, the town represented a vastly different world than existed in Savannah. Financed by the expenditures of the War Office, it had attracted 100–150 residents, including blacksmiths, wheelwrights, carpenters, shoemakers, bakers, a locksmith, shopkeepers, and other merchants, as well as traders and merchants from Beaufort, Charles Town, and elsewhere.[68] During those heady days, St. Simons merchant Henry Manley reproached the citizens of Savannah "for [being] a Pack of Fools to stay and starve, when at Frederica there was money enough, and everybody paid their money upon asking."[69]

Oglethorpe had personally ensured that people of African descent were excluded from St. Simons except as visiting sailors, and even then he was a stickler for formalities. On returning from a voyage in 1741, the general had the justice of the peace at Frederica arrest an African sailor on board "Mrs. Wood's schooner" and two on "Mr. Jeny's vessel." A fourth person was ordered seized, "a Girl also of Mrs. Lyford's, who was too cunning for them." In an appearance before the magistrate, the masters of Mrs. Wood's vessel and Mr. Jeny's argued they would not have brought Black sailors into Georgia had they been able to recruit white men and that they were still in port only because of a violent storm. After much wrangling, it was established that the so-called sailor on Mrs. Wood's vessel was in fact her own slave and had been hired out to the ship's master. That unfortunate person was sold out of the colony at public auction.[70]

Shortly after Oglethorpe's departure in 1743, Africans began to be auctioned when eager buyers from within Georgia and Carolina appeared as Frederica emerged as a small market able to sidestep the policy of the Georgia Trust. In what was now functioning as a semi-independent military colony, the commander of the Forty-Second Regiment of Foot, Maj. William Horton, insisted to Savannah magistrates that the colony would never prosper without slave labor and willingly overlooked infractions by his officers and others of a certain prominence. Because the regiment pumped thousands of pounds sterling into local markets and helped float Georgia's struggling economy, Horton possessed almost irresistible leverage.[71] With this kind of backing, merchants began bringing Africans into Frederica and auctioning them to an array of buyers, from Mary Musgrove, the part-Creek interpreter and confidant of Oglethorpe who resided on an isolated barrier island, to Carolinians who happened to be there on business.[72] Black captives were put into service under the guise of being indentured servants to support Oglethorpe's regiment. The terms of service were unspecified.[73]

Those participating included the unscrupulous Capt. Caleb Davis, who offered his sloops and schooners both to Maj. William Horton and to his successor Col. Alexander Heron as a "navy" for Georgia. He used the forthcoming letters of marque to jump back into an old pastime, privateering against Spanish and French vessels plying the waters in the Caribbean. Full of braggadocio, he claimed to have fitted out eighteen privateers.[74] Sizing up Davis's role, a young merchant from Philadelphia judged he had "none but Piratical Principles."[75] Seized vessels were brought to Frederica, judged by an admiralty court that had no legal standing, and the cargo sold for the benefit of Horton, Heron, Davis, and others in their tiny circle of friends.[76]

Among those put up for auction in defiance of the Trustees was John Peter, a Dutch-speaking sailor and a free Black man who had been seized by a privateer while sailing on a vessel in the Caribbean. Unceremoniously transported to Newport, Rhode Island, he was judged by an admiralty court to be a slave, taken to Philadelphia, and sold to Samuel Clee, a trader from Georgia. A Jewish merchant in Savannah, Abraham Minis, had sent his young partner to New York with £400 to settle outstanding accounts. Instead, the duplicitous Clee sailed to Philadelphia and used the funds to buy the sailor from Curaçao. Arriving at Frederica, he sold Peter to a planter from Beaufort and thereby skated around the prohibition on people of African descent in Georgia. The resilient sailor had no intention of remaining a slave on an island off the Carolina coast, made an escape in a large canoe with others he persuaded to follow him, and headed for St. Augustine. Caught, he was brought before the magistrate's court in Savannah. Claiming to be free, the articulate Peter, who spoke excellent English, threw the leading citizens of the town into a fierce debate about the nature of positive law and how it applied in the case of a literate Black man.[77]

The case of John Peter opens a door to another world, one where creolization and contraband went hand in hand. Curaçao was a small island in the
southern Caribbean that had become a major commercial center and a hub
of the Dutch Atlantic.[78] In an age of mercantilism when the great empires
imposed a restrictive system for controlling commerce to their advantage,
the Dutch opened the port of Willemstad to free trade, making Curaçao a
prime center of smuggling or contraband for traders willing to travel along
routes that were more direct or more efficient than the often cumbersome
official trade channels. Opportunities for illicit trade were all the greater because of the nearness of the Spanish mainland, known as Tierra Firme, today's Venezuela and part of Colombia. Home to half the island's population
by the mid-1700s, Willemstad offered rich opportunities for sociocultural
interactions across lines of race, ethnicity, social class, and even empire. Creolization went apace with a society that attracted people from all quarters of
the Atlantic. The layers were many: a small Dutch merchant elite; the largest and most prosperous Jewish community in the Americas; a broad base
of sailors of all ethnic groups; skilled slaves; and a large free colored population, who typically lived in a separate quarter that came to be called Otro-
banda. From the interplay of disparate cultures, languages, and ethnicities,
the island's sailors absorbed the vibrant new creole identities that emerged.
Peter was a prime example of this new identity.

His buyer was a Carolinian who hungered after the potentially rich rice
lands in the neighboring colony and was ready to pounce once the prohibition on slavery was lifted. John Mullryne had migrated from Montserrat,
established himself as a merchant at Beaufort, and had an interest in four
coasting vessels. Fellow Carolinians elected him as colonel in the militia.[79]
He traveled regularly to Frederica on business and used these occasions to
visit the mainland looking for likely rice-growing land. Mullryne purchased
the man from Curaçao as something of an afterthought but seemingly had
no idea of his character. Accustomed to making his way through and around
ports, John Peter stood in the mold of Francisco Menendez in that he could
fight within the prevailing legal system and still be ready to lead Black resistance outside that system. He was well aware of the sanctuary offered by
St. Augustine and of the continuing flights of runaways. Only three years
before, Carolina authorities had alerted Oglethorpe that a group of thirty
"sensible Negroes, fifteen of whom had firearms[,]" had escaped and were
headed for St. Augustine.[80]

As a sailor and free Black man from Dutch Curaçao, John Peter had the
confidence and technical expertise to lay out a plan of escape and recruit six

men from neighboring plantations on Hilton Head to follow him.[81] Gathering together one night, they departed in a large canoe, possibly a dugout capable of carrying forty or fifty barrels of rice, and relied on his maritime skills to carry them through the Inland Passage. At Tybee, a barrier island eighteen miles from Savannah, the canoe stopped for unknown reasons, and the group disembarked. The "lighthouse people," the handful of whites who facilitated shipping, spied them moving about. The lighthouse at Tybee, a ninety-foot structure made of durable long-leaf pine on cedar piles with a brick foundation, had been one of Oglethorpe's first projects. The lighthouse people were accustomed to intercepting freedom seekers and engaged in a firefight that wounded one African. The remaining men surrendered and were imprisoned in the Savannah jail.

The magistrates' court in Savannah convened in session to listen to a representative of several planters near Beaufort claim their rights to the property. After a brief "trial," six of the seven were remanded to the agent from South Carolina. Allowed to speak in his own defense, John Peter, a Dutch speaker who was fluent in English and possibly in Spanish, made an impassioned plea about his rights as a free Black person taken illegally on the "Spanish Main" and sold into slavery.[82] Whatever their thoughts about slavery, local officials were touched by a story that raised a fundamental question about the rule of law in a colony founded for humanitarian reasons. A minor official related to the trustees: "The Negro finding himself detained in cruel Slavery embraced the first opportunity to make his escape, and with some more of his colour who are always glad of a leader sate off in a Canoo."[83] This sailor, familiar with the workings of English law, found a receptive ear when he asked for the same rights as John Mullryne or Samuel Clee enjoyed under English common law. Peter boldly "asserted that he was a freed man and no Slave, and that altho' he had took the opportunity of coming away with the other Negro's in the manner he did, which was to escape from a Cruel and unjust Slavery . . . yet being a free subject of the States of Holland prayed he might have the benefit of the English laws of Mulrain who pursu'd him or of Clee who Sold him."[84] Impressed, the magistrates declined to return the man to Mullryne.

The chief magistrate, Henry Parker, a former weaver, emphatically declared for his audience he would not deliver up John Peter until word came from Curaçao about the man's status.[85] An amiable man who drank too much, Parker had another agenda. The magistrates of Frederica on St. Simons, center for the southern district of the colony, had long resisted the rule of Savannah and relied on the clout that His Majesty's Forty-Second

Regiment of Foot gave them in any dispute. This unprecedented act flowed not only from a genuine concern for the integrity of the Georgia Plan but also with the desire to punish Frederica for flaunting Savannah's authority. The trustees had long been engaged with Major Horton over his attempt to establish a military government in the southern part of the colony. Striking a blow at the illegal slave market on the island was an opportunity not to be missed.[86] Standing behind Parker was the thirty-two-year-old James Habersham, disciple of George Whitefield, manager of the Bethesda Orphanage, and fledgling merchant who had recently opened a mercantile house on Bay Street. More than any other person, he provided the muscle behind the defiance of the military, all the more remarkable since privately he was a leading advocate of lifting the ban on slavery in Georgia.[87]

In May 1746, the governor of Curaçao sent a bill attesting to John Peter's freedom and expressed himself in words described as "strong and particular in [John Peter's] favor as if he had been a Man of another Rank."[88] Clearly John Peter was a personage within the society of free Blacks in Curaçao. On hearing this, Habersham applied to the magistrates for a warrant to arrest Samuel Clee, the trader on Frederica. Clee was already being pursued through the court system by Abraham Minis for the stolen funds.[89] Swayed by the arguments, Parker granted warrants for the summoning of several individuals on the island. In the ensuing tug-of-war, Lieutenant Colonel Heron, the new commander of the regiment, came to Savannah and threw around his considerable influence to quash the warrants. Heron's presence notwithstanding, John Peter was released and presumably made his way back to Dutch Curaçao.

It was a stunning victory for the articulate creole in the face of a system heavily weighted against the Black man, but it was a Pyrrhic victory for those committed to the Georgia Plan. During the final years of the Trusteeship, Georgia continued to ban slaves and slavery but took few steps to counter a growing influx of Africans and African Americans, a nibbling around the edges that grew into a steady addition of people of African descent. Although most had left the colony after their final defeat in 1742, the Malcontents had sucked the lifeblood out of the Georgia Plan. A recent interpretation sees that fierce struggle as one between elites who wanted slaves to labor on large-scale plantations on the Carolina model and non-elites who saw their freedom threatened by men who wanted to impose a capitalist economy that would marginalize them.[90] Yet the desire for enslaved people was widespread among most Savannahians, if not the German Pietists around Ebenezer or the Highlanders around Darien. As many as nine hundred of the fifteen hundred people in the colony signed the four petitions favoring the adoption of slavery. Over 44 percent of the signers were charity settlers whose way had been paid by the Trustees or had gone as indentured servants.[91] The fiercest supporters of the Trustees were not in Savannah but among the German peasant farmers around Ebenezer and the Highland Scots in Darien, culturally as well as philosophically at odds with the majority of residents in Savannah. With the military rationale all but gone, Parliament no longer had an interest in underwriting what increasingly seemed like a failing economic experiment, and the Highland Scots did not feel so strongly about foregoing enslaved labor. The end of the Spanish threat was all-encompassing.

In the second half of 1748, the dispirited Trustees, many of whom no longer attended meetings of the council, reluctantly conceded the point that slavery was inevitable. To lay the groundwork, they ordered local magistrates to assemble a council of notables to discuss conditions under which that coveted institution might be introduced. In one fell swoop, the grand dream of a white man's colony in the Lower South was pronounced dead. A census taken in 1750 found that the province already held 202 Black men, 147 women, and an undetermined number of children out of 2,500 inhabitants, or about 17 percent of the population.[92]

For a brief moment, the colony turned into a society with enslaved people as opposed to the harsh enslaved society that existed next door. It more closely resembled the chartered colonies of the seventeenth century in which the unique laboring conditions gave Black people the kind of breathing room that led Ira Berlin to call them the "charter generation," where slavery was one form of forced labor among many others, notably indentured servitude.[93] As the last colony to receive a charter, Georgia arguably belonged to that group, but it was a fleeting moment. At the time that the Trustees petitioned the Privy Council for the removal of the ban on slavery, most Georgians of modest means, men and women, believed that the change would benefit them. Instead, the next decade would see their world turned upside down as Carolina planters crossed the river and, with their enslaved labor force, took the best lands.

Nevertheless, the Black sailors of Trusteeship Georgia left an indelible mark for those who came afterward. As Jeffrey Bolster argues when he draws on Olaudah Equiano's exceptional career, maritime slaves and freemen became forces for change because they grasped revolutionary ways of imagining the world and their place in it.[94] From the ranks of Captain Davis's vessels came men who were accustomed to trading across imperial boundaries, listened intently when the governor of St. Augustine announced the creation of a community for free Blacks, made their escape directly from their home port so that wives and children could accompany them, and probably fought against Oglethorpe and the British in 1740 and again in 1742. The Black sailor from Dutch Curacao, in his interaction with the magistrates of Savannah, gave voice to all his peers when he displayed a self-assurance and fearlessness in the face of the white power structure and revealed a gift for playing on the differences in that structure to obtain his freedom. The demand of John Peter for legal equality captured the essential thrust of Black aspirations in the long eighteenth century. That demand served as a precious legacy for sailors of color during the royal period. How those aspirations translated into a society that set about becoming a plantation economy like South Carolina's over the next quarter-century is a far different matter.

CHAPTER 2

The Journeys of Mahomet

In 1750, the dispirited Georgia Trustees reluctantly bowed to reality and approved a request to repeal the ban on slavery and terminate their troubled Trusteeship with the British Crown. Oglethorpe's grand vision of a colony for white men and women of limited means received its final coup de grâce. The effect was electric. Carolina planters crossed the Savannah River with hundreds of enslaved Africans to stake out claims to rich tidal lands along the coast. Impatient with the independent ways of his North American colonies, George II assumed direct control of the province and placed it under the authority of the Board of Trade, a powerful committee of Parliament that effectively shaped London's policy for the emerging empire.[1]

With the coming of the royal period and the resulting economic growth, enslaved Black sailors became an even more visible presence on the waterfront in Savannah, serving as a vital part of the fast-growing port town. They were to be found at work on vessels along the quays, walking around town with considerable autonomy, or perched in down-at-the-heel grog shops in the working-class neighborhood of Yamacraw. Between 30 and 40 percent of the estimated fourteen hundred "jack tars" who, in the course of a year, climbed the bluff to go into town after docking were African, a reflection of the overwhelming importance of the Caribbean to the commerce of the colony. Almost half of the vessels entering and leaving the ports of Savannah and Sunbury, a smaller entrepôt thirty-five miles to the south, came from the sugar islands of the Caribbean or the Bahamas and Bermuda, where

Black sailors were necessary in a world characterized by an enormous imbalance between races.[2]

No other colony in British North America went so quickly from near bankruptcy to economic boom, from a society with enslaved people to a fully developed slave society, and from a frontier outpost to an integral part of the Atlantic world as did Georgia. In 1750, there were approximately twenty-five hundred white and four hundred enslaved people. By 1775, the colony had exploded to roughly twenty-two thousand whites and eighteen thousand enslaved. It was now shipping 23,500 barrels of rice per year, three hundred thousand pounds of deerskin, and 2.1 million feet of lumber; and it boasted a government under one of the most effective royal governors in North America.[3] In terms of rapid growth over a short time, the province stood alone in British North America. The remarkable turnaround came at an unconscionably high cost: the abandonment of the Trustees' grand vision and its replacement by a firm commitment to a plantation economy modelled after South Carolina's. Thousands of people were uprooted from hundreds of communities across Africa, thrown into rude labor camps, and buried away in water and mud, all in the effort to transform marshland into hard profits for a tiny white elite.

In the process, Savannah acquired the look and feel of the towns of the Caribbean, an extension of the perverse culture of the sugar islands. Olaudah Equiano, author of one of the earliest and most influential slave narratives, captured the doubled-edged freedom and openness that a Black sailor now experienced in Savannah.[4] The young enslaved sailor from tiny Montserrat could walk the streets and wander along roads headed out of town; command a craft going up rivers in search of lumber to assemble a cargo; visit with an enslaved friend who had his own small house; and stand at City Market selling wares he had imported, sometimes no more than oranges, sometimes packets of sugar, and occasionally English manufactured goods. The appearance was deceptive. His encounters laid bare the seamy underside in which brutality and racism informed every aspect of life: the brutal attempt on his life by a drunken physician, his flight to Yamacraw to hide from a merchant determined to have him whipped around the streets of the town, and his escape from two white men who sought to sell him back into slavery.[5]

Nor was Florida a magnet for fugitive slaves from the English colonies as it once had been. In the early 1760s, Spain made an ill-thought decision to intervene in the global struggle between Great Britain and France and trust in the combined navies of the Bourbon powers to check the naval dominance of the English. A powerful British fleet and ten thousand soldiers landed near Havana, capital of Cuba and key to the Spanish Caribbean. In a remarkable campaign, they occupied the city after a seven-week siege. By the terms of the Treaty of Paris in 1763, Spain relinquished Florida, a two-hundred-year-old possession, as the price for recovering Havana, with its deep harbor and strategic location.[6] Under British control, the narrow strip of coastland east of the St. Johns River witnessed rapid development as a plantation economy with the same type of enslaved labor from Africa and the same mix of commodities as Georgia and South Carolina.

However, the phenomenal expansion of the enslaved community began in slow, random fashion. By 1760, the population of people of African descent in Georgia was still less than four thousand. Most had been forcibly marched from South Carolina by planters eager for new rice lands. In no other slave society in the British Empire did the core of its enslaved labor migrate across the boundary of an adjoining province. Georgia was the only colony in North America to benefit from so significant a transfer of labor from a neighbor. The ports of the British Caribbean and Charles Town provided hundreds more, but the great flood of Africans into Georgia began in 1766 when the first slavers arrived directly from West Africa. The three dozen vessels that came over the next eight years carried an estimated 5,349 captives into the colony, while another 3,910 passed through the Charles Town markets and then to Savannah or Sunbury.[7]

Among those thousands of human beings was a man named Mahomet or Mohamedy, "a short, well-made Negroe Fellow," a Muslim judging by his name, pitted with smallpox scars that offer a vital clue as to his identity.[8] That piece of evidence suggests he arrived on a square-rigged vessel, the *New Britannia*, under the command of an Irish captain, John Deane, who appeared off Tybee in 1769 with 125 people from the Gambia River. The captain was making his second attempt to break into this new, untested slave market. When Deane anchored, word quickly reached town that the people aboard were suffering from smallpox, a highly contagious disease that eventually struck dozens of people on board. The governor ordered the captain to place his vessel at the relatively new quarantine station on Lazaretto Creek behind Tybee Island, shave their heads, and burn their clothes. The two-story tabby structure was too small to accommodate the weakened human cargo, and the misery was compounded by a shortage of food and medical support. Twenty-three Africans and several crewmen died. Mahomet bore the scars on his face as a badge of a disease that did not discriminate.[9]

Mahomet's life serves as a measure of the type of man who chose to become a maroon twice and both times on the borders of Georgia, once before and once after the Revolution, in a memorable display of the continuity of life on the coast. The search for freedom and a new identity took him into or near Native American lands and, on a second occasion, to a remote corner of the Savannah River, passing through British East Florida. His eighteen-year career as a slave in Georgia illustrates the limited options that most faced, the opportunities and challenges that fluid borders offered, and the stubborn refusal of freedom seekers to accept defeat in the face of insuperable odds. His life speaks to the importance of Muslims along the coast and the religious imprint that they brought.

The cargo of the *New Britannia* joined a great wave of captives coming to Georgia from West Africa, a vast region distinct from Central and Southern Africa. The cultivation of rice made its people especially valuable for their agricultural skills while the proximity of the western coast to the Georgia Lowcountry minimized shipping costs for the horrific Middle Passage. Although Africans had been growing rice for hundreds of years in a variety of landscapes and employing a range of techniques, the great majority of people were raising millet, herding cattle, and engaging in other agricultural pursuits, trading along the rivers, or occupied as blacksmiths, leatherworkers, and other artisans.[10]

Among the more important West African ethnic groups were the coastal populations of the Wolof, whose centers at Jolof, Waalo, Cayor and Baol controlled the flow of commerce between the Atlantic and the interior; the Fulbe, who occupied the central and upper valleys of the Senegal River; and the Bambara in the far interior of what is now Mali. Alongside were other groups like the Sereer, Khasso, and Soninke. Yet similarities existed. The vast majority of Senegambians were cultivators, not warriors, and therefore possessed needed skills. The rivers and coasts of the area gave their peoples a strong set of commercial connections.[11] Mahomet, who was carried to a Wolof-speaking town on the Gambia River, was probably from the Bambara people in the interior and knew nothing or little of rice culture.[12]

An experienced slaver, Captain Deane had secured the backing of Joseph Clay, a prominent merchant in Savannah and the nephew of the acting governor, Joseph Habersham, an early pioneer whose skills as a merchant saved the virtually bankrupt colony. Habersham also bore heavy responsibility for introducing the slave trade.[13] In his nine trips to Georgia and South Carolina, Deane transported thirteen hundred Africans captured exclusively from along the Gambia River, the source of so many of Georgia's bondsmen.[14] "The Slaves from the River Gambia are preferr'd to all others with us save the Gold Coast," Henry Laurens, a central figure in the Carolina trade, reminded a correspondent.[15] Clay echoed the sentiment: "The Windward Coast Negroes say from Gambia to the Gold Coast inclusive are most liked in this country and will afford the best prices."[16]

The key to the captain's remarkable success was a woman, Fenda Lawrence, who lived in the town of Kau-Ur, one hundred miles upstream from the Gambian coast at the point where the water lost its saltiness.[17] Kau-Ur was a Wolof-speaking town whose inhabitants were principally but not exclusively Muslim and where the principal activity was rice cultivation. The town was ideally situated to connect to the Muslim commercial network that began in the western Sudan (today's Mali) and became a slave-trading entrepôt for Muslim merchants. The English had traded for decades with the kingdom of Saalum—or Saloum—at the mouth of the Gambia and sent large canoes and boats upriver for trading in inland towns.

That trade had been facilitated by the presence of an elite group of women, known as signares, who provided valuable services to merchants, sea captains, assorted sailors, and servants.[18] Often of mixed race, signares commanded capital to buy and sell provisions to the British; bought European products to trade; and provided enslaved people through their contacts in the African world. To finance their commerce, they typically sought to marry a European, and, if their husband left with no intention of returning, they were free to marry again. Fenda probably had a previous relationship with an English captain or sailor named Lawrence. She was an entrepreneur in her own right, a remarkable example of the Atlantic creole who served as an intermediary in the transatlantic slave trade, employing her linguistic skills, familiarity with the Atlantic's cultural conventions, and access to capital to mediate between African merchants and English sea captains. Successful in her working relationship with Captain Deane, she demonstrates the extraordinary fluidity of gender roles in Senegambia for those in the upper stations of life.[19]

Mahomet remains a puzzle. How does one reconstruct the life of an individual about whom little is known? Yet that puzzle can be partially resolved because of his religion. He might well have been able to read. Basic literacy was widespread among Muslims in West Africa. The ability to read and write passages from the Qur'an was considered essential to any believer and imparted even to peasants and girls. Nor did most Muslims drink alcohol, a characteristic that would have set Mahomet apart from the general enslaved population. He would regularly say the shahada or statement of faith that there is no God but Allah, one of the five pillars of the Islamic faith. He would pray five times a day or, after his capture, may have prayed in secret. Most telling is his ability to maintain his name, Mohammed, which planters interpreted as Mohamet or, in one case, Mohamedy. The Georgia Sea Islands became a reservoir of African Muslim names, a testimony to the disproportionate number of enslaved people taken from Senegambia and Sierra Leone and their resistance to assimilation.[20]

The captain of the *New Britannia* sailed directly to Savannah from Fort James on the Gambia River. He hustled Mahomet and his peers onto the deck of the ship, oiled them down for appearance, and sold him there or on the adjacent wharf or in a holding pen in the industrial neighborhood of Yamacraw or possibly inside a barn at a nearby plantation. Members of the differing ethnic groups may have bonded in the filth and horrors of the lower deck to become "shipmates" but their chances of staying together were not high. Many were sold singly or in pairs.[21]

John Graham, a Scottish merchant and slave trader who stood at the beginning of a new career as a planter, purchased the Muslim. Flush with their early success, merchants like Graham became the driving force behind the transformation of the sleepy plantations along the Savannah River into highly efficient, capitalist enterprises.[22] Within the space of seven years, he went from being the "master" of sixteen Africans and odd pieces of undeveloped land to concentrating 262 people on three plantations, two of them on the Savannah River.[23] At his newly acquired Mulberry Grove, he paid £4,865 to purchase eighty slaves and a valuable tract of twelve hundred acres.[24] At his second plantation on the river, New Settlement, Graham invested £3,800 and added another sixty people. On an inland plantation, he placed one hundred individuals, and a dozen were placed at his house in Savannah. A veritable mania for acquiring enslaved people had seized the tiny elite. "What is the matter that you have bought no Negroes for me this season," the English politician William Knox asked a close friend of Graham concerning his plantation not far from Mulberry Grove. "No pray don't let any of your confounded Punctillio get the better of your good sense and friendship for me in this business. Negroes I must have or I shall never forgive you."[25]

As a newly purchased African, Mahomet was given light work by Graham's overseer for the first few weeks to accustom him to the routine and help his body adjust to the wet, humid climate. Given the unhealthy conditions and the high mortality rate, the merchant invested heavily in young adult males. Mahomet found himself on a plantation where there were two men for every woman and virtually no children. Out of 126 enslaved people at Mulberry Grove at the time of the Revolution, only fifteen were boys or girls.[26] The African population was heavily male. Of the 141 people at Mulberry Grove, there were 84 men, 42 women, and 15 children.[27]

Once deemed "seasoned," he was put under military-style discipline in an enterprise roughly modeled after the sugar plantations of the Caribbean. Enslaved laborers waded knee-deep into swamps next to the Savannah River, cut down trees, cleared the underbrush, and built large embankments around wet fields. They divided the land into fields and subfields, dug ditches and canals, and created an elaborate irrigation system, a "huge hydraulic machine" as one planter phrased it. Women worked alongside men. Hoeing and weeding in the fields under a relentless sun in the summertime, they found their menstrual cycle disrupted, produced few children, and had difficulty keeping alive those that were born.[28]

Was Mahomet one of 190 field hands, managed by four drivers who had the right to use the whip and did so generously? Or was he one of the seventy-two people who were in skilled or semiskilled positions, including fourteen seamstresses and washerwomen, fourteen sawyers, twelve squarers and carters, eight house carpenters, five coopers, four gardeners, three boatmen, two blacksmiths, two cooks, a tailor, a bricklayer, a coachman, and a hairdresser? The range of skilled and semiskilled positions reflected the complexity of tasks on a large rice plantation.[29] For field hands, death came at an early age. Death was ever-present as a consequence of so many working knee-deep in marshes. John Graham ventured to guess that he lost 3–4 percent of his slaves per year on his Savannah River plantations, but William DeBrahm, the talented military engineer and the most knowledgeable of Georgians in terms of statistics, thought 5 percent a more appropriate figure.[30]

Uninterested in living conditions, looking only at profits, John Graham and his fellow planters allowed considerable autonomy for Africans buried in remote labor camps to piece together their own lives from the disjointed moments at their disposal. Many of the Africans lived in wattle-and-daub structures that mimicked their West African homes, planted vegetables common to their native land (like eggplant, okra, benne seed, and melons), and collected herbs and shrubs to create their own medicines.[31] Most were implacably hostile to Christianity and continued to embrace their traditional belief systems. Obeah men and women mediated with supernatural forces and used their assumed powers to help heal the sick, avenge wrongs, and resolve disputes by ferreting out the truth. Some males practiced polygamy. Most men and women practiced an animistic religion that emphasized spirits, conjurors, and the worship of ancestors.

If Mahomet followed the practice of most Muslims, he continued to pray and obey the strictures of Islam, at least in some truncated fashion. He could have followed three of the five pillars of Islam by repeating the shahada frequently, praying in secret and writing passages from the Qur'an in the sand, and fasting, as difficult as these may have been given his working conditions. In the early nineteenth century, Sea Island Muslims in Georgia and South Carolina did not hide to pray. They did so publicly and in some cases in front of their enslavers. His religious outlook may have been influenced by the association of Islam in West Africa with the Sufi orders, emphasizing the personal dimension of the relationship between Allah and humans, many rituals and devotional practices, and meditation. Reinforcing his outlook was the large number of Muslims present in the captive population, not merely peasants and laborers but also traders, clerics (marabouts), and even members of the "nobility."[32]

In 1771, Mahomet disappeared from Graham's Mulberry Grove at the very moment it was being converted into a ruthlessly efficient machine capable of producing eight hundred barrels of rice a year, several times what it had been producing.[33] He fit much of the profile of three-quarters of all freedom seekers in the Lowcountry: African-born, young, male, unskilled, and of recent arrival.[34] Most were captives who had not yet been fully incorporated into the plantation routine, were often without a job, and were reacting to the shock of being thrust into a militarized labor camp unlike anything they had experienced in Africa. They lacked the means, the requisite linguistic skills, and a sufficient familiarity with the realities of life outside their immediate environment to succeed on the outside. Often they fled their settlements in large groups, had little idea of the geography of their surroundings, and were quickly caught. While Savannah was a magnet for acculturated slaves who hoped to pass as free, "New Negroes" headed for the obscurity of swamps and forests along the coast or whatever inhospitable terrain promised cover.[35] Mahomet was one of the few who were successful, at least for a time, perhaps because he had been at hard labor for two or three years and had acquired needed skills and knowledge of coastal geography.

Africans on the Graham plantations were frequent runaways. In the *Georgia Gazette,* a planter-merchant described five of these fugitives as "New Negroe Men, of the Conga country" who had been in the colony for less than five months: Somerset, six feet tall, from "the Cormantee country" on the Gold Coast; Cuffy, with a bushy beard and red eyes; Stephen, a short fellow; Stepney, "a very likely black fellow, of a middling size"; and Robin, "a stout man-boy about 16."[36] In a second notice, he mentioned four of the six, suggesting that two had been recaptured. He added that he was also looking for Fortune, "a pretty tall, slim, black fellow" who had run away the preceding summer and, "after being out some months," had been captured at a Brier Creek settlement farther north.[37] A subsequent notice reported three runaways, also from the Conga country, with the freshly minted names of Ben, Peter, and Tom. They carried off "a canoe with three paddles and, it is supposed would go towards the sea." Since they spoke little English, their capture seemed certain unless they disappeared into the ocean in an attempt to return to Africa as occasionally some did.[38]

In September 1774, John Graham placed a notice for Mahomet stating that the African had run away three years earlier and had recently been seen "at a settlement near the Indian Line on Ogeechee," a boundary defined by treaty between the Creek Nation and the colony of Georgia. The notice said that Mahomet was marked by smallpox scars and an ear that had been partly cut off, a form of punishment in which the victim had his ear nailed to a whipping post and cut off in front of fellow slaves as an example. The possibilities are many. Perhaps he had attempted to run away on other occasions or resolutely defied the overseer at a critical moment or engaged in forms of insubordination that marked him as a subversive individual.

Mahomet had become a survivalist, a maroon staking out a place in a patch of territory near the point where Creek hunting lands began, a fluid zone where hunters, both Native and white, passed and where he may have worked at a white settlement for some kind of compensation or been part of a maroon community that traded with both white people and Natives. He would have enjoyed considerable autonomy but also run considerable risks. His options were limited.

He would have had reason to hesitate in deciding whether to advance beyond "the Indian line." Few Africans from the rice plantations of the Lowcountry took the path to Creek towns to escape their fate, at least if one considers the advertisements in the *Georgia Gazette* between 1763 and 1775. Of the 453 notices for fugitives, 148 gave destinations. Sixteen indicated "going upriver," "Backcountry," or "Indian Nation" as a goal, wide-ranging categories that include Indigenous and white settlements.[39] Fleeing to Indian country could be a risky bet. British officials had success in making it worthwhile for Natives to turn over Black freedom seekers. Those who delivered slaves to designated officials were to receive a gun and three blankets for each captured person. Authorities not only wanted to recover "property" but also, as importantly if not more so, prevent any possibility of an alliance between disaffected Blacks and red "savages." The expectation of being absorbed into a compatible but different culture had to be balanced against the risk of betrayal, enslavement, or death.[40]

Numbering fourteen thousand people on the eve of the Revolution, the Creeks formed a loosely organized confederacy of fifty to sixty towns that stretched from the Oconee River in present-day Georgia to the Tombigbee River in Alabama. The Creeks of the Upper Towns lived on the Tallapoosa, Coosa, and Alabama Rivers in present-day Alabama, and the Creeks of the Lower Towns lived on the lower Chattahoochee and Flint Rivers in present-day Georgia. The confederacy had come into being in the late seventeenth and early eighteenth centuries by welcoming the survivors from the collapse of older societies who spoke different languages or dialects and possessed different cultures. The dominant Muskogeans welcomed Hitchitis, Alabamas, Yuchis, Abihkas, and others in this evolving society that had become the dominant force in the interior of the South by mid-century.[41]

In his tour of the Southeast during the early 1770s, the naturalist William Bartram reported seeing Black slaves in many Native towns and mentioned fifteen at one site who waited on Boatswain, the headman of Apalachicola on the lower Chattahoochee, and tended his crop. A few women among the fifteen had married Creeks and gained their freedom as members of a family and clan.[42] Slavery was no new institution. Muskogeans considered all those outside their kinship networks as outsiders who did not have a recognized place in society. As intertribal warfare declined, they looked to enslaving Black people on their own terms. For men, it typically meant tilling the fields for corn and peas, an activity that warriors considered women's work, or herding cattle, or serving as a servant to a mico or chieftain. Yet they gained their freedom from the horrific discipline of a rice plantation, enjoying considerably more autonomy and freedom in their daily lives. For women, enslavement meant doing the most menial of tasks or, if fortunate, marrying a warrior and entering a clan, becoming an insider through a fictive kinship that tied her to all other members of the clan. In earlier times, children had the opportunity to become full members of the talwa or town, but those opportunities were shrinking as lifetime servitude became the norm.[43]

On occasion, Creeks from the Lower Towns welcomed Black refugees from coastal plantations. "Alick," a headman who moved around the edges of the plantations in St. Johns Parish, made contact with enslaved people on a regular basis. A planter referred to him as "that villain the Indian Doctor," a medicine man with valuable roots and herbs that attracted an audience. Plantation owner Lachlan McIntosh described Ben and Glasgow as the two most valuable individuals in his possession—"good Sawyers, Squarers, Boatmen & Shingle makers as well as Field Slaves"—the kind of jacks-of-all-trades who made a plantation hum with activity. According to their "master," Alick "conveyed" them to the Creek Nation, but McIntosh eventually managed to retrieve them, presumably paying a generous reward to Alick. Within short order, the two men sought their freedom, this time to Charles Town, where they were stopped, interrogated and held at the workhouse. McIntosh told their captor to sell them "as soon as possible to save any further Expence or risque." Both were from the Conga country; Ben spoke a little French, adding to the mystery.[44]

The surprise in Mahomet's escape, then, was his destination. He must have known that the most successful freedom seekers in the colony were those who deserted the rice plantations along the Savannah River and headed twenty or so miles north into the swamps and cypress groves farther upriver, a virtually impassable setting that made possible a community in the image of the maroon communities that existed in the Caribbean or Latin America. Since the end of the seventeenth century, Jamaican maroons had retreated to the fastness of densely covered mountains, established armed settlements at high elevations, and fought wars with the British that demonstrated their considerable skill at guerrilla warfare.[45] Here in the Georgia Lowcountry, the experience was on far smaller scale but with similar characteristics. Runaways hid in the wild, studiously avoided armed confrontation, and limited contact with other people, white or Black. Their purpose was defensive, to establish their autonomy from white society. That required the need for foolproof concealment, the exploitation of their natural environment, and occasional raids on farms and plantations for supplies.[46]

Like most of the enslaved population, Mahomet was well aware of maroon activities along the river because of the raids they conducted for food supplies to supplement their diet. Local authorities were frustrated by their humiliating inability to stop them. In 1765, the House of Assembly took note that "a number of fugitive slaves" had assembled in the river swamp on the north side of the Savannah River (South Carolina) and were making raids on the plantations on the south side, committing "robberies and depredations" to gain food and supplies and to "debauch" the women, according to one planter.[47] They were joining with their counterparts from Carolina plantations in a way that suggested a major threat to the planting elite.

Perceiving a growing menace, South Carolina sent a militia unit into the swamp to eradicate the community, always a high-risk task because of the hostile landscape. In a letter written to a neighboring planter, a captain in the militia wrote of how his unit had moved through swamps often waist-deep until they encountered three Black men who fled into the understory of brush. The militia came to a scaffolding where they found two men standing on the structure, one beating a drum and the other "hoisting Colours," possibly behaviors they learned as soldiers in Africa. The two discharged their guns and disappeared into the swamp. The soldiers at last arrived at a "town" with a square, around which were four houses, seventeen feet long and fourteen feet wide, kettles boiling rice on a fire, and an array of goods: blankets, pots, shoes, axes, "and many other tools[,] all which together with the Town they set fire to."[48]

The problem was a continuing one. In 1771, authorities learned that "a great number of fugitive Negroes had committed many Robberies and insults between [Savannah] and Ebenezer" and that the number of fugitives was said to be increasing daily.[49] The government discussed hiring Indians to apprehend the slaves and ordered Capt. Alexander Wylly, speaker of the House of Commons, to lead part of his militia company in a search. Six months later, the fugitives were still encamped in the swamps.[50] The Savannah River plantations, with their hyper development and concentration of "New Negroes," were a place apart. In no other location in the colony were maroons as frequent or as established as on the upper part of the Savannah.

Until recent years, historians judged that marronage was a relatively rare occurrence in British North America and the United States.[51] Independent communities of freedom seekers had been prevalent in Brazil, the Caribbean, and the American Southwest for centuries, ranging from tiny bands that survived less than a year to powerful states that survived for decades and longer. In Jamaica, rebels in different groups gradually merged over generations into two strong communities that burrowed down in the Windward and Leeward mountain ranges in the eastern and western parts of the island and waged two brutal wars with the British army in the eighteenth century.[52] For the Southeast of North America, it has taken longer to recognize the marronage that existed on the margins of plantation society. Enslaved people faced too many obstacles to form large and functional maroon communities in the style of the Caribbean.

In *Slavery's Exiles*, historian Sylviane Diouf makes a strong case that, even though white society had a monopoly of policing powers, a significant minority of enslaved people established themselves on the borders of plantations, able to visit family and survive on their own in the woods, with occasional raids on barns and granaries to supplement their meager food.[53] Their life was dangerous, restrictive, and stressful, with their movements confined to a small perimeter mostly accessible at night, but they knew how to exploit the fluid line that separated plantation and wilderness and roamed at nighttime along the many secret paths, trails, and waterways (in the words of one scholar, their "alternative territorial system").[54] Of the 453 advertisements placed in the *Georgia Gazette* between 1763 and 1775, a clearer picture emerges. Of that number, 45 percent were "New Negroes," recent arrivals from Africa, and another 30 percent were born in Africa and had been in North America for a period of time much like Mahomet. A majority (60 percent) were aged twenty-five or under. Most were males; women accounted for only 13 percent. Most were unskilled, and most ran away singly or in pairs. The reasons for running away were multiple: to visit family and friends on neighboring plantations, especially one's spouse or children or parents; to protest an onerous work regime or brutal mistreatment; to avoid physical punishment; or more simply to gain one's freedom as a human being with natural rights.[55]

Mahomet's forced return to Mulberry Grove raises an intriguing question. The notice of 1774 stated that he was living in a settlement near the "Indian line" without specifying whether it was an encampment of white people engaged in foraging, an outlying village of Creeks, or some other kind of community. Yet shortly thereafter he was back in bondage, wearing the shackles of slavery. Was he recaptured by agents working for Graham or, more likely, by white hunters or traders moving around a contested area and looking for the generous reward? Or did Native Americans sell him back to the authorities for an even more substantial reward paid by the government? The quasi-independence of maroons was a fragile state of being always under threat.

Between 1775 and 1782, little of Mahomet's existence is known, but we do know a considerable amount about the fate of the enslaved population on John Graham's three plantations—Mulberry Grove, Montieth, and New Settlement. When the Americans belatedly declared for the revolutionary cause in March 1776, John Graham fled Georgia with the royal governor and spent the next three years in London, mixing with other loyalists bitter at their fate. During those years when the new state of Georgia took its first steps, his plantations were placed under a manager who obeyed official orders to send a contingent of slaves to build defensive fortifications on the approaches to Savannah. Thirty-two people died during those years. "[This was] particularly owing to my Negroes being employed for a considerable time in erecting a fortification on a low marsh or morass in Savannah River which proved a grave to many," Graham wrote after the war.[56]

In December 1778, a British force of twenty-five hundred men made a surprise landing near Savannah and seized the town in a brilliant tactical maneuver that chased the American government out of Georgia, at least for a moment. On hearing the gladsome news, well over a thousand Black people fled their plantations to rush into Savannah in search of freedom under the protection of the British army.[57] Those of John Graham's plantations remained in place because of close supervision and could only listen to stories of the sudden freedom that many were now enjoying in an urban setting, where customary controls had all but disappeared. In July, Graham returned from London as lieutenant governor of a restored royal government and resumed control of his plantations, still intact.

In early September 1779, a French fleet with several thousand soldiers appeared off Tybee Island. Loyalist planters like Graham hurriedly rushed their enslaved population, including Mahomet, into the protective enclave of Savannah. A combined force of French and American troops surrounded the town and began a siege in September 1779. The American forces under Gen. Benjamin Lincoln, some fifteen hundred strong, compounded the danger when they began randomly confiscating people of African descent belonging to loyalists. With the arrival of enslaved people into town, the British army recruited the more able members into a pioneer corps of laborers to build redoubts and dig ditches while an unknown number were given weapons to serve as soldiers against the enemy. Pragmatism rather than principle dominated the effort. It is probable that Mahomet worked for the army strengthening defenses or as a sometime soldier on a picket line. Although planters like Graham were alarmed at this threat to the social and economic order, their fears proved to be fleeting. After the British victory, he and other planters hustled their enslaved people back to their plantations, confident that order had been restored.[58]

As civil war gripped the lands outside Savannah and rebel guerrillas began circling Savannah, Graham's estate became a special target because of his role as lieutenant governor. A lightning raid captured twenty-one men and women and placed them on American galleys; several died under the difficult conditions aboard the vessels. Subsequently, several dozen mounted guerrillas took another nineteen people—nine men and women and ten boys and girls—a loss that cut deep into the fabric of family life.[59] An unknown number had already died of yellow fever during the Siege of Savannah in 1779.[60] Altogether 27 percent of the Black people on Graham's estate disappeared either through death or kidnapping, an enormous blow to the community that had existed before the Revolution. This appalling number counts only those noted in extant records. It may have been a larger number.

To compensate for this unfolding tragedy, the merchant-turned-planter purchased "replacement" slaves in 1781, sixteen from the estate of his deceased friend James Habersham.[61] There were undoubtedly other purchases not recorded.

When the victorious army of Gen. Anthony Wayne marched into the streets of Savannah on July 11, 1782, a new kind of border crossing unfolded. Seven weeks earlier, orders had come from the commander of British forces in North America to cease resistance, setting in motion the relocation of thousands of loyalist Georgians and their enslaved people. The evacuation began in mid-July on Tybee Island, where Graham played a lead role in organizing the chaotic efforts of over three thousand people, Blacks as well as whites, to leave the state for St. Augustine and a new beginning in what they assumed would remain a British possession. Given his office, he commandeered enough shipping for 190 men, 128 women, and 147 children from five different estates along the Savannah River, by far the largest single body to arrive in East Florida. Most of the enslaved came in small groups of five or less. Only a handful numbered twenty or more. Most seemed to be in family groupings. At the very least, the number of women was almost the same as men, a noticeable difference from those from South Carolina where men greatly outnumbered women.[62]

Ever the merchant concerned with accounts, Graham placed Mahomet and his fellow laborers on land he already owned along the Matanzas River, some two thousand acres. He set them to clearing and draining the terrain to create an indigo and rice plantation, tying their fate once again to the hard labor involved in conjuring up incredible feats of water management in the sandy soil.[63] Loyalists like Graham expected that East and West Florida would remain British colonies on the Gulf Coast and the Atlantic and made their plans accordingly. They were soon disabused.

The preliminary treaty, announced on January 20, 1783, shattered the inflated illusions of the loyalists and restored the two Floridas to Spain. Signed in September, the Treaty of Paris gave British residents eighteen months to sell their goods, collect their debts, and leave the province or decide to swear allegiance to the Spanish Crown and make the enormous leap from Protestantism to Catholicism.[64] Once the evacuation began in earnest, John Graham decided to shut down his indigo works and rice plantation, dispose of his extensive estate, and return to England to reenter the mercantile world. His thoughts turned to selling his labor force in the Jamaica market, where he had extensive experience as a slave trader before the Revolution. On learning that prices had weakened and a better return was to be had in

Beaufort, South Carolina, his manager, Col. John Douglass, shipped over two hundred people to that nearby market.[65] At Beaufort, planters hungry for labor swarmed the auction site, eagerly bidding up the price.

Mahomet and his compatriots found themselves unceremoniously carted away to a grim, new labor camp on what had recently been the southern frontier. Godin Guerard, son of a prominent slave trader and brother to the governor, purchased a dozen or more of these victims. Appreciating the work ethic that they displayed in their first weeks of work, he willingly traveled to Florida and "purchased a considerable number of Negroes at St. Augustine."[66] The new surroundings were reassuringly familiar. Mahomet and his peers found themselves only forty miles away from their old homes on the Savannah River in a familiar setting of marsh, tidal creeks, live oaks, and pine barrens.

On May 1, 1785, sixteen individuals originally from the Graham estate, including five women, three children, and eight men, made a break for liberty and headed towards Belleisle Island (today Abercorn Island) on the Savannah River and a maroon community drawn from people coming from communities along the river.[67] As a survivalist and long-time maroon, Mahomet probably assumed the leadership of the group. Shortly afterward, a second group of enslaved people from Florida on the Guerard estate made a run, including four men—Frank, Sechem, Dembo, and Cook—and one woman, Cook's wife Peggy, raising the possibility of active communication between the two groups.[68]

News, stories, rumors, and gossip traveled along the Savannah River with remarkable speed, carried by canoes, dugouts, piraguas, and small sailboats, each on their own business. That flow of information was not intended solely for the consumption of white people. A second track flourished that fed off whispers, hidden conversations, and all the alternative places that Black people frequented. The information that traveled up and down and across the Savannah was as much for a Black audience as it was for a white one. The escapes from the banks of the river to Belleisle Island underscore how the maroons of Belleisle remained in contact with the fugitives from Godard's estate and how the fugitives may have communicated among themselves.

The noteworthy presence of women in a high-risk flight underscores their determination and courage. That three in the group on May 1, 1785, were children illustrates the willingness of women to engage in long-distance flight when there was a reasonable hope of escaping beyond the reach of white authority.[69] In weighing the odds, these women were making a reasonable calculation. They were headed to a well-organized, resilient maroon community

Abercorn and Bear Creek Islands on the Savannah River. Sixteen miles above
Savannah, the two connected islands were sites for a maroon community in the 1780s
that was one of the largest and longest-lived in the United Sates. "Sketch of the
northern frontier of Georgia extending from the mouth of the Savannah River to the
town of Augusta." By Archibald Campbell, engraved by William Faden, 1780. Courtesy
of Hargrett Rare Book and Manuscript Library, University Georgia Libraries.

that had achieved independence and autonomy through the careful shep-
herding of resources.

The origins of the community dated from the loyalist evacuation in 1782
when ten to twelve men and "a number of Women" hid in the fastness of
Belleisle Island eighteen miles up the Savannah River, not far from John
Graham's plantations.[70] Gen. James Jackson, a prime mover in the Georgia
state militia, identified its several leaders as "the very fellows that fought, &
maintained their ground against the brave lancers at the siege of Savannah,

& still call themselves the King of England's soldiers."[71] Former soldiers in the Black militia of the British army may well have made their way to the more remote regions of the Savannah River as they saw their comrades in Savannah dragooned back into slavery. A Charleston paper concurred: "In this country, it is said, that some of the Negroes who formed the late camp have been in a state of rebellion since the peace; and that some of them had been employed in arms by the British in the late war."[72]

The leader of this encampment was a talented African American named Sharper, whose background suggests he may have indeed been a "King of England" soldier. Seized by British forces during Gen. Augustine Prévost's raid into the Carolina Lowcountry in 1779, he was probably recruited into one of the fighting units defending the town against the French and Americans and made his way up to Belleisle after the withdrawal of British forces.[73] Knowledgeable in the art of fighting, he took as his nom de guerre "Captain Cudjoe," perhaps, as historian Jane Landers suggests, in reference to the famous Captain Cudjoe, a skilled and ruthless guerrilla warrior who led the Leeward maroons of Jamaica during the 1730s. Under his aegis, discipline was enforced, and, on the occasional raid for food, no buildings were burned nor crops set on fire nor white people killed.[74]

Over time, Belleisle became increasingly attractive to the surrounding population, much as other maroon communities along the river had in prerevolutionary times. With as many as one hundred freedom seekers at its peak, the island sheltered a well-organized encampment with small houses or huts, fields of rice and corn, as many as fifteen boats or canoes ready to be deployed, and carefully constructed defensive positions.[75] Arriving in 1785, the Guerard fugitives represented a tipping point for the community, already straining to support itself as more and more runaways appeared. Sizing up the growing need for food, Captain Cudjoe initiated raids on neighboring plantations on both sides of the river for rice, corn, and other foodstuffs and an occasional cow.

An earlier generation of historians viewed the maroons as revolutionaries with "a collective consciousness for large scale revolt" who launched a series of guerrilla attacks and carried on "the armed struggle for freedom."[76] Historian Alan Gilbert describes them as the last breath of the "second revolution," the battle for emancipation and equality.[77] Sharply questioning this bold narrative, historian Sylviane Diouf points out that if the maroons started raiding nearby plantations in Georgia and South Carolina, their actions were linked to the need for food, not to a more general struggle against slavery.[78] Diouf has the better of the argument. The reasons why the ma-

roons began raiding nearby plantations had more to do with their taking in
too many fugitives too rapidly, relative to what their modest economy could
sustain, not because of an armed struggle for freedom.[79]

After repeated maroon raids to steal provisions, the state ordered a militia company under Gen. James Jackson, a Revolutionary War hero, into the
swampy terrain of the river islands in search of the maroons. The soldiers located the settlement, but the first two parties of soldiers were beaten back in
an inconclusive exchange of gunfire. Jackson promptly led a third attempt,
found and burned numerous houses, and destroyed four acres of rice. Following classic maroon tactics, the inhabitants had already fled and regrouped
at a swamp in South Carolina, where they continued to raid plantations on
both sides of the Savannah River, carrying off substantial quantities of rice
to compensate for their losses.[80] In early 1787, Sharper and his followers returned to Belleisle Island at a more remote site on Bear Creek and constructed a sizable encampment, with twenty-one houses and land cleared for
rice and potatoes. Around this settlement, they built a four-foot high wall
out of logs and cane, created a narrow entrance, and posted a sentry along a
creek to give alarm, creating a veritable war camp.[81]

A quarrel between Sharper and his chief lieutenant, Lewis, though hastily patched up, weakened the group and led to a fateful decision that proved
the community's undoing at precisely the moment when the South Carolina militia had joined the hunt. Sharper had wisely dictated limited contact with the outside world and enforced his rule ruthlessly. Lewis violated
that edict at great cost. He brought into the hidden village a white man who
may have been a Pietist from the German community of Ebenezer eager to
trade. Captain Cudjoe ordered the unwelcomed visitor executed. The military discipline he imposed was unforgiving.

Despite this repudiation, Lewis made an even more crucial mistake. He
allowed himself to be persuaded by Mahomet and others among the Florida fugitives to go back to the Guerard plantation and liberate members of
their community still held there. That decision suggested the frequency and
depth of the communication between the maroons and people on the estate. Two large canoes set out toward dusk one evening. On the circuitous
way through tidal creeks and swamp, white patrollers ambushed the canoes,
killed two of the men, and wounded others. The rapid retreat of the maroons
to Bear Creek gave away the general location of the community.[82]

Rather than slip away as they had on other occasions, Sharper, Lewis,
and their lieutenants chose to lie in wait for the expected attack, confident
in their defensive fortifications and determined not to be forced away from

their food supplies.[83] The denouement stretched over eight days. In a series of firefights, at least ten maroons were killed, probably more. Several women and children were taken prisoner, among them Fatima and Hannah, who, when asked who they belonged to, replied "John Graham," not "Guerard."[84] Captured, Lewis was tried, interrogated, and condemned to be hung, "After Which his head to be Cut of and Stuck upon a pole to be sett up on the Island of Marsh opposite the Glebe land in Savannah River." From his testimony comes the wealth of information about the community that supplies so much of the historical narrative.[85]

Many others, however, made good their escape, seven of whom were thought to be headed "on their way to the Indian nation," possibly the Creeks but more likely the Seminoles. Not long afterward, a man named Sharper and his wife Nancy asked for sanctuary in St. Augustine. Historian Jane Landers speculates that it may be one and the same Sharper.[86] The fate of Mahomet was captured in a petition of Godin Guerard to the Carolina legislature that prayed "to be paid for sundry negroes killed in arms against the State."[87] Survivors may have regrouped in small bands or family units, others may have left the area altogether, and some may have made it to Florida.[88]

Mahomet demonstrated unwavering bravery and determination against the monopoly of power arrayed against him that lasted throughout his twenty years of servitude. As a Muslim uprooted from his faith community, thrown into a mostly male enclave with few women and children, he resisted the crushing of his soul at every step of the way. At Mulberry Grove, where men outnumbered women by a considerable margin and the mortality rate in the rice fields was high, his alienation seemed total. His years as a maroon in a remote part of the colony may have forced him to generate his own resources but provided an environment that enabled him to enjoy autonomy, self-sufficiency, and freedom of movement that only isolation can provide. The drama of recapture and the punishment that followed opened another long chapter. The Revolution brought a fresh set of trials. If Mahomet failed to flee the plantation during those years, his final years of life carried him to East Florida, then South Carolina, and once again to the margins of Georgia, where he demonstrated exceptional courage and sangfroid as a maroon.

Mahomet's experience during the Revolution leaves a puzzle. Why did this man who escaped under difficult circumstances in peacetime not succeed in slipping away during the seven years of revolutionary warfare when hundreds of others did so? Perhaps he did. That part of his life remains a mystery. For a high percentage of Africans, the Revolution in Georgia prompted unprecedented movement across the landscape of the Lowcountry, giving them a new sense of the geography of the Southeast. For the enslaved, the Revolution generated radically different choices in terms of how individuals interpreted the meaning of emancipation and equality and where they chose to go. The extraordinary upheaval that gave birth to the United States marks the beginning of a sustained forty-year-effort by Black Georgians to gain freedom and redemption in Spanish Florida and in Seminole and Creek towns. The irony of Mahomet's life lies in how the postrevolutionary period became the moment of final liberation through his death in battle. The story suggests the underlying continuity that ties together the history of the Georgia coast from the mid-eighteenth century to the second decade of the nineteenth.

CHAPTER 3

Hercules, Revolution, and British Florida

As the last colony to embrace the revolutionary cause, Georgia entered the grand conflict reluctantly and under the scornful eyes of Carolinians, appalled at its seemingly spineless response to events. The province had good reason to resist the rush to war. The creation of a plantation economy over the preceding quarter-century had lifted it out of virtual bankruptcy to an unprecedented economic boom that created a deep well of loyalty to the British Empire. The colony looked as much to Jamaica, St. Kitts, and the rest of the British Caribbean as to the North American mainland. It did not seem wise to enter into an uncertain conflict when a loyal British East Florida lay on its southern border and an increasingly hostile Creek Nation was only a few miles beyond the Ogeechee River.[1] As late as January 1776, the royal governor, Sir James Wright, a skillful tactician who had consistently outmaneuvered his opponents, tenaciously clung to power. Only gradually did the trappings of royal power unravel: first the militia, then the judiciary, and finally local government.[2]

Despite living on a barrier island, an enslaved African named Hercules was ever attuned to the rumors afloat in Savannah as the colony drifted toward war. Never an isolated figure, he found himself, circumstantial evidence suggests, an intermediary between the over one hundred people on Ossabaw Island and the larger world where new ideas were crowding in on them. As a builder and sailor of small craft, he was in and out of Savannah to deliver commodities and pick up supplies, make stops at Beaulieu, a plantation on the mainland across from Ossabaw, and carry out assignments to other plantations along the Ogeechee River. During his town visits, he conversed with fellow bondsmen at the wharf and store of John Morel, his enslaver, and was privy to news about unfolding events and Morel's election as a member of the Council of Safety.[3]

Like Mahomet, Hercules was an African who survived the Middle Passage and arrived in Georgia at roughly the same time, around 1768. His point of origin was a vast area called Angola in central West Africa where hundreds of different languages and cultures came into play.[4] Rather than being placed on a rice plantation as in the case with Mahomet, Hercules found himself in the middle of Ossabaw Island, eleven thousand acres of untapped upland that held valuable live oak trees for shipbuilding, room for cattle herds, and the kind of soil on which the indigo plant could grow.[5]

The life of Hercules offers a map for navigating the full spectrum of the landscape for Black people in revolutionary Savannah. His story is all about movement, movement between a barrier island and the mainland, around the battle lines in the Siege of Savannah in 1779, through a swampy area on the mainland in an ill-timed escape, and the final long-distance journey to British East Florida with his wife Betty and their two children. It is a story about hope, a hope qualified by the highs and lows of war—the separations, disruptions, and dashed dreams of people who thought self-emancipation a realistic possibility only to be returned to slavery all too often. His life offers a measure of the rise, fall, and the rise again of hope in a fluid situation where white authority, whether that of patriot or loyalist, was resolutely hostile, and the attitudes of the British officer corps unpredictable. Once the family arrived in St. Augustine, choices had to be made in a totally new setting. Those choices tell us much about the landscape of "freedom" beyond Georgia.

Their enslaver, Morel, had come as a boy with his family in the early days of the colony and then matured into an entrepreneur who saw enslavement from a different angle than most of his peers. Not yet forty years old in 1763, the successful merchant acquired full ownership of the barrier island to become one of the first planters in Georgia to cultivate and manufacture the rich blue indigo dye on a commercial scale. Having grown up as child in Trusteeship Georgia, he possessed a natural shrewdness about the conditions for success in this frontier colony. On his three plantations on Ossabaw, he produced indigo, raised cattle, grew provisions for the Savannah market, and had his labor force cut live oaks to build ships capable of crossing the Atlantic. Instead of acquiring slaves from the booming markets in Charles Town or from mariners sailing into Savannah, he worked out an arrangement to take

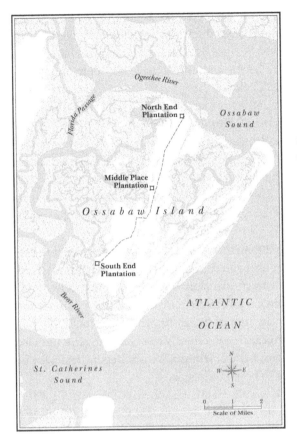

Ossabaw Island, late
eighteenth century

over the estate of Patrick Brown, a deceased deerskin merchant in Augusta, with its fifty-nine people.[6]

Originally from South Carolina, the men and women among that population had spent years at the trading post of Augusta and knew how to scrape skins, stack leather pelts in warehouses, load packhorses, and row the piraguas that carried the pelts to Charles Town. Brown's brother, a gilder in Dublin, inherited the estate on Patrick's death and moved the African Americans to the coast to attempt a rice plantation. When that effort failed, he sold them to Morel and returned to Ireland. Morel promptly moved them to the island in hopes of creating an agricultural empire based on indigo, timbering, and garden farming.[7]

Rather than a predominantly male group with few children like Mahomet's on Mulberry Grove, the community consisted of families, with as many women as there were men and as many children as there were adults. Unlike their peers from Africa who produced few children, these Carolinians created large families. Tom and Nelly boasted five sons and daughters—Tise, Abraham, Joe, Saffee, and Phebe—and were to have two more once on the island, Bacchus and Titus. Dick and Bess had six children; Carolina and Molly had four; and Sam and Venus were already parents to seven before setting foot in this new setting.[8] From Morel's point of view, the men and women who made up the Brown estate were much less likely to flee than were recently acquired Africans, understood something of the white world, and were accustomed to the give-and-take of negotiating with their "master" for the terms of work. They formed a community well on its way to developing a distinct identity at once African and American, one that promised benefits to both parties.

By the time of the Revolution, there were others from Africa, but the addition of outsiders did not alter the demographics of the settlement. Families still dominated, with thirty-two husbands and wives, twelve single men, and three single women with children. Living with their parents were seventy-six boys and girls, an astonishing 49 percent of the total.[9] New arrivals typically married into existing families. Many bore African names like Auba, Quamina, Mundingo, Larcho, Jemima, Tenah, Begora, and Dembo, but the majority were creoles born in Georgia.

The original families diligently maintained their position as the dominant group. According to an inventory in 1777, "old Charles" and his wife Rose had apparently died, but their son "young Charles" was now the driver for the main plantation, the most highly valued person on the inventory. The sisters of his wife, Diana, were married to principal figures on the plantation. Even an older couple like Joe and Nancy enjoyed a measure of importance in the community because of their daughter's marriage to Hector, a native of Angola and the indispensable blacksmith.[10] Betty, the daughter of Anthony and Kate, took as her husband Hercules, "a short thick fellow" from Angola.[11] The integration of outsiders into existing families was a distinctive feature of these Carolinians. As a craftsman capable of working with boats, Hercules brought valuable skills.

The community was hardworking, and the settlements on Ossabaw—North End, Middle Place, and South End plantations—were immensely productive. The several thousand pounds of indigo produced annually fed the rapidly expanding textile mills of England with a dye that was cheaper than the indigo grown in the French Caribbean but still commanded a good price.[12] Ossabaw's economy waxed and waned with the fortunes of the Industrial Revolution in England. The enslaved men who manned the beating vats developed the feel and touch of self-taught chemists producing for commercial markets. The indigo plant was no stranger to people from the immense Guinea region. For several hundred years, it had served as the foundation for numerous textile traditions in West Africa.[13]

Other products too connected this seemingly isolated island to the Atlantic world. Morel created a shipyard to take advantage of the ample supply of valuable live oaks whose curved features and dense wood made them ideal for specialty parts for vessels. African and African American craftsmen constructed the *Elizabeth*, an eighty-four-foot vessel with a twenty-four-foot width, a fully rigged ship with three masts, designed to carry barrels of rice to European markets.[14] The four hundred head of cattle that roamed freely across the landscape provided beef for the sugar islands in the Caribbean, while the provisions grown on the island made it a grocery store for Savannah.

As an artisan engaged in building watercraft as well as participating in the manufacture of indigo, Hercules was intimately bound to the Atlantic economy, and, although that did not alter his presence on an isolated island, it nevertheless brought him into the rhythms of the Atlantic world and the competitive demands that came with it.[15] His life moved in time with the market for indigo in London, the market for beef in the Caribbean, the demands of the shipbuilding world, and the need for provisions in Savannah. He was part of a community of enslaved people distributed across three plantations on an island, a fourth plantation at Beaulieu on the mainland, as well as in Savannah at John Morel's wharf, warehouses, and house.[16] Approximately twenty to thirty field hands worked each unit, with those too young or feeble adding to the numbers at each location. Almost as a matter of course, many in the community were accustomed to frequent crossing of the coastal waterways—in canoes, piraguas, yawls, or small schooners. Produce was transported to market and supplies regularly purchased while field hands were shifted from plantation to plantation and from island to mainland and back again as the needs of the enterprise evolved across the agricultural seasons. Families were split as young children grew up and were moved around to meet the labor needs of the growing enterprise.[17]

As a frequent visitor to Savannah, Hercules was well aware of the unraveling of the royal government under James Wright and the first signs that the Revolution might actually bear fruit for enslaved people. In early 1776, the British navy stationed a small fleet off Tybee Island in search of rice for besieged troops in Boston. Black fugitives began making their way through thick marsh and across tidal creeks and rivers to that three-mile-long sandbar with little more than a lighthouse and a lazaretto station. They had good reason. The brash governor of Virginia, the Earl of Dunmore, had issued a proclamation the previous November that promised liberty for all slaves of rebels in Virginia willing to join British forces and fight for the Crown. The promise became a reality with the creation of a several-hundred-strong "Ethiopian Regiment," whose members were rumored to wear sashes emblazoned with the indelible message "Liberty to Slaves."[18] Reacting to the news, a Georgia delegate, John Houstoun, warned the president of the Continental Congress, "The negroes have a wonderful art of communicating intelligence among themselves; it will run several hundreds of miles in a week or fortnight."[19]

Indeed, in the first months of the new year, several hundred bondsmen made the effort to reach Tybee where a small British fleet, looking for rice to feed the Boston garrison, was cruising. Separated from the mainland by a marsh rooted in sticky mud, Tybee was inundated twice a day by tides that rose six to eight feet, presenting myriad challenges for those seeking to make their way through the wetland. From the decks of the warship *Scarborough*, where he had taken refuge, Governor Wright witnessed the arrival of the fugitives and later estimated that some two to three hundred people had eventually made it to the vessels, declaring "they were come for the King."[20] Of the three individuals mentioned in a letter by a local merchant, one originated on an island across from Mahomet's plantation, another from the docks of Savannah where he worked as a cooper, and a third from the Ogeechee River near Ossabaw.[21] Despite an expedition by the Council of Safety to recover the fugitives, only twelve were secured. No massacre of freedom seekers occurred as has been suggested.[22] Instead, frigates from the Royal Navy carried refugees to St. Augustine, where the governor, James Grant, placed them under the supervision of various planters and merchants eager for additional labor. Their legal status remained a murky question mark, neither free nor enslaved.[23]

In March 1776, vessels of the Royal Navy slipped up the Savannah River, captured more than a dozen rice boats, and escorted them down to the entrance of the river at Tybee. The mission succeeded in securing much-needed rice for the hard-pressed British army in Boston besieged by Washington's forces. That minor engagement produced enough cannonading and smoke to allow the rebels to proudly call the Battle of the Rice Boats a signal victory. The skirmish was indeed important because it forced Georgians off the sidelines and into the serious business of reordering the onetime colony. For three uneasy years, the revolutionaries hammered out the essentials of a state government, debated how to control the many loyalists who remained be-hind, and fought a vigorous border war below the Altamaha River.[24]

As a newly formed state within the fledgling confederation of indepen-dent states, Georgia was vulnerable to attack. To the west lay the towns and settlements of the Creeks, many of which leaned toward the British. To the south lay the undiminished power of British East Florida where a military government was supported by a regiment of soldiers under the command of Col. Augustine Prévost. The vicious border war that followed left a deep scar on the landscape that lasted well beyond the war. It created an unfortunate template for the region that shaped much of its history over the next forty years. A vacuum of power invited individuals, small groups, and larger bod-ies to assert their influence in the absence of viable government.

From the onset of the war until the end of 1778, the lands between the Altamaha and St. Johns Rivers became a no-man's-land, where raids and counter-raids were common occurrences and a succession of American in-vasions of East Florida made life uncertain for every resident. In an opening bid, the newly founded state militia under Lachlan McIntosh went about "destroying every plantation between the rivers St. Johns and St. Mary," not only to achieve military objectives but also to help themselves to cattle and slaves.[25] A planter on the St. Marys, William Chapman, reported that thirty-five of the enslaved people on his plantation had been stolen or es-caped, a clue that some African Americans saw a silver lining and took the opportunity to make a bid for freedom. Americans carried off thirty bonds-men from the settlement of a London merchant and several dozen more from the estate of a Swiss planter. Loyalist planters fled south. Within seven months of their arrival from the Wright estates on the St. Marys, twenty-four men, women, and children had died, as had Charles Wright, their el-derly enslaver.[26] Starvation, disease, and death were ever-present among all those who tried to evade the American attacks.[27]

The aggressive governor of British East Florida, Patrick Tonyn, launched a counteroffensive after appointing the young, charismatic Thomas Brown as commander of the newly created Florida Rangers. A resident of Au-gusta bitter at having the soles of his feet burned by patriots in the opening months of the war, the newly minted colonel filled the ranks of the provin-cial company with loyalists from Georgia and South Carolina, a sprinkling of Black fighters, and occasional Creeks and Seminoles. Within short order, the Rangers expanded their role from protecting the border to raiding cat-tle, seizing slaves, and burning plantations and farms across the St. Marys, reaching as far as the Altamaha River.[28]

Adding to the misery of African Americans in southern Georgia were the guerrilla bands loosely connected to the Florida Rangers. By far the most fearsome and effective was that of Daniel McGirt and his followers, who oscillated between sheer banditry and serving as an organized fighting force. Calling out their effectiveness, merchant Joseph Clay lamented, "We are again much infested with Tonyns Banditti Stealing our Horses & Negroes & doing us all the Mischief they can as Thieves."[29] Later in the war, a patriot newspaper denounced "a large body of infamous banditti and horse thieves that perhaps ever were collected together anywhere, under the direction of McGirt . . . a corps of Indians, with negro and white savages disguised like them [including disaffected poor people from the back settlements]."[30] The interracial gang reflected the same egalitarian ethos that characterized other outlaw societies. Those enslaved that had been captured and brought to East Florida faced being sold out of hand. The "banditti" and loyalist fighters had a decidedly ambiguous relationship with Black people, incorporating a rare few into their band of brothers and profiting from the sale of the rest.

To end the raids, the State of Georgia launched two controversial invasions over the strenuous objections of the commander of the Continental troops, who rightly feared that shoddy logistics and lack of manpower would doom the enterprises. The first barely made it to Amelia Island before it fell apart due to disease and lack of supplies. In the late spring of 1778, the second reached the Alligator River in swamps inside East Florida but disintegrated in the face of harassing attacks, lack of supplies, and a hopelessly divided command.[31]

The one-hundred-mile strip between the Altamaha and St. Johns Rivers brought an uncertain existence. An economy based on herds of cattle and a few plantations did not survive, and the lives of fifteen hundred to two thousand Africans on both sides of the St. Marys were torn apart in the process.[32] Many individuals were captured, kidnapped, or succeeded in running away to an uncertain fate. Many more died through the hardships of dislocation and starvation. "Negro huts" were destroyed; clothing and other modest possessions disappeared; families were torn apart as armies and marauding bands of guerrillas roamed across the landscape. Of the original Black population in southern Georgia, some ended up in East Florida either through capture or through the migration of loyalist planters. Others were taken northward beyond the fighting, an undetermined number died from the shock of limited food and deteriorating living conditions, and still others fled to the Seminole Indians or made their way to safer zones, perhaps Savannah or St. Augustine.

Hercules found a space that gave him a taste of the border war while enhancing his knowledge of coastal geography. English merchants in St. Augustine stood ready to buy indigo bricks, a fairly lightweight and easily transportable commodity of high value. Indigo planters like the Morels were delighted to see a black market for their crops emerge from the trauma of war and more than willing to send small watercraft to British East Florida. Prominent planters like George McIntosh, member of the revolutionary Council of Safety in Savannah, and Thomas Young, a genial loyalist with friends on both sides of the political divide, took part.[33] The episodic border war invited the smuggling of commodities out of Georgia by planters anxious to evade the coastal blockade by the Royal Navy and overseers eager to milk an opportunity on their own.

According to court documents, one or more overseers on Ossabaw Island participated in the smuggling. A prosecuting attorney asked a witness after the Revolution, "Did not one Hodson the overseer at Ossabaw take a large boat and with one Ellis in a schooner carry off to Augustine some boxes of indigo, myrtle wax, and everything that was saleable?" A proficient waterman, Hercules was almost certainly a seaman on these adventures, picking up invaluable knowledge of waterways with their shifting sandbars and connecting creeks. In addition, privateers called "picaroons" raided plantations on the barrier islands for an easy chance to secure needed crops. An overseer on Ossabaw assisted their dark enterprise in return for a bribe. Hercules and his companions may well have internalized the connections with East Florida, the war serving as a vivid lesson in the coastal landscape.[34]

That scenario changed dramatically when, on December 28, 1778, a British army landed a few miles south of Savannah and overwhelmed the surprised, undermanned, and demoralized defenders of the town. Gen. Henry Clinton, commander-in-chief of the British armies in North America, dispatched somewhere between two thousand and three thousand British troops under Lt. Col. Archibald Campbell from New York to open a southern campaign in a bid to end the stalemate in the North. He looked to the South for fresh resources from three distinct groups: loyalists; Black people; and Creeks, Cherokees, and Seminoles, many of whose talwas or towns showed strong pro-British proclivities. The Revolution in Georgia was poised to become three parallel revolutions, white, black, and red.[35]

Already in the Upper South as well as northern states, the Revolution had turned into a momentous event that brought an enormous defection from slavery from a people thought by white southerners to be loyal, passive, and ignorant of the grand political currents sweeping British North America. Historian Gary Nash calls the moment the first mass slave rebellion in American history, the first attempt by enslaved Black people to wrest equality from a resistant white society, and the first large-scale construction of free Black life attempted until Reconstruction.[36] If his argument may overstate the case, it points the way to fresh thinking about the extraordinary upheaval in Georgia where people of African descent made clear their aspirations and had a voice in the outcome.

In response to the invasion, hundreds of enslaved Georgians left their plantations and sought the protection of the British army now in control of Savannah. It was an electrifying moment. The master-slave relationship was severely tested as Campbell found on a march northward toward Augusta. On January 9, 1779, less than two weeks after landing, the colonel noted, "The Bandittis of Negroes who flock to the conquerors . . . do ten thousand times more Mischief than the whole Army put together."[37] At the end of January, a "Board of Police" in Savannah, set up to reestablish "order" in the countryside, found 925 slaves left on abandoned properties between the Savannah and Ogeechee Rivers, considerably less than their population a few weeks before.[38]

When Wright returned from London in July as the reappointed royal governor, he was shocked at finding "vast numbers of Negroes" ("I may venture to say some or several Thousands") and called the leading planters and merchants to his house to address the "growing evil" of Black people "at loose" in the town.[39] Seeking the protection of the British army, Black Georgians had flocked to Savannah and radically changed the tenor of life, challenging the basis for white supremacy and the stability of the social order. White Georgians were horrified at the sight of Blacks wandering the streets of Savannah, sleeping in abandoned houses, sheltering in hastily constructed shantytowns, picking up odd jobs from the British military, and displaying an independence deemed insolent and threatening.

While loyalist planters were horrified at Black assertions of independence, the British army took a pragmatic approach. Ultimately, the military had no intention of overturning the social order and jeopardizing their relations with the loyal white population, but it intended to use the extra manpower to best advantage. General Prévost, formerly commander in St. Augustine and successor to the departing Campbell, commissioned his chief engineer, Maj. James Moncrief, to form a corps of pioneers from the floating population of African Americans to begin strengthing Savannah's fortifications. The corps set about building a series of redoubts around the perimeter and digging ditches to slow the advance of enemy troops in an expected counterattack. Eventually several hundred men and women were engaged in hauling supplies and military equipment, working in military hospitals, preparing food in kitchens, and washing laundry.

By the end of the summer, only three to four redoubts had been finished, while the wall around Savannah remained incomplete. The pace picked up when observers on Tybee spied a French fleet hovering off the coast with twenty-five ships of the line and nine frigates led by the Count d'Estaing, fresh from a stunning naval victory over the English in the Caribbean. An estimated thirty-five hundred troops landed at the Morel plantation on Beaulieu, lost valuable time slogging toward Savannah, and joined with an American army led by Gen. Benjamin Lincoln to begin a siege of the town. With a regiment of their soldiers seemingly marooned on Hilton Head, the British staff had begun to contemplate defeat.[40]

In this moment of crisis, an order from the royal governor called on planters to supply five hundred slaves to prepare the defenses for a last-ditch effort. Most willingly complied. A few resisted. Stubborn and headstrong, Mary Morel, John's widow, thought that the isolation of Ossabaw would give her an exemption, ignored the order, and counted on her connections to extract a pass. The governor and his council refused to bend to her entreaties and commanded her to send thirty laborers to Savannah equipped with hoes, axes, spades, and cooking utensils or face a steep fine.[41]

When Hercules stepped off onto the docks in Savannah, he witnessed a stunning sight. The town's population had exploded and now held between two and three thousand soldiers; hundreds of freedom seekers, most of whom were working to support the needs of the British army; hundreds more enslaved people taken in the Carolina Lowcountry on a raid by Prévost; and refugees from the countryside, both white and Black. On the wharves were stacked provisions, cannons, equipment, and wagons, all of which had to be lifted by cranes forty feet to the top of the bluff. Hercules and his companions encountered a mass of people on the narrow strip of land and lumber that formed the wharves: soldiers, officers, commissaries to handle supplies for the army, "wharf negroes," freedom seekers who had found employment with the army, enslaved workers, and planters bringing their enslaved people to town to keep them out of the hands of the Americans. It was a confusing if exhilarating sight, the first time that hope took a tangible form.

Ignoring the protests of a powerless Governor Wright, the British military began training volunteers for a Black militia to supplement their forces outnumbered by thousands of French and Americans. In a supreme irony, those soldiers faced a company of 547 free Blacks and biracial people from the French colony of Saint-Domingue who hoped that their service would enhance their status within the colony. The presence of the Chasseurs-Volontaires made the Siege of Savannah distinctive, with Black soldiers pitted against Black soldiers, although there is no evidence that they ever fired on one another or were even aware of each other's presence. Sadly, the hopes of the Dominican regiment were not realized.[42]

As a first step in manning the defenses, Prévost turned to a loyalist from South Carolina, William Hanscomb, a coach maker by trade who had already raised a company of Black pioneers to help build the network of redoubts around the town's perimeter. Accustomed to working with skilled Black craftsmen, he showed the respect and confidence that gained their loyalty. Faced with long odds, General Prévost armed the company.[43] Here was a concrete measure of hope that Black refugees could understand and embrace. John Zubly, son of the Presbyterian minister and a planter, noted, "During the siege 8, or more of my slaves were constantly in arms."[44] Minimizing the risk, the general placed his Hessian troops behind the company of Black soldiers, with loyalist units from North Carolina and South Carolina on the lefthand side and a unit from New York on the right.[45]

The siege, which began September 16, generated an enormous surge in the morale of Black participants, whether soldiers or pioneers, enslaved or free. At that heady moment all seemed possible. A letter submitted to the Claims Commission in London after the war offers a measure of the optimism that enveloped participants. In a memorial, Scipio Handley, a free Black soldier, described quitting Charleston when the royal governor departed in 1775 and making his way to the relative safety of Barbados. When he heard that the British had retaken Georgia, he had taken it on himself to board the first vessel for Savannah and resume his life in the Lowcountry under British rule. The arrival of the French and "rebels" on the coast thrust him into a situation he had not expected. "As [the town] was very bare of troops," he explained, "all that was in it were Employed both White & Black, in order to Endeavour to keep them off." The siege represented a tremendous collective effort in which every participant was working towards the same goal. Handley, recognizing that he and other people of color could have paid a heavy price, added, "If [the rebels] had succeeded in their attempt they would have had no mercy on many."[46] Officers in the American forces had been on the prowl for fugitive slaves. One reported that he had captured seven of his own slaves and hoped to find more once the town fell.[47]

If Hercules had been able to walk around the British lines, he would have seen how pervasive their service had become. Black soldiers not only fought as independent militia but also as an integral part of white companies. Col. Stephen De Lancey of New York recruited 18 Black men to fight alongside 228 whites. The Georgia loyalists incorporated 10 Blacks with 104 whites, and the Engineering Department, a nonfighting unit, had 41 Blacks and 39 whites. The records of payment of wages show that 235 Black people were in various fighting units, not counting those serving in the redoubts or on vessels of the Royal Navy in the Savannah River or four dozen who were simply listed as "volunteers." Historian Alan Gilbert calculates that over 450 people of African descent were under arms, roughly 10 percent of total imperial forces.[48] Archaeologists Rita and Dan Elliott are more conservative in their estimate. By their count, 620 African Americans were fed by the commissary general at the time of the siege, a mixture of soldiers and laborers hard to tease out. From several lists of payments for services, they tallied 218 "Volunteer Negroes," 54 people of African descent employed in the "Redoubts," 13 in the first battalion of the South Carolina Royalists, 20 in General de Wissenbach's battalion, and 36 "Negroes" as sailors and seamen, in addition to others.[49]

Circumstantial evidence suggests that Hercules was one of those soldiers. Col. Thomas Brown commanded the far-ranging Florida Rangers, a cavalry unit that Col. Archibald Campbell had at first dismissed as "a mere rabble of undisciplined Freebooters" (he altered his opinion when he witnessed their fighting ability).[50] Created to stop the Georgia militia from harassing the British, the Rangers evolved into an offensive force that struck farms and plantations throughout southern Georgia while incorporating Indians and people of African descent into its ranks as occasion demanded.[51] During the siege, Prévost stationed Brown and the Rangers on the far right side of the British line, opposite Lachlan McGillivray's rice plantation.[52] In addition to his normal duties, Brown assumed command of a Black militia unit. In the days that followed the defeat of the Franco-American force on October 9, a British officer recalled, "There was a good deal of skirmishing on Mr. McGillivray's plantation between some negroes and a party of rebels, and the latter were several times driven from the buildings on the plantation into the woods." Three were wounded and one killed.[53] Sometime later, a naval officer noted that "the armed negroes brought in two Rebel Dragoons and eight horses, and killed two rebels who were in a foraging party."[54]

The evidence of Hercules's presence in that militia is circumstantial but suggestive. When he escaped from Ossabaw Island with his wife and family and landed in East Florida many months later, he immediately went to the headquarters of Brown and placed his family under the protection of the colonel. The second family involved in the escape elected to travel to the Seminoles a few dozen miles west.[55] Hercules and his family remained with Brown for four years. The deposition of a British deserter from Savannah toward the end of the war testified that about 150 Blacks, "armed and equipt as infantry," served under a Colonel Brown.[56] It is not clear whether he is referring to the time of the siege or the closing days of the conflict. Nor was Hercules the only Morel slave who fought in the battle. When York escaped from Ossabaw in 1781, he was wearing "an old blue coat of the Hessian uniform" issued by Hessian auxiliaries.[57] The records of the Hessian troops under the command of Count Friedrich von Porbeck mention the work of African Americans as soldiers, laborers, and musicians.[58]

Sending those conscripts back to their enslavers was a slow process. Following the stunning victory against a superior force, a large contingent of Black militiamen remained stationed around the walls of Savannah while individuals walked about carrying weapons and showing a confidence that whites found deeply threatening. Offering a modest tribute to their contribution in a report to General Prévost, Governor Wright quickly shifted his tone and lobbied the commanding general to disarm the soldiers, curb the various freedoms that African Americans were enjoying, and discipline the "Number of Slaves [who appear] in Arms and behave with great insolence." Other notables trotted out "outrages" and hinted that outright rebellion was only a matter of time.[59] Leading the list of protesters were the most prominent slave merchants of the colonial era who had vast sums at stake with their London factors. The December presentments of the grand jury to the chief justice echoed their sentiments:

> We present as a Grievance, the great Number of Negroes, that are suffered to stroll about, both in Town and Country, many with Fire-arms, and other offensive Weapons, committing Robberies and other Enormities, to the great Terror and Annoyance of the Inhabitants thereof; and we recommend that those employed upon public Service should wear some Badge or Mark of Distinction whereby they may be known.[60]

A frustrated Governor Wright described for the secretary of state the wide range of freedoms that the hundreds of African Americans enjoyed in wartime Savannah:

> Many Inconveniences are complained of from Negroes occupying Houses under no Control from any White Person; selling and otherwise dealing

or trading without any Limitation or Check; and . . . many were skulking about in the Woods, who had no apparent Means of Subsistence but the Plunder of the adjoining Plantations; with many other Enormities, contrary to the Laws and Good Policy.[61]

In the aftermath of victory, official British policy in Savannah abruptly changed to one of returning self-emancipated Black people to their enslavers and enforcing the sanctity of the property rights of loyalists, whose support was critical to the army's success. In November 1779, General Prévost complained, "The works [construction of fortifications] go on but not so briskly as I wish. Since the news of the raising the siege of Savannah, most of the planters have retaken their negroes; and I am sorry to tell your Excellency that the Governor's negroes were the very first who went away."[62] Ultimately, Hercules found himself hustled back onto the island in the same fashion as other slaves to their original plantations. Planters like the Morels were quick to give their loyalty to the restored royal government. The months after the stunning and unexpected British victory at the Siege of Savannah saw a rapid shutting down of the avenues for escape as planters tightened their grip on the countryside.

Nevertheless, the growing civil war meant that those avenues were never completely closed off.[63] On Ossabaw, the Morels lost five of their Black laborers who chose a traditional pattern of flight and sought out either family members or a former home. According to a notice in the *Georgia Royal Gazette*, four were "formerly the property of Jonathan Bryan," Mary Morel's wealthy father who had given them to her on her marriage. Abraham and Billy fled to be with their wives, servants of Mary who had been moved off the island and were now residing on a plantation not far from her father. Billy headed to Yamacraw when he learned that his wife had been living "for the few weeks past" at Mr. Cade's house in that biracial neighborhood.[64] A married couple, York and Priscilla, disappeared to seek family and friends on the Bryan estate. [65] A fifth person, Joe, had been the "property" of Peter Tondee, a deceased taverner in Savannah. He refused to accept his forcible uprooting from an urban setting when sold to the Morels.[66] On the mainland, Thomas Gibbons advertised for eighteen Africans who had run away from his cousin's rice plantation during the twenty months since the British invasion.[67]

Mary Morel moved Betty and Hercules and their two children to a newly established labor camp on the mainland in an attempt to convert a large tract of marshy land into a rice plantation. Morel had received two thousand acres across from the island as compensation for several hundred head of cattle confiscated from her earlier in the war. From being an artisan with recognized skills, Hercules found himself and his wife in a primitive setting that required backbreaking labor clearing marsh and swamp without the benefit of the strong family community on Ossabaw. Within weeks, the family disappeared into the maritime forest. Quickly caught, they were returned to Ossabaw, where flight was more problematic.[68]

That experience spurred Hercules to think in larger terms. Back on the island in January 1781, he began a different set of calculations to measure out the risks and possibilities of reaching British East Florida by water. It was not a far-fetched gamble. During the years of the border war along the St. Marys River, he learned the route or routes to Florida through the smuggling of indigo bricks. In the early fall, he and Betty brought into their plot another family, Jupiter and Auba and their two children, as well as a single person, Jack. Jupiter spoke "good English" according to a notice placed by John Morel's son and was probably creole. His wife, Auba, may have come from Africa if her name is any indication. She had a "suckling" child whose name is not known.[69]

The presence of Jack raises a tantalizing possibility. Both he and Hercules were from the vast area called Angola and probably had close ties with each other since the majority of people forcibly brought to Savannah originated in the regions of upper West Africa—Senegambia, Sierra Leone, and the Windward Coast. But that is not certain. He may have come from the Kingdom of Kongo on the western coast, a strong centralized state that had developed a form of African Christianity from their contacts with the Portuguese. Or he may have had roots in the Kingdom of Ndongo, south of Kongo, where Christianity had scarcely penetrated and where the Imgangala, a marauding group allied to the Portuguese, pillaged villages in the search for captives. Or, just as likely, he could have been born into another group of people in the region.[70] Whether or not Hercules and Jack shared the same broad cultural background, it is not inconceivable that they were together on a vessel that made the Middle Passage and enjoyed a tight bond based on that experience. Aged forty-five and speaking "bad English," Jack was a singular person, the one member of the group that was not accompanied by family.

Experienced in shipbuilding as well as navigating the waters, Hercules was at work on a twenty-foot yawl on which pitch had recently been applied to seal the wood. The craft was still unfinished. With a set of four oars and a tiny sail, the yawl was a type of craft typically used in and around ports to go from shore to vessel or between vessels. Clothing and food were prepared; the flow and ebb of tides was considered; and the planners questioned whether to stay behind the islands and the relative safety they offered or to venture into the Atlantic. Nine people—five adults, three children, and an infant—crowded into a boat that depended as much on rowing as on one small piece of sailcloth in contending with waves and wind.[71]

Whether Hercules and company could pass unobserved on the waters to Florida was another question. In time of peace, a variety of vessels were seen moving up and down the coast, carrying rice, deerskins, indigo, provisions, and trade goods. Many were periaguas, dugout constructions made from a single log, the workhorse of coastal traffic whose construction Native Americans had perfected. Periaguas, often made from cypress, could move up tidal creeks with ease with little risk of grounding but those using them typically avoided the open ocean.[72] Two-masted schooners and single-masted sloops carried the heavier loads and were common sights. After the war, galleys made their appearance in raids along coastal Georgia, primarily from British territory. It would have been unusual to see a yawl, designed for use within a port, making its way down the coast. Hercules and the eight passengers probably stayed behind the barrier islands to keep out of sight as well as for protection from waves, winds, and ocean currents. One point stood in their favor. Africans in a modest-sized boat captained by one of their number were a common sight.

The small watercraft travelled the 135 miles from Savannah to St. Augustine successfully, a tribute not only to Hercules but also to the five other adults in the vessel. Nine people stepped off into a small town, characterized by typically Spanish architecture, that had blossomed into a war camp teeming with military activity, white refugees, and enslaved Black people, as well as Seminoles and Creeks who came for gifts and to coordinate actions against the rebels in the Carolina and Georgia backcountry.

How many Africans made it to British East Florida during the Revolution? Lord Hawke, a notable investor and knowledgeable about conditions, calculated for the British government that fifteen hundred African Americans entered the colony from the beginning to the end of the war.[73] An undetermined number of Black people were fugitives. The largest group consisted of the two hundred to three hundred freedom seekers from Tybee Island who had been carried to St. Augustine by the Royal Navy in 1776 and placed under the "protection" of merchants, planters, and others in the colony. They enjoyed a precarious status that allowed them a certain autonomy, with many working odd jobs around the waterfront and the marketplace. A second set came from farms and plantations in southern Georgia, especially those on the St. Marys River, who were forced to escape from the horrors of the border war.[74] Others used the confusion of war and of the demobilization to make their bolt for freedom. The commissioner of sequestered estates in South Carolina cited information that "many negroes, the property of gentlemen of Carolina . . . have made their escape to this province."[75]

Slaveholders led the largest number of Black Georgians and Carolinians who entered East Florida. Some were fleeing the region. Loyalist planters left South Carolina with large contingents of enslaved Africans. Charles Bissett transported 100 people over the waters, and George Bell carried 120.[76] Both sought to replicate the plantation economy of their colony. In Georgia, planters above the Altamaha River were less successful. A series of laws made the departure of enslaved populations illegal. Robert Baillie of Liberty County wrote his Scottish mother that "most of the Gentlemen from Savannah" went to Providence in the Bahamas, leaving behind their families and enslaved people. "As I had no way to support myself there," he explained, "I determined to push with part of my slaves to this province but as my Intentions were suspected I was so closely watched that I could make no Preparations or procure Boats to remove my family."[77] He managed a flight in a small watercraft with a few of his captives, leaving his wife, family, and the greater part of the workforce behind.

The great unknown is how many Africans were carried into British East Florida by the raiding parties that ranged across Georgia throughout the war, both before and after the invasion of December 1778. During the border conflict, Col. Thomas Brown and his Rangers were reputed to have brought back two hundred bondsmen from one assault on plantations along the Altamaha River. A guerrilla fighter loosely attached to Brown, Daniel McGirt, and his companions established an active pipeline via which slaves seized in raids in the Georgia and South Carolina backcountry were sold to slave-hungry refugees in St. Augustine.[78] And those raids did not cease with the British seizure of Savannah. An investigating commission set up by the royal governor found that civilian gangs, especially McGirt's, "had committed very great waste and destruction" and that "a considerable number of negroes were from time to time clandestinely shipped or carried off" to East Florida, where they were "converted to their own personal use and benefit."[79] In a subsequent report, Governor Wright affirmed that McGirt's interracial gang was "robbing, murdering, distressing, and breaking up the Settlements" in South Carolina.[80] In a later report, the governor complained, "McGirt & his Gang of Villains . . . were always a Pest to this Province."[81]

Throughout the war, the sale of slaves in St. Augustine was brisk. The population was ballooning as refugees streamed in, the army was a constant consumer of goods, and a booming wartime economy dominated.

For those who reached East Florida and possessed sufficient autonomy, there was a range of choices to be made, whether to seek odd jobs with the military, work along the waterfront, look for a protector, remain a "vagrant," or head toward Seminole encampments. Without hesitation, Hercules placed himself and his family under the protection of one of the most powerful and capable British officers in the province, Thomas Brown, commander of the King's Rangers, the provincial regiment present during the Siege of Savannah.[82] Hercules and Betty arrived in October 1781 and were still "in [Brown's] possession" four years later, in the same ambivalent position as the refugees from Tybee Island. That connection with the Black militia opposite the McGillivray rice plantation seems to have been real.

Named superintendent of the Creek and Cherokee Nations by London, Brown functioned as an influential mediator between the Creeks, Spanish, and British in the difficult transition of Florida from the control of one empire to another. The colonel pressured the Creeks to make an alliance with the Spanish, developed a strong relationship with the newly arrived governor, Vicente Manuel de Céspedes (Zéspedes), and helped convince Céspedes to give a monopoly of the Creek trade to a British trading firm, Panton, Leslie & Company. Brown proved instrumental in laying the foundation for the diplomatic revolution that replaced British influence with Spanish in the Southeast but left breathing room for the British government to intervene in later years.[83]

Jupiter, Auba, and Jack took another path, one that Hercules could have taken. They chose to flee to the Seminoles to ensure their autonomy, even at the expense of entering a vastly different cultural world. Freedom, the two families learned, depended on one's perspective. Hope came in different forms. The five people, including an infant and a young boy, joined those in St. Augustine who slipped away in the confusion to cross the St. Johns River and make their way to the Alachua Seminoles and a life in one of the Black villages next to the settlements of Seminole chiefs.[84] As the war loosened the ties that bound slaves to their plantations, others bolted to head west only a few dozen miles for a life that offered relative autonomy under Native protection.[85] The fact that the Indians still considered them technically slaves paled compared to the gains they made in obtaining considerably more control over their lives. Most Black people made good their escape. No better demonstration of the weakness of the colony could be found than the inability of either British or Spanish governments to challenge a Native people on whom they depended in so many indirect ways. St. Augustine still functioned as a military outpost with little authority beyond the St. Johns River into the vast interior of Florida.[86]

In July 1782, the British army departed from Savannah, accompanied by loyalists and their enslaved people. The first weeks of July saw hectic negotiations, a truce established, and an agreement reached between generals Anthony Wayne and Alured Clarke for the evacuation of loyalists and their enslaved people in the coming weeks. Starting in late July, thousands of Black and white loyalists gathered on Tybee Island. For those enslaved people waiting for transport on Cockspur and Tybee Islands, it was a disorienting and disheartening experience.

For three years, Black Georgians had been exposed to a life of disruption, transition, and turmoil. Many had made it into Savannah in 1779 and experienced a precious moment of liberty as a pioneer or fighter for the British army but had then been rudely returned to slavery, sometimes under the same enslaver but frequently under a new one. Others had seen members of their family or community torn from their ranks never to be seen again. Strangers had been introduced into their communities as planters struggled to replace losses of people. In the closing days of the conflict, many had been forced to relocate to new plantation sites as the American army closed in on Savannah and raids made staying in the Lowcountry untenable. If family life was disrupted beyond measure, there was hope for a new and more secure life in British East Florida. According to the various "returns of refugees and Negroes" recorded by the commissary for refugees, about thirty-seven hundred enslaved people from Georgia, along with a few freemen, made it to that province over the next ten months, along with seventeen hundred white loyalists.[87]

Beneath that troubled narrative lies another one that is typically overlooked. At the very moment when newly formed slave communities were beginning to coalesce, the Revolutionary War tore those communities apart and thrust their members into a succession of disjointed movements across the length and breadth of Georgia and beyond, movements caused by the border war with British East Florida, movements from plantation to town after the British conquest and sometimes back again, movements caused by the horrors of civil war in which both sides treated slaves as pawns to be sold and traded, movements into and sometimes out of British East Florida, movements into Creek and occasionally Seminole lands, and movements of those carried to Tidewater Virginia or upcountry South Carolina by their enslavers.

In the process, the war became a painful but important education for many in the geography of the Lowcountry and of its paths and waterways, a lesson in the contours of the Southeast and in the connections to the world beyond. Few Africans remained in one place along the coast. The Black experience during the Revolution effectively laid the groundwork for the waves of fugitives who would flee coastal Georgia in the decades to come.

CHAPTER 4

Entangled Borders

In the months after the end of the war in Georgia and South Carolina, over eighty-five hundred Black people, some free but most enslaved, stepped off a steady stream of vessels from Savannah and Charleston onto the wharves at St. Augustine, a sandy town ill equipped to receive a flood of people.[1] With a traditional Spanish grid pattern built around a central plaza, the town consisted of houses little more than shacks, a handful of more substantial buildings, and a few two-story structures displaying typical Spanish features like side entrances and loggias.[2] People of all backgrounds—Black, white, and Indigenous, including Creeks, Cherokees, and Choctaws—thronged the streets, walking with apparent ease in a center demobilizing after an exhausting war. Counting the white loyalists and those already in East Florida, the population—some sixteen to seventeen thousand humans—were pushing up against each other, trying to make do with limited provisions and groping about for a space on which to land.[3]

Loyalists expected British East Florida to become a haven for all those forced to leave the United States, naively envisioning a new colony made up of both East and West Florida that would be integrated more closely with the British Caribbean. News of the preliminary Treaty of Paris reached them in February 1783, only six months after their arrival, shattering their illusions and throwing them into despair. All the fierce lobbying could not undo the final signing of the treaty in September and the restoration of both Floridas to Spain. A brief uprising by John Cruden, a British official who plotted with fellow loyalists to seize an enclave around the St. Marys River and make it into an autonomous region, collapsed with no support from London.[4]

As the months passed and people scrambled to secure their future, the besieged governor, Patrick Tonyn, former military officer with a quick temper, found himself an unwilling spectator to the unraveling of the colony.[5] The announcement of Britain's departure gave rise to a spate of lawlessness as impoverished inhabitants, disbanded soldiers, and Americans coming into the province to claim fugitives and stolen slaves jockeyed to secure their future. Several units of the British infantry briefly mutinied on learning of orders to be transferred to hazardous duty in the West Indies. Former guerrilla fighters known for their ruthlessness put together marauding communities of war veterans, deserters, social outcasts, and "Negroes," and struck northern Florida and southern Georgia. Both sides of the St. Marys River in Florida and Georgia once again became an outlaw-infested no-man's-land.[6]

All the more galling was the role of Francisco Sanchez, a long-time planter and merchant in St. Augustine. Aware that law and order were breaking down, he conveniently shipped to Havana slaves stolen by Daniel McGirt, the nemesis of authorities on both sides of the border, and shared the profits. The governor of South Carolina accused Sanchez of responsibility for the theft of at least one hundred enslaved people from his state.[7] While Tonyn struggled to impose order and curb the activities of individuals like McGirt and Sanchez, planters began dismantling their plantations or holdings, made plans to evacuate their labor forces, and cast around for shipping. The theft of slaves and horses along the St. Marys River by border-crossing Georgians or those Floridians out for a quick profit made it difficult to distinguish who was law-abiding and who was not.[8]

Over the next four decades, the river was to assume enormous significance. Serving as the dividing line between Georgia and soon-to-become Spanish East Florida, the St. Marys was a slow-moving channel of water originating in the Okefenokee Swamp and emptying into Cumberland Sound and the Atlantic Ocean. The river basin contained extensive wetlands, interspersed with bottomland growths of cypress trees, and flanked by long-leaf pine forests that fueled a slowly developing logging industry. On the American side, marsh predominated and was submerged four or five feet at every high tide.[9]

For almost one hundred years, the river had functioned as the central feature of a borderland in which Spanish, British, Native Americans, and all those who fell outside any neat racial or ethnic definition met, fought, negotiated, and, more often than not, looked after their own personal interests.

St. Marys River, border between the United States and Spanish Florida, 1784–1821

The river was no impermeable boundary but a place of continual interaction, a contested space in constant upheaval. In the run-up to the War of Jenkins' Ear, it was the scene of repeated attempts by the Spanish and British to outflank each other. During the Revolution, the bloody border warfare saw rangers and guerrillas from Florida wreak havoc on nearby Georgians while a succession of invasions by ineptly led American armies ended in humiliating defeat. The borderland represented as much a process as a place, one where many cultures and ethnicities interacted and produced a constantly changing image.

In the second Spanish period (1783–1821), East Florida and southern Georgia evolved into one large zone of transition that stretched from the St. Johns River in Florida to the Altamaha River in Georgia. Despite the obvious differences in governance, language, and population, the two adjacent regions were inextricably linked by the frequent crossing of cultural, religious, and racial boundaries by their inhabitants. It was an ambiguous and often unstable realm where the boundary was also a crossroad. Creeks and Seminoles came down the St. Marys River at will to trade on occasion but more often than not to steal horses or cattle from people who had seized their land in shameful fashion. Indian traders casually flouted regulations as they moved between two radically different worlds. French refugees from Saint-Domingue were concentrated along the St. Marys on the Georgia side; British loyalists farmed modest holdings on the south bank of the St. Marys; Americans trying to escape debt reinvented themselves on both sides of the border, while cattle thieves flourished in this unregulated environment. A critical feature of this social and cultural mixing was the number of Black people who moved across the borders as fugitives or as slaves, from Georgia to Florida for the most part but on occasion from Florida to Georgia, an aspect that is often overlooked. The cultural intermingling and weak central authority created an ideal space for fugitives to find a path forward to a new life.

The British departure was messy, and in those first years the new Spanish government was short of staff and resources, with only a light footprint beyond the gates of St. Augustine. In June 1784, the new Spanish governor, Vicente Manuel de Céspedes, arrived to find the British colony in a state of turmoil, with Blacks and whites crowded into small houses and huts throughout St. Augustine and in small, primitive encampments along the banks of the St. Johns and Matanzas Rivers and with British authority unraveling.[10] Sensitive to the awkwardness of the situation, the veteran administrator offered additional time for evacuation. For over a year, the British and Spanish governors ran dual administrations, with Céspedes in control but in an increasingly strained relationship with his counterpart, who watched in frustration as his power over British residents slipped away.[11]

As the evacuation proceeded in fits and starts from 1782 to 1785, St. Augustine evolved into an active slave market where seasoned creoles rather than Africans were auctioned to a variety of slaveholders, especially Americans crossing into the territory to rebuild their labor force. Absentee landlords in England who had been swept up in the enthusiasm for what had been a great speculative venture sought to liquidate their holdings and redeem as much of their investment as possible. Lady Egmont offered a "gang" of sixty slaves, while the broker for a London notable touted that the seventy-six people in his estate divided almost equally between men, women, and children. The first governor of East Florida, Gen. James Grant, put up for bids the seventy enslaved people who were the heart and soul of his plantation that had produced some of the finest indigo in the colony. The broker described fifty of them as workers and "the rest, Children, some of whom were nearly fit for the hoe."[12]

Loyalists who had fled Georgia and South Carolina scrambled to trade away their labor force as they sought financial liquidity for their next move in the British Empire. Black families and communities were destroyed with scarcely a thought. Twenty-eight men, women, and children arrived from Augusta as the "property" of Alexander Patterson, including Hannah, March, and Monday. Their enslaver promptly traded two people as well as three cows for eight horses that he needed for the plantation he hoped to establish. When the evacuation began, the remaining twenty-six were offered in the market at St. Augustine. Those that could not be sold were loaded onto a ship for Patterson's next destination, Dominica. In the confusion, Monday, March, and Hannah managed to escape before embarking on a ship stationed in the St. Marys.[13]

The great outmigration of slaves from St. Augustine between 1783 and 1785 produced a stunning surprise. More Black people arrived in the United States and West Florida than in any other location in the British Caribbean, Canada, or England, a reality that is often overlooked. According to the meticulous records kept by the Commissary of Refugees in St. Augustine, planters and others transported 2,214 enslaved people to the Bahamas, another 714 to Jamaica, 444 to Dominica, 155 to Nova Scotia, and 35 to "Europe." Two hundred went to "other Foreign parts." Those same records show that 2,561 Black people were carried back to the United States, a stunning 40 percent of those on the British evacuation lists.[14] Far from being an exception, Mahomet, the recaptured maroon, was part of a sizeable movement of people. In his case, it meant shipment to Beaufort, South Carolina, for sale.

The British statistics hold another surprise. Governor Tonyn reported a category on the list for those who went "missing," white and Black people who apparently had departed from East Florida but whose destination was not known. These figures included 2,692 whites and 4,756 Blacks, people he surmised disappeared into the vast territory of Spanish West Florida, the Creek Nation, and the United States.[15] Historian James McMillin estimates that, out of all the different categories, a total of 1,500 African Americans entered Georgia during the three-year period following the Revolution, an assumption that sounds reasonable. There were probably more.[16]

Georgians came in person or sent brokers to St. Augustine to bid on the human flesh being offered in what became an important slave market for a very brief period. Leading the way were two of Washington's most capable generals, Nathanael Greene and "Mad Anthony" Wayne, who had been awarded prize plantations along the Savannah River by the legislature in gratitude for their role in liberating Georgia. Greene received Mulberry Grove, the former property of John Graham. Wayne received Richmond and Kew, once the plantation of the royal governor's son.[17] The irony was palpable. Only four years before, a hard-pressed Greene had written to the governor of South Carolina that Black men "would make good soldiers," described them as the natural strength of the state, and argued that freedom rather than wages should be their reward.[18] Of the one hundred five Africans purchased, Greene took fifty-eight men, women, and children, including sixteen sawyers, two coopers, one carpenter, two tanners, cooks, and seamstresses, the type of skilled and semiskilled labor that formed an important component of any plantation.[19]

Gen. Anthony Wayne claimed forty-seven of the enslaved and quickly instructed his broker to purchase another twenty-three from an Englishman who had relocated his estate from Florida to the Satilla River in Georgia.[20] In 1786, his overseer submitted a memorandum that included a list of the "Negroes" a year after the purchase. Out of the pages leaps a tale of incredible cruelty and indifference. Of the original forty-seven, nineteen had died—"4 taskable hands & 15 Superannuated blind Idiots & Children," the overseer maliciously noted. He complained he was left with twenty men, three of whom were too old to be useful. And then there was Pompey, "the worst of the bad Negroes"; Sam, unfit for service; and Adam, who was blind. The women fared better in his estimation, and he made no comment on the children.[21]

The arrival of fifteen hundred or so African Americans in Georgia, most to the Lowcountry to supplement the losses incurred at the time of the evacuation, represented more than a simple addition to the labor force. The presence of these people who had spent one, two, or more years in Florida seeing and absorbing a different world, one where constraints were loosened, raises questions about the kind of cultural impact that they had on the enslaved communities on the Georgia coast. What narratives did the loyalist Africans of Florida carry with them? What perspective on life did people like Pompey and Sam offer? Each had his or her story, and collectively they shared a common set of experiences. They had witnessed the aftermath of the defeat of British arms and the resulting collapse of British power. They had seen a plantation economy come unraveled. They knew someone or had heard of someone who had received a certificate of freedom or escaped to the Seminoles or found a niche as a free Black person in the confusion of the evacuation. Most found themselves in a setting in Florida where con-

trols were looser and greater autonomy was possible. Others knew people
who had been kidnapped and sold to Havana or been subject to arbitrary violence. If nothing else, their memories gave them a powerful sense of the region in which they lived. They could not go back to thinking of themselves
as part of small, self-contained communities isolated from the outside world.
Those fifteen hundred men and women would not fail to leave an imprint on
a population that numbered 13,261 in the Georgia Lowcountry in 1790.[22]

On his arrival in July 1784, Governor Céspedes had issued a proclamation
that required all white people having Black people "in their power," slave or
free, to register them. In addition, it required that all Black people or people
of mixed race without a known owner or without papers present themselves
to the governor, clarify their status, and obtain a work permit.[23] Those failing to do so would be claimed by the Spanish government and put to public works or sold into slavery. Céspedes thought the measure a way to clear
out the "wandering vagrants" who proliferated around St. Augustine. The
British viewed it as an attack on their property rights as guaranteed by the
Treaty of Paris. It was an embarrassing reminder. Few British citizens possessed clear property titles to their enslaved people, as the chief justice, John
Hume, pointed out to a glum Patrick Tonyn: "Your Excellency well knows,
that five out of six of the Slaves in the Country, are held without any title
deeds, and Bills of Sale were never given with New Negroes: parole Sales,
and possession is all they can shew, which was sufficient Title by the Laws
of this Province."[24]

Of the over 250 people who eventually came forward, most were in possession of certificates of freedom from the British commanding officer, Gen.
Archibald MacArthur, in recognition of their service in South Carolina.
More than half of that number belonged to thirty-eight family groupings.
Even in flight, family ties remained central to their lives. The largest family
came from Savannah, Bacchus and Betty Camel and their seven children,
although they had embarked from Charleston before coming to St. Augustine. Disputes broke out between British citizens and the authorities. Katy,
an enslaved women that John Milligan, a Savannah loyalist, claimed to have
bought for his wife, presented herself "unknown to her master or mistress"
to MacArthur, told her story, and obtained a certificate of freedom.[25] Céspedes was resolute in defending the basic principle of recognizing the free
status of those who had some proof, however slender, and eventually issued
certificates of freedom, mostly to individuals who had fought with or given
aid to the British in South Carolina.[26]

As the evacuations got under way, planters in Georgia and South Carolina journeyed to St. Augustine in an attempt to reclaim slaves taken or "stolen" by Loyalists.[27] Hopes rose when the Spanish governor took office and expressed a desire for amicable relations with the United States. Nevertheless, Céspedes made clear that his government would never hand back fugitives and reaffirmed the old policy of sanctuary that offered freedom and a recognized place in Hispanic society to fleeing slaves in return for conversion to Catholicism.[28] It was not only the case in Florida. Royal orders to Spanish governors in the colonies of Trinidad, Venezuela, Cuba, and Santo Domingo as well as Florida continued to encourage the immigration of freedom seekers from British, Dutch, and other foreign colonies throughout the 1780s. An increasingly impotent Spanish Empire refused to back down from a century-old policy.[29]

East Florida presented a remarkable test case. Spain had few troops, few citizens, and little in the way of resources to defend its restored colony, but there were sound political and cultural reasons for activating the policy. The province was desperately undermanned, short of workers and skilled laborer, and stood to benefit by welcoming any and all comers. More significant was the diplomatic leverage offered vis-à-vis the United States in the face of the great territorial issues of the Mississippi Valley. Spain held as much territory as did its neighbor in North America and saw the policy as a useful diplomatic tool.[30] At a deeper level, the stance reflected the uniqueness of Spanish society and its legal codes, which accorded limited rights to slaves, including the right to own property, testify in court, and negotiate for manumission or liberty.

Among the first to respond to the open door were enslaved people who had been part of the African Americans carried from Florida into Georgia. Returning to a space they knew and appreciated for its greater freedoms was a natural instinct. Prince Whitten and his wife Judy had been taken from their neighboring plantations outside Charleston in 1780 by Col. William Young and a guerrilla fighter, "Wild Bill" Cunningham, and carried back to East Florida with as many as two hundred other captives. Prince could have been one of the colonel's "colored Dragoons" that American guerrilla leader Francis Marion reported that he fought against later in the war. It is more likely that he remained an enslaved person since the property of Peter Whitten was "plundered as the spoils of war" and eventually sold.[31] After three years in Florida, Prince was purchased by Jacob Weed, a wealthy rancher, land speculator, and agent of the federal government whom the Spanish used to represent some of their interests across the border. With thousands of acres in Camden County, Weed took the lead in organizing the small trading and shipping port of St. Marys.[32] Whitten's skill as a carpenter and a shaper of lumber was highly valued by this timber merchant. In December 1786, only eighteen months after arriving in Georgia, Prince's family of four boarded a canoe and made their way several hundred yards across the river into Spanish Florida to seek asylum and ask for freedom.[33]

Weed was less surprised by the fact of their escape than by their chosen destination. The family had already made attempts to flee to South Carolina but been caught. He was on the point of selling Prince back to Peter Whitten, his original "master," and had agreed on terms to sell "the wench & Children" to a Mr. Kenty, her original enslaver in South Carolina. Prince's flight was a heartfelt effort to keep his family together in the face of an oppressive system that tore families apart with scarcely a thought for lives destroyed. Learning that the four had headed south, he placed a notice that gave a fair measure of the family. According to Weed, Prince Whitten was a striking individual, 6 feet tall, "strong built and brawny," talkative, a skilled carpenter, about thirty years old, from Africa. His wife Judy was "a smart, active wench," about thirty, a creole, and their children, Glasgow, "a well-looking boy of open countenance and obliging disposition", eight years old, and his sister Polly, six, with "lively eyes and gently pitted with the pox."[34]

Others who had been part of the reverse migration to Georgia followed. Six men who escaped from St. Simons in a canoe and made it to St. Augustine were part of the estate of a former deerskin merchant, James Spalding, who left St. Simons Island for St. Augustine at the beginning of the conflict and earned his considerable wealth providing supplies for the British army. In 1785, he moved back to the island, site of his original home, and began planting black-seed cotton that developed into the highly successful Sea Island cotton, a long, silky, strong fiber that commanded a premium price and helped fuel Britain's Industrial Revolution.[35] From a neighboring plantation on St. Simons, a man named Primus entered the slave quarters of Alexander Bisset, who had accompanied his father from South Carolina to East Florida with one hundred bondsmen before the revolutionary war. A pragmatist, Bisset decided to throw in his lot with the new republic when the war concluded. Primus had little difficulty in persuading Sancho, James, Mary Ann, Ned, and John to join him in a flight to East Florida. It is probable that there had been extensive conversations over a period of time.[36]

Between 1787 and 1790, over two hundred fugitives escaped and made their way, most by water, to East Florida.[37] If one adds those who fled between the end of the Revolution and 1797, the total probably came to over four hundred people, a figure that suggests more freedom seekers may have reached Flor-

ida in this brief period than during the several decades before the War of Jenkins' Ear. The total does not count the many who were successful but were
never reported to the authorities or the many others who had the misfortune
of being caught before crossing the border. If one counts the enslaved people
who came as fugitives between 1783 and 1786, the number climbs higher still.
Most remained in Florida, but at least fifty-seven Black fugitives were sent to
Cuba on the vessel *Diana* in accordance with orders.[38]

The effect on coastal planters was profound. By October 1788, the grand
jury of Chatham County, sifting through typically local issues, was startled
to receive an angry petition from ninety citizens demanding action and responded in kind: "We present as a grievance of a most oppressive and alarming nature the frequent instances of negroes absconding from this state to
East Florida, and the protection they meet with from the Spaniards, in violation of the laws of nations." The petition demanded restitution of this
"property" and called for the building of a boathouse on St. Simons "or some
more southern station."[39] Reports to the governor highlighted the "passing of negroes" into East Florida and their role in contributing to the general disorder that prevailed along the entangled border. A young revolutionary war hero with a plantation on the coast, James Jackson, now a general in
the state militia, could scarcely restrain himself. He led the Georgia militia
against the maroon encampment on Belleisle. Station a unit of the militia
near St. Marys, he urged, and a host of problems would be solved: people of
color would find no way to cross over, the plague of outlaws would be ended,
and the Spaniards would learn respect.[40]

Fugitives to Florida were cut from a different cloth from most Black
freedom seekers who fled their plantations singly or in pairs to see family and friends or chose to shelter in secret spots around the margins of
the formal world. The men and women who headed to Florida left in surprisingly large groups, sometimes families but more often bands of friends.
They were willing to cut ties with their communities, risk crossing an international boundary, and face the uncertainty of a land where the official language was different from their own. Most chose to flee over water. The enslaved communities on barrier islands and coastal lands had deep ties to the
tidal and marsh ecosystem that supplied the fish, oysters, and other marine
life on which they depended.[41] Most fugitive groups included one or more
skilled watermen who showed a keen understanding of maritime culture.[42]
In South Carolina, 60 percent of skilled slaves who fled their enslavers had
maritime experience, while slave boatmen accounted for 10 percent of all
male enslaved people advertised as runaways.[43]

Boat sailing out of Charleston Harbor, circa 1900. Black watermen on the Georgia coast used similar vessels to escape with family and friends to Spanish Florida. Courtesy of the Charleston Museum, Charleston, South Carolina.

The dash to Florida in large groups did not come about as a sudden decision. To escape required one or more boats or canoes, ample provisions and water, a set of goals that were generally understood, and thoughtful planning, nautical and otherwise. The psychology of flight brought forth a ruggedness and fortitude in fugitives that overcame the haunting doubts that gripped many at the outset of their venture. On May 8, 1789, sixteen slaves, nine of them from the plantation of John Davies, six from his neighbor Ferdinand O'Neil, and one the "property" of Alexander Creighton in Liberty County, put into play a carefully designed plan. The adults placed their baggage, including clothing, food, and water, in a vessel of some size and rowed away until it was safe to hoist a sail.

Shortly afterward, the planters caught wind of what was afoot and launched a vessel manned by two planters and other armed white men. The pursuing boat discovered the fleeing Blacks crossing the Cumberland Sound and ran them ashore between the Satilla and Crooked Rivers. The fugitives jumped out and took off on foot into the thick underbrush and swampy wa-

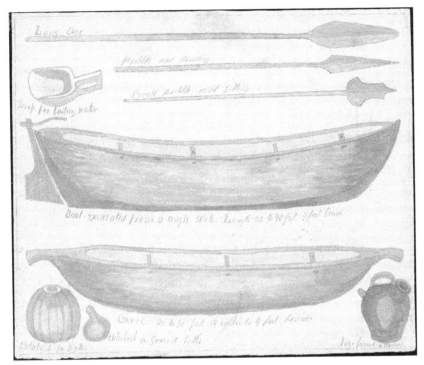

Two African dugout canoes with accessories. Many of the flights from Georgia took place in canoes made of cypress. The dugouts reflected both Native American and African influences. Courtesy of Albert and Shirley Small Special Collections Library, University of Virginia, MSS 14357.

ters, hoping to lose themselves in the saw palmetto of the maritime forest and the Spartina cordgrass of the marsh. One by one they were picked off by their pursuers until all had been caught except for three men—Harry, Hector, and Isaac. Those three kept forging ahead, eluded their pursuers, stole a boat, and completed the dangerous journey to Amelia Island. The fact of sixteen desperate people fighting through swamp and palmetto to elude armed men personified the kind of heart and commitment necessary for success.[44]

Canoes seemed to have been the most common watercraft thanks to the availability of cypress suitable for dugout construction and a set of techniques based on Indian and West African technology. Neither South Carolina nor Georgia had invested in the shipbuilding industry during the prerevolutionary period and residents relied instead on canoes, boats, and periaguas to bring the produce of plantations to market down tidal creeks and on to Savannah or Sunbury.[45] Hugging the coast or traveling the inland

route behind the Sea Islands, these craft navigated the waterways from Savannah to St. Augustine with relative ease.

Case after case involved flight by canoes. Lt. Pedro Carne on Amelia Island reported that nine fugitives had arrived from Savannah in a canoe with
a rudder, four oars, a mast, and a sail. In the craft were two boxes of clothing, a small cask of water, a cauldron for cooking, and two wooden plates.[46]
Prince Whitten used a canoe to power his family across the St. Marys to
Spanish territory. The six men from Spalding's estate and the other six from
Bisset's are likely to have used canoes in their escape from St. Simons. Five
enslaved people in the town of St. Marys boldly swam out into the river,
boarded a Spanish canoe passing through, and reached the opposite shore.[47]
Four fugitives from South Carolina were forced to land on Jekyll Island,
where a planter saw opportunity and enslaved them on his estate. Several
months later, Dick, Fortune, March, and Prince took another canoe or boat
and finished their journey.[48] Christopher Paysan, resident of Amelia, captured three fugitives from Charleston, sent them to St. Augustine, and confiscated their canoe and several weapons for his own benefit. The governor
allowed him to keep the guns but not the canoe.[49]

James Spalding used his considerable authority to reach St. Augustine and
present his case for restitution to the governor. Much to his surprise, the governor accorded him the privilege of speaking directly with his former captives. And much to his dismay, he watched as they laughed contemptuously
in his face. The governor had promised freedom, they pointed out in high
spirits. Before leaving St. Augustine, he penned a hastily written letter appealing to Céspedes's sense of justice and pointing out that the governor's
decision was setting a bad example: "It will be easy for the rest of [my] slaves
to follow their companions into this country in hopes of also being made
free." This would deprive him of his means of support.[50] Or so he pleaded.
Céspedes returned the canoe but not the men. In need of watercraft, Spanish officials often kept the American-made canoes and sometimes, as an act
of concession, returned a locally made substitute, to the anger of Georgians.[51]
An influential figure like Spalding recovered his boat while others did not.

Since the commander of the garrison on Amelia Island typically initiated
reporting on fugitives, the official correspondence in the East Florida Papers records only a few flights overland. Given this scenario, it is likely that
the number of fugitives is higher, perhaps significantly higher, than what has
been put forward. Georgia planters, frustrated by their inability to seize their
"property" so close by, threatened to invade Spanish territory in an effort to

grab their enslaved, a reminder that many freedom seekers never went to St. Augustine but secured work or hid in the countryside between the St. Marys and St. Johns Rivers.[52]

The commander of the district, Carlos Howard, asked Céspedes to make preparations to counter any invasion. Relations between East Florida and Georgia reached a nadir as preparations for armed conflict were made on the Spanish side, while Georgia showed a galling indifference to reining in the freewheeling adventurers and planters who dominated this frontier world where legal processes were notably absent.[53] The turmoil delayed the settlement of Glynn and Camden Counties, as planters attracted to the possibilities of new lands decided to wait and see whether military-style labor camps with little possibility of escape could be created. Pierce Butler, one of the larger slaveholders in the Carolina Lowcountry and owner of valuable lands on St. Simons Island, told his manager that he would not move his workforce to Georgia until the Florida question was settled.[54]

The American side of the St. Marys River was no less a part of the borderland that encompassed the region. In 1790, only 304 Black people lived in the entire fifty-one-mile strip between the Altamaha and St. Marys Rivers, compared to the 13,115 who lived in the sixty-five miles between the Savannah and Altamaha Rivers. Glynn County, where St. Simons and adjacent islands were to boast some of the largest rice and cotton plantations in later years, held only 193 whites and 220 blacks, including five free blacks. In Camden, there were more whites, 221 in all, and 84 blacks, including 14 free blacks.[55] Eight years after the war ended, there were fewer enslaved people and fewer plantations than before the conflict.[56] The legacy of a bloody guerrilla war had taken its toll, as had the sanctuary policy of the Spanish government.

James Seagrove, a former Philadelphia merchant who had spent time in Havana, took a lead role in organizing the county and was one of the founders of the town of St. Marys. He confessed to the Spanish governor that the port had become a magnet for smuggling and added the obvious: "There are numbers of suspicious and bad characters passing and repassing the river with property for sale such as horses, cattle, and Negroes etc., which in many cases have been stolen on both sides of the river."[57] His call to put a monitoring station on Amelia Island was ignored. Within Camden County, there was little check on those who operated outside the law and considerable tolerance of those who pushed social norms, a frontier-like setting where individual egos found considerable space for expression.

Loosely organized groups of men, united by kinship networks but little else, traded in stolen cattle, horses, and occasionally enslaved persons. On the Spanish side of the St. Marys, the Rain cousins and John Bailey cooperated with Nathaniel Ashley and Richard Lang on the American side. Most had been loyalists during the Revolution and enjoyed a camaraderie rooted in military experience. During the late 1780s, Lang used an appointment as a customs official by the Spanish working on the American side to admit four hundred cattle illegally into Florida. Ashley gained notoriety for smuggling horses purchased in Creek territory, some of which had been stolen from Georgians.[58]

Native Americans added to the feeling of insecurity on both sides of the river. Many decades before, a Scotsman had set up an isolated trading post, known as Trader's Hill, only thirty-five miles from the mouth of the St. Marys and a few miles shy of the Okefenokee Swamp and made it into an important location for Indigenous people to obtain supplies, clothing, and provisions.[59] Not far away on the other side of the river but farther south into East Florida, the Scottish firm Panton, Leslie & Company, licensed by the Spanish government, had set up another of their several stores in the Florida Panhandle.[60] Their clientele aimed at the nearby Seminoles, then in the process of evolving away from their Creek roots.

Native hunting across farmlands became a common occurrence in a region where deer were increasingly scarce. During the latter part of the 1780s, incursions took on a more threatening appearance. At the western end of Camden County, a large party of Natives led by an Indian of mixed parentage suddenly emerged to surround a pair of white men rounding up their cattle. They killed the horse on which one was riding and held both overnight, threatening to murder them. Because James Bryant, one of their captives, was a sometime Indian trader who spoke Hitchiti, they decided otherwise and departed with the cattle, a substantial windfall by any measure.[61] Then there were the occasional "rogue" warriors like the three men painted in black who raided a home on a small farm in the county, dashed out the brains of a three-year-old, and scalped a boy, all without apparent motive. Nothing else in the house was touched.[62] That kind of apparently irrational terror left deep marks.

Concerns of the white elite about the dangers posed by Black and Native peoples in a lightly policed region were paramount. Before a justice of the peace in Glynn County, John Hornsby testified that his house had been attacked by a "mulatto" at the head of three or four Black men armed with muskets. He claimed they had pointed their muskets at his chest, rifled through the house, and helped themselves to guns, rum, bolts of cloth, and provisions. Apparently the victim was a merchant. In the process, they commandeered an unfinished canoe twenty feet long and three feet wide. Hornsby saw a second canoe come out of the shadows. After loading, the two canoes disappeared into the muddy currents of the Altamaha. The merchant suspected that the thieves had gone to East Florida and had his deposition sent to Spanish authorities.[63]

Even in Florida the simple presence of Black freedom seekers was enough to generate outsized fears, especially among Anglo-American planters. Insertion into a slave society was never easy. When Prince Whitten crossed the St. Marys with his family, he found a place as a contract worker on a farm on the southern banks of that river. William Pengree, a prominent planter, complained that "the negro Prince and his family, who in reality belong to Colonel Weed, have behaved with such shamelessness and presumption since they have moved to the River, that two of my negroes, have fled with the idea of becoming free; I have been able to catch one and have sent to Georgia for the other."[64] Pengree had once lived in Camden County. It is likely that the two men who escaped his grasp were headed back to the communities from which they had originally come.

Nor were white farmers, accustomed to having slaves at their beck and call, impressed with the work ethic of free Black men. Charged with constructing public facilities on the banks of the St. Johns, a manager explained his delay to the Spanish governor with the revealing note, "Supervising runaways takes a lot of time." Indeed, assembling a work force of men who came to Florida in search of autonomy and creating an efficient work unit under white men accustomed to slavery was a challenge. The Anglo supervisor expressed his frustration at not being able to control their movements. Those free Negroes were in the habit of visiting enslaved Africans on plantations across the river from where they worked "at all hours of the night," much to the discomfort of the white inhabitants.[65]

In this loosely defined environment, confrontations reinforced the stereotype of the "Negro" as a criminal element in society. Magistrates were on the lookout for a Black man who had slipped out of jail in St. Augustine and stolen a horse. When two deputies approached an individual who fit the description riding northward, the man pulled a knife and lunged at one of the two but missed his target. When a deputy aimed a gun and told him to surrender, "The Negro positively refused to do so, and on jumping about was fired at by Mr. Blunt." He was subdued. Standing before the justice, the African American claimed to be free since he had been in the "Black troop in

the American War" and was being unfairly targeted. To the magistrate re-
cording the incident, the status of being a veteran of the "American War"
had lost its power to command attention.[66]

Incident after incident underscored the vulnerability of African Americans in northern Florida. William Cain, an Indian trader and sometime
farmer living on the St. Marys River, lodged a complaint of how an outlaw,
with three stolen horses in tow, aimed a pistol at his head and robbed him
of his own horse and the "Negro man" accompanying him. The robber met
up with accomplices who had meanwhile kidnapped a "Negro woman" from
a nearby planation. Together, the party crossed the river and headed to the
Creek Nation to find a market for their horses and enslaved people. It was a
lucrative trade.[67]

For freedom seekers, that landscape changed quickly and unexpectedly in
a decidedly unfavorable way. In a surprise move, King Charles IV of Spain
issued an edict on May 17, 1790, that withdrew the century-old policy that
had governed the fate of fugitive slaves from foreign lands since 1693. No
longer would runaways from the United States be accorded their freedom
in return for converting to Catholicism and embracing Hispanic society. A
feeble ruler had given way to a set of ministers who were anxiously trying
to navigate the treacherous waters of an unraveling empire. Local officials
in Florida had long been advising the Spanish government to do so, pointing out that few fugitives ever converted to Catholicism and that, when they
did, it was for show. The policy, they pointed out, antagonized more powerful neighbors with little gain to show for it. By a letter dated August 28, 1790,
Governor Juan Nepomuceno de Quesada, the newly appointed governor of
East Florida, informed newly appointed Secretary of State Thomas Jefferson
that the Spanish monarch had given orders "not to permit, under any pretext, that persons sold in slavery in the United States introduce themselves,
as free, into the province of East Florida."[68] And so a turning point had been
reached.

The pivotal change reflected geopolitical concerns that went far beyond
the politics of East Florida. No indication had been given that Madrid was
considering a major step repealing a century-old policy. In fact, there was every indication of the opposite. An edict published in Spanish Trinidad only
a few months earlier had welcomed runaways from the English and French
colonies while Jamaican planters continued to be worried by Africans making their way to Cuba to gain free status under the protection of its governor.[69] The edict of May 17 came as a surprise to virtually everyone in North

and South America. Geopolitical concerns in both hemispheres had flowed together in an unexpected way, perhaps triggered by the Nootka Sound Crisis, a confrontation between Spain, Great Britain, the United States, and Native Americans over sovereignty claims and maritime rights and trade in the Pacific Northwest.[70]

Georgia planters welcomed the news but guardedly. If the new policy promised to halt runaways from the United States in the future, it explicitly declined to take any action on those who were already in Florida. The many enslaved people who had crossed the international border before 1790 would indeed be lost. Jefferson and Washington were cautious about embracing this hardline stance. They had no desire to pick a fight with the Spanish Empire when the larger game concerned navigation rights on the Mississippi River. Governor Edward Telfair dined with the president in an effort push him into taking a strong stand. Washington's instructions to James Seagrove, the federal collector of the port of St. Marys, however, gave the newly designated diplomat ample running room. Seagrove was to ensure that Quesada fully enforce the king's order to stop sheltering fugitives from Georgia, seek the return of slaves who had come since the proclamation of the edict, and, lastly, attempt to recover slaves lost since 1783. "This last instruction," the president knowingly warned, "will require peculiar delicacy, and must be entered on with caution and circumspection, or [is] not to be taken up at all."[71]

Seagrove's opening position was blunt. He forcefully demanded a return of all fugitives who had arrived in Spanish East Florida before May 17, 1790, arguing that it was an act of justice for all property owners no matter where they resided.[72] The final agreement fell far short of that mark. Quesada agreed to issue an order to his officials to detain fugitive slaves but never specified how they were to be returned or whether they were to be delivered in St. Augustine or on Amelia Island or elsewhere. Moreover, he demanded proof of ownership, a significant hurdle for many if not most planters. Nor would the Spanish government pay for the feeding and housing of prisoners, while all questions about their upkeep would have to be funneled through George Fleming, a loyalist merchant in St. Augustine. Finally, he stated that only those runaways who came after August 9, 1791, the date of the agreement, would be returned. Checkmated at each turn, Seagrove had no choice but to accept.[73]

Seagrove's agreement was a sobering reminder of how little power the United States actually exercised over this borderland region. It was also a hint that freedom seekers were not to be so easily halted at the border on St.

Marys River. The period between 1791 and 1797 saw a continued flight into Spanish Florida although at a reduced flow of people. The circumstances say much about how the borderland on either side of the river was evolving. Indeed, as has been mentioned, the borderland was as much a process as a place, foreshadowing the uneven spaces on either side of the Ohio River in Kentucky and Ohio.

CHAPTER 5

A Maroon in the Postrevolutionary Southeast

For Black Georgians in the postrevolutionary period, Spanish Florida was a beacon of freedom; but for those who made it into the colony, choices had to be made. Where did they go and how did they integrate into the life of this new world during the second period of Spanish rule when such great diversity characterized town and countryside? That question took on different meanings as waves of people made it into the province during the 1780s and 1790s. Freedom seekers adopted differing models of behavior in the presence of the tension between Hispanic culture and government and the strong population of Anglo-Americans. "Freedom" was a relative term that depended on the merging of the varied aspirations of individuals and the circumstances in which they found themselves once in Florida.[1]

The exploits of a man named Titus represent choices that illuminate the several faces of marronage on the Georgia and Florida coasts and the fluidity of the borders between Georgia and Florida. His career and his mobility illustrate the many cracks in the region's system of slavery. In the course of a long-distance run over twelve years, Titus created three different communities of people, each with its own inner logic yet each demonstrating underlying commonalities. His experiences as a maroon offer what Richard Price calls "the living proof of the existence of a slave consciousness that refused to be curbed by the master's conception or manipulation of it."[2] They also offer a close-up look at the movement between a republic and the province of an empire. To understand Titus's life, we must first appreciate the larger context in which he operated.

The town of St. Augustine was a welcoming place for freedom seekers. Its heterogeneous population representing diverse cultures made assimilation considerably easier than in the countryside. Spanish officials and those of Cuban or Spanish extraction ensured that Spanish law and language as well as the Catholic faith were the dominant features of the town, ensuring a culture that closely resembled that in every other Spanish town in the Americas. The great majority of residents were Majorcans, Italians, and Greeks, the surviving indentured servants of Dr. Andrew Turnbull's indigo plantation at New Smyrna and now shopkeepers and artisans, devout Catholics, and strong supporters of the new regime. At the southern end of town were the barracks housing a regiment of troops from Cuba, together with those who catered to the military trade—petty merchants, artisans, and wineshop keepers. Foreign residents included Britons, French, Swiss, Italians, Corsicans, and Americans, mostly elite merchants, clustered in the core of the city around the central plaza. An undetermined number of slaves worked as house servants or laborers on the waterfront. Some sixty to one hundred freemen found space in the poorer neighborhoods on the periphery of the town, although several found places in the central district through the special protection of high officials or merchants.[3]

Once in St. Augustine, Prince Whitten and his wife Judy, refugees from Georgia, took full advantage of the support offered by the Catholic Church in its role as the primary vehicle for Black assimilation into the life of the town. The two priests, Fathers Thomas Hassett and Miguel O'Reilly, both Irish, were adamant in their instructions to their white parishioners to treat Black people as "brothers in Christ." The Whittens' son, Glasgow, was baptized as Francisco Domingo Mariano Witten, and their daughter, Polly, as Maria Rafaela Witten. The protective priests placed them in a Catholic school for basic literacy and the tenets of the Christian faith. There they were with children of all social classes, although they sat separately from the others in the classroom. When the parents' baptism took place sometime later, Prince became Juan Bautista Whitten, and Judy became Maria Rafaela Quenty. Significantly, their godparent was Manuel Fernandez Bendicho, a prominent Spaniard who lent his influence and patronage, ensuring their social acceptance. In turn, Prince acted as godparent to twenty-three men and Judy to thirty-one women, transforming themselves over the years into loyal Spanish subjects and popular leaders in the Black community.[4]

However, Euro-Americans in St. Augustine did not always see free people of color in the same positive light as they did the Whittens and harbored deep-seated fears of a slave insurrection being plotted in the shadows of the town. This fear was a permanent feature of the landscape. In 1792, a judge was called on to untangle accusations that "free Alick" had gone into the household of John Sanders to meet with Diana, the cook and also his wife, and six others—two from another household—to conspire. While they were talking in the kitchen over a period of days, a white man who lay sick in an adjoining room overheard discussion of plans to commandeer a boat, rally "Negroes of both sexes, free and slaves," and escape to North Carolina, killing anyone who tried to stop them. Pleading innocent, Alick related how he had been brutally seized by a band of North Carolina patriots during the Revolution, sold for the benefit of the state, and, not "liking" his new "master", made it to Florida and a new life. Told that he had to convert to Catholicism, he claimed to have memorized pages from the catechism and studied Catholic doctrine but gave up after four years of effort since he understood little. Although Alick never formally converted, Céspedes granted him his status. At the conclusion of the trial, the judge found that the alleged conspirators were covering for each other and remanded the seven to the presidio for whipping and Alick to be exiled to Havana "for the scandal he has caused."[5]

For people of African descent outside St. Augustine, the situation was considerably more fluid. Black people could use the law to their own advantage.[6] Spanish law and custom, based on thirteenth-century Castilian slave codes, acknowledged enslaved Africans as human beings with a juridical personality. One of the most significant benefits of this was the possibility of manumission through *coartación*, a process by which a slave could file a lawsuit to have a judge establish a price at which he or she could purchase his freedom.[7]

Born in West Africa, Felipe Edimboro had originally been a slave of Francisco Xavier Sanchez, a merchant, rancher, and slave trader whom the governor of South Carolina had fingered as the orchestrator of a pipeline that fed more than one hundred Carolina enslaved people to East Florida and eventually Havana. Edimboro and his wife became members of the Catholic Church, had their children baptized, and remained close to their one-time owner. Skilled at butchering cattle, Edimboro sometimes served as overseer of the main estate, San Diego, when Sanchez was away on business in Havana. Granted one hundred acres of farmland, Edimboro acted like his white counterparts and invested his income in slaves to work the land. Black slaveholders in Florida seemed to have had the same relationship to their bondsmen as did whites. They rented them out, sold them on a regular basis, and posted them as collateral for bond.[8] Skin color did not necessarily determine the treatment of enslaved people.

For most people of African descent living in the countryside, the fluid conditions throughout the region led to other kinds of choices given the lay of the land. In the late 1780s, the Florida between the basins of the St. Marys and St. Johns Rivers remained exclusively Anglo, with a small population that was predominantly American-born and Protestant. Resistant to authority of any kind, disruptive and sometimes violent, they were described by one official as "men without God or King." The land was a place of small farms and a few plantations, cultivated by the handful of British subjects, mostly loyalists who had stayed behind when the colony was evacuated. It was a wide-open space. Most farmers were to be found along the banks of the rivers growing provisions and herding cattle, the majority of the farms did not exceed thirty-six acres, and few households held slaves. Freemen and freewomen were to be found working for wages. When he first crossed the St. Marys, Prince Whitten had been one of those. A loyalist, William Pengree, had a plantation with fifty-two enslaved people, and a Swiss-born planter, Philip Francis Fatio, made his New Switzerland plantation into a model of efficiency with its eighty-six enslaved people.[9] In 1790, Governor Céspedes estimated that there were forty-four white families with two hundred members and seventy-one slaves in the St. Marys district of the colony.[10]

In this setting, most fugitives followed a different path and chose not to apply for free status. Many, perhaps the majority, worked on farms or plantations for wages paid through a formal work contract. Céspedes complained more than once to his superior, the governor-general of Cuba, that fugitives only went through the motions of conversion.[11] Anglo-Floridians in the northern part of the colony feared the precedent being set for their own slaves. William Pengree leveled a charge against Prince Whitten while he was under contract to another planter, accusing him of setting a dangerous example. Pengree had only to point to the two of his slaves who had already run away, one of them to Georgia. When Juan Nepomuceno de Quesada arrived as the governor to succeed Céspedes, he proposed dealing with the issue head-on. On September 2, 1790, he issued a "Proclamation of Good Government" that ordered all unattached Black people to enter the service of a propertied person within one month of the announcement. The aim was a simple one, to control "the multitude of foreign blacks" in the rural areas. In the background were the voices of members of the elite assigned administrative duties for a region, known as *regidores*, who frequently complained of the misconduct of fugitive slaves residing in Florida.[12] For his misbehavior, a freedom seeker from Georgia named Alexander was sentenced to two

months on public works, and he was placed on half rations when he continued to be disruptive.[13]

Other fugitives were grimly determined to establish more fully their autonomy and independence in the new setting. In the lingo of Spanish of-
ficialdom, they were "dancers", moving from site to site, hard to catch, and
free of white control. James Seagrove, by this time the southern superintendent for Indian affairs, wrote the governor that his slave, Will, had run away
from his house in Georgia: "[He] has been seen several times between the
St. Marys and St. Johns rivers. . . . I believe he is skulking about near the
plantation of McQueen on the St. Johns."[14] The refugees maintained ties
with the enslaved on neighboring farms and plantations and emerged to
trade with whites and people of color for clothing, food, and tools. When an
agreement with the State of Georgia was in the works in 1795 and fugitives
were at risk, a Spanish official wrote the governor of his hesitation "to pick
up the maroons dispersed throughout this province," saying that "putting a
hand on a few without doing it to all would cause some of them to hide and
others would flee to the Indian Nation." Better to wait, he said: "to give it
time until knowing the name of everyone and to be able to nab them in one
blow or as prudence dictates."[15]

Marronage was part of a long-established phenomenon. The word "maroon" was derived from the Anglicization of the Spanish word "cimarrón,"
meaning wild and untamed, and was used to describe fugitives hiding on the
fringes of the plantation world or further into the woods and swamps in inaccessible terrain. North America never had the equivalent of the powerful
communities that had existed in the Caribbean or Spanish America, like the
separate enclaves of Captain Cudjoe and a woman warrior known as Nanny
in Jamaica, or the legendary Palmares in Brazil, a close-knit federation of
villages made up of thousands of people that lasted for over one hundred
years until their defeat by a large Portuguese army.[16]

In North America, the one great community that appeared after the Revolution was on Belleisle and neighboring islands on the Savannah River. Belleisle comprised 2,081 acres in a remote, uninhabited section of the Savannah
River, virtually impassable given the thick, subtropical vegetation that flourished. The settlement lasted four or five years but finally succumbed to the
combined assault of Georgia and Carolina militias, assisted by Catawba Indians.[17] In contrast, the Great Dismal Swamp between Virginia and North
Carolina offered maroons a waterlogged terrain that proved welcoming for
a period of more than one hundred years, with two thousand square miles
of a vast natural wetland studded with small islands or hammocks. Recent

"Osman the Maroon in
the Swamp," *Harper's
New Monthly Magazine*,
September 1856, claimed
to have been drawn from
a real-life figure in the
Great Dismal Swamp of
North Carolina/Virginia
by David Hunter Strother.
Schomburg Center
for Research in Black
Culture, Photographs
and Prints Division,
New York Public Library
Digital Collections.

research has shown that no permanent settlement of maroons took root, no
serious threat to southern slavery ever emerged, and many of the maroons
were indirectly tied to the Atlantic economy. That fragile connection came
through the production of shingles and other wood products for the slave labor camps devoted to timbering in the swamp.[18] Nevertheless, the very existence of an independent space where an individual Black person could find
autonomy posed a threat to the institution of slavery.[19]

All maroon communities, however big or small, short-lived or long-
lasting, borderland or buried in the hinterlands, shared commonalities. Their
members lived in exile; they chose inhospitable, inaccessible areas in which
to hide; they exhibited extraordinary survival skills in the face of limited
resources and frequent threats; they lived in a state of continuous crisis; a
skilled leader invariably emerged in the communities that survived; and, if
there was not always a commitment to guerrilla warfare in the way that existed in the Caribbean or Spanish America, they showed a willingness to
fight in self-defense.[20]

Emblematic of these maroons was Titus, mentioned above, a Black Georgian who crossed boundaries and frontiers for at least twelve years. Born around 1769, Titus grew up in a large family on Ossabaw Island where the Savannah merchant John Morel had established three indigo plantations. His parents, Tom and Nelly, were two of the several dozen enslaved people purchased from the estate of a deerskin merchant and spent their early years laboring in the deerskin trade in and around Augusta. Titus was the youngest or next to the youngest of seven children in one of the leading families on the island; the other children were Tice, Abraham, Joe, Saffee, Phoebe, and Bacchus.[21] By the time he came of age, he spoke good English, was familiar with the ways of the white world, and enjoyed the security offered by a large family. Titus emblematizes those who rejected white authority in search of self-determination, empowerment, and autonomy. He exemplifies how goals, ambitions, and motivations evolved over time, with each person's experience distinctive when it came to the decisions made at each point in the journey.[22]

Very much a cross-cultural creole in outlook and upbringing, he was given the dubious privilege of becoming "waiting man" to John Morel (son of the original John) at age sixteen on a recently purchased rice plantation, Tweedside, on the Savannah River. The young Morel had acquired the plantation by purchasing property confiscated from a loyalist and making the main house the center of activity, a chance to impress the coastal elite with his rice cultivation debut.[23] Titus was admitted to the most intimate details of the private life of the family, the personal conversations, the moments of tension, and the normal give-and-take of any household, in return for giving up his privacy and leaving behind family and friends. Within months of going to Tweedside, the frustrated young man headed for Yamacraw, the biracial neighborhood where sailors, Black people, and local whites regularly repaired to find drink and entertainment or someone to buy their stolen goods or provide other illicit services. Described as being "of a black complexion, smooth skin, 5 feet 6 inches high, well known about Savannah," Titus joined a childhood friend from Ossabaw Island named Jesse. For both men, it was their introduction to an adult world that provided ample opportunity to make new friends, experience different forms of pleasure, and find a place to sleep.[24] After two months, they were captured and returned to their respective plantations.

Four years later at age twenty, Titus made another attempt, this time with a radically different destination in mind, East Florida, rarely mentioned in the advertisements in the *Georgia Gazette*.[25] It is not clear whether he was on Ossabaw or at Tweedside. As a twelve-year-old in 1781, Titus had lis-

Tabby cabins on Ossabaw Island, circa 1930s. Originally built for enslaved people in the 1840s, the cabins probably stood where huts were erected during the 1760s for the first captives. Courtesy of Georgia Historical Society.

tened to the spirited conversations in the settlement about the flight of Hercules and Betty to St. Augustine as news sped from cabin to cabin. A few months later, he was somewhere on Ossabaw when a galley full of loyalists, sailors, and roustabouts from St. Augustine made a stunning raid that hauled away thirty-three Black slaves, took two thousand pounds of indigo, and burned a ship under construction.[26] Negotiations secured the return of most, but the very mention of Florida called forth a flood of ambivalent feelings and meaning.[27] In 1789, Titus recruited Hector, the valuable blacksmith; Patty, a nineteen-year old with a baby; and Daniel, Patty's fourteen-year-old nephew, to escape with him. Four men at the plantation of Bryan Morel at the north end of Ossabaw left at the same time, probably in concert.[28] Throughout his career, Titus never moved alone.

How many set out is not known, but Titus and at least three others crossed the border into northern Florida to find an ideal setting for sustaining an existence relatively independent of outside support. Once embedded in the landscape, the Georgia fugitives never applied for free status, never converted to Catholicism, and never embraced Spanish culture as had so many others. Nor did they make an attempt to escape to Seminole country and a new life in alliance with Natives who would have valued their skills. They chose to live the life of maroons, hiding in swamps and forests or perhaps more openly in a land where settlements were still sparse, free from any form of white control, emerging to secure provisions and foodstuffs.[29]

Titus and his companions had to learn a new geography in a land where Spanish was the official language and to function as strangers in an alien world, buoyed only by the fact that the region was a borderland where many enslaved people and planters spoke English and where other fugitives lived with an ambiguous status. It is probable that the sparsely populated land south of the St. Marys River offered ample room for this group to trade with whites, to steal on occasion when supplies ran short, and maintain its ability to move across the landscape without constant fear of being intercepted. As Sylviane Diouf so aptly phrases, autonomy was at the heart of the maroons' project, and exile was their means to realize it.[30]

Communication with families on Ossabaw seems never to have been interrupted and may have prepared the way for another grand escape from the Morel plantations. In September 1791, two boats, probably twenty-five to thirty feet long, one of them with six oars, landed on Amelia Island with nine men, one woman, and a boy, all from Ossabaw or the network of plantations around Savannah where Titus had family and friends. Titus and the three other maroons surfaced at that very moment to meet them, an extraordinary testimony to the ability of Blacks to communicate across long distances.[31] The new arrivals came from seven different plantations and had been acquired by two sets of families—the Morels and the Bryans, related by marriage.[32] It is impossible to tease out who knew whom and how, but it is clear that these people were part of a much larger network than one plantation, had moved back and forth between multiple sites, had been acquainted with each other for a long period of time, and were disillusioned by changes in their current masters.

What these new fugitives had in mind is not clear. They might have become maroons in the same fashion as Titus and his friends; they might have sought to blend into the variegated Spanish landscape and find protection and perhaps wages; and some might have made a break for the Seminoles. Those options never materialized. By 1790, Spain had concluded that the usefulness of runaways as pawns in international diplomacy had ended and that the empire had little to gain by antagonizing the United States.[33] The negotiations of August 1791 between the U.S. commissioner, James Seagrove, and the new governor of East Florida, Juan Nepomuceno de Quesada, produced an arrangement for the return of fugitive slaves.[34]

Spanish soldiers were well prepared to carry out the mandate. They surrounded and arrested the fugitives shortly after they landed on the island, much to their surprise. Journeying to St. Augustine as the representative of the planters, the young Bryan Morel presented to the governor affidavits from the six planters who claimed ownership.[35] The legal documents were nothing grander than sworn statements before a justice of the peace in Chatham County in which each holder gave little information about the slave or his claim. Adam was described as "a lusty, stout fellow, of a black complexion"; Cesar was said to have a ring in his ear and be "much addicted to drinking"; Sam was "a well-made fellow of a yellowish cast"; and Tom was said to speaks good English. By Spanish standards, it was thin gruel, but Governor Quesada did not quibble. It was important to successfully conclude the first test of the August agreement. In January 1792, all fifteen were returned to Savannah and re-enslavement.

That marked the beginning of Titus's second experience with marronage. For two years he had tasted a life that spoke to his deepest aspirations and refused to accept becoming chattel property, condemned to being deferential and obedient, having to endure countless humiliations, including occasional whippings. His Spanish experiences conditioned his new existence. He remained a "dancer," only now on a grander scale. After several months, he found an opportunity to escape from John Morel and resumed his life as a permanent fugitive on the outskirts of settled communities, receiving food from sympathetic slaves, stealing from plantations, occasionally robbing people, and staying in constant motion.[36] The distinguishing feature of this new life phase was the incredible mobility of the man. He constantly moved in an arc that took him fifty miles from one end of his accustomed travels to the other and back again.

He roamed a broad expanse of land, "a known villain," in the words of his aggrieved owner, "concerned in most of the robberies committed on the inhabitants of this city and the neighborhood," moving surreptitiously among the hammocks on the coast bordering Chatham and Bryan Counties, that part of Carolina facing Chatham County, and in the swamps of the Savannah River "as high as Purrysburg [in South Carolina]."[37] In *Slavery's Exiles*, Diouf takes Titus as an example of what she describes as the "hinterland" maroon, that person who lived in the wilderness in secret, was not under any form of control by outsiders, and sought autonomy in a limited sense.[38] Her analysis focuses on the final community created in 1797, but his presence along the river during these earlier years provides a striking demonstration of those same characteristics.

His travels provide a map of the informal connections that linked the region. First, Titus knew the geography extremely well. This was not a case of a man finding an inaccessible spot in the wilderness and clinging to it. He ranged from the plantations along the Ogeechee to his childhood home on Ossabaw Island to the rice plantations along the Savannah to the Carolina side of the river, today the site of the Savannah Wildlife Refuge, and almost to Purrysburg, still a viable if dwindling community. He was easily covering fifty miles or more in his jaunts. Secondly, he was moving by water. Did he have his own boat or canoe? Were other people with him? At the very least, he emerges as a waterman of considerable skill and strength. Lastly, he was touching base with a large number of enslaved people along two of the great waterways in coastal Georgia. One wonders what kind of communications took place. What news did he carry? What did he learn at each of his stops? Surely, he must have become a folk hero to the Africans and African Americans who fed and supported him.

At every turn, Titus's character stands out as a rejection of white authority and indeed of white society, and his burning desire for self-determination is evident. Gifted with extraordinary survival skills, he simultaneously demonstrated a strong sense of community as seen in his orchestrating the landing of his compatriots in Florida. To that list, one must add loyalty to his extended family that never disappeared. In late 1794, he learned that the Morel brothers were planning to sell dozens of their enslaved people to stave off an impending bankruptcy that stemmed from over a decade of poor investments and high living. By this time, the brothers were struggling to maintain their father's legacy in the face of financial constraints generated by prewar commitments, postwar ambitions, poor management, and multiple lawsuits.[39] Members of Titus's family were included in two lots of forty-eight and thirty-seven people that the Morels were planning to put on the block.[40]

Concentrating on the problem at hand, he and others secured a boat large enough to hold eight people, six from one of the Morel plantations together with him and his wife. They took with them supplies of rice and other provisions, clothing, and at least one shotgun. A second group followed suit, drawing their numbers from the estate of Bryan Morel at the north end of the island.[41] Entire families boarded the two vessels. The men were seven in number: Titus; Tice, probably his brother; Jeffrey, John, Mingo, Lester, and Summer. There were five women: Nelly, the wife that Titus took during his years in Savannah; Betty, the wife of Tice; Beck, a mulatto skilled in tailoring women's clothes; Rose, and Sue. And there were three children: Bess, Elsey, and Phoebe, the daughter of Nelly and Titus. Nine of the group came rate fale till THURSDAY next, the 29th inftant, for ready money; if not fold by that time, they will then be expofed to public fale on THAT DAY, if the weather permits, for cafh on the titles being executed. Inquire of William Stephens, Efq.

One Hundred Dollars Reward.

RUN AWAY from the fubfcriber, from off the ifland of Of-
fabaw, on the night of the 12th inftant.

The following NEGROES:

TICE, a ftout black fellow, about 5 feet 7 inches high, has a wide mouth, is well made, 26 years of age, and country born.

JEFFRY, a ftout black fellow, about 5 feet 6 or 7 inches high, full faced, rather knock knee'd, and parrot toe'd, 25 years of age, country born.

JOHN, a lad from 15 to 16 years of age, well grown, about 5 feet 5 inches high, rather of a yellowifh complexion, country born.

ROSE, a likely wench, about 17 years of age, of a black complexion, flutters a little, and is about 5 feet 5 inches high, country born.

BECK, a fair Mulatto wench, 20 years of age, rather likely, about 5 feet 7 inches high; and her CHILD, a Mulatto girl a-bout 4 years old.

The above Negroes carried with them a fmall two oared canoe, their pots, blankets, and clothes; their drefs white plains; and are well acquainted in this county, efpecially in Savannah, on the river a few miles above, and at Mr. Netherclift's plantation, Placentia, at which places they have connexions, and where it is fuppofed they may be harbored. A REWARD OF TEN DOLLARS will be paid for each of the grown Negroes, on their being delivered to the fubfcriber, or lodged in the gaol of the city of Savannah.

FIFTY DOLLARS are alfo offered for the fubfcriber's Negro Fellow TITUS, a known villain, who has been concerned in moft of the robberies that have been committed on the inhabit-ants of this city and the neighborhood for thefe three years paft. It is fuppofed that the foregoing Negroes have been inveigled away by this fellow; his haunts are on the hammocks on the fea coaft bordering on this and Bryan county, that part of Caro-lina adjoining Chatham county, and on the fwamps of Savannah river as high up as Purrysburg. JOHN MOREL.

Savannah, Chatham County, January 15, 1795.

N. B. If the above Negroes are apprehended going fouthward-ly, which may be the cafe, any reafonable expence will be paid for the guarding and fecuring of them to this place.

Ten Dollars Reward.

ROBBED and RUN AWAY, from
on board the fchooner Abigail, of Bofton, commanded
by Capt. Solomon Hopkins, lying at Alexander Watt's
wharf, DANIEL LEACH, mate, and WILLIAM and JOHN
HOLMES, feamen. Daniel Leach, the mate, is an American

"One Hundred Dollars Reward," notice by John Morel, Ossabaw Island. Titus, a maroon originally from Morel's plantation, led six people to East Florida in a "two-oared canoe," replete with pots, blankets, and clothing, in late 1794. Thanks to his ability to escape and cross borders, Titus became a major concern to Spanish and American authorities. *Georgia Gazette*, January 12, 1795, February 26, 1795.

from the plantations of John Morel while two, Lester and Summer, were "New Negroes" from Bryan Morel's estate.[42] Most were in their twenties and "country-born."

The composition of the group tells yet another story. In the constant waves of Blacks headed to Florida, creoles were dominant, not individuals born in Africa, as was the case for the majority of runaways from Lowcountry plantations. The presence of women and children harked back to revolutionary times when the confusion and chaos of the war created opportunities for whole families to flee, an indication of the strength and depth of feeling that animated this unusually cohesive community.

The geopolitics of the region was treacherous. Spanish Florida had little trust in the integrity of Georgia, whose citizens were bent on territorial expansion and eager to see the Spanish government fall so that they could add the peninsula to the "Empire of Liberty" that Thomas Jefferson was to extoll as president. Nor did Georgia trust the Spaniards, whom they considered deceitful and superstitious and who had supplied the Creeks with the arms and ammunition in the recent raids along the extensive border of the state. Indeed, contempt for the other was the common frame of mind.

Titus had had no qualms about returning to the territory where he had been captured. He was aware that the agreement of August 1791 had broken down in a welter of mutual accusations, with the Spanish accusing Georgians of coming across the border to steal slaves while refusing to return Florida slaves who escaped into Georgia, and the Americans accusing the Spanish of allowing a fresh wave of fugitives to cross the border without consequence.[43] Both sets of charges were true. Over one hundred enslaved people were successful in escaping to the colony during those years, and a handful of Florida-based escapees were in hiding in Camden and Glynn Counties.[44]

The circumstances that had preceded Titus and his party's voyage in 1791 were repeated in a nasty twist of fate. In the weeks before Titus, Nelly, Tice, Betty, and the others landed on Amelia Island in February 1795, Spanish and Georgia negotiators had come to an informal agreement to resume the former practice of mutually returning runaway enslaved people. Both sides were eager to bury the issue once and for all. St. Augustine had issued orders to the garrisons of soldiers stationed on the northern tip of Amelia Island to halt and hold any fugitives by force of arms. Unknowingly, Titus and the others stepped into a trap. When a small garrison confronted the seven men, five women, and three children, the creoles and two Africans put up a spirited fight. One was severely wounded and, within minutes, the outgunned freedom seekers surrendered.[45]

Col. Carlos Howard, commander of the military post at San Vicente de
Ferrer at the mouth of the St. Johns River, was in the middle of punishing
a set of freeman for their "excesses" and wanted to keep the fugitives from
becoming heroes to the Black population. His greatest concern was Titus,
who was known from his earlier time there. "He is of such notoriety," Howard explained to the governor, "that I consider it to be prudent to put him
in chains here and then to consign him to work in chains."[46] The colonel arranged for the group to be lodged in the outbuildings of a nearby plantation
belonging to John McQueen, a former Georgian. McQueen was the uncle
(by marriage) of John Morel and quite familiar with Titus's reputation.

At this point, Titus turned to the only resource left, a party of Seminoles
who were making their way through the region hunting game. Between the
St. Johns and St. Marys Rivers, there were no fixed boundaries as such, and
plantations and farms on the west bank of the St. Johns were especially vulnerable to having their livestock stolen.[47] Hunting parties occasionally appeared among the settlements, making planters and farmers nervous for their
property and fearful for their own safety should something go awry. The appearance of a Seminole hunting party led by Cohiti, a chief or headman, near
the post at St. Vicente de Ferrer and McQueen's plantation gave Titus his
opportunity. Security was lax, and he already was slipping out at night to visit
his compatriots in scattered outbuildings near the main house.

Cohiti was leading a party of ten or twelve men, with several women
and children, ambling through the countryside supposedly hunting for deer.
The Seminoles were accompanied by two Black fugitives of Governor John
Houstoun of Georgia, fugitives who—like so many of their peers—were
serving as translators and cultural brokers between the Natives and Euro-
American society. Farmers and ranchers feared that the Indians were looking for opportunities to steal livestock, slaves, and valuables. Colonel Howard put out feelers and learned that Cohiti was a medicine man from a
Hichiti-speaking town who had chosen to go into exile when townsmen
had turned against him. It seems that predictions the headman had made
had not come true and had had placed his settlement into a difficult position. But the exile was temporary. Cohiti was planning to return at the
time of the Green Corn Festival in late summer, when the town fire was ex-
tinguished and a new one built, past misdeeds were forgiven, amnesty extended, and ceremonies marked a new beginning in the cycle of life.[48]

Appearing at Colonel Howard's residence with several horses carrying
furs, Peter, one of Houstoun's fugitives, told the commander that the Natives
wanted to sell the skins to sailors on a nearby boat for rum. Howard refused

permission. At this point, Cohiti rode up to the post and entered into a spirited discussion that set forth the points for debate. When the colonel asked in frustration why the Natives would dare hunt among the plantations along the St. Johns River, burn fields in the search for game, and enter private houses when they knew it was against Spanish policy, Cohiti gave a spirited reply that blamed the Americans for pushing Natives out of their land and asserted that the territory west of the St. Johns belonged to the Seminoles. "These Negroes already speak the Indian language," Howard wrote to Quesada, "and were going about spreading word around the slaves in the neighborhood of the happy life they could live with the Seminoles."[49]

The "happy life" that Peter described to his enslaved peers in East Florida was indeed privileged in the sense that Black Seminoles lived in villages attached to Seminole towns, retained control of their daily lives to an extraordinary degree, and performed certain services for their captors—from giving a small portion of their crops to acting as interpreters and cultural brokers with the white world. Some historians considered them as genuine maroons loosely attached to the Seminoles, a relatively recent coalition of Native groups that retained older forms of captivity with looser forms of control. Historians continue to debate their status, but it is worth noting that the Indigenous Seminoles viewed Black Seminoles as enslaved people, even if they required little from them and eventually fought side-by-side with them in the Seminole Wars of the nineteenth century. The subsequent history of the two groups down to the present day reflects this reality, with Black Seminoles claiming recognition as members of the Seminole Nation and "blood Seminoles" refusing to accord that status.[50]

Slipping out of his place of imprisonment, Titus freed Nelly, his wife; John, Nelly's brother; and Mingo from their outbuilding and fled with them in search of Peter and the Seminoles.[51] Cohiti and his men were pleased to add to their numbers and planned to pull up stakes and leave the area with their rich prize of four new Black people as quickly as possible. On learning of their escape the next morning, McQueen moved quickly, dispatching two professional slave hunters, a Mr. Thorp and a Mr. Fitzgerald, together with their English hunting dogs, to track the four.[52] Howard instructed that, if McQueen's men discovered the fugitives already with the Natives, they were to negotiate for their return, it "being notorious that the Indians easily return any stolen property that they find [in return for money]."[53] The bounty hunters discovered the four with Cohiti and, for a goodly price, arranged for the Seminoles to return them to the McQueen plantation.

Cohiti and his men brought back the fugitives, but, for reasons that re-

flected their deep aversion to humiliating people who demonstrated bravery, refused to tie their hands and delivered them at the plantation house
free of restraint. Titus was far from cowed. Standing in front of the house,
he refused an order to go inside, and pulled a knife. McQueen would write
to Howard, "[Titus] swore that if [the overseer] tried to lay a hand on him,
he would cut his guts out and immediately grabbed [the man]." On seeing
McQueen and his foreman appear, the fugitive moved behind the screen offered by the eight Native warriors and dashed into nearby underbrush. The
foreman discharged his shotgun but missed as the escapee disappeared into
a dense thicket. Titus doubled back but was captured that night hiding under his wife's bed.[54]

The Spanish governor hoped to return him to Georgia as quickly as possible. That was not to be. At the very moment the transfer was being arranged in late June 1795, the Georgia-Florida frontier exploded in violence
as a disjointed fighting force of American adventurers, supported by disaffected American colonists in Florida, attempted a clumsy uprising that collapsed under the weight of a Spanish counterattack.[55] Some of the leaders of
a failed invasion in 1794 rallied a few dozen Anglo planters who were dissat-
isfied with their lack of protection from raids by the Seminoles and the mer-
cantilist restrictions on trade that reduced them to smuggling goods from
Georgia. The attempted coup ended talks between the two governments and
resulted in Titus spending two years imprisoned in the fearsome Castillo
de San Marcos in St. Augustine, with its thick tabby walls and dungeon-
like rooms. Never losing hope, he made a bold but futile attempt to escape.
For his troubles, he was placed on half rations.[56] Despite the Treaty of San
Lorenzo between Spain and the United States in late 1795 that opened the
Mississippi River to American vessels, the crudely mounted coup on the St.
Johns River delayed a settlement on fugitive slaves until early 1797.[57]

In that year, the U.S. commissioner, James Seagrove, and the new Spanish governor, Enrique White, took advantage of the turn of events and began a conversation that led to the exchange of lists of enslaved people held
in the two territories. Realizing that both sides had little to gain from pro-
longing the tension, they worked out the terms of agreement with surprising ease.[58] An understanding reached in May 1797 provided for the return
of Florida fugitives in Georgia and Georgia fugitives in Florida. The return
took place rapidly. On May 22, 1797, the sloop *Harriet* brought twenty-seven
of the failed freedom seekers to St. Marys, where they were said to be "safely
lodged in the new prison in this town, until proof be made by their owners." Another eleven remained in St. Augustine as "hostages" until the re-

turn of an equal number "now detained in Georgia." Unable to budge planters in the Lowcountry, Georgia had to compensate Spanish slaveholders for
the fugitives that they adamantly refused to release and shipped thirty-four
hundred Spanish dollars to St. Augustine.[59] News of the agreement motivated Titus to make a new attempt at escape. He made his way past guards
at the seventeenth-century fortress and headed northward toward Georgia.
Always in search of followers, he recruited two English-speaking field hands
to join him.[60]

The remarkable escape, a rarity in a century-old masonry fortress, inau-
gurated the third phase in his career as a maroon. In July, Seagrove reported
to the Spanish governor, "The notorious fellow Titus, with some negros
from Florida, made their way along the sea coast until they got into Savannah River and among the rice plantations where he was well acquainted.
There Titus soon formed a party with some other outlaying negroes who
became very troublesome to the people by plunder and as a receptacle for
runaways."[61] Within short order, this quintessential maverick had created a
wholly new community around the rice plantations of the Savannah River.
Maroons in the neighborhood joined him, and runaways began to appear,
with the group evolving into an unstable community whose survival depended on raiding nearby plantations at a time when a network of support
had not yet been built.

Until this point, Titus had surrounded himself with family members and
friends from the Morel and related plantations. Once back in Georgia, he
began welcoming other maroons and runaways. The recruitment of outsiders represented something new, as if he had adopted the model of marronage that the so-called soldiers of the King of England had embraced toward
the final days of their settlement. It is hard not to draw the conclusion that
imprisonment in the Castillo de San Marcos had profoundly changed Titus
and that he was an angry man ready to throw caution to the wind. Predict-
ably, the new formula drew the intervention of the authorities. For the white
community, individual maroons and even small numbers of them were often
too inaccessible to make it worthwhile to root them out. The presence of a
growing number of maroons who struck at nearby plantations and impeded
travel on rural roads brought back white Georgians' memories of the exis-
tential threat that the Belleisle community had represented in the 1780s.

Within short order, a company of the Georgia militia was dispatched
with orders to kill those who did not surrender. Although they discovered
and fired upon Titus's band, most of the maroons escaped, "it being a very
thick swamp." They suspected they had killed one of them given "a great

quantity of blood found on the ground," but they were not able to confirm this. Trackers, presumably with dogs, headed into the marshes and managed to capture several people who were taken to the jail in Savannah. Seagrove noted to the Florida governor, "A Negro belonging to Mr. Maxey may still be with his friend and patron, Titus, in the woods but parties are constantly after them and there is little doubt they will be taken or killed."[62] Both Ben and Plato, from the estate of Robert Maxey in Florida, were eventually captured, but there is no evidence that Titus was taken. At that point, the historical record falls silent.[63]

Charismatic, bull-headed, blessed with an indomitable spirit, and possessing a proud sense of his Black features, Titus had made the sanctity of his own group his primary focus. Over the years, that focus changed. At the beginning, he led a community built around the conventional model of men creating a highly gendered society in a place of safety. He then led a second community in which the family was paramount and women and children were present. It appears that the flight to Florida in 1795 was less about him and his wife, Nelly—they had been successful maroons outside of Savannah for three years—and more about saving their loved ones from sale by the Morel brothers. In the third and last iteration, he created a short-lived community that became a magnet for runaways and other maroons in the region and showed himself willing to stake out a claim for broader recognition within the Black world.

The year 1797 marked the turning point for Spanish-American relations on the Georgia border. Henceforward, Spanish authorities detained and returned escapees when caught, although for years to come Georgia newspapers carried the occasional notice that a fugitive was suspected to have gone to St. Augustine. Not all fugitives were intercepted, nor did authorities in Florida have the time or interest in pursuing them. If tensions subsided and a relatively cordial working relationship emerged during the next decade, the border remained a lawless area. Smuggling cattle, cotton, and slaves was always a staple of business on both sides of the frontier.[64] With the change, fugitives now headed directly to the Seminoles. Many took the well-worn Mikasuki path that crossed the St. Marys River at several points below Trader's Hill and wound around the outer edge of the Okefenokee Swamp into Indian territory.[65] The Seminole people and the role they accorded to fugitives in leading a relatively independent life remained a source of considerable angst among whites.

One can argue that Titus bore only a distant relationship to Prince Whitten and his friends, who took full advantage of the opportunities offered by the Spanish government, Spanish law, and the Catholic Church. Whitten's family became valued members of the St. Augustine community, skilled artisans who constituted a critical part of the colony's defensive forces. Indeed, Titus more nearly fits the image of the "hinterland maroon" that Sylviane Diouf draws in *Slavery's Exiles*, the fugitive who relied on the difficult terrain of dense forests and treacherous swamps rather than on man-made works to elude the white world.[66] His was a much less complicated quest to establish absolute autonomy free of any form of outside control. When the Spanish consul in Savannah interrogated Ben, one of the fugitive slaves he had recruited from a Florida plantation, Ben stated that he had fled "at the instigation of the notoriously perverse Titus, of the same color, who made them [Ben and Plato] believe that here they would spend a life entirely different from the yoke of slavery."[67] That life was to be more nearly the life of a survivalist, not a participant in a community rooted in the culture of Spanish America.

Nevertheless, Titus's exploits cannot be fully understood unless they are placed in the larger movement of African Americans from the Georgia Lowcountry to Spanish Florida across a span of forty years. In searching for freedom, he sought the same basic goal that animated Jupiter and Auba during the Revolution, Prince Whitten and his family during the 1780s, and the fugitives who attached themselves as "junior allies" to the Seminoles. Titus's remarkable ability to traverse the width and breadth of the Lowcountry, cross international borders, and seemingly appear and disappear at will represented an accentuated version of what hundreds of other Black people were doing across a long period of time. Although negotiating a place in white society was foreign to his thinking, Titus remained an integral part of the Atlantic world. His interactions with Spanish authorities, Georgia planters, Seminole Indians, Florida enslaved, Savannah-region maroons, and enslaved people still living on the Morel plantations showed his remarkable connections to this larger world and his ability to read the political and cultural landscape according to his own deeply held beliefs. Far from an isolated actor, he played a leadership role in a relatively large-scale movement of fugitives into Spanish territory between 1785 and 1797.

Another lesson is apparent. Not only was Titus aware of this larger world, but so too were the enslaved people along the Georgia coast. Far from being isolated and cut off on rice plantations in swampy terrain, many of them remained connected with the realities of the Atlantic world as filtered through the adjacent borderland. Too many of their family, friends, and acquaintances made their way to Spanish Florida for them not to be. Too many raids by Creeks and Seminoles into coastal areas reminded them of both the dangers and possibilities. The occasional slave stolen from a Lowcountry plantation and hustled across the frontier provided another marker; and the occasional Florida freedom seekers heading north provided yet another. And in the background was the underground pipeline of information that traveled up and down the coast such that Titus could stay in touch with the Morel slaves during his years as a maroon in Florida.

Few Black people were tempted by the life of Titus or his followers. But they were well aware of the possibilities that existed, and hundreds of them did choose to make their way across the frontier over a forty-year period. The ties between Lowcountry Georgia, Spanish Florida, and the Seminoles were substantial and nowhere more so than in the understanding that pervaded slave quarters along the coast. The movement of Black people was an important element in creating a sense of a larger region among those who remained in place, one that included knowledge of the Spanish, the Creeks, the Seminoles, and perhaps even the British. In the backdrop were the geopolitical calculations of many governors, three empires, and one republic. Marronage during the concluding years of the eighteenth century bore a transnational perspective, stemming in large part from the incredible mobility that the juxtaposition of a colonial society, a newly created republic, Native lands, and a watery world of swamps and tidal creeks made possible.

Beside the movement of maroons like Titus and freedom seekers like Prince Whitten, something new was happening along the border that separated an increasingly self-confident state, flush with an expanding population, and a colony that was only beginning to find its footing and stood in desperate need of manpower. In 1791, the governor of East Florida received belated approval of a policy already in place in West Florida and threw open the gates of his province to all settlers willing to give an oath of allegiance to the king of Spain, accept Spanish law, and worship as Protestants only in private homes. It was a generous offer that required little, while land was virtually for the taking. A new generation of American planters with their enslaved people made an appearance, and a different dynamic took hold. Suddenly, enslaved people from Georgia found themselves thrust into a Hispanic landscape.

CHAPTER 6

The Florida of
Don Juan McQueen

At the very moment that Titus was attempting to create an autonomous community for family and friends in East Florida and Georgia, entire settlements on the Georgia coast were being abruptly uprooted and relocated to Florida. At the beginning of the 1790s, hundreds of enslaved people found themselves deracinated with little warning, carried across the St. Marys River in a mass migration, and planted on largely unsettled spaces in East Florida, facing a new life in a Hispanic context.[1] The forced migration reflected a radical change in Spanish land policy that pushed the colony toward a genuine plantation economy. Africans and African Americans, whether recent arrivals or not, faced a new reality as the first moves of the Spanish government toward a plantation economy raised questions of how Hispanic culture, law, and society would accommodate the new reality of American planters playing a driving role and how those same planters and their enslaved would adapt to the changed setting.

East Florida governor Vicente Manuel de Céspedes had been closely watching events in West Florida, using the province as a model for opening up East Florida to settlers who could breathe economic life into what remained not much more than a glorified military outpost. By a royal order issued in 1787, Spain formally allowed loyalists who retained their British citizenship to settle along the rich alluvial lands of the Mississippi River, while opening the door to a controlled flow of Americans in search of opportunity.[2] Céspedes embraced this vision with enthusiasm. Northern Florida, he claimed, was being infiltrated by American frontiersmen "distinguished from savages only in their color, language, and the superiority of their de-praved cunning and untrustworthiness." By admitting farmers and planters, Spain would create "a living wall of industrious citizens" and build an export economy around cotton, rice, and timber.[3]

His reliance on cultural stereotypes may have reduced a complex dynamic to simple terms, but, for that moment, it had the ring of truth. On November 20, 1790, the Spanish government issued a decree enabling foreigners to migrate to East Florida and receive land grants based on the headright system, with each head of family eligible for one hundred acres and each dependent, whether slave or free, fifty acres.[4] In return, settlers were to follow the same requirements as in West Florida: giving an oath of loyalty to the Spanish Crown, obeying Spanish law, and confining Protestant worship to the home.

The effect was electric. During the following three years, some 348 white men, women, and children entered East Florida, bringing with them at least 921 enslaved Black people and probably more.[5] Although Americans formed a little less than one half of the settlers, they were the source for most of the enslaved. Many, like John McQueen, the planter who had imprisoned Titus, were one step ahead of their creditors and chose Florida rather than face bankruptcy and the loss of their human property.[6] According to the magistrate for the St. Marys District, many of the wealthier immigrants intended to remain only until matters could be "made up with their creditors."[7]

The infusion of Black and white people between the St. Johns and St. Marys Rivers promised to create a vibrant export economy, bring to an end the relative lawlessness of that area, and, it was hoped, call into being Céspedes's image of a living wall of industrious citizens. To an extent it succeeded. More than half of the settlers came from England, Scotland, Ireland, Italy, and France. Most were Protestant. Of the Americans, not a single Catholic was among them if one does not count McQueen, who converted after arriving. Almost 40 percent of both Americans and those of other nationalities came as single individuals without family.[8] In some cases, they left wives and families behind, as did McQueen, whose spouse, Anne Smith McQueen, continued to reside in Savannah under the protection of her father and John's brother, a merchant. Most of the others did not hold enslaved people.[9] They were simple farmers or artisans or mariners who blended into the maritime community in St. Augustine.[10] The Black population of East Florida more than doubled, from 588 enslaved people and 63 free Blacks in 1788 to 1,527 enslaved and 126 free Blacks, a step on the road to a full plantation economy.[11]

Such a policy carried huge risks. The central question became whether Americans would give their loyalty to the government and accept the rule of Spanish law or in turn become disloyal and sow the seeds of rebellion. The role of John McQueen, a land speculator and planter in Florida until his death in 1807 at the age of fifty-seven, testifies to the presence of a small but important group of Americans who embraced Hispanic values to a surprising extent, remained loyal to the Spanish government, and opposed the intrigues of settlers conspiring to overthrow it. His flamboyant career as the largest slaveholder in East Florida, as a Presbyterian who converted to Catholicism, as an advisor to the governor, and as a backer of the free Black militia serves as a window through which one can peer into the conflicted lives of enslaved people who participated in this latest migration, as opposed to the freedom seekers whose story dominated the previous decade.[12]

McQueen was no stranger to a multicultural society. His father ranked among the top deerskin merchants in Charles Town before the Revolution, while the son's own openness owed much to the cosmopolitan upbringing he received. When his father died an early death, the mother took young John to England for his education. Sometime during his late teens and early twenties, he became a sea captain, and his maritime credentials would catch the eye of Carolina legislators. When the Revolution began, he was named commander of the small patriot navy for South Carolina. His greatest skill seemed to have been in making himself useful to powerful figures. As a twenty-six-year-old, he greeted the nineteen-year-old Marquis de Lafayette when Lafayette landed in South Carolina on his way to Washington's army, and he kept up that friendship after the war. On subsequent missions to Philadelphia, he was introduced to George Washington and Benjamin Franklin, and toward the end of the Revolution he provided intelligence and provisions to Gen. Nathanael Greene, a close friend until the general's early death.[13]

At the conclusion of the war, McQueen reverted to his speculative ways and placed a high-risk bet on the purchase of Sapelo Island, one-half of St. Catherines, as well as Little Cabretta and Blackbeard Islands from the State of Georgia, a total of twelve thousand acres that had been confiscated from loyalist merchants.[14] Young John moved aggressively to claim a stake in "live oaking" at a time when navies throughout the Atlantic were rebuilding their fleets using this wood with exceptional tensile strength and graceful curves that made it ideal for specialty parts on a ship. He sent some of his best enslaved timbermen to Cumberland Island to help Nathanael Greene initiate timbering on the extensive property the general had purchased there. The bet did not pay off.[15] Despite the lobbying of Lafayette, the French Ministry of War made a half-hearted offer to buy his pieces but only if delivered to a French port, a financially ruinous condition.[16]

It remains a mystery how and why McQueen assembled an enslaved population of almost three hundred people on the Sea Islands during the 1780s when he was first and foremost a timberman with a taste for land speculation. Inheritance, opportunism, and debt on McQueen's part shared in equal measure in explaining the three distinct groups that made up the population. The core set of families came from a substantial rice plantation on Horse Savannah Creek in South Carolina that the timber speculator inherited at his father's death in 1762. At that time, they numbered well over one hundred people, but there is no indication of how many families or individuals were still present eighteen years later.[17] These were men and women who gave a certain cohesion and stability to the whole community. Harry, his body servant, who had been with him since the age of twelve, belonged to this cohort. He offered a fierce loyalty to his "master," was entrusted with considerable responsibility that included sailing on his own from West Florida to Havana back to St. Augustine, and eventually became a freeman with a small farm and a member of the prestigious free Black militia. When McQueen died, he supervised the burial and noted that the enslaved had wept over "the loss of such a good owner."[18]

The second group came from the manner in which McQueen took advantage of the confusion at the end of the Revolutionary War to seize unattached Black people and enlarge his holdings through subterfuge. The governor of South Carolina had placed in his care 120 enslaved people turned over by the British as they departed Charleston and asked that he hold them until claimed by their "masters."[19] Although enslavers appeared and made their claims, he benefited in the exchange and retained a few. One of these presented a letter from the British military that certified her freedom and became the basis for a long-running court battle in St. Augustine during the 1790s. How many came this way is unknown. Certainly they were the smallest of the three groups. Finally, McQueen purchased a large number of Africans during the 1780s from Thomas Shoolbred, an English slave trader in Charleston to whom he was deeply indebted, a financial obligation that hung over him for the remainder of his days.[20] These were recent survivors of the Middle Passage on slavers coming from West Africa.

McQueen had mortgaged his property on the Sea Islands to acquire additional timber-rich lands around Augusta and dozens more African captives, failed to pay taxes in three counties at a time when authorities had become less forgiving, and faced down creditors in court, notably Shoolbred.

His hopes momentarily brightened when two young Frenchmen, the marquis de Chappedelaine and François Dumoussay, looking for an investment safe from the turmoil of revolutionary France, bought the islands. The complex sale, replete with lawsuits, did not solve his problems.[21] The bet on St. Catherines and Sapelo ended in bankruptcy. At that point, he entered into conversation with Governor Céspedes, an acquaintance he had made during a diplomatic mission taken on behalf of the Georgia legislature. The soon-to-depart governor used these discussions to prod the captain-general of Cuba into approving the same land policy for East Florida as for West Florida. He let drop that "a certain Don Diego MacQueen," with as many as five hundred slaves, had declared to him "his determination one way or another to become a Spanish citizen by moving his entire estate to the island of Trinidad" ("since he has not been allowed to settle here as a vassal of the King").[22]

When news of the change in land policy reached McQueen, the Georgian discretely assembled schooners and sloops and departed for St. Augustine in April 1791. Self-assured, this cosmopolitan figure meant to transform himself into a dominant figure on a smaller stage in a new cultural setting. He had a fair claim. The 280 enslaved people that accompanied him represented almost one-half of the entire slave population of East Florida as enumerated in the census of 1788.[23] Landing with his labor force in the schooners and sloops, he strode to the government building facing the plaza of St. Augustine and took an oath of allegiance to the Spanish Crown, with the new governor, Juan Nepomuceno de Quesada, as a witness. This complex man who embodied so much of the revolutionary generation—with his patriotic credentials, his taste for land speculation, his friendship with leading public figures in the United States, his stake in the emerging national economy, and his Presbyterian roots—changed loyalties with dizzying speed. A few days later, McQueen played on the excitement by announcing his desire to convert to the "One True Faith" and embrace an institution that was the ultimate expression of Hispanic values. Two months after his arrival, the assembled ranks of the priesthood in St. Augustine came together to baptize this longtime Scottish Presbyterian into the Catholic faith.[24]

The victims of this migration were the Africans whose sudden removal from the Sea Islands had come as one more unpleasant surprise. McQueen had studiously avoided giving advanced warning to anyone of his departure for fear of tipping off the creditors. Bewildered and shocked, the families received minimal notice, were forced to depart without a farewell to family members or friends on other plantations, and had no choice but to leave behind livestock, gardens, and material possessions in the rush. Shortly after landing, at least five of their number voted with their feet and escaped over the St. Marys River to be reunited with extended family in Georgia. Quickly caught and returned, they served as a cautionary tale. Their capture was one more indicator of McQueen's high standing along the coast since Georgia planters were notorious about incorporating fugitives from Florida into their own labor force.[25]

Where did such a large body of Africans and people of African descent go once they disembarked in St. Augustine? How were they housed and maintained? For the tiny government of Spanish Florida that was already short of cash, the logistical challenge was enormous. Probably they were placed in different locations outside the town and encouraged to raise their own provisions despite the late May start. Conditions were miserable for these forcibly uprooted people who were expected to cope as best they could. But they did not have to wait long before John McQueen obtained a huge grant of land, made all the sweeter through an extraordinary adventure in keeping with his outsized personality.

In late 1791, Governor Quesada was in a state of panic because thirty-one-year-old William Augustus Bowles, a former loyalist armed with a vague expression of support from the British government, was aiming at nothing less than the overthrow of Spanish rule in Florida, the creation of an independent state among the Creeks and Seminoles, and the reintro-duction of Great Britain as an active force in the Southeast.[26] He was sail-ing around the Florida coast to reunite with his father-in-law, Kinache, the most powerful Seminole leader in the Apalachicola region and arguably in the entire network of decentralized towns that made up the still coalescing Native people. After the British defeat at Pensacola late in the war, Bowles had deserted his unit and sought refuge with Natives led by Kinache. He married the chief's daughter and intended to build on the resulting relation-ships to create a veritable state anchored in the grievances felt by Natives. With two vessels supplied by the governor and a makeshift crew recruited along the waterfront, an emboldened McQueen sailed to the west side of Florida, seized several prizes, and came close to tracking down the would-be revolutionary.[27]

If the expedition failed to secure the man, the demonstration of Span-ish "naval" power was important in saving face for a weak government. Que-sada responded by granting McQueen the whole of Fort George Island at the mouth of the St. Johns River, several thousand acres of mostly marsh but with valuable uplands at the northern and southern ends.[28] For the first few months, enslaved men and women were put to work raising provisions to

The McQueen-Kingsley House, built in 1798 by John McQueen. A leader of the Americans who immigrated to Florida in the early 1790s and an adviser to the Spanish governor, McQueen constructed the house on Fort George Island and made it the center of several plantations that held over 280 enslaved Africans. Courtesy of State Archives of Florida.

feed themselves and building "Negro huts" thatched with palms. At the site of a former indigo plantation, McQueen installed several metal vats for the manufacturing of the dye but soon reverted to form. His laborers were diverted to cutting timber, always a dependable source of income, and building sawmills at the north end, still known today as Los Molinos de McQueen.[29]

According to an inventory at McQueen's death, Los Molinos sheltered ninety-three slaves living in seventeen wooden cabins. Most of them raised Sea Island cotton, although timbering always remained a staple commodity produced by a water-driven saw. Dominating the plantation was McQueen's own well-furnished house, surrounded by other wooden structures, including one for cotton gins, a water-driven saw with two working blades, a blacksmith's forge, a kitchen, and livestock pens.[30] The population included forty children or adolescents, forty between the ages of fifteen and forty-nine, and thirteen who were fifty or older. Most lived in fifteen nuclear fam-

St. George Street, St. Augustine, circa 1890. The street functioned as the center of
town for the Spanish period. John McQueen, an American immigrant, maintained
his in-town house on the street next to the house of the governor, with whom
he frequently spoke. Courtesy of University of Florida Digital Collections.

ilies, but on the plantation as a whole men outnumbered women by fifty-
one to forty-two. The largest family had eighteen members, including the
grandparents, Jacob and Amy, sixty-five and fifty years old, two other men
and three other women, and eleven children or adolescents. Jack and The-
resa, both thirty years old, had four young children, aged nine, eight, four,
and two. As a carpenter, Jack was the most highly valued enslaved person (at
600 livres) other than the blacksmith. Seven people were listed as "mulatto."
Nancy, twenty-eight years old, bore that designation as did her ten-year-old
daughter, Sophia, but not her two younger children, Sam and James.[31]

Other grants followed as the government looked with favor on McQueen,
an extraordinary individual whom the captain-general of Cuba described as
"a wealthy, intelligent, expert man, one partial to the Spaniards."[32] Within
three years of his arrival, McQueen had assembled an estate that spanned
sixteen thousand acres of land, claimed another ten thousand acres, and received a favorable response to setting up a sawmill near the southern tip of

the peninsula to export lumber to Havana with claims on thousands of surrounding acres. His empire of sand, mud, water, and timber matched those of John Graham and Governor James Wright in prerevolutionary Georgia.[33]

Of the two plantations established on the St. Johns River, the first, called Canefield, later Shipyard, spanned over a thousand acres and housed fifty-eight enslaved people in nine cabins, a few miles south of today's Jacksonville.[34] As the name indicates, Shipyard had a stock of wood and heavily wooded grounds around it, together with carpenter tools. The enslaved families included an equal number of men and women and tended to be younger than those at Los Molinos. In their twenties, Paul and Bina were raising four young children. Forty-five-year-old Clarisa had three teenagers in her household. Nevertheless, four individuals were listed as eighty years old, two were ninety, and one was said to be one hundred five years old. If the five young single males were to marry, some would have had to search for their wives on other estates. The single women like Clarissa were older and had either lost their husbands or had husbands on other plantations.

The second plantation on the St. Johns, San Pablo, near Cowford, the crossing point now at the heart of Jacksonville, covered 2,266 acres and sheltered 106 people living in twenty-eight houses. The least productive of several enterprises, San Pablo contained the highest number of people fifty years or older, many in their sixties and seventies and older, just shy of one-third of the population. It may well be that these were from the plantation of McQueen's father on Horseshoe Creek in South Carolina, reflecting his disposition never to sell enslaved people even when hard-pressed financially but rather to duck and weave in order to hold on. According to the inventory at his death in 1807, the humans located at San Pablo represented considerably less value than those on his other plantations. Another twenty-three people worked on a smaller plantation on a creek off the St. Johns, and ten bondsmen raised crops on a farm on Amelia Island.[35] On virtually every unit, enslaved people produced lumber, always the cornerstone for McQueen's success; others raised Sea Island cotton and provisions like corn and peas; and a small number herded cattle. Rice was a minor crop.[36] Government contracts provided a ready market for the lumber.

Harry McQueen, John McQueen's faithful and supportive body-servant, had witnessed his owner's transition from a southern planter of the eighteenth century who demanded absolute obedience to a man with a more paternalistic approach, showing concern for the well-being of enslaved people, sometimes real, more often for show, but always self-interested. In letters to his family in Savannah, John McQueen expressed his concern for the health of particular Black people, described their illnesses, and spoke movingly of their deaths.[37]

His son shared those sentiments. John McQueen Jr. had come to Florida to be with his father and to serve in the trading firm of Panton, Leslie. From St. Augustine, the son advised his sister, Eliza, who was in Savannah, not to marry Bryan Morel, the much younger brother of John Morel, describing him as "a hard Negro Master," a sign of "a little mind & bad disposition."[38] What made the father and son unusual was the way they worked within a Spanish context and their embrace, however partial, of Hispanic values and norms, especially of a three-caste society in which free Blacks had a prominent role. The father was not alone in this respect and provided leadership to a small group of American planters who adapted as well. Peter Carne and Andrew Atkinson, captains in the militia for the northern district, were two of his leading supporters.

Harry was almost certainly a baptized Catholic. McQueen demanded as much. The planter met each week with Father Miguel O'Reilly, participated in the many rituals of the Catholic Church, prayed on a daily basis, and provided opportunities for his enslaved people to convert. In 1788, a bishop had conducted an ecclesiastical visitation of the entire province and observed "with great pain" that almost all the slaves and free Black people lived without the sacrament of baptism and "were denied the happiness of being Christians."[39] When Father Hassett, the second priest in St. Augustine, made a tour of the province in 1793, he noted that McQueen had 44 of his "children" baptized and eventually saw to the baptism of 110 children and adults, more than for any other planter in Florida, Spanish, or non-Spanish.[40] McQueen served as godparent in a number of instances and was a witness to many marriages, a sharp departure from American practices in which the marriage of slaves had no legal basis. McQueen's conversion to Catholicism was no cynical ploy as is frequently suggested, and his concern for the spiritual life of the enslaved set him apart from his peers.

But his paternalism had sharp limits. The other side of the romantic image of "Don Juan" McQueen was visible in a man who pursued escaped slaves with English hunting dogs, used his position as judge of the northern district to maintain the violent and oppressive nature of a slave society, and participated in the African slave trade in a desperate attempt to right his shaky finances.[41] His embrace of the trade was no less vigorous than his commitment to capturing runaways. When the Georgia legislature banned the trade from Africa and the Caribbean from January 1, 1798, he obtained a license from the new East Florida governor, Enrique White, to bring a vessel carrying seventy-seven captives—thirty-three men, twenty-one women, and twenty-three children—into Florida and sell the human cargo primarily to U.S. citizens coming across the sound.[42] Indulging the planter, White authorized Georgia slave traders to come to Amelia Island and broker the sales to fellow Georgians duty-free, a considerable enticement. Alexander Watt, the leading dealer in Savannah, was present at this event, as was Edward Swarback, a Savannah slave trader of German descent, and, surprisingly, James Seagrove, the U.S. agent to the southern Indians, who had dabbled in the slave trade before settling at St. Marys.[43] McQueen was dissuaded by Robert Mackay, his son-in-law and slave trader in Savannah, from joining a subsequent plot to smuggle Africans into Georgia.[44]

In a province with a legal system rooted in Roman and canon law, enslaved people were able to stand up to their "masters" by having recourse to the courts or at least to the local justice of the peace, on a range of issues. It may have taken a strong person to follow through and pursue a legal challenge to the person who controlled his or her fate, but many did, whether it was protesting unfair treatment, asking for a price to be set for the purchase of one's freedom, or enforcing a contractual relationship. Isabel McCully, who later called herself Nancy, was an extraordinarily strong-willed, determined woman who fought for her legal rights against John McQueen, one of the most powerful men in East Florida, in a Hispanic legal system of which she had little knowledge. She took the lead role from her husband and conducted herself with considerable self-confidence. Seized by McQueen in South Carolina in the aftermath of the Revolution, McCully clung to a letter that testified to her and her husband's freedom for service to the British army in Charleston.[45] The military had issued certificates of freedom to enslaved people who escaped from patriot planters and came into British lines to participate in the defense of the crown. Unfazed by McQueen's dismissal of the letter, Nancy refused to let the question of her status as a free person be pushed aside and forgotten.

The Siete Partidas, a compilation of Roman and canon law whose origins lay in the Middle Ages, recognized the slave as a human being and gave enslaved women as well as men the right to sue.[46] One year after her traumatic removal to Florida, Nancy filed suit against her enslaver and laid out a compelling story. She related to a judge how she and her husband had fled to British lines when their master and his widow in South Carolina had died, and she and her husband had earned a certificate of freedom from the military for their service. As the war ended, the British turned them over to the Americans as they made haste to evacuate. At the governor's direction, the two were carried to the McQueen plantation in South Carolina to join the 120 individuals sheltered there. Apparently she had the opportunity to leave the compound but elected to stay "because she was pregnant, sick, and starving." When she was well enough to leave, McQueen ignored her plea and carried her and her growing family to St. Catherines Island in Georgia along with others who had not been claimed.[47]

When McQueen finally sold her and her family to a Spanish don, as much to rid himself of a nuisance as for financial gain, she filed a second suit and again produced the paper she claimed granted her family freedom. And once again McQueen discounted the value of this "freedom paper," saying that it only promised to maintain the family in the same job with the British army and nothing more. And therein lay the ambiguity of the Philipsburg Declaration issued by General Clinton in 1780, promising limited freedom without a formal promise of full freedom. In 1784 and 1785, Gen. Archibald MacArthur, once British commander in Charleston and then in St. Augustine, ultimately stood behind several hundred of those certificates when pressed by Céspedes at the time of the evacuation. McQueen described how MacArthur had turned over to the governor of South Carolina hundreds of Black people in 1782, of which the governor turned over 120 to him. "They all came to my plantation, were fed and supported and some of them for many months at my expense," he noted in the Spanish court, "Every week or two their respective owners came and claimed them away. At length they were all taken."[48] At best, this was a half-truth. He had confiscated those for whom there was no clear title.

The semiliterate Nancy stood toe-to-toe with a man who belonged to an international elite that had included George Washington and the Marquis de Lafayette, boldly disputing his attempt to discredit her arguments point by point. When he said that her Carolina owners had attempted to reclaim her, she replied that they were deceased before the end of the war. When he said her slip of paper was signed by a simple soldier, she countered that it had the full faith of the British army behind it. She challenged him to produce any proof of ownership, which he could not. She cited the support she had received from the Marquis de Chappedelaine, who had bought St. Catherines Island, and urged the court to contact her previous master's family and friends now living in Philadelphia. McQueen's strongest point hinged on the piece of paper that Nancy McCully had carefully guarded over the years and presented in court. "But on the so-called certificate being produced," he told the judge, "it proved to contain nothing more than a note of some hanger-on of the army, that they were under his protection to prevent their being imployed in other departments." Her sale to the intendant was allowed to stand. An illiterate field hand, she showed a remarkable ability to conduct her case in court but had little or no grasp of Spanish institutions and law and of the need for powerful allies like the Catholic Church.[49]

Paradoxes abounded. During the "Second Spanish Period" (1784–1821), many American planters in East Florida embraced the use of armed Black militiamen in defense of the province at precisely the moment that their peers in the United States were burrowing further into a racist ideology that saw no room for Black people other than as bonded labor. Don Juan McQueen stood at the center of this enigma. While fighting Nancy McCully in court, chasing freedom seekers in northern Florida, and importing Africans from West Africa, he embraced wholeheartedly the idea of a free Black militia that could defend the integrity of the Spanish colony. He accepted Black soldiers as capable fighters, reliable and tough human beings with a full range of emotions and talents. McQueen himself defied the odds when he led Black troops into a skirmish against Georgians involved in a clumsy rebellion in Florida in 1795.[50]

McQueen's brief moment leading the Black militia was a little-known episode during a mini-invasion of the colony by a group of adventurers out of Camden County. Historian James Cusick notes that, during the postrevolutionary period, the Spanish borderlands of East and West Florida and Spanish Louisiana comprised an area of constant turmoil. Between 1778 and 1818, fourteen different conspiracies, revolts, or invasions occurred, many carried out by small groups of white men who drew their support from across international boundaries. In areas of weak authority, these adventurers were motivated by a desire for self-aggrandizement, contempt for Spanish regulation, personal feuds with Spanish functionaries, clan loyalty, and the ability to whip up support among discontented settlers. Seven of those events shook East Florida.[51]

The background lay in a failed invasion in the spring of 1794 by American adventurers, backed by French money and naval vessels.[52] The revolutionary government in Paris had dispatched an emissary to Charleston, Edmund-Charles Genêt, to dispense funds and recruit troops in an effort to topple the government of both provinces in Florida and expand the revolutionary movement to the Americas.[53] For many Georgians, a full-fledged assault, whether under French sponsorship or American, offered an opportunity to resolve the question of runaway slaves to their satisfaction, spike Spanish influence over Native Americans, and create conditions for eventual annexation of the territory.[54] A hastily called council of war in St. Augustine put the regiment from Cuba on alert, called up all the free "Negroes" in the province, and summoned the Black militia inside and outside of St. Augustine.[55] The French threat collapsed when a change of government in Paris produced a radical change in foreign policy and support evaporated overnight.

The clumsy, brutal handling of the scare by Governor Quesada backfired badly when he ordered the houses of suspect collaborators south of the St. Marys to be burned as part of an ill-conceived scorched-earth policy.[56] Almost immediately, a handful of American settlers in Florida fled to the safety of Camden County and began fomenting a new plot to overthrow a government they held in utter contempt.[57] On June 29, 1795, a small group, joined by eighteen Georgians from Camden County, launched an assault on the tiny military post of Juana on the St. Johns, where they were greeted like heroes by the militia stationed there.[58] Matters took a more serious turn when the momentarily triumphant rebels captured Fort St. Nicholas, located on the southeastern side of the St. Johns and guarding the all-important road from Georgia to St. Augustine. In a vigorous counterattack, an assault force launched by the Spanish government mirrored the multicultural nature of Floridian society: a brig captained by an Englishman with a crew of English, Black sailors, and others, forty veteran soldiers of the Third Cuban Regiment, thirty-two free Blacks and mixed race men, including Prince Whitten and Felipe Edimboro, and thirteen from the white militia of St. Augustine. For the first time, an organized unit of freemen, composed primarily of freedom seekers from Georgia and South Carolina, participated in the defense of the colony, an evocation of the stirring memory of Captain Menendez and the freemen of Fort Mose in 1740.[59]

After the rebels fled Fort St. Nicholas in the face of the superior firepower and retreated to the safety of Camden County, Quesada appointed McQueen commander of the naval forces on the St. Johns River. When word came that Gen. Elijah Clarke, Revolutionary War hero and unrepentant expansionist, was assembling his frontiersmen on the St. Marys for a fresh chance at dismembering the province, McQueen was asked to lead the Black militia in the place of John Leslie, the successful deerskin merchant and perhaps his closest friend.[60] The war council in St. Augustine ordered the arming of all freemen still not under arms and the deployment of a hundred troops from the Third Cuban Regiment. McQueen was instructed to find arms for those freemen who did not have any weapons.

In the final episode of the mini-rebellion of 1795, McQueen personally led the Black militia against a fresh incursion by a small number of diehards. A handful of the followers of General Clarke crossed the St. Marys, raided the home of a farmer who supported the government, and made off with three enslaved people.[61] The enslaved were promptly sold to residents of Camden County. With 150 frontiersmen and adventurers at the tiny village of Temple on the upper part of the river, Clarke led an advance party of thirty men across the St. Marys to probe Florida's defenses. A member of the McGirt family was captured. Had the defenses at Fort Saint Nicholas been strengthened? Yes, Daniel McGirt replied matter-of-factly. Were the loyal militiamen being paid any better than they had been? Yes! Were there any free Negroes among the defenders? Yes! The interrogator must have breathed deeply when he observed, "I reckon they will fight Dam strong." It was clearly recognition of their emerging reputation as fighters and their preference for dying rather than return to slavery.[62] When the Spanish force reached the hammock where Clarke was thought to be, only campfires were found. Once more, the frontiersmen and adventurers melted away rather than risk battle with Black troops and white militiamen.

McQueen's military skills were used to best effect when Spanish Florida faced a new challenge from William Augustus Bowles, the loyalist who escaped from house arrest in the Philippines in 1799 and returned to the Apalachicola region to carry through his vision of creating an independent Indian state under British influence.[63] When the Seminoles launched a series of attacks against the plantations along the St. Johns in 1800, McQueen coordinated the actions of the governor and planters in mounting a defense. For the northern district, he hurried about looking for gunpowder for the militia in the area, set up a defensive position near the crucial crossing at Cowford, and asked the governor to "strengthen us with the Black gen'l [Georges Biassou] and his colored troops," a measure of his respect for this veteran of the Haitian Revolution. Known for his military skill as well as brutality, Biassou, an early leader of the slave insurrection in Saint-Domingue, had built an army of thousands and had been enjoying an awkward retirement in Spanish Florida with his followers. After Biassou died from natural causes, McQueen suggested to the governor that, for those planters nervous about their exposure to the Seminoles, "nothing would quiet their minds so effectively as your establishing a post of free negroes [if regular troops cannot be spared]."[64]

After Bowles was captured and imprisoned in Cuba, East Florida entered into a decade of spectacular growth. Motivated in part by the closing of the slave trade in the United States, American and foreign settlers poured into the colony to take advantage of the huge reserves of unclaimed land, rich natural resources, and resistance to Anglo-American hegemony.[65] In an unprecedented migration in 1803, sixty-three new settlers brought into the province 2,270 enslaved men and women and their children, a greater influx of Africans than Georgia ever experienced in any one year before the close of the slave trade.[66] That injection of labor, prompted by fears for the closing of the African slave trade, fueled a booming trade in lumber, cotton, and rice, resulting in a record level of prosperity. The town of Fernandina on Amelia Island appeared as if out of nowhere and emerged as the second largest in the colony, the port of choice for Georgians who wanted to escape the severe disruption in trade caused by Jefferson's Embargo Act.[67]

With the influx of this entrepreneurial set of planters, many of them British citizens and former loyalists, McQueen saw his position in the colony diminished. A restless person, he was a speculator by temperament. His operation could no longer sustain itself with a man at its head more interested in timbering than planting. Flailing about, he removed the overseer of his Amelia Island farm for attending "more to his own interests" than to McQueen's affairs and noted that none of his cotton had been ginned for the market.[68] The Georgian could never resolve the underlying problems that indebtedness created and turn his four plantations into efficient, profitable operations. Despite the extensive land and labor that he had amassed, he never developed his enterprises to the point that he could pay down his debts in Savannah or Charleston of £60,000 ($300,000) by the turn of the century.[69]

His creditors kept up a steady drumbeat of threats and lobbied the governor to help their cause. Notable among these was Shoolbred, who sold slaves to Florida planters and enjoyed a certain leverage over local officials. At one point, McQueen grandly promised to sell his entire estate of 260 people except for 22 bondsmen that he proposed to keep for one of his plantations to maintain himself in comfort.[70] That never happened. It was another stalling tactic. When he died in 1807, the average age of his enslaved people was unusually high. Some 22 percent were over fifty years old, a rare phenomenon on coastal plantations where black mortality was elevated.[71] Clearly he had chosen not to sell those coming from his father's plantation.

When McQueen faced bankruptcy once again near the end of this life, he chose a novel way of addressing the dilemma that spoke to those deeper values. Instead of commodifying his "property," he sold the land on which Los Molinos and San Juan stood for $28,000 and rented the workers at the two plantations to the new owner, John Henry McIntosh, once imprisoned in Cuba for his involvement in the intrigues of the mid-1790s and a member of a prominent coastal family. "I have hired him the Working Negroes here,"

McQueen told his son, John Jr., "for 120 dollars the head . . . I begin to take new Courage and on your plan I hope yet to leave my poor Negroes to my family."[72] McIntosh was to pay ten dollars per person per month. McQueen chose to hold on to "his people," partly out of loyalty, partly in the knowledge that his son would inherit the most valuable part of his estate.

When he died in 1807, his body servant, Harry, emerged as the pivotal person who supervised the burial at Los Molinos plantation. A solemn procession of twelve Black people carried his coffin to the gravesite. The faithful body servant was manumitted by the terms of the will, became a subsistence farmer through a government land grant, and joined the free Black militia, where he found himself in the company of Prince Whitten and Edimboro, part of that tight-knit circle of men who set the tone for the free Black community of East Florida.[73] His path to emancipation lay through devotion to his enslaver but ironically ended in the company of those free Blacks who had escaped their Georgia planters and went on to fight those same Georgians.

McQueen's death marked the loss of the one American leader in East Florida who unabashedly championed Hispanic values. His conversion to Catholicism and devotion to the liturgical life of the Catholic Church suggests as much. His active role in serving as godparent to so many Black people, his tolerance of mixed marriages, and his acceptance of the necessity for a free Black militia was at considerable variance with American practices as well.[74] Increasingly he found himself in the minority. The growing number of settlers from the United States, small farmers and frontiersmen for the most part, brought with them a sharply bifurcated view of Blacks and whites that had no room for the three-caste system of Spanish society and a law that viewed the enslaved as legal personalities.

Some years before his death, John McQueen had welcomed the arrival of Louis Joseph de François Richard, a French refugee from Saint-Domingue, and his family, together with twenty enslaved Blacks, and was impressed enough to employ his son, Francis Richard Jr., as the manager of the extensive lumbering operation at Shipyard with its massive sawmill. Mirroring the attitudes of the Hispanic elite, Francis had two and possibly three enslaved consorts during his lifetime and fathered thirteen children by them.[75] McQueen had stood as godparent to the fourth child, embracing the color line as a flexible instrument that was as much a matter of personal convenience as a perceived law of nature. It was an unthinkable public display for coastal Georgians, who kept their sexual exploitation of Black women well hidden from public view. Although there is no evidence that McQueen had a mixed-race family, his housekeeper in St. Augustine was Maria, mother of three children, one of whom, also Maria, was listed as a "mulatto."[76] European-African unions were common and accepted throughout the length and breadth of Florida. Many of the wealthiest ranchers, planters, government officials, and merchants had large mixed-race families and recognized their mixed-race children. Prominent among them was John Leslie, close friend of McQueen and a partner in dominant Panton, Leslie, & Company.[77]

"French Negroes" also posed an issue in the changing society of Hispanic Florida. Dominic, a favored captive on the Richard plantation, cut a striking figure for a style of dress more characteristic of Saint-Domingue than Florida, his casual use of French, and the unaccustomed autonomy that he enjoyed. Philip and William Dell, a father and son who lived close by, were appalled. Eager to exploit a new frontier, these eager Americans had arrived in 1802 with an indentured servant, eight slaves, and attitudes at considerable variance with those of Spanish society. They worked a small farm and had bid on property owned by Richard that apparently led to a disagreement that colored their subsequent dealings.[78]

One Sunday, Dominic took his wife and children across Pottsburg Creek for an afternoon away from the plantation visiting friends. As they were waiting for the canoe that served as the ferry to carry them back, William Dell arrived at the same time and demanded to see his pass. Dominic replied that he did not have a pass, had never used one, and that he had always been allowed this freedom by Mr. Richard. Incensed at what he deemed impudence, Dell grabbed a wooden stick and beat him fiercely, pushing the defenseless man into the creek in front of his horrified wife and children. The family was forced to watch as their husband and father was humiliated and emasculated. Lycurgus, the Black ferryman, maneuvered his canoe to grab Dominic and shove him and his family into the boat. The planter pursued in his own canoe, forcing the victim to jump into the water rather than running the risk of causing the boat to tip over and endangering the life of his family. Dell continued to hit him whenever he surfaced until Lycurgus, fearing that he would drown, rescued the injured man.[79]

In a hearing before a justice of the peace, Francis Richard demanded satisfaction for his injured worker and for the services that he lost during Dominic's recovery. Dell retorted that, if he were in the United States, he would not care a whit if the slave had drowned. "If he caught him, he would have learned him [how] to speak to a white man," said one David Sweeney in a deposition.[80] Although Capt. Andrew Atkinson testified that Dominic had been severely beaten and manhandled and that he had seen the injuries, the examining doctor, another American, insisted that he found no evidence of bruising. The justice of the peace, an American as well, seized the opportunity to dismiss the charges.[81] Two worldviews were colliding, and the cruder, harsher view based on a purely racial definition of slavery was gaining the upper hand along the banks of the St. Johns River. William Dell would participate eagerly in the Patriot War that took place in 1812 as a priceless opportunity to rid the country of "savage" Indians and "the Spanish yoke." He died violently in a skirmish during that ill-fated attempt.[82]

For most of the captives on the McQueen plantations, one last migration across an international boundary awaited. The father had left massive debts. Creditors were quick to assert their claims. John McQueen Jr. handled the estate with an insider's knowledge of Spanish procedure grounded in the time he had spent in St. Augustine and Pensacola as an agent of Panton, Leslie. The plan was risky: delay the legal process as best as he could, offer land in settlement of as many debts as possible, and find a way to smuggle as many of the 280 enslaved people back into Georgia as possible. The key to success if creditors were to be held at bay was shipping these human beings across the St. Marys as quickly as possible without attracting attention. On board a vessel off Amelia Island, Robert Mackay, McQueen's brother-in-law and cotton broker, wrote his wife, Eliza McQueen MacKay, "I am busy removing the Negroes into Georgia as fast as possible and hope soon to finish, as I am really tired of being here and wish much to be in Savannah."[83] The challenge was the constant petitioning by those whom he would prefer not to take back—the old, the feeble, the difficult, all the people he preferred to leave in East Florida as economic liabilities:

> The Negroes all seem glad to go to Georgia, but I have been dreadfully pestered by many of those that were sold [to Floridians], begging to be taken back, saying they were enticed away by wicked people. In one case, I have given way to keep peace with a large family. Old Minah who was sold with her daughter to Richard, says it was all a plan of his to get her, and her other children making such an uproar about separation I have taken her back. She is of little value and it makes not much odds but makes it pleasant to preserve peace and quiet. And I am sure it is very agreeable to me to make them comfortable and as happy as they can be.[84]

It was an impressive exercise in self-deception. McQueen's son-in-law found himself in a position of power to decide who was worth keeping and who could be left behind, mistaking the swelling chorus of pleas from those whom he had sold with expressions of undying loyalty and devotion. Those pleas were less about loyalty to a family than having second thoughts about having agreed to be sold to Francis Richard, an apparently benevolent man, and seeing their own relatives and friends depart for Georgia. While basking in the faux praise of Minah and the daughter, McQueen was shuttling the rest over to Cumberland Island, where the descendants of his father's old friend Nathanael Greene held them on their Dungeness estate. While this operation proceeded, the young man sat on a vessel off Amelia Island grandly dinning on fine turtle from the Bahamas, chicken from Savannah, and turnips, carrots, beets, and cabbage from Dungeness.[85]

A missing element in the story of the McQueens and their enslaved population is the presence of Native Americans, never far away from the fluid boundaries of Spanish East Florida, itself a tiny intrusion into the vastness of the Southeast. The attempt by Titus to escape from John McQueen's plantation by fleeing to the camp of Cohiti and the Seminole hunting party is a testimonial. He came close to succeeding. Five years later, in 1800, a small party of Seminoles suddenly appeared at the Richard property, next door to McQueen's Shipyard plantation. The Natives grabbed three field hands finishing their labor in the field as the sun was setting, threw them on the back of their horses, and rode into the dusk. Dominic was among them. One of the other men escaped that same night by waiting until everyone else was asleep. Dominic was ransomed two years later. The third never returned, perhaps because he chose to stay.[86] The McQueen enslaved were fully aware of the dangers and sometimes opportunities that raids by Indigenous people posed for them.[87] Native Americans, whether Creek or Seminole, posed a different kind of choice for the Black population along the coast of Georgia and East Florida, one that required weighing difficult options.

CHAPTER 7

War Captives of the
Creek People

In the two decades after the Revolution, Black people on the Georgia coast came to harbor a more nuanced feeling toward the Creeks on the Chatta-hoochee and Flint Rivers than they did for the Spanish. Slaves on the coast were well aware of the range of possibilities once they crossed the St. Marys River, whether becoming freemen and freewomen in St. Augustine, con-tract labor or maroons in a lightly populated region, or even as unfree peo-ple in a society where Spanish law offered easier if unevenly applied condi-tions. Coastal communities still contained members who had been in East Florida during the Revolution, many individuals knew or at least had heard of someone who had fled to Florida, and a few were able to communicate with acquaintances there.[1] Some and perhaps many were aware that a Black militia had faced up to American aggressors in the 1795 rebellion.

If Spanish Florida excited hopes and sometimes dreams, the Creek town-ships that stretched along the rivers offered a less certain and less predict-able future to enslaved people.[2] The nearest Indigenous settlements were the Lower Towns of the Creek Confederacy that extended along the Chatta-hoochee River valley, the banks of the Flint River, and even below the fork where the two streams flowed together to form the Apalachicola River. Ap-proximately twenty-five talwas or towns and their related villages dotted the landscape, embracing as many as 6,400 Indians in 1793 according to one re-port; dozens of white men, many of whom were traders with stores; a residue of slaves from other Native groups; and a growing number of Black people who were primarily enslaved servants of deerskin traders or slaves of chieftains.³ The Lower Towns had fewer inhabitants than the Upper Towns, with their 8,715 inhabitants in forty-eight talwas along the Coosa and Tallapoosa Rivers in today's Alabama. They spoke a wider variety of dialects than did those in the Upper Towns, and they were settled in more widely dispersed communities that weakened the role of the traditional town councils.⁴

The two hundred miles between the coast and the Lower Towns had few settlements as such but, in that contested space, there was constant movement through the grassland and longleaf-pine ecosystem. Hunting parties seeking deer and other game moved systematically through the pinelands during winter. Black slaves from Native settlements shepherded strings of horses and herds of cattle to the coast, often without supervision. At the western end of Camden County, Trader's Hill emerged as a major trading post on the St. Marys River for those Creeks located south of the "mother towns" of Coweta and Cussita, site of present-day Columbus, Georgia.⁵ The Muskogean-speaking towns of Coweta and Cussita continued to trade with Augusta as they had before the war, while those on the lower Chattahoochee, where Hitchiti, Yuchi, and even Yamassee were spoken, depended heavily on Trader's Hill for their supplies.

A small trading post of a Scots-Creek mestizo, Jack Kinnard, on Kinchafoonee Creek, and that of Timothy Barnard, an English-born trader with a Yuchi wife, on the Flint River, tied the Native country to Trader's Hill in multiple ways. Trains of packhorses moved continuously between the coast and the interior. The white traders carried goods and information (if sometimes rumor) from place to place, moving through Indigenous towns and occasionally attempting to ransom captives for their slaveholders. Black couriers as well as Black cowboys or herdsmen in Creek communities made occasional appearances in white communities on the coast and found themselves in a position to pick up vital information.⁶ For Native Americans, that space had been their hunting ground over the centuries, all the more important because the Okefenokee Swamp rendered so much of the territory unproductive.⁷

Black people on the coast were realists who well knew that the Creek people had functioned as slave catchers before the war, seized war captives time and again during and after the Revolution, regularly traded Black slaves among themselves or with the Spanish, and continued to hold most of their peers in some form of captivity.⁸ They were now having to rethink their attitudes. They were aware that their counterparts in the Lower Towns often enjoyed a better life in terms of the labor required, the autonomy granted, and the possibility of being adopted into a family or even becoming free.[9] They understood that agriculture for Indigenous people, whose main commodity was easy-to-grow corn rather than cotton or rice, was not about creating an ever-increasing surplus with an ever-increasing demand for forced labor.

What they did not understand was that many Creek chieftains were moving away from Native conceptions of slavery toward a racially based conception rooted in the commodification of Black people. The older idea of captives who stood outside a well-defined system of kinship (clans) was fading away. African men and women worked in the fields growing crops as did Creek women but lacked the rights, obligations, and status that came with clan membership.[10] As perpetual outsiders, they were vulnerable. However, in this traditional culture, slavery was not necessarily a permanent condition but could end with the death of the mother, the freeing of her children once they were grown, and their incorporation into a family and a clan. Intergenerational slavery was a new phenomenon.

A central figure in this evolution was Jack Kinnard, the son of a Hitchiti-speaking mother and a Scots trader who had established Trader's Hill many decades before. Although Kinnard had made most of his fortune as a rancher with over a thousand head of cattle, he possessed a sufficient number of enslaved people to have qualified as a major planter, traded goods and slaves with aplomb, and showed himself a skillful diplomat in the tangled web of Native, Spanish, and American intrigue.[11] Considered fully Creek in a matrilineal society, he embraced his Celtic heritage with pride, boasted of his white blood, and negotiated with the Spanish in Pensacola and the Americans as a social equal.[12] As a fluent speaker of the Hitchiti language, Kinnard occupied a special space in the Creek world of the southernmost towns since Hitchiti rather than Muskogean was the most common dialect.

His activities shed precious light on several related questions about the type of enslaved person Creek warriors seized in their raids on coastal plantations during the 1780s, the reaction of Black people to attacks that were psychologically terrifying, the need to distinguish between war captives and genuine freedom seekers, the degree of success of slaveholders in recovering their captives, and the extent to which the Lower Towns were eventually integrated into the slave trade along the Georgia coast. Kinnard's flamboyant life was pivotal, nowhere more so than in deciding the fate of the recently negotiated Treaty of New York.

In September 1790, Maj. Caleb Swan, an American military officer, sailed from New York to St. Marys to travel through Creek towns and report on

"the state of manners and arts in the Creek, or Muscogee Nation." His was a
mission to ensure the success of the treaty and to end the many years of raids
and counter-raids between Natives and Georgians known as the Oconee
War. Negotiated between Alexander McGillivray, a dominant leader in the
Upper Towns, son of the deerskin merchant Lachlan McGillivray and a
Creek woman of the powerful Wind Clan, and Henry Knox, secretary of
war, the treaty made the federal government rather than individual states responsible for Indian affairs.[13] By the terms of the treaty, the Creeks received
a federal guarantee of their sovereignty over the vast interior of the South
in return for ceding most of the land between the Oconee and Ogeechee
Rivers, parts of which were already overrun by American settlers and cattle
herders.

For most Creeks, the treaty was viewed as a disaster, a giving away of
the treasured lands between the Ogeechee and Oconee and the shifting of
Creek interests from the supportive Spanish to the hated Americans. Especially infuriating to all levels of Native society was the stipulation in Article 3 that stated, "The Creek Nation shall deliver as soon as practicable to
the commanding officer of the troops of the United States, stationed at the
Rock-Landing on the Oconee River, all citizens of the United States, white
inhabitants or negroes, who are now prisoners in any part of the said nation."[14] For one brief moment, "Negroes" were identified as citizens of the
United States. Article 3 was a red flag that touched as much on the Native
sense of honor—for those were captives won in fair contests in their eyes—
as any other provision. The Lower Towns had no intention of giving up their
war captives or freedom seekers who had escaped from coastal plantations.

Swan hoped to test Creeks' willingness to return both war captives and
fugitives. He and his party landed at the small town of St. Marys and made
their way along "Kinnard's path," a well-known trail to the Creek towns
along the lower parts of the Chattahoochee and Flint Rivers. After many
days, the major and his companions arrived at the house of Jack Kinnard on
a tributary of the Flint River near present-day Albany, a geographic point
that permitted its owner considerable influence in both the Creek and Seminole worlds. "Kinnard is a noted trader, farmer, and herdsman," Swan dryly
commented. "He has two wives, about forty valuable negroes, and some Indian slaves. He has from 1200 to 1500 head of cattle and horses, and commonly from 5000 to 6000 Spanish dollars at home, which are the produce
of cattle he sells." In a few words, the major captured the nature of the new
generation of leadership emerging in Creek country.[15]

"Hopothle Mico, or the Talassee King of the Creeks." Of mixed parentage, Hopothle Mico was one of the Creek chieftains who accompanied Alexander McGillivray to New York City to negotiate the Treaty of New York in 1790. He remained active in the Creek Nation through the Creek War of 1813. New York Public Library Digital Collections.

The forty-odd "Negroes" under Kinnard's rough hand placed him in a unique spot in the Lower Towns. He had gained many of these Africans as a noted warrior, unlike so many of the mestizos in the Upper Towns who did so by inheritance from their fathers or by purchase. "He accumulated his property," Major Swan commented, "entirely by plunder and freebooting, during the American war and the late Georgia quarrel."[16] "Plunder" and "freebooting" were relative terms, at least during the Revolution. Responding to Governor Patrick Tonyn's call on behalf of the hard-pressed British, the young Kinnard joined other Seminoles and Creeks in patrolling the border along the St. Marys River and conducting raids into Georgia that reached as far as the Altamaha and into Liberty County. The strikes were highly effective. The war parties became an essential part of the extensive pipeline that drained Black people out of Georgia and into Florida and the Creek Nation.[17] As an effective war leader, Kinnard received his due from British officials in the form of slaves presented as "king's gifts" in recognition of his service. [18] As a war chief during the late 1780s, he had participated in raids along the Georgia coast that brought dozens of enslaved people into the Lower Towns of the Creeks.

Those raids came in retaliation for the continuing push into Creek lands framed by the fraudulent treaties of Augusta, Galphinton, and Shoulderbone, negotiated in 1783, 1785, and 1786. Millions of acres passed from Native to white hands through the complicity of a handful of chieftains.[19] Over the three years from 1786 to 1789, Kinnard took part in what historian Joshua Haynes calls "border patrolling," the discrete use of violence along the frontier to push back the offending settlers.[20] The many towns of the Creek confederacy, both Upper and Lower, agreed to send out parties of warriors along the three-hundred-mile frontier to harass and intimidate settlers. They stole horses and cattle, burned crops and outbuildings, and occasionally kidnapped enslaved people along the coast. Young warriors rode out in small parties to carry out these limited aims, but in the excitement of the moment, and as a warrior culture came into play, matters could take a different turn, especially along the coast where sizeable plantations presented greater opportunity.

Of the over three hundred raids that occurred between 1786 and 1789, seventy-eight were in coastal counties. If the majority were aimed at Wilkes, Greene, and Washington Counties because of their proximity to the Oconee lands, raiders in the coastal counties of Liberty, Glynn, and Camden made a particular point of stealing slaves from plantations or helping them to escape.[21] Over a period of almost two years, Creeks made off with 110 slaves,

55 from Liberty County alone, and killed 10 others. By way of contrast, they put to death 72 whites, wounded 29, and took only 30 as prisoners. Clearly, Black individuals held more value than whites, but the raids themselves were more about the taking of livestock than people. During that short time, 984 head of cattle and 643 horses were stolen and hundreds of hogs destroyed in Camden, Glynn, and Liberty Counties.[22]

The strategy was a success, at least in the short term. Whites abandoned their plantations along the coast in panic and headed for safety on the Sea Islands. The foreman of a grand jury in Glynn County, the old Scotsman James Spalding, sent a chilling description to authorities. "[Inhabitants] have been drove from their plantations and homes," he said, "robbed and plundered of their property; several of our citizens murdered and others carried into captivity; their homes burnt and themselves and their families confined to the sea islands."[23] A planter in Liberty County warned that two large Indian parties were in the vicinity and that four or five plantations had already ceased operation: "People in general appear so discouraged that unless some [military] support is immediately offered then I am persuaded the County will break up."[24]

Attacks by Indians were a terrifying experience for Black people, whether they were in the field or around their huts or cabins or walking a distance from their settlements. The attacks happened unexpectedly and with dire consequences. If the raids were about taking cattle and horses, the witnesses were helpless spectators. If the raids included slaves, those taken represented a more or less random choice. An armed guard standing over a field may have deterred some attacks, but the guard often headed for the main house to alert others and put himself out of harm's way, abandoning the field hands. Small farmers resorted to taking their families and enslaved people to one of the two or three forts along the Altamaha or other rivers and sometimes wrote of how they had "forted" their own property.[25]

Working in the fields, Black Georgians were more at risk than the planter who was lodged in his house in relative safety or in distant Savannah. Most were horrified at the thought of being spirited away from family and friends and delivered into a strange world where the outcome could result in a new form of slavery. James Smith of Liberty County witnessed this panic when he set out to inspect his rice plantation on a warm day in May. "While approaching his people who were then at labor," it was stated in a deposition, "he discovered them running in all directions, and several approached . . . with [the] overseer Mr. Solomon Harper (now dead) and requested to know what they should do." About two hundred yards away, Smith and Harper helplessly watched as twelve Natives took thirteen slaves—seven men and six women.[26]

The fighting could be brutal. Of the people on John Burnett's plantation, two of four whites were wounded, an enslaved person killed, a second one scalped, and five others taken and carried off.[27] When they tried to capture bondsmen at work, the enslaved ran: "[They] run and hollowed out to the Guard, which run immediately to their relief." As a warrior seized one enslaved man and tried to tie his hands, "he made so much resistance that [the Creeks] found the guard would be upon them. [The warriors] shott a ball through him and cut his throat and Scalped him and run off."[28] Even the makeshift forts or stockades were vulnerable. Natives picked off people who wandered too far beyond the walls. At Fort Williams on the Altamaha River, Creeks seized an unsuspecting white man named McAphee, a Black man named Byron, and two Black women, one of whom was heading to a nearby fort to pick up a sack of potatoes to feed the sheltering families.[29]

Most Black people resisted capture, and some fought back. In 1789, three small Creek war parties crossed the frontier in Liberty County, coalesced into a larger fighting force, and laid siege to Woodmanston, the plantation of Dr. John Eatton LeConte, a prominent person who had married into the tight-knit families of Midway whose lives revolved around their Congregational church. LeConte had concentrated his Black families behind a stockade next to the main house. When the first hands left to go into the fields the next morning, the Creeks tried to seize them, but the men and women ran back into the makeshift fort. Six Black men came out with guns and positioned themselves to fight, while several others in the "fort" began firing, together with LeConte. After the shooting began, the warriors retreated to a fence where they rallied and commenced a heavy fire of their own for some time. The plantation house and slave quarters were successfully defended, but three of the six men outside the stockade were taken, and two others were seized elsewhere in the quarters, for a total of five Black people—Jimmy, about forty years old; his wife, Phiana, about forty-five; Tomboy, twenty-five; Samson, eighteen; and Peggy, fourteen.[30]

During the periods of danger, Black Americans became the effective managers of most threatened plantations. White families typically retired to Savannah or Darien or one of the Sea Islands until the danger passed. When an attack was imminent, even the overseers departed. Militia commander John Berrien reported that the "latest Indian alarm" had thrown a lightly populated corner of Chatham County into a panic: "[Thus] we are obliged to abandon our fields to the management of our Negroes."[31] In exposed areas where whites were relatively few, enslaved people found that they exercised considerable authority.

Not all Blacks were fearful. Some saw the arrival of warriors as an opportunity to break out of their oppressive condition and join the Natives in a new life free of the arbitrary violence to which they were subjected. When a party of Creeks attacked the plantation of Andrew Walthour in Liberty County, they killed three enslaved people—January, "a prime fellow"; Miley, "a valuable wench"; and Miley's four-year-old child. They carried away another five people, Cooper, Rachel and her two children, and Sary, a girl of five. But in his claim for compensation, Walthour mentions that three "Negroes" had run away seven weeks before—Pearce, Isaac, and Orange—and were present on the night of the attack. Presumably, they led the Natives to the settlement and guided their efforts. Rachel and Cooper may have been husband and wife and fled as a family with their friends and companions.[32] On a second Liberty County plantation, Creeks seized five women and a boy and three days later came back to take seven "Negroe Fellows," perhaps with encouragement from the women.[33]

The evidence is circumstantial but suggestive. We are dependent on letters asking for compensation from the state government by planters and other slaveholders who had every interest in establishing that their "property" had been seized by marauding Indians. It is probable that a number of war captives were in fact freedom seekers, and it is highly likely that many freedom seekers never found their way into the written records.

The people carried into Creek country represented a broad cross-section of the bondsmen in coastal Georgia, a mixture of African-born and "country-born" or creole, field hands, and semiskilled and skilled people. One planter reported that of the four people he lost on two separate occasions, the first pair were creole, the second from "the Calabar country" and Angola.[34] Of the five taken from Woodmanston, LeConte noted that three were African men and two were creole.[35] At the Girardeau plantation, four of the eight people carried off were African, two from Angola, one from Gambia, and the last from "Kessy Country."[36]

The majority of those seized along the coast were field hands, but Andrew Maybank reported having lost several good boatmen, prime house "wenches" and cooks, washers, ironers, and spinners. Enslaved women on his enterprise were spinning cotton, an activity usually reserved for white women.[37] From the plantation of John Girardeau, a raiding party took hold of Pompey, a waterman and tradesman; Cate, Pompey's wife, noted as a good cook; Agrippa, a "good house servant"; and Rose, "a valuable house wench," and her two sons, adolescents.[38] Later another party captured "London, a boatman, trader, sawyer, and a valuable manager on the plantation" as well as Sam, a boatman and sawyer. The Creeks seemed to have grabbed Black captives as opportunity presented and rarely hesitated to take children.[39]

Age-wise there was no pattern. At the Maybank plantation, the thirteen kidnapped people were in their teens, twenties, thirties, and forties. Two were listed as "fifty," a euphemism for men and women well past their prime. For the most part, the Creeks seized Black people on the fly, snatching whomever was found nearby. Most Natives placed their captives on horseback and rode into woods in fear that a posse of white men might follow.

The year 1790 brought an end, albeit temporarily, to the travails along the borders of Georgia and the leverage that Spain had enjoyed with the Creeks. In a stunning reversal of positions, the forty-year old Alexander McGillivray, a mestizo who was the closest approximation of a leader in a loosely constructed alliance of Creek towns, turned to George Washington to negotiate a treaty that achieved the reconfiguring of the geopolitical framework of the entire Southeast to the manifest disadvantage of the Creeks and Spanish.[40]

There was a deeper reason for his reversal of positions than the miscalculation of the ability of the federal government to halt settler colonialism. The historian Claudio Saunt details how McGillivray, son of a Scottish deerskin merchant and Creek mother, emerged after the Revolution as the embodiment of a new and controversial economic order in the Creek nation all while playing the leading role in the fight against American expansion. Familiar with the intricacies of plantation management and Atlantic commerce, he modeled himself as best he could after the planters he had known in Augusta and Savannah working for his father before the Revolution. Always rich in land, livestock, and slaves, he represented the emergence of an elite in Creek society determined to embrace the values of a slave-holding society while defending Creek autonomy and setting sharp limits on the degree of cultural assimilation. He had two plantations, one at Little River near Mobile and a larger one at a site called Little Tallassee, up the Coosa River near its junction with the Tallapoosa, with cabins for sixty enslaved people. Across the river, he had a cowpen with large stocks of horses, hogs, and horned cattle and retained two or three white men to superintend the livestock while employing a white overseer to supervise his plantation on the Little River.[41] John Kinnard was a lesser version of McGillivray but with one critical difference. He

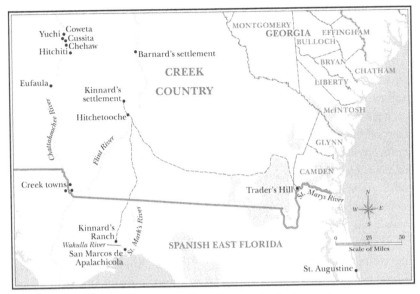

Trading paths from the settlement of John Kinnard,
Scots-Creek, to the coast, circa 1790s

remained in touch with local headmen and was more skilled in negotiating his way through the maze of loyalties and sentiments.

The newly named commissioner for southeastern Indians, James Seagrove, a resident of St. Marys and the agent responsible for federal relations with Spanish Florida, needed allies to help secure acceptance of the treaty's unpopular provisions. It was only natural that he turned to Kinnard, one of the most pro-American chiefs among the Lower Towns, particularly with the more militant Hitchiti and Chehaw towns to the south. From Seagrove's perspective, it was a devil's choice. Kinnard was a known figure who was guilty of the very practice that the commissioner was to end.

Major Swan had found Kinnard to be temperamental, egotistical, and prone to outrageous behavior. "He is a despot," the officer remarked, "shoots his negroes when he pleases, and has cut off the ears of one of his favorite wives, with his own hands, in a drunken fit of suspicion."[42] The cutting off of the ears of an unfaithful spouse was an older form of Muskogean punishment. Virtually illiterate, the entrepreneur employed an ever-changing repertoire of "secretaries" who took down his dictations. In the handwritings of his surviving letters, one sees the varying levels of education of his many amanuenses, but one never misses his energy and imprint.[43] Despite his seemingly arbitrary ways, he never wavered in struggling to preserve the political autonomy of the Creek people while being quick to find new ways to survive economically in the face of a declining deerskin trade.

In his new role as an arbiter of a treaty despised by Creeks, Kinnard began modestly by collecting stolen horses and sent twelve of the valuable animals to Trader's Hill to be delivered to their owners "on proof being made."[44] For a fee, he brokered the return of enslaved people, but it was contingent on his good humor. When a dispute broke out with his factor in St. Marys, the mestizo wrote to a correspondent, "My friends need not to write to me anymore to get their Negroes and horses that is strayed or stolen in this country. . . . As you know I have always done everything in my power for white people and now my things is taken from me."[45] Nevertheless, he had cast his lot with the Americans. An itinerant trader reported that during the difficult months following an attack on an American trading post, Kinnard still had "the United States standard flying in his yard," and Kinnard himself reported, "I have talked until I was exhausted [in an effort to maintain peace]." Timothy Barnard, a white trader living on the Flint River, noted that, although headmen from most Lower Towns were opposed to the Treaty of New York, "John Kinnard and his people have left no stone unturned [in its support]."[46]

The patch of borderland that stood at the juncture of Creek, Seminole, Georgian, and Spanish lands exploded in violence in March 1793, less than two years after the signing of the Treaty of New York. Raiding parties that included Black warriors set out from several Chehaw villages on the Flint and Chattahoochee Rivers to strike Trader's Hill, gateway to coveted goods on the St. Marys River and a humiliating symbol of Creek dependence on the Anglo world. On the upper reaches of the river where Kinnard's trail began, the store effectively tied together the economic and physical geography of the region while providing important access to the Atlantic economy for the Natives of the Southeast. On March 11, a party of Chehaws entered the store to trade deerskin for dry goods. After a seemingly amiable transaction, they roughly shoved the storekeeper, Captain Fleming, against the counter and scalped him as well as another white man who had the misfortune of being present. The warriors spent several hours plundering the store of some two thousand pounds sterling of goods, an unprecedented sum.[47]

In the final moments of that desperate scene, a Black fugitive stepped out of the nearby woods, where he had been patiently waiting for a chance to make himself known. About thirty years old and speaking "plain English," he was described as "country-born" or creole, thick-set, short, and with the initial "N" on one cheek and a "W" on the other. In an unusually cruel form of torture, his original enslaver had branded him with a red-hot iron that left scars an inch long. The victim was no field hand but a sawyer, cooper, and tanner by trade, a skilled craftsman, victim of a succession of inhumane planters. He had fled the farm of Nathan Atkinson, a man known for his violence and willingness to push the boundaries of the law. The Chehaw warriors carried him back to their town.[48]

The two leaders of the raiding party, John Galphin and the Black Factor, were well known on the frontier. The hot-headed, mixed-race Galphin, whose parents were George Galphin, the largest deerskin merchant in pre-revolutionary Georgia, and Metawney, the daughter of "the Great Warrior of Coweta," was angered by a succession of slights by white authorities. Echoing pan-Native arguments that were gaining currency among southern Indians, he renounced his earlier loyalty to the United States and became one of the chief advocates of war on the frontier to unite Native Americans east of the Mississippi.[49]

"The Black Factor," whose Creek name was Philatouche, was even more of an enigma than Galphin. Historian J. Leitch Wright identifies fleeting references to him that imply he was indeed a Zambo but speculates he may have been fully Black, a supposition that at least one contemporary believed to be true.[50] He had fought with the British at the final military engagements around Savannah during the Revolution and was now the mico of a settlement called Chiaja, located among the network of Hitchiti towns at the confluence of the Chattahoochee and Flint Rivers.[51] John Forrester, a white trader, reported to the governor of East Florida, "A black half-breed by the name of Black Factor is, it seems, the chief of this town, as big a pirate as Galphin."[52] According to an interpreter for the Spanish governor of Pensacola, Julian Carballo, the small settlement consisted of around 110 "free and maroon negroes," most from Georgia although a few from Pensacola, in essence a collection of former war captives and fugitives.[53] The story of Chiaja remains wrapped in mystery, but that there was an outpost of maroons and war captives near Kinnard's settlement seems likely.

Additional groups struck along the frontier, one from a Chehaw town that attacked a family moving to East Florida in a single wagon, killing four of its seven occupants, and another hitting farms and plantations on the Spanish side of the St. Marys River.[54] That second party included Black warriors as well as Indians, a testimony to the acceptance of Blacks as equals within the structure of a raid.[55] Kinnard confirmed for the governor in St. Augustine that it was led by "the Little Black Factor," a Zambo (person of mixed African and Indigenous ancestry) whose Indian name was Ninnywageechee.[56] In explaining that the Black Factor himself was not on this raid, a trader described Ninnywageechee as "the half breed negro who lives low down on Flint River."[57] The Indians swooped in on a planter plowing his field, ransacked his house, and carried off an enslaved family: Isaac, his wife Sarah, and their four children.[58] Other farms were hit and more than one hundred cattle taken. Over the next two months, other raids carried off two dozen enslaved people from the Georgia Lowcountry. The lost workers of James Smith were said to have been "as prime a parcel as he ever saw, young, healthy, and orderly," a formulaic phrasing meant to obtain the highest possible compensation from the state government if their return could not be secured.[59]

In the traumatic series of incidents in 1793, Black warriors were visible in at least one other major event. In October 1793, 130 mounted Americans crossed the Oconee River and proceeded toward a Chehaw town on the Flint River to recapture lost slaves and livestock. "They expected a large body of negroes and property," Seagrove told the secretary of war. Instead, as they were fording the river opposite the town, Creeks counterattacked, killed two of the militia, and wounded two others. The militia lost their taste for a fight, abandoned the dead, and rode back to the safety of their stockade. Seagrove made a point of informing Henry Knox, secretary of defense, that the enemy consisted of sixteen Creeks and four "negroes."[60] Militia general James Jackson voiced the opinion of many when he speculated that there might be a "Negro rising" on the coast but added that the proof had not yet come in.[61] Anger was at such a fever pitch along the St. Marys that Natives who ventured too far down the river risked their lives. When four Creeks came with talk of peace, residents along the St. Marys River killed two and badly wounded the others, who barely managed to turn around their horses and make it to safety.[62]

The attack on Trader's Hill exposed a Creek land that was in shambles. The killings represented years of disruption inflamed by the failed treaty. Despite the discouraging reality, Kinnard and Seagrove worked tirelessly to restore a semblance of peace and, at great personal risk, prevent the war party from gaining the upper hand.[63] Over the next two years, a token number of Black people were returned and delivered at designated strong points on the frontier, but even here the process was fraught with difficulty. At his trading post on the Flint River, Timothy Barnard warned James Jackson that "a large Body of Indians were prepared to set out for the Frontiers to take back the Negroes they had given up; that they would first hunt about the Saw Mills, from thence on the head of the Canoochie & from thence go for the rice Plantations." A level-headed Englishman, Barnard surmised that this was not the Creek Nation generally but "the Cheehaws & others of the old Gang & which Kinnard wished punished some Years since."[64] Not surprisingly, the Chehaws had been a powerful pillar of support for the British during the Revolution.[65]

In June 1796, a delegation of 147 headmen, warriors, and even women gathered at Colerain, along the St. Marys River not far from Trader's Hill, to meet with commissioners for the United States and the State of Georgia. Unavoidable pressures had forced the Creeks to the negotiating table: the backing off of diplomatic and military support by Spain, the irreversible decline of the deerskin trade, and the continuing trespassing of Americans on Native lands. John Kinnard played a significant role in persuading his peers in the Lower Towns to attend the gathering with representatives from the United States. Present in the crowded encampment were all-too-eager planters who came in hopes of recovering their lost "possessions."[66]

The resulting Treaty of Colerain did no more than reaffirm the provisions of the Treaty of New York six years before, but the landscape had changed so dramatically that this drew grudging approval from the assembled Creeks. Tucked away in the text was Article 7, a verbatim repetition of one of the most hated articles in the Treaty of New York. All white citizens, Negroes, and property taken before 1790 were to be restored, as were those taken after that date.

In early 1798, Benjamin Hawkins, U.S. senator from North Carolina, replaced James Seagrove as federal agent to the southeastern Indians. He promptly submitted his first report to the governor of Georgia from the newly established Creek Agency on the Ocmulgee River. Fluent in the Muskogean language, the former delegate to the Continental Congress dared take their side even more forcibly than had his predecessor.

The report echoed what Kinnard had been saying to James Seagrove. The former commissioner had already called on the Creeks to return war captives, Hawkins noted, "and they delivered all the horses and negroes they could get except such as were deemed legally their property, according to the Rules of War, and which they had rec'd from the British for their services, or such negros as had fled to them and which they were not bound to restore." With that, he touched the key points: the British "gifts" to the Indians as part of cultivating their support during the Revolution, the belief of many warriors that the Black people seized during the border wars of the 1780s were theirs by dint of the "Rules of War"; and their repugnance at returning those brave souls who had made their way to Creek territory to secure their freedom. In all three instances, the return represented a violation of deep-seated cultural norms based on their warrior ethic.[67]

A new game emerged, with Georgians loudly demanding the satisfaction of the clause on war captives and the Creeks sidestepping and insisting that they had only agreed to return those taken after the signing of the treaty, not before, an interpretive twist that infuriated Americans.[68] Kinnard personified the conundrum. As an influential chief, he was acting as a broker for slaveholders in the search for former slaves located somewhere in the scattered network of the Lower Towns and had just enough success that he earned their respect while benefiting from the fee paid. Yet ultimately he did little to shake the tree. He was a war profiteer who had no intention of surrendering his own captives gained over the years, some of whom he claimed as "gifts" from the British and some of whom came directly to him as a leading warrior on the Georgia frontier during the Revolution. Major Swan thought Kinnard had done equally well in the border wars of the late 1780s when he again led raiding parties against settlers moving into Camden and Glynn Counties.[69] When it came to his own holdings, the mestizo defended the Creek position that these Black men and women had been taken under the "Rules of War" and were not subject to be returned despite the clear meaning of Article 3 of the Treaty of New York.

In the push to gain war captives, Georgia planters found themselves plunged into a labyrinthine world where cultural dissonance confounded the traditional byways of negotiation between whites and Native Americans. "The negroes cause great dispute among us in our land with respect to returning them," a chieftain explained, "as some are sold or bartered from one to another and property paid for them consumed by those who got it."[70] With no legal titles, each change of master dimmed the claim of the Georgia planter. An Indian trader hired to tease out the fate of five people taken from the plantation of John Whitehead discovered that one person, a woman, had been sold to Panton, Leslie & Company at its store on the Apalachicola River and was now out of reach in Spanish territory. He reported that Hector and an unnamed woman belonged to Jumalathluychee or "Big Eater," who refused to part with them.

The biggest problem Whitehead encountered was Kinnard himself. The Scots-Creek had purchased two of the women, Cloe and Dido, from Jumalathluychee, who in turn had purchased them from a white trader.[71] The women proved their value by giving birth to six children. Kinnard refused to part with either the mothers or the children, pointing out that they had been sold and resold in the Creek Nation and hence could not be considered as "owned" by the white planter.[72] His statement reflected the reality that most of the captives, like the stolen horses, had been sold by their captors shortly after their return from the Georgia Lowcountry. Such sales helped offset the decline of the deerskin trade. In effect, they became trade goods for Creeks who had no interest or ability in handling a slave. It was a quick way to generate the means of purchasing household goods, tools, and rum. The market was brisk. Buyers were typically chiefs or traders. Nor was it unusual for Indian enslavers to resell slaves casually and quickly when they needed to pay debts or obtain cash. For all Creeks, the internal exchange of money or livestock for enslaved people obliterated any claim of ownership by a Georgian. Offspring belonged to the current master.

Andrew Maybank of Liberty County hired a trader, "a prudent and discrete person," to go into the Creek Nation and offer a generous reward for several slaves who had escaped. The trader found the men and women in the possession of Kinnard, but the Hitchiti chief refused to hand them over. It was a potentially awkward situation since he functioned as the point person for the federal government. "If [Kinnard] is not made to give up the property in question," Col. Daniel Steward sternly warned Governor John Milledge, "will it not ultimately invite all artful slaves to leave their owners, just as a whim capricious or fancy may take them[?] I am of opinion that a precedent of this nature . . . will be attended with serious consequences."[73] The irony was especially poignant. The governor to whom he wrote was married to John Galphin's half-sister, Martha Galphin Milledge, daughter of George Galphin's white wife. The leader of the war party that sacked Trader's Hill and rode into Spanish Florida had a half-sister at the very center of the state capital.[74]

The process of negotiating for the return of formerly enslaved people became a complex maze that frustrated the most determined planters. Creeks from one town returned to Andrew Walthour two of the three Africans that they held but kept back the third person for unknown reasons.[75] When James Smith of Liberty County lost thirteen enslaved people from his rice plantation during the course of two attacks in 1791, he secured the return of Sarah within a matter of weeks by working through an Indian trader and paying $63 for her. He had to wait another four years until James Seagrove arranged for "talks" with a party of Creeks at Beard's Bluff on the Altamaha but was disappointed when only three more people were recovered. After the Treaty of Colerain, the ever hopeful Smith secured a passport for traveling in Native lands, hired an interpreter, and visited several towns. The expedition was a failure. In one last effort in 1807, he secured the return of four more people, including Mary, sixteen years after the event. In the negotiations, he demanded the return of all four of her children, not just one. Kinnard refused on the grounds that they had been born in his town and were hence his property. American civil law rooted in the belief that the offspring of the mother belonged to her master did not translate into an Indigenous setting. Three of the children—Rachel, Eley, and Fanny—were not returned.[76]

White traders who lived in Native towns proved a serious obstacle to recovering enslaved people. They typically purchased captives from warriors anxious to monetize their gain, or, more simply, they acted as more-or-less honest brokers between Creeks. When John Girardeau attempted to recover the people taken from his plantation, he discovered that a trader named Lucas had carried Prince, Rose, and her children to the "Notichies" to exchange for livestock and returned with several horses in tow.[77] A trader hired by Girardeau discovered that a seven-year-old boy, Billy, had been sold to a mestizo family, the Marshalls, who later traded him to a white man named Thomas Martial, with a small store in a distant Native town, and was eventually carried to Cuba in exchange for goods.[78] The dry accounting language involved in the loss of property covered up the trauma and horror that a young boy experienced as he was handed off to unknown parties, white and Black, speaking multiple languages, to become a child slave in Havana. Many traders kept their own enslaved people, providing shelter and food in return for work in the store and cultivating a patch of ground, a typically loose arrangement.[79]

Mestizos like Jack Kinnard held by far the greatest number of enslaved people and were pushing the Creek Nation toward an economic model loosely based on American practices. The forty or so slaves that belonged to the Scots-Creek were primarily engaged in raising livestock and enjoyed a degree of freedom in tending cattle and managing a stock of valuable horses, altogether some twelve hundred to fifteen hundred animals, according to Swan. On making his way from the St. Marys River toward Creek country, the major noted, "Supplied ourselves with fifteen fresh horses, taken from J. Kinnard's negroes, whom we met in the woods, bound to St. Mary's with a drove for sale." [80] Those "negroes" were apparently unsupervised and enjoyed considerable freedom in setting the pace of travel. But they were met in town by an Indian trader turned merchant, David Garvin, who held them to strict account.

Many Creeks did raise cattle and hogs, not for their own consumption but for sale. Garvin was a regular buyer of Kinnard's livestock and came to act as a factor for his commercial involvement along the Atlantic coast.

Livestock was driven to markets in St. Marys, Savannah, St. Augustine, and Pensacola and then sold on the hoof. Natives in the Lower Towns adjusted to this new way of life by separating from their talwas or towns and dispersing their settlements in outlying villages of twenty to fifty families over the countryside. On Kinchafoonee Creek, Kinnard's estate was spread out rather than concentrated in the traditional Creek square. The town of Eufala spread down the Chattahoochee to its confluence with the Flint River. Archaeological evidence demonstrates that towns along the Flint were a response to the demands of free-range ranching, which benefited from the large limestone plain underneath the lower Flint and the large stretches of river cane and reed that made the area valuable for herding.[81]

Investment in lands in Spanish Florida was a critical part of the strategy of the Kinnard family. Together with his brother William, Jack had continued to spread his holdings into Florida and created a sizable farm at the head of the Wakulla River that emptied into the Apalachicola. Enslaved people worked in relatively unsupervised conditions, producing corn for a nearby Spanish fort as well as for the Seminoles in Mikasuki. They enjoyed considerable free time since corn did not require the intensive labor of rice or cotton. It was a cat-and-mouse game between enslaver and enslaved. Always anxious to increase their wealth, the Kinnards rented out Africans for work at the fort, an assignment that placed them in difficult work conditions.[82] The several farms in Creek territory and Spanish Florida helped feed their large number of dependents but generated only a modest surplus from a vast enterprise.

The question remains of estimating how many enslaved people made a break for freedom on their own and found a measure of breathing space in Indigenous society. The chance to find greater autonomy and independence as well as a better life convinced many to make the attempt to escape the indignities and mortality of planation culture on the Georgia coast even if they knew the conditions in Native society were dubious. The determination of those who chose to do so was astounding.[83]

A skilled craftsman who escaped from Nathan Atkinson made his way to Trader's Hill as the surest way to link up with the Creeks. To his astonishment, he found himself in the company of a war party that pillaged the store and set off fears of a coming war. A free man for a few precious days or weeks, he told a member of a party of white people who came to settle a dispute with that town about how he fled the "ill-usage" of Atkinson, been carried to a Chehaw town by the warriors, and sold to a warrior who in turn sold him to Hoopawnee, a headman of some influence. When Atkinson learned of his location, he swore the man was worth $500 and commissioned traders to offer $100 for him, an above-average rate. When the Black crafts-man learned of the price put on his head, a trader recalled, "he confessed that he belonged to the said Atkinson but he would not go back if he could help it."[84] His spirit of resistance refused to dim even in the face of a web of Na-tive and white ownership.[85]

When Atkinson learned that Hoopawnee had come to St. Marys on business, he took advantage of this seeming good fortune and arranged for a meeting in the presence of a trusted interpreter. The headman pointed out that he had purchased this craftsman from another Creek and would only consider selling him if he received the money that he had originally paid, six hundred chalks, or the equivalent of many dozens of deerskins measured out by the number of chalk marks on the trader's account book, a significant sum by the prevailing standards. Atkinson agreed to the terms, but Hoopaw-nee, using a technique favored by Natives placed in an untenable situation, agreed to the deal and then vanished, never to reappear. In the early years of the nineteenth century, Atkinson made one last attempt, then filed a depre-dation claim for five hundred dollars. The unnamed creole preferred life as a slave in an Indigenous society than returning to the rigors of plantation slav-ery. It was an easy choice.

Few accounts of flights to the Creeks exist, primarily because farmers and planters could not claim compensation for their losses and had little reason to document the outward flow of people. The stories that are extant point to the continuing hemorrhaging of the labor force on Georgia Lowcountry plantations. In the first years of the nineteenth century, four individuals es-caped by their own means from the Maybank plantation in Liberty County, two men and two women, presumably husbands and wives. Andrew May-bank had lost over a dozen people to a raiding party in the early 1790s and recovered only a small number despite repeated offers. It may well be that the four who fled were motivated by news coming from their long-lost com-patriots among the Creeks of a life that was better than on a rice plantation. The governor of Georgia confirmed as much when he wrote the "Chehaw King": "[Slaves who fled] will very probably be concealed by some negro fel-lows who are in the nation and run away some years ago."[86]

In 1799, another family of four slipped away from a white planter "low down" on the Altamaha River. They crossed the river and, to their misfor-tune, encountered a party of Creeks "who acted very honestly and carried them to Fort James," apparently preferring a cash reward to the task of car-rying them back to their town and attempting to commodify them there.

Fort James was a stockade recently erected on the banks of the Oconee River as a result of the Treaty of Colerain. As described by Gen. James Jackson, the father in the family was an African, thirty years old, with a yellow complexion and country marks, or decorative scars made on his face, and scars from whipping on his thighs ("as he is a great villain," Jackson wrote). Was the father willing to abandon his family, or did he have some other plan? It was clear that life among Indigenous people was preferable to the alternative of repeated whippings and other forms of torture. And it was clear that the man could count on protection from Black refugees among the Creeks. In his letter to the "Chehaw King," Jackson's point was clear: "harboring runaway blacks breeds ill-blood and makes the chain [of friendship] rusty."[87]

Large groups could organize themselves in attempting long-distance flight. From South Carolina, "a horrid band of Negroes" fled the Lowcountry heading west toward Creek territory when they were sighted not far from Saunders Swamp in Liberty County. Members of the state militia were alerted and rushed to intercept them. An African American was killed; two more were wounded, but another five escaped. The soldiers recovered their arms, "thirteen weight of powder," and their supplies for the journey. This was no ordinary flight but a carefully planned journey that showed the ability of Africans and African Americans to secure weapons and think through what it would take to cross a large territory that was hostile.[88] Coming shortly after the incident at Trader's Hill, the event deepened the sense of unease in the Georgia Lowcountry.

By the turn of the century, Jack Kinnard symbolized the way that mestizo planters were embracing slavery in the American style, with bondage as a transgenerational phenomenon. Unlike earlier times, the descendants of captured slaves were now bound to a lifetime of servitude, but Black slaves, like Indian captives, still found themselves living and working under a range of conditions. Captivity under the Creeks was evolving away from a spectrum of loose practices to more rigid and fixed forms that reflected a growing acceptance of white attitudes and practices toward African Americans. Racial attitudes were beginning to percolate into the fabric of the Indigenous world. Where once the offspring of slaves had been considered free, now they remained enslaved. The children and grandchildren of Black people taken during from the Revolutionary era remained in captivity.[89] An Indian might make a captive a part of his or her family or as a servant or extra labor but still be willing to sell him or her if needed. A chief needed multiple laborers to help him maintain political power and high status in the way that Kinnard achieved a singular position in his large neighborhood.

By 1800, the Lower Towns were active participants in the slave trade along the Georgia coast. The demand for Black herdsmen and laborers, combined with the rapidly declining ability to seize slaves by surprise raids, drove the process.[90] The entrepreneurial Kinnard regularly imported slaves who could not be sold in Savannah because of their foreign origin. In the spring of 1798, he traveled to Savannah to purchase five "French Negroes" who had been shipwrecked en route from Grenada to Cuba and captured by a privateer that took them to Savannah to be auctioned. Three were masons, one a cooper, and one a carpenter. Their protestations that they were freemen earned them little credit with their new "master," who used them to pay off debt to the Panton store at San Marcos on the Apalachicola River.[91] Again and again, Kinnard served as a distribution point for "French Negroes" whose presence aroused deep fears that they would prove carriers of the ideologies motivating revolutionaries in Saint-Domingue, soon to be Haiti. When thirty-six Africans were picked up on a sinking vessel at sea and brought to Savannah in 1801, the city council had them lodged in the jail on the assumption that they were brigands. The aldermen passed an ordinance permitting their sale to David Garvin, a trader who had lived in the Creek Nation but now used his contacts to sell cattle and horses coming out of the Lower Towns. He disposed of six of them with Kinnard.[92]

Occasionally, African Americans refused to go quietly into Creek country. Garvin sent up seven men from St. Marys to Kinchafoonee Creek, escorted by two whites, to be sold by Kinnard. The market was active. "When the negroes came, the red people wanted to buy," Kinnard told Garvin in explaining the curious circumstances of why the sale did not go through. The men had little relish for the prospect of being consigned to headmen and warriors in distant towns and villages. When buyers looked them over, the men gave out the same line of talk, which the Indians readily grasped. Kinnard explained, "The negroes said they did not know how to work but give them guns and they would go to war. They knowed how to do that." Whether it was a ruse or a genuine desire to fight, it worked, or so it appeared. The chief had to provide their food and that of the two white slavers who had accompanied them at his own expense for two months. "Nobody would buy them," Kinnard explained to Garvin, "so I bought four at 300 dollars and so I paid Aiken and Smart [the slavers] 1200 in cattle and horses." James Aiken and his companion returned to St. Marys with the three unsold slaves.[93]

Black slaves in Creek country fled to Florida in search of freedom but encountered the same long hand reaching across the border to re-enslave them as did those running from white enslavers. When the white traders who sold Kinnard the men were returning to St. Marys with the other three, one called "mulatto Lucy" slipped away and headed southward to the Spanish fort of St. Mark's. The Scots-Creek sent word to the commandant of the fort, who jailed Lucy without asking questions. Kinnard travelled to the fort, paid twenty dollars for his release, and sold him to one of the partners in Panton, Leslie.[94] More typically, John Galphin, the mestizo who had led the attack on Trader's Hill and the farms on the Spanish side of the St. Marys River, dared write the governor of East Florida in an effort to reclaim one of his own slaves, Simon, who now called himself a free man in Florida.[95]

Lucy's flight underscores an essential change. The direction of those fleeing through the borderland was increasingly southward towards a people who only then were coalescing into a coherent polity with their own customs and ways of looking at outsiders. The Seminoles were former Creeks who had broken away from the Lower Towns during the mid-eighteenth century in search of greater autonomy as well as the open spaces of Florida that favored the grazing of cattle. Creek headmen referred to them contemptuously as wanderers, even outlaws, people who had moved beyond the reach of recognized traditions. Those wanderers were willing to accord Black people considerably more freedom and allow them to create their own villages adjacent to Native towns.

Yet the Seminoles remained intimately connected to the Creek towns along the lower part of the Chattahoochee and Flint Rivers. They spoke Hitchiti in common; they engaged in trading relationships; hunters and warriors routinely ignored the boundaries; and many presumed Seminole headmen signed treaties as Creeks.[96] It was indicative that the raiding parties led by "the Black Factor" and the mercurial John Galphin contained Natives from both Chehaw and Seminole towns. The vast region where the Chattahoochee and Flint combined to form the Apalachicola was evolving into a remarkable frontier in which the chief actors were Creeks who were moving toward a more centralized system of governance and former Creeks who treasured their autonomy and saw their relationship with people of African descent in starkly different terms. Maj. Caleb Swan wrote, "The Seminolies are said to be principally under the influence of Jack Kinnard, a rich Scotch half-breed, living on the neck of land between Flint and the Chattahoosee rivers." The reference to Kinnard may have been an exaggeration, but it hinted at the ties that bound Hitchiti speakers along the waterways of the Chattahoochee-Apalachicola River system.[97]

CHAPTER 8

Flight to the Seminoles

Within a relatively short time, Black Georgians came to see the Seminoles as their best hope for securing freedom, a phenomenon that goes to the heart of profound changes in the Creek people during the last decades of the eighteenth century. The Seminoles were a relatively recent creation, fashioned out of dissident Creeks who had migrated from the interior of the South into the largely uninhabited spaces of northern Florida.[1] The interior of northern Florida belonged to these migrants who trickled in from different spaces and for differing reasons.[2] When asked whether the Florida Natives were part of the Creek Nation, Alexander McGillivray, the Upper Creek mestizo, described them as "wanderers," while other leaders called them "renegades and vagabonds."[3] After multiple visits, one Carolinian observed, "it has been generally understood that this tribe of Indians were formed originally by a casual association of fugitives and outlaws from the Creek nation"; their name was said to signify outlaws.[4] Indeed, the term "Seminole" was an Anglicization of the Spanish slang for "wild" and used in reference to cattle lost in the woods or runaway slaves.

The number of Seminole Indians was always small, and their dispersed settlement pattern reinforced a basic lack of unity. "They are more unsettled, in their manner of living, than any other district of people in the nation," Major Swan commented on a tour through Creek country. "The truth is, they have no government among them."[5] Despite this lack of governance, they were evolving into a people with a distinct culture and social organization.[6] The Seminoles were skillfully adapting their Creek culture to fit the

MICO CHLUCCO the LONG WARIOR
or KING of the SIMINOLES

"Mico Chlucco the Long Warrior, or King of the Siminoles." Micco Chlucco shared leadership of the Alachua band of Seminoles with Ahaya (Cowkeeper) during the mid- to late 1700s. This etching appeared as frontispiece for the William Bartram's *Travels* (1791), based on a drawing by Bartram. Courtesy of State Library and Archives of Florida.

environmental and economic conditions of northern Florida, occupying the grasslands of the prairie once used by the Spanish for cattle herding.

Among the first to appear were Ahaya (Cowkeeper) and his brother Long Warrior, who, according to one source, led 130 families—some 450 Creeks—from the Oconee River to a site in the Flint watershed and then, by the 1750s, onto the rich grasslands of the Alachua Prairie near St. Augustine.[7] It is probable that he had appeared alongside Oglethorpe during the War of Jenkins' Ear in 1739 and was returning to where he had captured Yamassee Indians and still held many as slaves. His great determination was to maintain his independence, and so he began a cautious realignment with the Spaniards in Florida. In addition to hunting deer and other game, the Indians raised cattle on the grassy plains and sold the beef and hides to the Spanish, creating an economy that marked a sharp separation from Creek life.[8]

Other groups broke off from the Lower and Upper Towns of the Creeks and crossed into the Apalachicola basin farther west, some as far as the Tampa Bay region. Originally, they functioned as satellite towns (talofas) of the communities from which they came, but they gradually built their own square grounds, council houses, and sacred fires, elevating themselves to the status of autonomous talwas.[9] Together the various settlements represented an ethnic minority within the Creek Nation. All spoke Hitchiti rather than Muskogee and jealously sought to guard their independence from the Creek Confederacy.

From the Revolution onwards, the Seminoles absorbed growing numbers of Black people, most as fugitives from Spanish Florida, Georgia, and, to a lesser extent, South Carolina; others as war captives taken by raiding parties; and a few as slaves purchased in the markets of St. Augustine and Pensacola, usually by a chief exchanging his cattle.[10] Their relationship with the new masters set them apart. The Seminoles retained older forms of captivity that allowed them to embrace people of African descent and create a pluralistic society that made room for diverse groups of newcomers. Blacks lived in separate villages next to Native settlements, cultivated their own fields, paid an annual tribute in the form of provisions, frequently served as interpreters and cultural intermediaries, and, in time, fought alongside Seminole warriors. Other than a share of agricultural produce, the chiefs expected little from their captives, leaving them, in the words of an American observer, "at liberty to employ themselves as they please."[11]

Observers in the 1820s and 1830s were astonished at the independence of the Black towns or "Negro villages" as they called them and puzzled over the paradox. Wiley Thompson had been a trader among the Seminoles since the first years of the nineteenth century and was a federal agent when he knowingly wrote, "They live in villages separate, and, in many cases, remote from their owners, and enjoying equal liberty with their owners." But he went on to note that they annually supplied to their "owners" a small amount of their crops, typically corn. The house or hut in which a Black family lived was theirs, and Thompson noted, "Many of these slaves have stocks of horses, cows, and hogs, with which the Indian owner never assumes the right to intermeddle."[12] Another knowledgeable observer, W. H. Simmons, pointed out to his American audience, "The Negroes uniformly testify to the kind treatment they receive from their Indian masters, who are indulgent and require little labor from them."[13]

Scholars have ever since puzzled over how to call them, whether they should be considered as maroons who lived autonomous lives, half-slaves still owned, partners in an unwritten alliance, or, in Christina Snyder's felicitous phrasing, "junior members" of the several chiefdoms. Together, she argues, Native and Black Seminoles created a new society, one that increasingly iso-

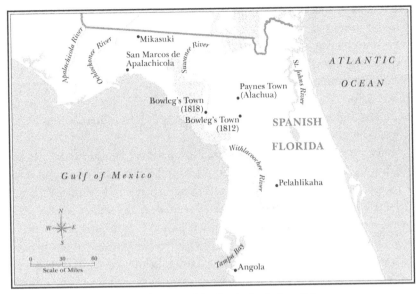

Principal towns of the Seminoles before 1818

lated them from other Southerners, white and Native.[14] That isolation owed much to the geopolitics of the region.[15] The presence of Black Seminoles in the heart of the southeastern borderland defined this region in a way that had no parallel in American history. The very act of fleeing across the St. Marys or down the Flint or Chattahoochee exposed the stunning vacuum of power that characterized this unique borderland. To their frustration, the Great Powers were unable to control much of anything that transpired in the interior of northern Florida, a failure that extended at various times into the southern portion of Georgia. Black people were the beneficiaries, able to use the setting to join these idiosyncratic Natives and become players in the delicate balance of power in the Southeast.

This unique set of circumstances evolved into a setting in which Black men originally from Georgia found themselves fighting white Georgians, besting them in a critical engagement in the Patriot War of 1812 and provoking unfounded fears of a slave insurrection in the Georgia Lowcountry. The progression was a measured one, from acting as cultural brokers and interpreters to participating in raids as recognized warriors to emerging fully as Black Seminoles who fought alongside "Blood Seminoles" in substantial numbers. By the first decade of the nineteenth century, they had become integral to the calculations of power in the Southeast.

In their twenty years of ruling East Florida (1763–1783), the British had been no more successful than the former Spanish government in projecting power beyond the St. Johns River. This astonishing impotence was on display from the very moment that the British plunged into transforming East Florida into a booming plantation economy built around the rapid infusion of English capital. Governor James Grant and his administration oversaw the addition of as many as fifteen hundred Africans through the Atlantic trade and another one thousand or so from South Carolina and elsewhere in the Americas.[16]

Benefiting from the exchange of trading goods for deerskin and cattle, officials were willing to tolerate a certain level of flight as a safety valve of sorts. Lt. Governor John Moultrie admitted to his superiors, "It has been a practice for a good while past for negroes to run away from their Masters and get into the Indian towns, from whence it proved very difficult and troublesome to get them back."[17] When four Black freedom seekers from a plantation near St. Augustine met up with a Seminole hunting party on the west bank of the St. Johns River, the slaves were made to accompany the hunters as quasi-servants as the latter continued their hunt. Confronted by whites, the Indians gestured that they were merely giving food to hungry men and surrendered their prizes without a struggle.[18] If fugitives reached a Native town or village, an extended negotiation between Natives and British might be successful or not. Given the small numbers of Seminoles and their sparse settlement pattern, the British saw these Indians as more of an annoyance than a threat and rarely applied significant pressure. The exchange of trading goods for cattle and deerskins more than compensated total losses.

The onset of the Revolution produced a radical change in attitude. Desperate for manpower, Governor Patrick Tonyn of East Florida negotiated with Ahaya for warriors to enter the conflict and agreed that, if he sent raiding parties into Georgia, they might keep all the horses, cattle, and slaves they took, although privately he was determined to minimize contact between Native Americans and Africans.[19] Reality dictated otherwise. During the war, Ahaya travelled to St. Augustine from the Alachua Prairie with cattle to trade for slaves and made his purchases unhindered.[20] Captives from the raids in Georgia were taken back to his town.

Meanwhile Black people were voting with their feet. Great numbers were escaping a war-torn economy in Georgia where the reins of authority were loosened. When Jupiter, Auba, and Jack landed at St. Augustine from Ossabaw Island in 1781, they chose to head to "Indian country" and join all those who found that the wartime conditions in the capital offered excellent opportunities to flee a white-dominated society and embrace a vastly different cultural world. The numbers departing testified to the weakness of a colony that still functioned as a military outpost with little authority beyond the St. Johns River in the vast interior of Florida.[21]

The return of the Spanish to Florida in 1783 changed the equation once again. As soon as Governor Vicente de Céspedes announced the restoration of the sanctuary policy and the granting of freedom to those fugitives who converted to Catholicism, freedom seekers from Georgia and South Carolina determined to make their way to St. Augustine or, at the very least, to blend into the Florida countryside. "Indian territory" seems to have been less frequently a destination during the 1780s, although no definitive judgment can be made, given the paucity of sources. But the promised sanctuary for freedom seekers was no more than an interlude. The period of grace lasted until the edict of May 17, 1790, when the Spanish king abolished the decree in the Americas and left the door open to a settlement with the United States, which occurred a year later.[22]

During the final decade of the eighteenth century, enslaved men and women in Spanish Florida pioneered the way. Jesse Dupont had arrived in East Florida in 1791 with his wife, eight children, and an unspecified number of slaves. Within months, two of them had run away. Dupont wrote to the governor: "[An] Indian negro Stole a wench and Child, and since she has been amongst the Indians she has had a second." The story ends there, unfortunately, and we are left with the tantalizing possibility that the "Indian negro" had been her husband. Sometime later, a party of warriors burned Dupont's rice fields and stole three "valuable" horses as well as cattle.[23]

Spanish officials had a self-serving explanation for why their enslaved people were so willing to take flight. Governor Enrique White pointed the finger at Black Georgians who had made it to the safety of Seminole towns and "dedicated themselves to instilling in the minds of the pacific Spanish slaves ideas of the advantage of liberty."[24] In fact, Black Seminoles were instrumental in spreading the word on plantations when acting as interpreters and cultural intermediaries on hunting parties that passed through white settlements. In the late spring of 1795, Col. Carlos Howard, commander of the northern district, confronted a small band of Hitchiti-speaking Indians, ten men with women and children, passing through the countryside near the tiny village of San Vicente de Ferrer at the mouth of the St. Johns River. When he saw several of the men stagger off a docked boat after having traded deerskins for rum with sailors, he expelled them from town. A short time later, a "Negro interpreter," a man who had either fled or been captured on a Georgia plantation, arrived alone at his office. Howard began lecturing him on the illegal trading of skins and telling him to lead the Seminoles away and not return. Howard wrote, "He told me, laughing in my face, that he would come back, that the Indians were coming behind him and they would make me see reason."[25]

Colonel Howard had his own reasons to be uneasy. The Seminoles were hunting among the plantations on the east side of the St. Johns River, burning woods and fields to frighten deer into the open, and occasionally entering the houses of the inhabitants. Of as great a concern were the two Black men who accompanied them, stolen or liberated from the Liberty County plantation of Governor John Houstoun of Georgia some years before, fluent in the difficult Hitchiti language, now serving as interpreters and cultural brokers. The lead interpreter, Peter, conveyed the words of the headman in a way that showed his delight in being able to tweak the nose of the commander. Howard was less concerned about his own dignity than the role of the two men in recruiting Black people: "Here, let me add that the Negroes . . . go around thinking about the slaves of the neighbors, [telling about] the happy life that the people of their color enjoy in the Nation, where they eat the same food as their masters, and work as much as they want alone without fear of punishment."[26] Blaming the loss of Black people on freedom seekers from Georgia was a common practice among Spanish officials.[27] Peter and others like him had a story to tell, and tell it they did.

Once fugitives from Georgia had crossed the St. Marys River, they had an important choice to make. An individual could go due south to the settlements on the Alachua Plain (Payne's Prairie), only a few miles distant from the St. Johns River, or to the southwest along the Mikasuki Path that wrapped around the eastern flank of the Okefenokee Swamp and on to the towns that lay on the banks of the Apalachicola River or near that river. With a strong sense of self-worth, Seminole towns and villages remained considerably more fractious and independent of each other than was true of Creek towns, where the national council gradually if fitfully set about undermining the authority of local chieftains. As Major Swan observed, there was no effective government over the estimated two thousand Indigenous people, not even a process for consultation among the various towns. That choice placed African Americans in towns with widely differing geopolitical outlooks.[28]

Through the early 1790s, the Alachua towns retained their primacy as the destination for freedom seekers from Georgia. If proximity was a key factor, so too was their prosperity. In 1788, Chief Payne, referred to as King Payne by whites, succeeded his uncle Ahaya as headman of the Alachua Seminoles. It was a daunting challenge. In his long tenure as chieftain, Ahaye had stood up to the Spanish, the English, and the principal leaders of the Creek Confederacy.[29]

Shortly after assuming the leadership, Payne abandoned Cuscowilla and founded Paynes Town a few miles away, constructing it plantation-style rather than around the time-honored square ground of Creek towns.[30] A superb diplomat rather than a warrior, Payne was keenly aware that his network of settlements was too small to be a military power and too close to the forces that surrounded it to be anything other than unaffiliated. His understanding of power was conditioned by the Spanish military garrison at St. Augustine, the frontier militias of Georgia, and the marauding war parties of the Creeks of the Lower Towns. Over time, he led the settlements on the Alachua Prairie to a remarkable level of prosperity and could boast of possessing fifteen hundred head of cattle, four hundred horses, untold numbers of sheep and goats, and twenty enslaved people.[31]

But there was another choice that could be made by a freedom seeker. Small bands of Creeks had entered northern Florida before, during, and after the Revolution, founding towns along the Apalachicola and Suwanee Rivers and farther south in the Tampa Bay area. The town of Mikasuki (by the waters that now form Lake Miccosukee) and the town of Talahasochti on the Suwanee River were larger and more substantial than those on the Alachua Plain and possessed a point of view that differed in many ways from their eastern neighbors.[32] The formidable Kinache, chieftain in Mikasuki and dominant figure in the Apalachicola region, had arrived only after the Revolution from the Lower Towns of the Creeks and remained a fierce partisan of the British, nursing a deep resentment of both Spanish and Americans. Best known as Tom Perryman in his early life, the mestizo did not hesitate to assert the independence of his people against the two dominant powers of the region.[33]

As chief, he commanded a substantial population that contained 180 to 200 men capable of bearing arms and a sizeable "Negro village" one and a half miles away, the largest such pairing in the whole of the Seminole polity. In a report some years earlier, Major Swan had described this "half-breed chief" as a man possessing as much property and influence as Jack Kinnard, with three young wives in tow. "For size and strength, [he] has never yet found his equal," Swan concluded, "He is master of the art of English boxing—and has been the Sampson of these Philistines from his youth upwards."[34] A prominent leader, Kinache was dismissive of the relatively passive Payne, who remained uncharacteristically silent when in the presence of the forceful military leader.[35]

The Seminoles at Mikasuki and in the Apalachicola Basin enjoyed greater freedom from outside influence than did those to the east, while nourishing as deep a hatred for the Spanish as for the Americans. Kinache's warriors resented the presence of the military outpost at Fort St. Marks and its control of trade. They complained vociferously about the high prices, low quality, and limited range of goods available at Panton's long-time store not far from the fort. As allies with the British during the Revolution, the Natives never lost their preference for things English and hoped fervently for their return. The Mikasukis continued to make periodic raids against Spanish plantations near St. Augustine for slaves and horses and compounded the terror they inflicted by occasionally killing an unfortunate victim, Black or white.[36]

In a wrenching change to the geopolitics of the region, Kinache stumbled into an unexpected opportunity to realize his dream of expelling the Spanish and extending his influence over neighboring towns, Creek as well as Seminole. In 1799, his son-in-law, the long-missing William Augustus Bowles, made a surprising reappearance in Mikasuki after an absence of six years. Now thirty-five-years old, he had fought for the British at Pensacola as a young loyalist from Maryland. Disciplined for insubordination, he had reinvented himself after fleeing to a Creek settlement on the Chattahoochee River, marrying the daughter of mestizo Chief Perryman, the future Kinache, and establishing trading relationships with British merchants in the Bahamas. He was quick to pick up on the pan-Native currents circulating among Native Americans in the eastern part of North America and put forth a call for an independent "United Nations of the Creeks and Cherokees." The quixotic effort spoke to his shrewd reading of the revolutionary ideas of the age as well as his own outsized ambitions. After a three-year chase, the Spanish government had captured the improbable adventurer through a clever ruse and exiled him to the Philippines.[37]

Undaunted, the persuasive Bowles escaped five years later and caught a vessel to London where he won tacit support from a cautious government, deftly spinning a vision of a British protectorate over an independent Indian state that might give Britain a new role in the American Southeast. He announced his readiness to refloat his bold vision of the State of Muscogee but built this time around the Seminoles rather than the Creek people and with room for dissident Creeks, Black runaways, and disaffected whites in the region.[38] Always a brash, self-interested adventurer, Bowles was capable

William Augustus Bowles (1763–1805). Bowles, also known as Estajoca by Native Americans, was a Maryland soldier and adventurer. Seeing action as a loyalist during the Revolutionary War, Bowles later formed an alliance with the Creek people and attempted to establish an independent Indigenous American state with British support. Courtesy of the Museum of Early Southern Decorative Arts.

of turning himself into a visionary who grasped the basic outlines of a newly emerging world rooted in the revolutionary Atlantic.

With Bowles's reappearance, Kinache saw in his son-in-law a new chance to secure a reliable source of reasonably priced goods while checkmating his most hated enemy, the Spanish government. Kinache arranged Bowles's re-election to his old position as director-general of the State of Muscogee while tacitly embracing the idea of creating a sovereign Indian nation carved out of territory claimed by Spain and the United States.[39] The newly installed director-general proceeded to churn out documents declaring war on Spain in the name of the newly formed state, made known his intention of rallying marginal peoples in the Southeast, including Black people and dissident whites, and stated his aim of organizing twin military forces, a navy and an army. As the American surveyor Andrew Ellicott dryly noted in his journal, Bowles was "a man of enterprise."[40]

For almost three years, the nebulous forces behind the State of Muskogee raided plantations along the St. Johns River, attacked Spanish shipping through letters of marque issued to Bahamian mariners, attempted to recruit dissident whites on the Georgia side of the St. Marys River, and assaulted Fort San Marcos. Capitalizing on easy victories early on, Bowles built a pseudo-government that tapped into themes running through the revolutionary Atlantic and energized an unprecedented coalition of Seminoles, Creeks, members of other Indigenous societies, African Americans, and whites of various origins.[41]

In the summer of 1800, raiding parties set out from the Seminoles to attack plantations along the St. Johns River. James Seagrove, the federal Indian agent in Georgia, warned his friend John McQueen that a party was headed his way composed of "from twenty-five to thirty Indians, Negroes, and infamous whites all of them direct from Bowles headquarters" with orders to "plunder and break up all the settlements in Florida."[42] A party of warriors carried off three Africans and fourteen horses from the plantation of François Richard, the refugee planter from Saint-Domingue and Mc-Queen's neighbor. Another took five enslaved people from George Fleming, a loyalist who had stayed in Florida.[43] Mikasukis canoed across the St. Johns and met up with four other Seminoles and two "hostile Negroes."[44] According to an associate of McQueen, the "hostile Negroes" went voluntarily with the Indians and acted as guides when they took Captain Fleming's enslaved workers, an apt description of how war captives transformed themselves into liberated people. Nor were Black slaveholders exempt. A pillar of the free Black community in St. Augustine and a baptized Catholic, Felipe Edimboro was a part-time farmer who raised pigs for his butcher's shop. A raid carried off his slave Jack as well as eight members of a free Black family whose farm lay next to his.[45]

That fall, Bowles unleashed an extraordinarily ambitious plan to rally white and Black Georgians in the St. Marys region, whose frontier-like conditions gave him room to maneuver and launch yet another coup to topple the Spanish government. The presence of a pool of frustrated filibusterers, horse thieves, and unregulated deerskin traders seemed a promising source of manpower to overthrow the Spanish in St. Augustine. The abortive attempt to organize an invasion of East Florida offers a measure of Camden County as an unsettled borderland where people of multiple cultural voices interacted in a drama involving an imperial power, a republic that functioned much as an imperial power, and a putative state that threatened both.

The focal point for much of the mischief that beset the region was the small port town of St. Marys, established by ambitious land speculators in 1787 at the entrance of the St. Marys River on Cumberland Sound. The end of the Revolutionary War had seen the frontier between Florida and Georgia explode into a bandit-ridden no-man's-land, raided by Americans coming south and ravaged by quasi-loyalist gangs from the remnants of British East Florida. After its fretful birth a few years later, St. Marys stood at the center of this curious borderland. Eventually fifty to sixty houses along the riverside sheltered a mixed population of Carolinians (trying to escape debt), Spanish citizens, Americans who claimed both Spanish and U.S. citizenship, French refugees from Saint-Domingue, Georgians looking for quick money, and shippers who engaged in a variety of legal and illegal activities, including smuggling Africans into Georgia. According to the 1790 census, there were 221 white people, 70 enslaved people, and 14 free Blacks. Ten years later, the population had increased substantially to 1,681, of whom 735 were enslaved people.[46]

Maintaining order along the banks of the St. Marys River was beyond the capabilities of Americans or Spanish authorities. The smuggling of slaves was a frequent occurrence made inevitable by the vacuum of power. A white Georgian operated a house on Tyger Island in Spanish Florida that served as a holding pen for people of African descent brought to him by residents of Camden. When confronted about a case involving Robert and James Ross, Samuel Mercer confessed his involvement in such a scheme. "He did so," it was said, "without asking any questions because he was in the habit of receiving negroes from the Ross brothers."[47] The pipeline from the town to Tyger Island was a reality. Indian traders lived on both sides of the river in a largely successfully effort to escape local authority. They engaged in a wide range of illegal activities and counted on the influence of chieftains like Jack Kinnard to keep them out of harm's way.[48] Purloined goods or livestock often reappeared on the other side of the river through one means or another. Creek and Seminole raiders regularly stole horses in Camden County and sold them to white traders or brokers who turned a good profit in East Florida.[49] Professional horse thieves like Bob Allen were caught and locked up in the tiny jail in St. Marys. Allen was adept at escaping, and no one seemed overly concerned.[50]

Bowles turned to a born schemer, Richard Lang, leader of the failed 1795 rebellion, who, after initially hesitating, accepted the proposal for a fresh offensive against St. Augustine. He counted on tapping into a pool of young men eager for land and slaves.[51] Lang had originally migrated from South Carolina as a debtor and moved to Spanish Florida to obtain land. He was involved with wholesale cattle smuggling from Georgia while trafficking in goods and people across the border illegally. When he was found plotting with would-be revolutionaries in St. Marys to invade East Florida, he lost his estate and fled across the river. In 1795, he put those plans into action and took the lead in an actual rebellion that cost the lives of three Spanish soldiers before his tiny force was chased back across the St. Marys River by a path-breaking coalition of Spanish soldiers, the free Black militia, and a white militia.[52]

In October 1800, Bowles, the director-general, marched on the village of Colerain, located on the St. Marys River, to meet with Lang and finalize plans for the coup. Black people were present at each stage. A Spanish official reported that Bowles's immediate party consisted of eight whites and eight Blacks and that one of the latter served as a captain.[53] A Florida planter led a posse in pursuit and neared the spot where it was rumored that the rendezvous was to take place. They encountered a Black man walking toward them, "one of the Negroes of the Bowles party." The African readily revealed that their leader planned to link up with Lang and expected to be joined by three hundred Georgians who were "to go into Florida and plunder and kill and take possession of Florida in the name of the King of England." It was not long before the McQueen party picked up the trail and was almost on an encampment of Bowles and his party early one morning. Hearing noise in the underbrush, the director-general and his three Black companions leaped up from the fire where they were cooking breakfast and escaped, leaving behind horses, clothing, arms, and even papers. Stripping off their clothes, they dived into the river and swam to safety.[54]

Lang weighed the odds of Bowles's project succeeding and quietly with-drew his offer of support—but not before becoming drunk and leaving Bowles's colorfully worded letter about invading Florida lying on the floor of a shop. That letter was soon in the governor's office, eliciting a proclama-tion that forbade anyone cooperating in any way with the director.[55] David Garvin, a trader with the Creeks, was deputized to go to every store in the town of St. Marys and buy up all the ammunition and powder still available to prevent African Americans and Native Americans from having access. Taking the threat seriously, Governor James Jackson issued a spirited proc-lamation that no Georgian could cooperate with this "vagabond and scoun-drel" and expect support from the state.[56] It was the last nail in the coffin of Bowles's Georgia adventure.

Among those arrested in St. Marys in the aftermath of this fiasco was the "notorious horse thief" Bob Allen, the freebooter who passed back and forth between Florida and Georgia as opportunity arose.[57] Taken with him were "three vagabond negro men, (stiling themselves free) from their Town in the Lotchaway country," according to local sources.[58] Their presence is of spe-cial interest since the Alachua chief, Payne, remained neutral in this contest. That three Black Seminoles in the surrounding villages of Alachua were par-ticipating with a man known as a horse thief in Georgia speaks to the net-work of relationships that made the region so unsettled and anxious.

Well aware of these efforts, Black Georgians responded to Bowles's vision of a multiracial society. "Many negroes have allredy made an attempt to run from the Overseer, but have been taken," a justice of the peace in St. Marys warned Governor Jackson.[59] The Spanish governor reported at least one fu-gitive from the state hiding on the Little St. Marys River only a short dis-tance south of the border and speculated there were probably more.[60] The state of alarm in Camden County rose dramatically when two Black men sent by Bowles strode into town by themselves and announced that they had letters for the governor. They were summarily thrown into jail, then released when no evidence could be produced that they were anything more than couriers.[61]

The drawing power of Bowles's vision was immense. A Camden planter showed a remarkable naiveté in writing to the director-general for his help in recovering Caesar, "a stout, likely young fellow about 25 years of age," who had run away from his plantation and was said "to be in the vicinity of [Bowles's] neighborhood."[62] When a Georgia planter asked for compensa-tion for a slave supposedly kidnapped by the Creeks, Indian agent Benjamin Hawkins detailed the reality for a state official. The bondsman had in fact run away to East Florida but was intercepted as he passed through Creek country, perhaps caught by Natives eager for a reward. Slated to be returned to his master, he "confounded" the jailers and made good his escape to Florida. The African was later said to have been killed fighting alongside Bowles against the Spanish.[63] If the State of Muskogee showed no overt ideological opposition to slavery, its welcome of freedom seekers and determined opposition to American and Spanish expansion constituted a substantive challenge to that institution, to the very idea of organizing society according to racial hierarchies.[64]

Although the State of Muskogee emerged as a multiracial, polyglot society that reached out to the marginal and disaffected, Kinache was pursuing his own agenda. He remained a traditional war leader rooted in hatred of the Spanish, devoted to older concepts of clan and family, and more than willing to use his son-in-law to achieve those long-standing aims. He provided a refuge to those alienated by changes in the Southeast, including young men from the Upper and Lower Towns—Coweta, Tallahasse, Apalachicola, "Hitcheta," Uchee, "Ooseooche," Oconee, "Eufaulau," and "Oketeyeconne."[65] A knowledgeable planter wrote to his wife that the newcomers included "an assorted pack from all the nations—Chiahas, Cowetas, Hitchitis and a number of High Creeks, who are American, as well as those of Alachua."[66] Many among the Creek Indians were people convicted of crime or who came out of curiosity or saw an opportunity to fight when no such opportunity existed in their own towns. Whatever their motives, most Natives preferred their own towns and independence, not a fictive state with abstract powers.

After the initial taking of Fort San Marcos and its subsequent loss, Kinache planned a series of terrifying raids along the St. Johns that followed the traditional pattern: sudden surprise strikes, limited goals in terms of plunder, and no intention of killing white or Black people but with a focus on taking slaves as prizes. He went one step further. When Governor Enrique White arrested Mithology, Kinache's cousin and confidant, for multiple misdeeds and locked him in nearby Fort St. Marks, an infuriated chieftain struck back.[67] Jack Kinnard had advised the governor to release Mithology or expect dire consequences, and in this he was accurate.[68] In August 1801, Seminole warriors swooped down on New Switzerland, the model plantation of Francis Phillipe Fatio, and carried off eight Black men, eight women, and twenty-two children. On his own authority, he had launched a raid that captured thirty-eight Africans as revenge against the Spanish government for the imprisonment of a valued member of his clan.

The matter was serious enough to prompt an attempt by the Alachuans to mediate matters. Bowlegs, Payne's nephew, left his town to visit Mikasuki with horses loaded with goods supplied by Fatio in an effort to negotiate the release of the captives. Instead, Mikasuki warriors jeered him and asked why the owners of these people did not come themselves. Bowles stepped forward to disclaim any responsibility for the raid but then, in his grand theatrical style, proclaimed that the capture was legal since the Spanish were the ones who were stealing their "negroes, horses, and provisions."[69] On returning, Bowlegs relayed that the "Negroes" were being kept all together and that a girl had died on the march and another was close to death. The captives were complaining of inadequate food, while Mikasuki families were bitter about the provisions they were having to give up to feed them.[70]

In a second round of negotiations, Francis Philip Fatio Jr. accompanied Payne, leader of the Alachua Seminoles, to continue the delicate discussions. Taking full advantage of the occasion, Kinache and Bowles humiliated the young Fatio verbally, allowed his horse to be stolen, and made threatening noises to the point that the slaveholder feared for his life. A seemingly timorous Payne said nothing in the public assembly of warriors. Few of the bondsmen were ever returned. Records from the 1830s at the time of the Seminole removal to Oklahoma indicate that many of Fatio's captives were still present, listed as slaves belonging to individual warriors.[71]

Nor was Kinache sated with the New Switzerland raid. When Governor White remained adamant in his refusal to release Mithology, his warriors struck again in January 1802 to force the governor's hand. They broke into the modest home of a Majorcan family on the St. Johns River, where all but the father, Bonnelli, was present. The warriors killed the eldest son and took the wife of Bonnelli and their three daughters, one of the few instances where white people were kidnapped. The Indians seized ten enslaved workers on a neighboring plantation. The white family was eventually ransomed; the bondsmen remained.[72]

Bowles could not sustain his charade of creating an independent state much longer. His base among the Seminoles and Creeks was rapidly contracting in the wake of his blatant failure to obtain English trading goods for Seminole towns as well as the many military setbacks he had experienced. A dramatic encounter in April 1803 revealed not merely his loss of standing but also the continuing influence of Creeks from the Lower Towns with the Mikasuki Seminoles. The influence of Kinache, mico of Mikasuki, and Kinnard, dominant figure among the Hitchiti-speaking Creeks, extended over a wide-ranging set of villages and settlements united by language, customs, and traditions. Kinache was the aggressive warrior, Kinnard the Machiavellian diplomat, constantly playing ends against the middle. Although known for his pro-American sentiments, Kinnard assiduously cultivated the governors of both East and West Florida and was called on to mediate multiple crises. Their overlapping leadership was part of a larger whole. Hunters hunted across the region. Towns were connected in various ways. And Hitchiti-speaking Seminole and Creek warriors sometimes participated in the same raids and shared the plunder as in the case of the attack on Trader's Hill.[73]

Kinnard and his two brothers shared a farm on the Wakulla River in Spanish Florida. The house on that farm became the site of an extraordinary meeting that revealed Kinache's withdrawal of support for his son-in-law. Florida planters had hired a young Indian trader, Wiley Thompson, to go into various towns that held captives and negotiate a ransom. Only twenty-one years old, Thompson had the intelligence to travel first to Kinnard's settlement on Kinchafoonee Creek among the Lower Towns to secure his blessings. The Scots-Creek was blunt. Not only was the going rate $50 for each captive, he also demanded a special fee for his warriors to travel from village to village in the attempt to free the captives. Present in the farmhouse were Thompson, the three Kinnard brothers, and Jack Kinnard's son. Facing them were three Mikasuki warriors who sat glumly in a corner, William Augustus Bowles, and, most importantly, Jack Philips, a free Black accompanying the director of the Muskogee Nation. Philips had escaped from the Panton store at San Marcos.[74]

With the Kinnards sitting beside him, Thompson offered to ransom Philips and return him to his enslaver. Clearly, this was a test case for the status of all fugitive slaves in the Florida hinterland. The scene swiftly descended into confrontation. With his accustomed brashness, Bowles announced that no Spanish enslaved person would be returned under any circumstance and warned that Thompson risked "losing his hair" if he should go in and make such foolish requests elsewhere. Jack Kinnard interrupted to insist that all Black captives be restored to their owners as stated in the Treaty of Coleraine as agreed to by the assembled chiefs. It was a pointed statement. No Seminole chieftain had in fact signed that document. He added that Bowles was the one whose hair was at risk. Kinnard's brother Billy then ordered Jack Philips to be taken as a fugitive slave and clapped in irons. Bowles jumped up to shield Philips. John Kinnard promptly ordered his two brothers to seize Bowles while his son took a thick stick and began physically beating the defenseless man. The three warriors sat stoically in their corner, not budging, a certain sign that Kinache was no longer vested in his son-in-law. The taking of Philips and the chastising of Bowles underscored the erosion of the grand vision of an independent Indian nation and the hope for free Blacks in this community.[75]

After the confrontation, Kinnard charged a brother-in-law and his own "confidential negro Joe" with escorting Thompson through various Seminole villages as the young trader negotiated for the ransom of captives. Out of as many eighty-two people, the trader obtained the release of only three. If Kinache refused to make the slightest bow to Spanish authorities or elite planters, the reality remained that Bowles's ability to command had vanished. At a meeting of Upper and Lower Creeks in the meeting town of Tuckabatchee the following month, the adventurer was arrested and turned over to the Spanish. He died the next year in a cramped Spanish prison in Cuba.[76] The odyssey was over.

After Bowles's removal, the old Spanish-Seminole alliance that had come apart in so short a time snapped back into place as Americans emerged as the preeminent threat to both groups. In Seminole towns, life resumed its normal rhythm if it had ever changed at all. In the long run, the addition of some eighty Black people taken as war captives and the continuing stream of fugitives only strengthened the emerging pattern of life. Black Seminoles farmed their own plots of land, owned their own livestock, and were free to sell cattle and crafts to the Spanish. When two free Black men from St. Augustine went through Seminole towns on a buying expedition on behalf of the Spanish government, they purchased 18 out of 125 from Molly, a fugitive from Georgia who owned the livestock and kept the proceeds for herself.[77] Women as well as men had these precious rights.

Of the men, William H. Simmons, a traveler through Seminole towns and a keen observer of customs, observed, "They dress and live pretty much like the Indians, each having a gun, and hunting a portion of his time. Like the Indians, they plant in common, and farm an Indian field apart, which they attend together."[78] Enjoying relatively light servitude, Black Seminoles served as laborers, interpreters, and, increasingly, military auxiliaries. They retained their own cultural distinctiveness. Most intermarried among themselves. Many began to adopt Native Seminole dress, as Simmons testified, but others secured the plain cloth they had always worn. Significantly, they preserved their African roots through a creole language, speaking Hitchiti or Muscogee with the Seminoles and English with white Americans. Because of this cultural blending, it is difficult to make the argument that the Black

Seminoles were in fact another example of maroons in the North American continent. There was sufficient interaction between the communities that usual definitions of marronage do not fit.[79]

Yet their freedoms had limits. Black Seminoles did not live in an egalitarian society. On the most basic level, chieftains were open to returning fugitives if the ransom price was sufficiently enticing. James Cashen sent an Indian trader to Bowlegs Town to recover four of his people. Three of them had run away six years before. The trader was to offer $25 and, if this were not enough, to suggest trading cattle, perhaps as many as forty head per person. Cashen was prepared to ransom the fourth person, Jacob, only for money because he had fled a short time before and was not "corrupted" by years spent in a Seminole town. Twenty-two years old, Jacob had been born in Charleston and was described as "very knowing and talkative." He was living in a hut with one of the earlier runaways by the name of Harry, suggesting that Jacob had been in communication with the former fugitives or had found a ready-made support system once he reached Seminole territory.[80] We do not know if Cashen was successful, but other efforts were.

As chiefs had become ranchers with substantial herds of cattle, they had begun to accumulate wealth and used those resources to buy enslaved people. When Spanish officials auctioned off the assets of those planters who participated in the 1795 rebellion, Seminoles were among the buyers. Kinache purchased an African American from Bahamian trader Richard Powers for $400 Spanish dollars. Payne, nephew of Ahaya and his successor, boasted that he owned twenty slaves.[81] When the Black Seminoles were expelled from Florida in the late 1830s as a consequence of the actions of Andrew Jackson, the emigration records list only 18 free people out of a total of 390.[82] Ironically, the title of "slave" indicated a dependent relationship that concealed considerable freedoms.

The red Seminoles and Black Seminoles were creating a relatively inclusive society unlike any other on the North American continent that defies easy categorization. Scholars continue to debate how to interpret the independence that the people of African descent enjoyed. They were certainly not maroons in the classical sense of that term if one considers that their existence did not include the full ability to shape their own lives but was qualified by dependence on a chieftain. Nor did they fall into the category of "half-slaves still owned," as one contemporary argued. Their freedoms were too great to fit within the description of half-slave. Were they partners in an unwritten alliance with the Seminoles? Again, at the turn of the nineteenth century, they were still subject to being ransomed and returned to their original enslaver. Christina Snyder, historian and ethnologist, comes closer with her description of the Black Seminoles as junior members of the several chiefdoms, whose requirement of some form of tribute may have been a distant echo of the type of relationships that existed in Mississippian societies.[83] Of course, that junior membership came attached with many qualifications.

It is more likely that this unique people were at the beginning of a long, slow evolution toward becoming more like the Seminoles.[84] If one scratched the surface of any village, one would likely have found free people who had adopted certain Native customs, full-fledged slaves, runaways recently arrived like Jacob who held to their old way of life, and a few who had intermarried with Natives—in short, a diversity of conditions. In this setting, there was a degree of cultural blending on the Florida frontier that the Second Seminole War cut short.[85]

The period from 1803 until 1812 marked the high point for the delicate balance that existed between Seminoles, fugitive slaves, and the Spanish government. East Florida reached a state of prosperity that exceeded the level in many parts of Georgia. In the course of the early years of the century, dozens of planters migrated to the colony and brought with them several thousand enslaved people. Large plantations built around the latest management techniques took shape. A slave trader and planter from the Caribbean, Zephaniah Kingsley, created a series of model plantations with cotton, orange groves, and fields of corn, peas, and sweet potatoes. A representative of a notable Georgia family, John Houstoun McIntosh, purchased much of John McQueen's estate and moved his enslaved labor force across the St. Marys. Lumber, rice, and cotton were the primary commodities.[86]

The newly founded town of Fernandina on Amelia Island, with its six hundred inhabitants, emerged as the major shipping port for commodities produced in Florida. The economic sanctions imposed by Congress on British commerce—the Embargo Act, Non-Intercourse Act of 1809, and Macon's Bill #2—diverted a significant amount of trade into its harbor. Dozens of British ships were seen floating in the harbor, many visible from the town of St. Marys. While those vessels became a source of much anger on the American side, Floridians were pleased with their newfound prosperity and had little desire to risk their affluence in asking for change.[87]

Inland, the Seminoles benefited from the upheaval of the Bowles era by the influx of warriors, war captives, and fugitive slaves. Payne and Kinache continued as the acknowledged leaders among the loosely connected network of Seminole towns or settlements. The relative prosperity of the towns was indicated by the amount of cattle, deerskins, and other commodities sold to the Spanish through the Panton, Leslie & Company stores in northern Florida or to Cuban fishermen in the Tampa Bay area. Free Blacks from St. Augustine often conducted the trade in cattle, traveling through Indigenous settlements for weeks at a time.[88]

That prosperity came to an abrupt end as southerners awoke to the vacuum of power on the Georgia border and the opportunities that it presented. The idea of a march on St. Augustine had always been popular in Georgia and a seemingly logical outcome to the issue at hand. Georgians never questioned their notion that the Spanish government was a corrupt, inefficient bureaucracy responsible for the lawlessness that prevailed in the St. Marys region. They feared the status of the Catholic Church in a society that violated deeply rooted American beliefs about the separation of powers. Above all, they deemed dangerous a legal system that recognized enslaved people as human beings holding certain legal rights. For proof, southerners had only to look at East Florida as the ultimate sanctuary for runaway slaves and a haven for an armed Black militia. White Georgians had no intention of tolerating the Spanish deployment of Black soldiers, "the vilest species of troops" in the words of Maj. Gen. John Floyd.[89]

The balance of power in the Southeast was now shifting. For Georgians, the Seminoles were the most pressing issue. Bands were slipping into Camden County and stealing livestock without residents being able to cross the Georgia-Florida border in pursuit. Towns were continuing to shelter Black fugitives whose semi-independence presented a frightening example for their slaves. Seminole chieftains were now acting in alliance with the Spanish government as an effective buffer against American expansion. In the opposite direction, the presence of British vessels in Fernandina was a direct affront to America's defense of the freedom of the seas and an implied threat to control of the land. As war came closer, it seemed possible, even probable, that Great Britain would take possession of Florida from a faltering Spanish state already in the hands of Napoleon. Georgians heartily subscribed to the belief that the region east of the St. Johns River and the fertile lands of the Alachua Seminoles were ready for incorporation into the Empire of Liberty.[90]

In 1810, those hopes took a more tangible form. Settlers in the Baton Rouge district of the Louisiana Purchase rose up against their Spanish rulers and staged a mini-revolt that put President James Madison in position to secure the cession of a portion of West Florida to the United States. The valuable lands stretched from the Perdido River in today's Alabama to the Mississippi River and included the towns of Mobile and Natchez. Madison's idea of "conquer without war" seemed a promising template for East Florida and well within their grasp.

The president asked George Matthews, the former governor of Georgia who had engineered this striking success, to hold a similar conversation with the governor of East Florida and suggest to him a peaceful transfer of power. When the Spanish governor stood firm and refused to betray his country, Matthews went to St. Marys on the Georgia-Florida border and whipped up an impromptu rebellion of a handful of settlers with grudges against Spanish authority. A tiny force of Anglo-Americans in Florida and land-hungry adventurers from Camden County occupied Amelia Island on March 12, 1812. Taking over the port from a frightened Spanish garrison, the self-styled patriots created a shadow government clumsily named the Board of Officers for the Constituted Authority of East Florida. Units of the Georgia militia soon followed to back them up. American naval units hovered off shore, and one hundred men from the federal garrison at Point Peter joined in despite the fact that they had no orders to do so. Madison preferred to overlook the matter.[91]

From Fernandina, three separate columns of Americans fanned out across northern Florida to complete the occupation in what appeared to be a surprisingly easy task. Several hundred young men, eager for land and slaves, planted themselves in front of St. Augustine, ready to march into the town. One hundred U.S. troops set up camp two miles north of St. Augustine. Units from the Georgia militia positioned themselves on the St. Johns River near the strategic crossing known as Cowford. In total, eight hundred American troops were scattered across East Florida, with little coordination among them. Refusing to be intimidated by this show of force, the newly appointed governor of East Florida, Sebastián Kindelán, retreated with his forces inside the virtually impregnable walls of the fortress at St. Augustine, where he commanded a regiment of Cuban soldiers, four hundred Pardo (mestizo) and five hundred Moreno (Black).[92]

The declaration of war on Great Britain in June rendered moot any thought of committing U.S. troops to a border war started by Americans. The president ordered the federal troops not to engage in any offensive action but declined to order a withdrawal, leaving the lone unit on its own. Caught in a web of their own making, President Madison and Secretary of State James Monroe could not bring themselves to make a clean break and so pursued a policy rooted in ambiguity, making worse an already tragic situation. The three different commands were left sitting in possession of most of northern East Florida without clear guidance.[93]

Eager for action, officers judged that the orders not to engage in offensive action did not apply to the Seminoles and that eliminating the threat from Indigenous people was now a reasonable goal. Maj. Gen. John Floyd, an otherwise cautious man, wrote to an approving Senator William H. Crawford, "An Indian uprising would afford desirable pretext for the Georgians to penetrate their country and Break up a Negro Town; an important Evil growing under their patronage." He judged, "The Number of these Negroes from the lowest calculation Exceeds 500."[94] The general's estimate was probably near the mark.

In an instant, the war aims dramatically shifted. Destroying Seminole towns and eliminating the Black Seminoles were easy goals to justify, at least in the minds of Georgians frustrated by two decades of inaction. The army commander, Lieutenant Colonel Smith, lent his authority to the conspiracy theories floating about: "[The Seminoles] have, I am informed, several hundred fugitive slaves from the Carolinas & Georgia at present in their Towns & unless they are checked soon they will be so strengthened by desertions from Georgia & Florida that it will be found troublesome to reduce them."[95] The governor of Georgia, David Mitchell, upped the stakes. The campaign in Florida was a necessity, he told the president, because the "insolence" of its Negro population threatened to induce rebellion among the Black population in Georgia.[96] "It is also a fact," he told Monroe a few days later, "that most of our negroes on the Sea Board are restless and make many attempts to get off to St. Augustine, and many have succeeded, which renders it necessary to have constant guards and patrols."[97]

In many ways, it was a self-fulfilling prophecy. By the end of 1812, in the midst of the Patriot War, Black men originally from Georgia found themselves fighting white Georgians and besting them in critical engagements. They showed themselves an organized and disciplined fighting force capable of standing up to the American military. The first encounter took place at Twelve Mile Swamp in an ambush of supply wagons guarded by marines making their way from outside St. Augustine to a resupply station on the St. Johns. Thirty-two Black Seminoles joined with six Native Seminoles and twenty-five men from the free Black militia to waylay the wagon train and inflict a stinging defeat on the marine unit. Of the twenty-two men with the commander of the marines, Capt. John Williams, eight were wounded and one died, and Williams himself succumbed to his multiple injuries less than two weeks later.[98] It was a humiliating and unequivocal defeat for federal forces.

In the main encounter, Col. Daniel Newnan, commander of the Georgia militia, led 116 men and an African American boy in a retaliatory raid on Paynes Town. His troops were a collection of state militiamen whose enlistment was about to expire, federal soldiers, and a handful of patriots who volunteered to guide. A few miles from the town, the party encountered a band of Seminoles who were filing down the same path unaware of the approach of the enemy. In the accidental encounter, a fierce gun battle took place that lasted seven days. Newman's forces retreated into a crude shelter they erected and survived on limited provisions. Several men were killed and many more wounded. A desperate retreat enabled the beaten soldiers to make it back to the remaining American forces. Writing a long report to Governor Mitchell, Newnan offered a remarkably balanced account of how his men fought three engagements and suffered through a week of intermittent sniping. He observed tellingly, "[The] negroes . . . are [the Seminoles'] best soldiers."[99]

Newnan's comment is notable. The Black Seminoles gave the Indians a competitive edge and inspired a wholly new kind of fear among white Georgians as word spread. Despite the small numbers involved, the American military had suffered a major blow. Black soldiers and warriors, many of them former fugitive slaves, had shown themselves the equal of U.S. marines and provided a stunning challenge to the racial stereotype that Blacks could not fight. The short war revealed how the role of the Black Seminole had evolved over the preceding twenty years from interpreters and cultural brokers to fighters in the Mikasuki War to the disciplined warriors of the Patriot War capable of holding their own against federal troops and Georgia militiamen. Native and Black warriors, in concert with Spain's Black militiamen, had undone the half-hearted patriot rebellion and its attempt to take possession of Florida.

Retaliation came quickly. In January 1813, U.S. Army troops and the Georgia militia, together with Tennessee volunteers eager to fight, marched into East Florida with several hundred men to extract a final settlement with a troublesome Native American polity.[100] The surprise was on the Americans. The entire population of the Seminoles on the Alachua Plain had melted away into the swamps and thick understory of the land, leaving their villages deserted. Nor were the escaped slaves who populated the "Negro villages" to be found. However, the army exacted revenge by virtually destroying the Seminole economy. According to the official record, the troops burned 386 houses, took away three hundred horses and four hundred head of cattle, consumed or threw away between fifteen hundred and two thousand bushels of corn, and spoiled or carried back two thousand deerskins, the most important medium of exchange for the purchase of goods through Panton,

Leslie & Company. The first steps in the cruel removal of the Seminoles to Oklahoma in the 1830s had been taken.

With the destruction of the Seminole towns and Negro villages, the Patriot War effectively ended, but the ramifications were immense, not only for the Seminoles but also for Spanish East Florida. The government in St. Augustine reestablished its authority slowly and only with difficulty in the face of outlaws who roamed the northern part of the colony with impunity for several months and a plantation economy that stood in ruins. The naked aggression of the United States laid bare the desperate condition of Florida, with its lack of support from Madrid, its dependence on a Black militia in an increasingly racialized South, a nearly bankrupt treasury, and an Anglo population of decidedly mixed loyalty. That lesson fed the spate of rumors running through the Georgia Lowcountry about the heightened dangers of slave insurrection at a moment when coastal rice and cotton plantations were still trying to digest the infusion of enslaved Blacks from Africa, the Chesapeake Bay, and the French Caribbean.[101] It was a distinctly unsettled moment as planters along the Georgia coast increased surveillance over the lives of their enslaved people as they introduced more efficient means to increase production in a rapidly changing Atlantic economy based on cotton.

CHAPTER 9

Erasing a Borderland

During the second decade of the nineteenth century, the rapid succession of conflicts on Georgia's borders—the Patriot War, the Creek War, the War of 1812, and the First Seminole War—created unparalleled opportunities for Black Georgians to play a role in the swiftly changing balance of power in the region. It was a riveting climax to decades of continuous flight when twenty-five hundred to three thousand people between 1812 and 1817 took advantage of the political and military crises to cross boundaries into these new worlds.[1] Those final years of instability produced the last and arguably the largest wave of individuals to escape across porous borders and connect with communities that offered a measure of freedom or, at the very least, a form of servitude that promised greater autonomy and a recognition of their humanity. Ironically, those same wars marked a time when the struggle for dominance in the Southeast was decisively settled in favor of an ever-expanding United States and when much of that flight was necessarily scattered and defensive in nature.[2] War forced the trajectory of that multicultural region into a more narrowly linear path.

The first notable movement during this troubled period consisted not of Georgians but rather of Black Seminoles who relocated within the Florida Peninsula in the aftermath of the Patriot War. In their march into Florida in January 1813, American forces, as noted, had decimated the economy of the Seminoles, destroying houses and taking livestock and deerskins. To their great frustration, they found the "Negro villages" deserted except for a few women, children, and one old man and, after much searching, killed several warriors and captured nine men.[3] Many African Americans accompanied Bowlegs, the younger brother of King Payne, to a refuge on the Suwanee River, where a new settlement took shape. Many of the Alachua Seminoles followed a younger leader, Micanopy, to Okahumpka in central Florida's Lake Country.

Other Black Seminoles broke away from the Seminoles and made their way to the rolling savannas of west central Florida, where they founded a settlement along the Manatee River, a place that offered an easily defensible position near fertile farm land and not far from rich hunting grounds.[4] There they built a significant free Black community that served as a refuge of freedom not only for the victims of the Patriot War but also for many African Americans who were later routed by the string of conflicts that convulsed the Southeast. Known as Angola by Cubans who fished nearby, the coastal settlement testified to the deep African roots that shaped its culture. Reporting on the presence of Black people in the area, Benjamin Hawkins, the federal agent in Creek territory, noted, "The negroes [are] now separated at a distance from the Indians on the Hammocks or the Hammock not far from Tampa Bay."[5]

Archaeological digs have confirmed that Angola was indeed an all-Black community with ties to Cuban fishermen who regularly visited the Tampa Bay area and Bahamian wreckers who prowled the coast looking for wrecked sea vessels to salvage. The first residents were refugees from the Patriot War, but more, many more, came after the destruction of the British-built fort on the Apalachicola River in 1816 and the First Seminole War in 1818. During the latter conflict, Gen. Andrew Jackson's invasion of Florida forced the inhabitants of Bowlegs Town as well as the Mikasuki settlements to decamp farther south. Angola was a fiercely proud community that sheltered warriors and soldiers who had proven their mettle against Americans and pro-American Creeks.[6]

As a counterpoint, elite planters, unsettled by the deteriorating security in East Florida, carried their labor force back into Georgia in the aftermath of the patriot invasion. When his desperate gamble to establish an independent republic failed, John Henry McIntosh, member of a prominent Georgia family and president of the ephemeral Territory of East Florida, moved over seventy men, women and children to the Satilla River, reporting, "Negroe soldiers on St. John's have an entire ascendancy [and] treat the white inhabitants with the utmost insolence."[7] More to the point, none who escaped from his control during the upheaval had been returned. Disgusted that white supremacy as he understood it was not to be the order of the day, he retreated to wait for the moment when Florida fell to the United States.

Others saw opportunity in the anarchy that followed the invasion and participated in the stealing of slaves and their sale for quick cash in St. Marys, Savannah, and Augusta.[8] It was a reverse pipeline. Samuel Alexander, a self-styled "colonel" and adventurer, assembled an odd collection of sixty frontiersmen, bandits, and thieves recruited in Georgia at Trader's Hill and led them across the St. Marys in a spree through northern Florida. Taking advantage of the vacuum of power, his men plundered, pillaged, and stole slaves and valuables, targeting former loyalists still in that colony. In the most notorious raid, several dozen men crossed over to Amelia Island, occupied the plantation of Richard Cashen, and set about leisurely robbing the estate of its valuables. Twenty-six enslaved people were carried back to Savannah and sold at auction.[9] A resident of Amelia Island accused Alexander of bringing into Georgia "large bodies of negroes stolen from the Floridean planters," while a resident of St. Marys told the governor about the widespread prevalence of slave stealing and kidnapping by Georgians and Floridians. According to them, several ploys were being used, including luring free Blacks across the St. Marys River under pretense of high wages, then grabbing and selling them. So brazen were these operations that a free Black man and his family living eight miles from St. Augustine were kidnapped and auctioned in Georgia, as were fighters who deserted from the Black militia.[10] As in earlier periods, the movement of African Americans on the Florida-Georgia coast included forced migration.

Alexander and his confederates were able to cover their tracks by a carefully coordinated campaign in which Georgians on both sides of the river wrote letters describing the threat posed by African Americans. Jacob Summerlin delivered the starkest warning when he intoned that the Black militia welcomed any and all fugitives who joined them. "The Negroes publically say that they will rule the Countrey," he noted in a deposition.[11] The reality was considerably different. Governor Sebastián Kindelán of East Florida kept three companies of "Havanna coloured troops" confined to St. Augustine after word arrived that the leader of the insurgents, Buckner Harris, and his lieutenants were in the office of Georgia governor David Mitchell soliciting the launch of another invasion. When rumors spread of the concentration of "colored troops" on Amelia Island, a local merchant pointed out that, of forty-two supposed soldiers, seventeen were mulatto sailors whose ship heading to St. Augustine had been blown off course by a hurricane, while

the remaining twenty-five were militiamen who had been sent to help restore order in the wake of the storming of Richard Cashen's plantation.[12]

Despite the chaos, or perhaps because of it, the breakdown in authority in East Florida triggered a new surge of flights from Georgia. Six men
fled from a plantation near Darien for the river forty-five miles distant. They
made it as far as the town of St. Marys, where the frontier-like conditions
promised enough space to allow them to act as if they were part of the local
scene, but the group was stopped, interrogated, and jailed. During the night,
a fugitive named John quietly slipped out of the converted house that served
as the jail and found a way to cross into Florida.[13] As a former sailor, he spoke
Spanish, English, and French and, once across the border, adopted the surname Spaniard as a testimony to his embrace of Hispanic culture. He was
stepping back into the world from which he came. Other groups followed.
Planters John Couper and James Nephew were taken by surprise when seven
people from their adjoining plantations on St. Simons banded together to
steal a boat to reach Amelia Island.[14] Women were probably participants
since the group was large, and older patterns of escape continued to hold true.

A worried Governor Mitchell warned President Madison, "Most of our
male negroes on the seaboard are restless and make many attempts to get
off to Augustine, and many have succeeded."[15] In his letter, the governor
stressed the need for constant guards and patrols along the Georgia coast
because of the disproportionate number of Black people to whites and the
ease with which the enslaved could slip away by water. A merchant on Amelia Island, Jose Hibberson, pointedly told the district attorney in Savannah,
"[If Spain were to reinstitute the policy of sanctuary,] in all probability one
half of the negroes of your sea coast would be over the St. Marys River in
less than a month."[16] Georgians too felt aggrieved. An American witnessed
two runaways arriving in a boat at Cowford, the crossing that is the center
of today's Jacksonville, and reported how the captain of the Black militia stationed there, himself a former fugitive, purchased the boat and gave them a
pass to St. Augustine to petition for their freedom.[17]

Matters took a dramatic turn when the British, looking for opportunities
during the War of 1812, began to spill into southern waterways. In the years
leading up to the war, maritime commerce and attendant rights on the high
seas had brought Great Britain and the United States to the point of conflict
over the impressment of American sailors by the Royal Navy and the restrictive Orders in Council intended to cut off trade with Napoleonic Europe.
Adding fuel to the fire was the resistance of Native peoples in the Northwest
Territory under the magnetic leadership of Tecumseh and their reaching out

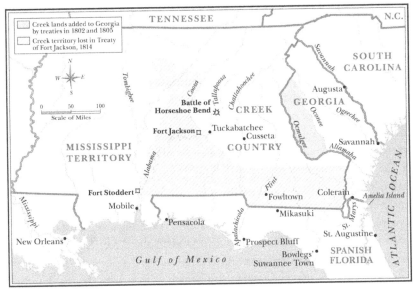

Georgia, the Southeast, and the War of 1812

to the British of Canada across national boundaries. For white southerners, Tecumseh's initiative reinforced their article of faith that the British were positioning themselves to seize East Florida and use it as a jumping off place for an invasion of the United States. Southerners in turn used that potent thought to cloak their dreams of territorial expansion into the Floridas.[18]

In fact, Great Britain was pursuing a strategy far different than the one imagined. Enmeshed in the final phases of the Napoleonic Wars and financially hard-pressed, the government under the Earl of Liverpool was more interested in harassing than in conquering America. During 1813 and 1814, British forces conducted a massive amphibious assault on the southern coasts of the United States that included an attempt to siphon off a sufficient number of slaves to undermine the American will to fight. The remarkably bold campaign stretched from the Chesapeake Bay to the Sea Islands of Georgia to Spanish West Florida and climaxed in Louisiana with the assault on New Orleans.[19]

Initially stationed off Chesapeake Bay, the Royal Navy under Admiral George Cockburn had limited aims that required no great commitment of ground troops. He sought to destroy American seaborne commerce, raid the many exposed towns and villages on the coast of Virginia and Maryland, and, most importantly, destabilize the plantation economy by welcoming the enslaved as soldiers and sailors.

The aim of recruiting a few Black soldiers, always an explosive issue, gradually expanded into something much larger. With a hard-won approval from London, Rear Admiral Alexander Cochrane, commander-in-chief of the North American naval station and Cockburn's superior, issued a proclamation on April 2, 1814, that announced freedom to all enslaved people who made it to vessels of the Royal Navy or to units of the British army operating along the coast. The proclamation was carefully nuanced in its promise that all fugitive slaves along the coasts of the United States could choose between entering "His Majesty's Sea or Land Forces" or "being sent as FREE Settlers to the British Possessions in North America or the West Indies, where they will meet with all due encouragement."[20] The two admirals claimed that any enslaved person who made it to a British ship, British territory, or British-occupied land would be granted freedom.[21] Walking a tightrope in their coastal offensive, the British looked to weaken the American will to fight without inciting a slave insurrection.

Despite the racism endemic to the British officer corps, several hundred fugitives were enrolled in the newly created Black Colonial Marines, a military unit with white officers. They had fled plantations along the Chesapeake Bay and were concentrated on Tyger Island in the bay, where they received training. In their first engagements, they acquitted themselves well, especially in the sacking of Washington, D.C., while those not used as soldiers or sailors found roles as guides, laborers, and spies.[22] For the first time since Lord Dunmore's Proclamation in Virginia in 1775, the large-scale recruitment and organization of fugitives into formal military units was being attempted on American soil, raising fundamental issues of race, freedom, rights, and military service. By the second decade of the nineteenth century, the use of Black troops, a commonplace in the British and Spanish empires, posed a terrifying prospect to Americans.[23]

In May 1814, a British expeditionary force landed at the Apalachicola River in West Florida to create a diversion for the American military and promptly dispatched Indians with Cochrane's proclamation of April 2. The response was immediate. The proclamation popped up on trees and buildings around Fernandina in East Florida, presumably posted by British merchant sailors eager to spread the news across St. Marys Sound into Georgia.[24] The citizens of Greene County registered their dismay at the invitation to the Black population to abandon their owners, while the Georgia General Assembly voiced its fears that the British might take St. Augustine and give protection "to all the outcasts of society ... ruffian bands [and] merciless savages, red and Black."[25] Their fears took on a concrete shape as news reached the state that the British were building a fort on the Apalachicola River and using it as a base to recruit a regiment of Black soldiers.

The expeditionary force on the Apalachicola River expanded into a supply base and stockade that officials in Spanish West Florida were in no position to resist. In May, British Admiral Alexander Cochrane had begun shifting his naval forces from the Chesapeake Bay to the Gulf Coast in preparation for an assault on New Orleans, key to the Mississippi. The fort began as a modest effort intended to slow the concentration of the American military on New Orleans and played on the rapidly developing racial tensions in the Southeast.

Cochrane put ashore George Woodbine, a sometime merchant who was brevetted as a captain in the Royal Marines, with instructions to recruit and establish a "Regiment of Colonial Marines from the American Blacks," five hundred strong, as well as Creeks fleeing the carnage of a civil war in which the Americans had intervened.[26] The fort opened a wide range of opportunities for people of African descent while threatening the racial balance in the region by offering the possibility of an alliance between African Americans and Natives.[27]

Woodbine recruited a cadre of Creeks and Seminoles to distribute Cochrane's proclamation throughout the Southeast, and, although the effectiveness of this initiative cannot be measured, the news of the fort spread rapidly. A few days after arriving on the Apalachicola River, Woodbine was already reporting, "Negroes are flocking in from the states." Reports surfaced of "a party of negroes, upwards of 200 men," who had "run away from the States" and were on the march.[28] To a planter in Camden County, the ever-vigilant Benjamin Hawkins identified a Mikasuki chief as giving "encouragement to negroes to run to them."[29]

Command of the outpost on the Apalachicola soon passed to a regular officer of the Royal Marines, Lt. Col. Edward Nicolls, who brought a deeply felt antislavery ideology forged by witnessing desperate scenes of fleeing slaves in West Africa and warfare in the Caribbean. He appeared with one hundred seasoned Royal Marines and a personal commitment to the abolitionist cause that made a deep imprint on the emerging community at Prospect Bluff. Stationed off the Gulf Coast in preparation for the New Orleans campaign, Admiral Cochrane urged Nicolls to "encourage ... by every means the Emigration of Negroes from Georgia and the Carolinas."[30] Recruiting enslaved people throughout the entire South became the overriding goal, even more so than appealing to the dissident Creek population. To a Creek chief, Benjamin Hawkins denounced the English officer as a second Bowles whose "negro stealing" had to be stopped and urged that Native Americans "take or destroy all white and Black people" found armed.[31]

By the end of 1814, enslaved people on the Georgia coast were well aware of the fort on the Apalachicola. In successive trips to St. Augustine, Woodbine brought back several dozen African Americans. One observer noted that, after his stay in St. Augustine that included a visit to the governor, "many negroes deserted from their masters and many complaints were made about him and soon after his departure, no less than eighty followed him . . . and . . . in passing thro' Indian towns within the Jurisdiction of Florida he picked up a few more."[32] The appeal went beyond his physical presence. Individual families set out on foot. Boatswain, Rose, and their two children escaped from the Perpall plantation on the St. Johns River and made their way to the Bluff "in consequence of having understood, that all negro slaves joining the British troops in the Floridas or America would be made free." Nor were they all field hands. Robin, a carpenter and skilled craftsman who worked in an urban setting hiring himself out, preferred freedom in an unknown setting to his relatively autonomous status.[33]

The Creek War of 1813 and 1814 complicated the opportunities and dilemmas that African Americans faced in the Southeast. Ever since the American Revolution, the Creek Nation had been undergoing an acute identity crisis as it grappled with the challenges of how best to adapt to multiple pressures forcing change. The issues revolved around the erosion of Creek power relative to expanding American settlements, the crumbling of a fragile hunting economy as deer became scarce, and the mounting pressures for assimilation generated by the "plan of civilization" drawn up by the Indian agent, Benjamin Hawkins. In 1813, a fateful year for the nation, a majority of warriors in the Upper Towns rose up against both American encroachment and an emerging elite of Natives who embodied the acquisitive instincts so at variance with an older world.[34] Called "Red Sticks" because of their brightly painted war clubs and animated by Tecumseh and other prophets of pan-Nativism, they repudiated white culture by killing thousands of cattle, burning houses and outbuildings around Native plantations, destroying spinning wheels and forges, and harassing the "old chiefs" whom they deemed betrayers of their nation's heritage.[35]

The war split towns and social groupings apart.[36] What began as a civil war soon morphed into a regional conflict that led to the involvement of Americans only too anxious to intervene. Three separate columns of American troops from Georgia, Tennessee, and Mississippi advanced into Creek country to protect American interests in principle but more easily to take advantage of the circumstances and expand territory. Skirmishes and raids by the Red Sticks ensued almost nonstop, not with the aim of defeating the Americans militarily but rather to force advancing settlers back behind the actual boundaries. In March 1814, a final, climactic battle took place at To-hopeka (Horseshoe Bend). Gen. Andrew Jackson inflicted a crushing de-feat that cost the Creeks as many as eight hundred casualties and extracted twenty-two million acres of land in the devastating Treaty of Fort Jack-son that took land even from pro-American Creeks who had fought for Jackson.[37]

Many of the defeated Red Sticks and their Black allies headed south into Spanish Florida, where they rallied around the small British force in the fort on the Apalachicola River. Numbers of enslaved people in the Upper Towns slipped away as well to join their peers at the Prospect Bluff fort. A slave of Chief J. Stedham disappeared, then returned with "negro March" to recruit and lead fourteen of his peers to the British.[38] Hawkins reported to Jackson that five of his slaves had either run off or were stolen, while his neighbor Timothy Barnard lost five as well.[39] More disturbing, Hawkins relayed news that a war party of twenty-eight people, half red and half Black, had been sighted on their way to attack a white settlement.[40] Hawkins was told by his Indian "spies" of a nefarious plan to "free and prepare for war all our Blacks in this quarter" and relayed this twisted information to a receptive Jackson.[41]

Excitement built up on the Georgia coast when rumors raced through the Lowcountry that Capt. George Woodbine was advancing toward St. Marys at the head of several hundred Indians, rumors that made real the emergence of an Indian-Black alliance around Prospect Bluff.[42] The threat, however, came not from Native Americans and their allies but from the Royal Navy. On November 24, 1814, a British frigate appeared off Jekyll Is-land escorted by a brig and a schooner. Royal marines went ashore, seized livestock and crops, and liberated twenty-eight slaves, including Big Peter, the driver for the DuBignon plantation.[43] Soon thereafter, at the begin-ning of 1815, Admiral Cockburn's entire fleet appeared off the Sea Islands of Georgia. His aim was quite modest: to support Admiral Cochrane's attempt on New Orleans by creating a diversion. He was to occupy the Sea Islands, encourage enslaved people to desert their masters, and threaten an attack on Savannah in the hopes of drawing away American forces from Louisiana.[44]

For the first time since the Revolution, enslaved Georgians saw Black sol-diers in a position of relative power.[45] Cockburn led a contingent of Black marines onto Cumberland Island and set soldiers and sailors to digging en-trenchments and building forts on the estate of the venerated revolution-

ary war general Nathanael Greene. The enslaved population watched in awe
as a mixed force of Black marines, resplendent in red uniforms, secured the
site alongside members of the Royal Marines. A naval surgeon recalled years
later how the 149 slaves on the plantation stepped forward as one body to
take advantage of the chance to "emigrate" and gain their freedom. It was
a quiet, orderly process. "The overseer, a Black man, carried the keys of the
outhouses to his mistress yesterday," the surgeon recalled, "and told her he
intended to join the British."[46] It was a decorous proceeding, so opposite to
the scenes during the chaotic days during the Revolution when the British
invaded Savannah.[47]

Among those stepping forward was fifty-year-old Ned Simmons, who
enrolled without hesitation in the putative "Black Company" and four weeks
later formally enlisted in the Third Battalion of Colonial Marines. He received a red uniform designed for the Colonial Marines and a weapon and
then began his training as a soldier.[48] The Colonial Marines were the brain-
child of the fertile mind of Cockburn, who was seeking a way to acquire
the manpower so desperately needed. They "are really very fine fellows," he
later wrote. "They have induced me to alter the bad opinion I had of the
whole of their race and now I really believe these we are training, will neither shew want of zeal or courage when employed by us in attacking their
old masters."[49]

The ranks soon filled out, with African Americans from all the Sea Islands stepping forward and assuming the responsibility of men called on
to fight for their freedom and for their liberators. When a Florida planter,
Zephaniah Kingsley, arrived on Cumberland Island to claim the several
dozen people that had fled his plantation, he remarked on "the magical
transformation of his own negroes, whom he left in the field only a few
hours before, into regular soldiers, of good discipline and good appearance."
He speculated what a few hundred more Royal Marines might have accom-
plished, "notwithstanding all the care and vigilance that was used to prevent
desertion."[50] His intuitive grasp of the issues found little echo among his fellow planters.

General Greene had acquired Ned Simmons shortly after the Revolution, either as part of the original group he had purchased in St. Augustine
or from the brief time that Greene spent in South Carolina.[51] He worked
at Mulberry Grove, the rice plantation that the loyalist John Graham had
turned into a showcase and a grateful state had given to Greene. In 1791, Simmons was selected as one of the handful of men to carry President George
Washington from Mulberry Grove to Savannah and through the streets of

Black Colonial Marines on Cumberland Island, February 1815. During the War of 1812, Admiral George Cockburn formed a corps of formerly enslaved Black soldiers to serve alongside British troops on the Georgia coast as well as in the Chesapeake Bay. Illustration by Frederick Mast.

the town, a celebratory journey filled with cheering crowds, fireworks, and artillery salutes.[52] It was a moment Simmons would remember throughout his life with great pride. After Greene died of a heatstroke, his widow, Caty, remarried and eventually moved with her new husband, Phineas Miller, and her three children to Cumberland to recoup the family's fortunes.[53]

Simmons's roots were deep in the slave community. A Baptist, apparently he was influenced by the missionary work of the Savannah River Association of Black Baptist Churches, a dynamic religious movement that was reshaping the cultural life of Black people along the coast and had reached all the way to the St. Marys River. Those from Cumberland Island who eventually migrated to Trinidad and Nova Scotia under British auspices created Baptist churches as part of re-creating their lives in a new setting.[54] Until the War of 1812, Simmons had lived within the bounds of a plantation system where monotony, routine, and harsh treatment were the norm and made himself a valuable member of the enslaved population of Louise Greene Shaw, an early advocate of a paternal system of management meant to incorporate slaves into the larger "family." Ned Simmons had no hesitation about turning his back on a system that was oppressive by definition and denied his humanity. The precious clues of his life point to a man animated by a fierce drive to assert his identity, nothing more so than his attempt to learn to read at age one hundred.[55]

Black Georgians on St. Simons Island shared Simmons's joyful reaction when, in 1815, three British naval vessels landed at the main dock to offer a long-hoped-for chance at freedom. No groups had more cause to break the chains of oppression than the enslaved of Pierce Butler, former senator from South Carolina, by this time resident of Philadelphia, who had assembled the largest slave force to be found on the Georgia coast. He held in bondage five hundred people by 1806 and several hundred more by the time of the war. Immensely talented but with an arrogance to match his talents, Butler aimed at creating nothing less than agricultural factories on St. Simons, Little St. Simons, and Tide islands, an empire of mud and water that rivaled in size and output the biggest of the plantation complexes in South Carolina. A man of giant ambitions and emotions, he personified the growing desire to produce commodities of high quality for the English market, generate a handsome profit, and exercise direct control over the lives of his enslaved people.[56]

Under the tutelage of Roswell King, a businessman turned plantation manager, the Butler slaves may have been some of the best clothed and fed on any plantation but they were under constant surveillance, their movement limited, and their every action controlled. The profit-conscious King became an extreme example of a new kind of discipline on plantations along the Georgia coast. The most distinctive feature was an absolute prohibition against visitation of neighboring plantations, keeping his labor force self-contained and isolated. Although the Cannon's Point plantation of John Couper was separated from Hampton by tiny Jones Creek and a narrow belt of marshland, to most of Butler slaves it was unknown territory.[57] The wife of a planter in Darien commented decades later, "The Butler negroes were a race apart. They never, until years after the [civil] war, mingled with other negroes."[58] King broke the power of Butler's long-time drivers by trading away their leader and grinding down the others, with Hampton and the plantations on Little St. Simons and Butler Island evolving into forced labor camps with no exit. He could boast to his watchful employer that no enslaved person had run away for over several years, a clear exaggeration but close enough to the truth to underscore the type of community that the settlements had become. An old habit had seemingly been eradicated.[59]

In 1815, virtually the entire enslaved population of Hampton Plantation, the centerpiece of Butler's empire and the people whose loyalty and contentment King had long boasted, walked off, never to return.[60] It was a peaceful moment when families were faced with the necessity of making hard choices about uncertain futures. With the British defeat at New Orleans on January 8, the whole effort of Cockburn on the Georgia coast had lost its military purpose. The British admiral remained determined to inflict as much pain as possible on the Americans. Naval forces continued to liberate enslaved people. Locked up for several days by a naval officer for his outspoken opposition, Roswell King was troubled by reports that his slaves appeared to have "a wish to try their New Master."[61]

After his release, King hurried to intercept one last group trudging down the road from Hampton Plantation to the small community of Frederica, where naval vessels were docked ready to take them to Cumberland, then Bermuda. In characteristic fashion, he planted himself in front of their path and argued why they should return. He reported to Butler: "I tried to reason with some of the most sensible of the Negroes not to be so foolish and deluded ... I found none of the negroes insolent to me, they appeared sorry, solemn, and often crying, they appeared to be infatuated to a degree of madness.... Many went off and left their children, others carried off children from their parents and all relations, some left their wives and others their husbands."[62] His report to Butler captures a key feature of the departure, the consciousness of what was at stake and the lack of anger on the part of the enslaved. Theirs was a thoughtful, considered decision. The last part of his statement suggests that families did not necessarily leave together, but the fact that virtually everyone on the Hampton plantation quit that space shows that King missed the point. Those departing included 34 children, 36 adolescents and teenagers, 57 men and women, and an additional 11 over forty-five years of age, for a total of 138 people.[63]

Among them were older people who had served Butler long and well at his home in Philadelphia as well as on St. Simons, like Molly, "a very deserving, good woman," and Old Betty ("who is free already [and] does as she pleases"), while being provided a home and food. King was crushed that only eight field hands had elected to remain. Virtually all of the skilled craftsmen, from shoemakers and tanners to blacksmiths and bricklayers, had decamped.

He could only find consolation in describing how Sancho, an artisan, stubbornly refused to go, even when his mother took all his clothes and blankets from him, leaving him "naked" and alone.[64]

The only success in halting the flight of the Black population came not from white managers or planters pleading their case in the fashion of Roswell King but rather from the lead driver at Cannon's Point belonging to the Scotsman John Couper. Tom was a practicing Muslim thought to be from a village on the Niger River in the "Foolah nation." He planted himself in the path of those departing and described his experiences as a slave in the British Caribbean, where the brutal discipline of the sugar plantation made for a strong counter-narrative. He raised the paralyzing prospect that some might find themselves back in slavery through trickery by an untrustworthy people and persuaded many of the fugitives to turn back.[65] He had touched on a sensitive point. When Admiral Cockburn recruited escaping slaves to fight for the British in the Chesapeake, he found that few if any would volunteer for the West Indian Regiments for fear of being dragooned into slavery in the British Caribbean, where conditions were exceptionally harsh and life expectancy short.[66] About a third of the Couper slaves turned back.

The one company of the Colonial Marines who engaged in combat with Georgians were from the units originating in the Chesapeake Bay, already trained, veterans of several engagements, and eager to go into battle. That moment came when Cockburn sent them to assist in the taking of the town of St. Marys on January 13, 1815. Their mission was to secure it for the arrival of Maj. Edward Nicolls and his mixed force of British soldiers, Native American allies, and freed Blacks thought to be advancing eastward from the stockade on the Apalachicola River. As the marines moved into the woods ringing the town, a rear guard of American forces delivered the first fusillade on men made conspicuous by their bright red uniforms. "The Yankee riflemen fired at our men in ambush," a white officer wrote to a relative. "Blackey, on the impulse of the moment, left the ranks and pursued them into the woods, fighting like heroes." One incident caught the mood. "A poor Yankee, disarmed, begged for mercy. Blackey replied, 'He no come in the bush for mercy,' and immediately shot him dead." The Black soldiers had no idea of giving quarter to captured Americans, the writer noted, and it was with great difficulty that the officers prevented them from putting prisoners to death.[67] The encounter was the first such inside the state of Georgia since the Revolution, made all the more remarkable by the fact that Black troops had outnumbered the Whites.

In his time on Cumberland Island, Admiral Cockburn had become so committed to the idea of punishing the Americans for their seemingly reckless war that he continued raiding well after learning the news of the British defeat at New Orleans. By the third week of January, the news reached Cockburn as did the announcement of the peace terms at Ghent, yet he did not stop his raids until mid-February and continued to accept runaways on his vessels until March 18, the day on which he sailed away.[68]

The numbers of freedom seekers were staggering. On Cumberland, virtually all the slaves, 236, placed themselves under British protection. On St. Simons, the three principal plantations lost 436 people, 138 from Butler's Hampton, 238 from the Hamilton Plantation of James Hamilton; and 60 from the Cannon's Point Plantation of John Couper.[69] According to military records, 1,455 people left with the fleet and another 250 died before the departure for a total of 1,705 Black people from the Sea Islands and adjacent areas on the mainland; this was in addition to 200 from Spanish Florida.[70] The admiral allowed slaveholders to board the vessels that held their "property" and make an appeal to return, but virtually none did so. A truce between the admiral and representatives of the United States specified that only those persons present on a vessel of the Royal Navy at 11:00 p.m., February 17, the moment the treaty was signed in Washington, were recognized as free.[71] All others would be returned to their masters. Eighty-one people were put ashore on Cumberland. Tragically, Ned Simmons, still serving on the island in the Colonial Marines after February 17, was forced to surrender his red uniform and weapon and resume his status as a slave belonging to the Greene estate because of this maddening technicality. He did not gain his freedom until the Civil War, when, at age one hundred, he crossed St. Marys Sound to federally occupied territory in Florida.[72]

Cockburn's departure from the Georgia coast left the planters on the Sea Islands ever more convinced of the ingratitude and fickleness of Black people. Roswell King summed up the widespread feeling of betrayal when he wrote his employer, "To treat Negroes with humanity is like giving Pearls to Swine, it is throwing away Value and giving insult and ingratitude in return."[73] Elite planters interpreted the bolting of their labor force as proof of their fickleness, laziness, and ingratitude. They were incapable of seeing any other motive. By way of contrast, white Georgians in the interior of the state never felt threatened and never saw the episode as anything more than a naval incursion. News of the negotiations coming from Ghent had a tremendously calming effect.

The threat that focused everyone's attention was the fort at Prospect Bluff on the Apalachicola where hundreds of African Americans from many directions were assembling, many from Georgia. The white population had good reason to be concerned. Even if Admiral Cockburn's hostility toward slavery was implacable, its impact was necessarily limited. Col. Edward Nicolls's antislavery crusade threatened to plant a bomb whose impact had the potential to touch all of the South. In the twelve brief months that he commanded the residents of the fort, Nicolls succeeded in creating a community with a disciplined military force, an organized polity, and the ability to sustain itself through agriculture and trade.[74]

As orders came to withdraw his troops in the late spring of 1815, the abolitionist reminded the residents of Prospect Bluff that they had earned their freedom in service to the British military and could look forward to perpetual freedom and lands in Canada and Trinidad. He left an arsenal of weapons in a powder magazine and, just as importantly, the assurance that these men and women were subjects of the British Empire. Prospect Bluff became the largest and most successful maroon community to exist in the United States, resembling those in the Caribbean yet one of a kind in its commitment to a formal antislavery ideology.[75] Unlike any other, it reflected the revolutionary currents sweeping the Caribbean and Atlantic worlds.

When Nicolls and his soldiers withdrew in April, the fort sheltered approximately five hundred former slaves. Estimates vary, but historian Nathaniel Millett believes that three hundred to four hundred men were organized into a fighting force, and the presence of women, children, and men incapable of military service carried the total number to six hundred to seven hundred people at its height.[76] The presence of Red Stick Creeks seeking refuge from the disaster of their civil war may have brought that number to nearly one thousand residents. When the British departed, the Creeks disappeared into the Florida landscape.

The remaining community embraced a remarkable cross-section of the Black population in the Southeast: many who had escaped directly from Georgia, others from East Florida, Africans from West Florida who spoke Spanish and were often of Caribbean origin, those coming from Indian country, slaves stolen from Louisiana, and a number from Mississippi and Tennessee. In December 1815, a leading deerskin merchant, John Innerarity, grumbled, "A considerable number of negroes have escaped from Georgia to that occursed hornet's nest at Prospect Bluff."[77] The following April, Gen. John Floyd reported to the governor of Georgia that the number of "refugee" slaves from the state was rapidly growing and that the seeds of emancipation were being planted insidiously. "Since the restoration of peace," he warned, "many of the most active and intelligent male slaves have fled from their owners, and joined these outlaws . . . as to render its frequency alarming." During the previous week, three "fellows" had gone over from plantations along the Satilla River, while rumors circulated that a Mrs. Gibbons had "not a fellow left on her plantation."[78] In the extraordinary mix of people, every element of the African diaspora was represented, a potent mixture of cultures, languages, and backgrounds. Their hopes reflected a blending of all the events surrounding the War of 1812, Nicoll's fierce antislavery rhetoric, and the ideas astir in the revolutionary Atlantic.[79]

For the Spanish, the "Negro fort" revealed the near collapse of their authority in all of Florida in a way that could no longer be hidden from view. For Black people and Indians, it represented a chance to establish an independent community based on a seeming British promise to return and assist their allies. For Americans, its very existence was a provocation, an invitation to enslaved people to throw off the chains of servitude, spreading the dangerous rhetoric of antislavery and acting as an unwelcomed brake on their expansionist aims.[80] To General Floyd, the danger was pressing: "The seeds of Emancipation are already sown, and are taking a strong hold in a Situation so well Calculated to encourage its growth."[81]

The existence of the mixed-race fort at Prospect Bluff was brief. In the spring of 1816, the U.S. Army established Fort Scott at the confluence of the Chattahoochee and Flint Rivers as a first step in containing the real or imagined threat from Prospect Bluff. The following summer, a flotilla of U.S. naval gunboats made their way up the Apalachicola River to reduce the fort while a small party of soldiers approached from the eastward side. When a flag of no-surrender and a British flag were raised over the bluff, followed by a warning shot, the lead gunboat returned fire. Of the first five shots, one ball that had been heated in its galley apparently rolled into the powder magazine and caused a massive explosion that was heard as far away as Pensacola, sixty miles distant. In one stroke, the fort was virtually erased. In line with other histories, Gene Allen Smith and Frank Owsley suggest that 270 of the 334 defenders died, while Nathaniel Millett, who has exhaustively studied the maroons at the fort, speculates that most of the defenders had already melted away into Seminole lands.[82] Twenty-six Blacks were captured and returned to slavery. The leader of the maroon community, Garçon, survived but was taken by the pro-American Creeks and tortured to death in unspeakably cruel fashion. By the end of the summer of 1816, the borders of freedom around Georgia had been reduced to a shadow.[83]

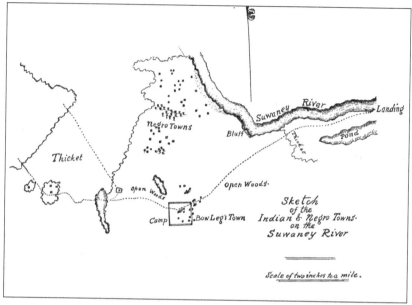

Hugh Young's map of the Black villages around Seminole settlements, 1818.
It is thought that Captain Young, a topographical engineer with General
Andrew Jackson, made this sketch showing the relationship between Seminole
and Black settlements on the Suwannee River during the First Seminole
War. Source: Alan K. Craig and Christopher S. Peebles, "Captain Young's
Sketch Map, 1818," *Florida Historical Quarterly* 48, no. 2 (Fall 1968): 1–4.

In the following months, the final phase in a forty-year period of movements across the Southeast was more nearly a retreat from the Black communities that had dotted the borders of Georgia. Survivors of the disaster
at the fort fled to various points deeper into Florida. One group headed to
the maroon community of Angola near Tampa Bay in southwestern Florida,
providing a valuable addition to those who had already come from Paynes
Town and other villages in the Alachua Prairie.[84] Others headed to a new
community called Fowltown, part of the Mikasuki network of villages but
located near the Flint River on territory by this time claimed by the United
States by virtue of the Treaty of Fort Jackson. Most, however, came to the
villages under the direct authority of Bowlegs, the much younger brother
of King Payne killed in the Patriot War.[85] A planter in Chatham County
claimed to have upward of forty slaves at the Suwannee towns and a few
around Mikasuki and speculated that at least two hundred slaves were there
from his "neighborhood."[86]

At Bowlegs Town, the refugees replicated the world that they had known at Prospect Bluff.[87] Rebuilding as best they could their maroon community, they founded loosely associated villages along the Suwannee River and Lake Miccosukee, planted crops, and re-created the political and military structure of the fort. For their leader, they chose a fellow refugee, Nero, who eventually became a chief adviser to Bowlegs while his colleague Abraham became a remarkable Seminole leader who achieved national prominence during the Second Seminole War.[88] Soon after their arrival, a Seminole told a mestizo friendly to the Americans, George Perryman, that the maroons were mustering arms, parading with regular discipline, and "very strict in punishing violators to the military rules."[89] Woodbine returned from the Bahamas in the fall of 1816 and again in the spring of 1817 to encourage their efforts, leading one resident of nearby Camden County to worry, "He will no doubt use his influence to do the worst he can."[90]

In retaliation for the destruction of Prospect Bluff, the refugees joined with Seminoles and Red Stick Creeks in making raids along the Georgia frontier. Reports regularly came to the Americans at Fort Scott of the many horses, cattle, and hogs taken from settlers in Camden County by "negroes and Indians" who spoke "in the most contemptuous way of Americans."[91] The most notorious incident took place in Camden when a party of Creeks killed and scalped a Mrs. Garrett and her two children in retaliation for the murder of Big Tom, a Creek in Seminole country, by whites who had crossed the border for plunder.[92] Throughout the year, the raids continued without pause.

Situated on the eastern side of the Flint River across from Fort Scott and now inside Georgia on land seized through the Treaty of Fort Jackson, Fowltown became the flash point.[93] When the commander of the fort received intelligence that the Seminoles were being strengthened by "the addition of every runaway from Georgia able to get to them," he made humiliating demands on its chief, Neamathla. When the chief refused to comply, he sent 250 men across the river to clear the settlement. In the ensuing firefight, four warriors were killed, while the rest executed a swift retreat to the safety of their towns in East Florida.[94]

The pressing question became whether the American forces at Fort Scott would advance into Florida and, if so, under what rules of war, since this act meant crossing an international boundary with hostile intent. The ambush of a U.S. naval vessel making its way up the Apalachicola River made the question easier to resolve, at least in the minds of Americans. In a brutal assault motivated by a desire for revenge, the warriors from Fowltown boarded the boat, slaughtered over thirty soldiers, and captured and tortured to death women and children in Spanish waters.[95] That event changed the equation.

Receiving instructions, Andrew Jackson departed from Nashville and arrived at Fort Scott on March 9, 1818, with approximately twenty-five hundred men, consisting of federal troops, militiamen from Georgia and Tennessee, and pro-American Creeks.[96] Interpreting President James Monroe's orders in the broadest possible sense, the general crossed into Spanish Florida, destroyed the network of Mikasuki towns, occupied the Spanish fort of St. Marks, and, after a short pause, launched out against the towns under the authority of Bowlegs and the Black settlements around them. The Battle of the Suwannee proved to be the decisive engagement. Black and Native warriors held their position on the Suwannee River's west bank long enough to permit their families and themselves to escape into the peninsula. Millett suggests that more than three hundred Black soldiers fought skillfully and bravely before executing the well-planned escape. In the aftermath, the town was destroyed, as were the surrounding villages. The Scottish merchant Alexander Arbuthnot, who supplied Native Americans with provisions and arms originating in the Bahamas, had written to a young Englishman, "The main drift of the Americans is to destroy the Black people of Swany." Arbuthnot instructed the Englishman to tell Bowlegs to beware, but the man failed to follow through.[97]

The last grand movement of free Blacks in the Southeast was a purely defensive effort. While the Seminoles retreated farther down the Florida Peninsula to avoid a major loss of life, many Black Seminoles found shelter in the maroon community of Angola, east of Tampa Bay. In August 1818, only a few weeks after Jackson's incursion, an aide to Jackson reported, "The negroes and Indians driven from Micosukey and Suwaney towns have directed their march to that quarter." The aide warned, "The bay of Tampa is the last rallying spot of the disaffected negroes and Indians and the only favorable point where a communication can be had with Spanish and English emissaries."[98] If the primary purpose of the expedition was to eliminate the "Negro villages" of the Seminoles, it failed. Angola remained in contact with Edward Nicolls in the Bahamas and with Spanish officials who on at least one occasion funneled ammunition to them. Constant flight had not dented the steely resolve to resist. A literate shipwright named Harry, originally owned by Forbes & Company in West Florida, followed a circuitous path. He escaped from slavery to the Prospect Bluff fort, lived there a year, fled to Seminole villages along the Suwannee before they were blown up, and then, after Jackson's invasion, decamped for the Tampa Bay area, where he was last reported to be drilling one hundred warriors.[99]

Making Jackson a hero to the American public if not his own government, the spectacular incursion into Florida in 1818 accelerated the ongoing talks between John Quincy Adams, secretary of state, and Luis de Onís, the Spanish minister in Washington.[100] Within months, Onís and Secretary Adams reached an agreement whereby Spain ceded East Florida to the United States and renounced all claim to West Florida. The Treaty of Adams-Onís in February 1819 transferred all of Florida to the United States, but Spain delayed the actual conveyance to maintain a degree of leverage in its dealings with the Americans. Named the first territorial governor in 1821, Andrew Jackson immediately asked for permission to send federal troops to disband Angola, and, when permission was refused, he arranged for a party of Lower Creek warriors to wipe out that community. Raiding Natives from Coweta took 120 prisoners and carried many back to be restored to their masters or resold into slavery. Survivors made their way to the Florida Keys, where fishermen picked them up and took them to the Bahamas. Many ended on Andros Island, the largest of the Bahamian islands, where they succeeded in creating a permanent community at Red Bays that sustained itself through cutting timber, gathering sponges, and picking up wrecked property.[101]

At the same time, prosperous Amelia Island and the port of Fernandina proved a tempting target for an assortment of adventurers, filibusters, and privateers attracted by the collapse of Spanish authority. They mirrored a whole class of people who had appeared throughout the Americas at the end of the Napoleonic Wars and trumpeted revolution while pursuing private ends. The decaying Spanish empire attracted ambitious revolutionaries from other countries in the Americas searching for power and plunder, and Amelia Island was no exception.[102] As part of this breakdown, Black sailors, soldiers, and adventurers made one last appearance a few miles from the Georgia coast.

In June 1817, Gen. Gregor MacGregor, acting in the name of Latin American insurgent forces, landed on Amelia with one hundred sailors and adventurers, established a shadowy government, and created a base for privateering attacks on Spanish shipping.[103] A flamboyant Scotsman, he had served with the Duke Wellington in the Peninsular War and Simón Bolívar in Venezuela and left when he quarreled with Bolívar over advancement. Desperate for money from the moment of his arrival, he arranged for the sale of thirty-one slaves of Spanish planters who fled the island when he arrived, and he authorized small parties of volunteers who degenerated into roving bands that plundered the mainland on their own account. When one such party approached a plantation on the Matanzas River to seize field hands as prize booty, the careless insurgents mistook soldiers from the Black militia for laborers only to be quickly captured.[104] When the United States disrupted supplies from reaching the island, MacGregor turned over command to his lieutenants and sailed away for adventures elsewhere.

The vacuum was quickly filled. On September 17, another revolutionary and privateer, Luis-Michel Aury, landed on Amelia with a force of "about one-hundred and thirty brigand negroes" ("a set of desperate and bloody dogs") to pick up the pieces of MacGregor's enterprise.[105] With the coming of a multiracial, international band of sailors and pirates, Aury represented a more serious challenge to Spanish authority. An adventurer of the first order, he was a well-established privateer who had served with revolutionary governments in Latin America, participated in an attempt to overthrow Spanish rule in Mexico, and had a tenuous claim to represent the Republic of Mexico. Backed by a loosely associated group of Americans in New Orleans who were interested in ending Spanish rule in all the Floridas, Aury occupied Amelia and Galveston Islands simultaneously.[106]

Of the approximately four hundred sailors and soldiers who accompanied Aury, Blacks made up probably less than a quarter, but that number still represented around eighty to one hundred armed free Black men on the border of the United States. Further alarming Americans was the news that many came from Haiti and were assumed to be animated by the same ideologies that had inspired the Africans who participated in the German Coast uprising in Louisiana in 1810, the largest slave rebellion in American history. Newspapers referred to the men on Amelia Island as "St. Domingo Rovers" and the "brigands who participated in the horrors of St. Domingo."[107]

Aury's downfall came from his not-too-subtle attempt to convert Fernandina into a major slaving depot and funnel Africans into the new Alabama Territory and Georgia. In an attempt to evade U.S. naval forces, his men used rowboats to convey two or three Africans at a time, headed small craft up tidal creeks, and managed to take larger craft up the St. Marys to offload them in a remote corner of Camden County. Of the ten vessels known to be carrying slaves into Fernandina, the USS *Saranac* intercepted six but missed four, with five hundred to six hundred men, women, and children on board.[108] Georgia intercepted another eighty "African negroes" on the border of Creek territory. They had been purchased on Amelia Island, taken up the St. Marys River, carried along the Chehaw trail, and seized near the Creek Agency of federal agent Benjamin Hawkins, where they were to be funneled into the newly declared Alabama Territory.[109]

President Monroe initially followed a wait-and-see attitude toward MacGregor and Aury, but, as pressure built up, he ordered a combination of U.S. naval and army units to invade and occupy the island. The unopposed landing took place on December 22, 1817. Overpowered, Aury's mixed force of Haitians and adventurers were allowed to sail away peacefully. Debate over the wisdom of the U.S. invasion dominated public discussions throughout the United States in the first months of 1818, fueling a battle between Congress and the White House that laid the groundwork for the eventual takeover of Florida through the Adams-Onís Treaty. Although the agreement was signed in February 1819, Spain delayed surrendering Florida to the United States to gain better conditions and finally turned over the colony in 1821.

As the old order gave way, a significant part of the free Black community in St. Augustine sought refuge in Havana. A notable contingent of free Black (Moreno) and mixed-blood (Pardo) militiamen in St. Augustine understood all too clearly that the racial policies of the United States would limit their freedoms and reduce many to slavery. They and their families elected to accompany the Spanish back to Cuba. It was a sad voyage that paralleled the experience of an earlier generation of former fugitive slaves who chose to accompany the Spanish to Havana after the British had occupied Florida at the end of the Seven Years' War.

However, the parallel was only partial. In 1763, several dozen Pardo and Moreno families had accompanied families of Spanish descent in Florida to make new lives in Havana. They found themselves assigned to marginal land outside the capital eking out an impoverished existence. That mistake was not repeated. Most of the families settled in the Barrio Colón in Havana, where many of the men worked as stevedores on the docks or as artisans. Families clung to families. The center of gravity consisted of the sons and daughters of the dead Isaac Bacas, who had escaped slavery in Georgia at the end of the Revolution: Andres and his wife Eva Fish (and their four children); Justo with his four children; Catalina (Kitty), married to Juan Morel from Ossabaw, and her family; and Teresa, wife of Pedro Ysnardy, the illegitimate mixed-blood son of Florida's royal treasurer, Miguel Ysnardy. John or Juan Morel, an Ossabaw fugitive who had arrived by 1797, may well have been inspired by the example of Titus.[110] All these men had been part of the Black militia serving under the dominant figure of Prince Whitten. It was a cohesive community that had embraced Hispanic culture, although many still spoke English as their first language.[111]

The acquisition of East Florida by the United States signaled the shutting down of the "borders of freedom" that had surrounded Georgia for forty years, the rapid amalgamation of the Southeast into American culture with its devastating racial classification of people, and a dramatic reduction of ties with the Atlantic world that limited the spatial reach of the region. Atlantic history narrowed into the channels set by the rise of a cotton-dominated economy and an expanding slave system controlled by a powerful planter class and a slave population growing through natural increase.[112]

Underground Railroad

By the conclusion of the First Seminole War, the taming of a troublesome borderland for white Southerners was far from complete, but the outcome no longer in doubt. From the moment the Revolutionary War concluded, the United States had pushed relentlessly to expand the southeastern boundaries of the republic to secure supremacy over an intricate web of multiracial and multicultural societies. Hispanic peoples, French Creoles, Muskogeans, Seminoles, former loyalists, ambitious adventurers, and African Americans who had discovered a niche with other people found their room for maneuvering either eliminated or seriously constrained. The multiple conflicts involved in the War of 1812 created the last great set of opportunities for Black Georgians to escape into this other world. The tragic aftermath marked the decisive moment in the transformation of the emerging cotton frontier and the consequent closing off of most avenues of escape.[1]

In the wake of the bloody Creek War, Congress granted independent territorial status to the newly designated Alabama Territory and touched off an onslaught of backwoods settlers and speculators elbowing their way not only into the territory along the Alabama and Tombigbee River valleys but also the lands and villages of the Creeks. The cotton frontier moved westward as settlers led carts full of their possessions, including enslaved people, onto former Native lands.[2] The Seminoles were equally hard-pressed following the transfer of Florida from Spain to the United States in 1821, opening the way for American settlers to move into fertile sections of what had been East and West Florida. The large Mikasuki bands near the Apalachicola moved to a location west of the upper Suwannee. Bowlegs's band headed farther south near today's Lake Harris in central Florida. Micanopy and his Red and Black Seminoles settled at nearby Pekaclekcha. Some thirty towns were scattered throughout the Florida peninsula from the Georgia border to Tampa Bay and continued to shelter "Negro villages," as Americans called them. As conflicts between newly arrived white Floridians and the Seminoles became endemic, territorial authorities began plotting how to move the Natives onto reservations or, failing that, how to remove them from Florida.[3]

After the signing of the Transcontinental Treaty of 1821, the free Black community in St. Augustine faced a frontal assault on its rights and liberties. The new territorial legislature outlawed manumission, restricted the right to carry firearms, imposed head taxes on males, and instituted draconian punishment for those who could not pay. It eventually required every free Black person to place himself or herself under a white guardian, as was the custom in the southern United States.[4] Northern Florida once again became a world in flux but a different kind of flux as immigrants of a new type—fiercely independent, white, ambitious, crude in manners, and thoroughly racist—pushed their way in and jockeyed to impose their ideas and values.

As the windows on the borders of freedom were slamming shut, the flight of hundreds and eventually several thousand Black Georgians in the postrevolutionary era nevertheless left an important legacy for generations to come. Despite the image of the Gullah-Geechee people created in the twentieth century, Black people living on the coast of Georgia were never isolated or clueless about events in the republic or in the greater Atlantic. They shared in a collective wave of hope and fear that came from the realization that they were living in a time of profound change.[5] Over a forty-year period, freedom seekers sought out the competing visions offered by the many racial, ethnic, and religious groups in the Southeast. How they defined freedom may have taken on an infinite number of shapes and forms depending on the circumstances in which they found themselves, but they possessed one clear goal—freedom from bondage.

As a region, the Southeast offers a vital connecting link between the Black self-emancipation that occurred during the American Revolution and the growth of the Underground Railroad in the final years of the antebellum period. In many respects, what took place from 1776 to the end of the War of 1812 can be understood as an early version of the Underground Railroad, that grand metaphor describing how thousands of enslaved people fled the Upper South between 1830 and 1860 for northern cities, Canada, and, as recent scholarship has shown, Mexico and the British Caribbean in extraordinary acts of bravery.[6] The similarities are many. In both time periods, the process of making a successful flight required incredible fearlessness, daring, and boldness in the face of long odds. Men and women of both periods were in search of a society that recognized their humanity and accorded them a measure of equal treatment. In both instances, families played an important part in deciding who was to go and how to make the run for freedom.

In the earlier period, escape was primarily by water or by Indian trails. In the latter, it was small groups of Black people who were assisted by a vast and largely informal network of free Black people and sympathetic whites as well as those still enslaved in the South. Nevertheless, historians of the Underground Railroad are now recognizing that, to better understand the phenomenon, increasing emphasis must be on a narrative of self-emancipation rather than the story of high-minded white people assisting frightened and helpless African Americans.[7] That brings the story several steps closer to the experience in the South several decades earlier.

However, the apparent similarities of the flights take us only so far. Pursuing freedom in the Lower South required a different mind-set than it did in the Upper South. For both sets of people, the decision to make a clean break with an enslaved community and a culture in which one had grown up was a costly emotional one. All freedom seekers no matter the period of time had to calculate the personal sacrifice involved in leaving places and people they knew for the uncertainty of the unknown and the risk of being retaken and either severely punished or sold away. African Americans in the Southeast faced an additional challenge. They had to be prepared to enter a different world, speak a different language, and operate by cultural norms that were foreign by definition. They had to possess the adaptability to integrate themselves into societies for which they had little or no familiarity. In the words of historian Ira Berlin, they had to possess "cultural plasticity" in order to navigate borders, boundaries, and frontiers.

As they filtered across those borders, Black Georgians played a notable but largely unnoticed role in the shifting balance of power in the region. The Southeast may have evolved from a place of many cultures and peoples to a dominant culture where slavery was racialized, non-English Europeans were marginalized, and Natives were dispossessed of their lands, but that reality does not diminish the value of what Black Georgians brought to this struggle. Fugitives strengthened Hispanic and Native societies in distinct ways: the addition of manpower in areas with a static population, a willingness to accept prevailing cultural norms and act as participants, and their unrelenting commitment to resist, by force of arms if necessary, settler colonialism.[8] They played an underappreciated role in resisting the push by American frontiersmen and settlers to eliminate Native groups and expel the Spanish from the continent.

Black men and women were willing to pick up weapons to defend their rights and engage in combat, a remarkably different phenomenon from the landscape of people fleeing to Philadelphia and New York or Cincinnati and Canada. In the revolutionary and postrevolutionary age, African Americans were tenacious fighters against white oppressors when there was a realistic hope of making a stand. This meant reliance on the British, Spanish, Creeks, or Seminoles, whether organized in the defense of Savannah in 1779 or at the Prospect Bluff fort in 1815–16, whether with the Black militia of Hispanic Florida or the Black Seminoles, or accompanying warriors from the Lower Towns of the Creeks. In virtually all cases, the fighting was defensive in purpose, even in maroon communities. Unlike the Upper South, the Southeast spawned a spectrum of independent maroon communities that showed a diversity of goals and aspirations that arguably matched those in the Caribbean while sharing in the universal quest for autonomy and self-determination.

The Southeast offers a vital link between the stories of Black self-emancipation that occurred during the American Revolution and the growth of the Underground Railroad in the final years before the Civil War. That narrative has been obscured by the absence of chroniclers of their flight, the episodic geopolitical events that raised larger issues, the relative lack of documentation of Native societies, and the archival silence that exists when looking into southern slavery in the late eighteenth and early nineteenth centuries. An epic story, it is a potent reminder of the strength of Black resistance in the postrevolutionary South, a remarkable gauge of the depth of feeling and commitment that existed among African Americans. Their constant movement marked the closing act of a chaotic eighteenth century when empires struggled for position and Native peoples resisted the relentless advance of nations bent on eroding their lands and freedom. In a larger sense, the story marks the passing of the torch of liberty from the generation of the Revolution to those who belonged to the era of the Underground Railroad, a grand connecting arc that stretches over a forty-year period.

NOTES

Abbreviations

ASPIA	*American State Papers: Indian Affairs*, 2 vols.
CGHS	*Collections of the Georgia Historical Society*
CILTT	*Creek Indian Letters, Talks, and Treaties, 1705–1839*, 4 parts
CRG	*The Colonial Records of Georgia*, vols. 1–19, 21–38.
DLG	Digital Library of Georgia, dlg.galileo.usg.edu
EFP	East Florida Papers, Library of Congress
FHQ	*Florida Historical Quarterly*
GA	Georgia Archives, Morrow
GHQ	*Georgia Historical Quarterly*
GHS	Georgia Historical Society, Savannah
HAR	Hargrett Rare Book and Manuscript Library, University of Georgia Libraries, Athens
HSP	Historical Society of Pennsylvania
JSH	*Journal of Southern History*
LBH	*Letters of Benjamin Hawkins, 1796–1806*
LOC	Library of Congress
NARA	National Archives and Records Administration, Atlanta
NAUK	National Archives (United Kingdom)
NRS	National Records of Scotland
PKY	P. K. Yonge Library of Florida History, University of Florida
SCHM	*South Carolina Historical Magazine*
WMQ	*William and Mary Quarterly*
WCL	William L. Clements Library, University of Michigan, Ann Arbor

Introduction

1. The story of Hercules and Betty comes from two notices in the *Royal Georgia Gazette*, January 11 and October 11, 1781, and one in the *Gazette of Georgia*, October 10, 1785. For background, see Paul M. Pressly, "The Many Worlds of Titus: Marronage, Freedom, and the Entangled Borders of Lowcountry Georgia and Spanish Florida," *JSH* 84, no. 3 (August 2019): 549–50.

2. Notice of John Morel, January 4, 1781, *Royal Georgia Gazette*, in Lathan Windley, comp., *Runaway Slave Advertisements: A Documentary History from the 1730s to 1790* (Westport, Conn.: Greenwood Press, 1983) 4:82–83; Petition of Mary Morel to the Council of Safety, October 22, 1776, in *Revolutionary Records of the State of Georgia*, comp. Allen D. Candler (Atlanta: Franklin-Turner, 1908), 1:210–11. Mary Morel, a widow, moved Hercules and his family to a new site on the mainland that she received from the government for compensation for cattle removed from Ossabaw Island. The family immediately fled and were returned to the island.

3. Notice of John Morel, October 11, 1781, *Royal Georgia Gazette*, in Windley, *Runaway Slave Advertisements*, 4:100.

4. Notice of Peter Henry Morel, October 20, 1785, *Gazette of the State of Georgia*, in Elizabeth Evans Kilbourne, comp., *Savannah, Georgia, Newspaper Clippings ("Georgia Gazette"), 1775–1775* (Savannah: E. E. Kilbourne, 1999) 2:444; Edward J. Cashin, *The King's Ranger: Thomas Brown and the American Revolution on the Southern Frontier* (New York: Fordham University Press, 1999).

5. James W. Covington, *The Seminoles of Florida* (Gainesville: University Press of Florida, 1993), 3–37; Christina Snyder, *Slavery in Indian Country: The Changing Face of Captivity in Early America* (Cambridge, Mass.: Harvard University Press, 2010), 213–34.

6. Notice of John Morel, May 20, 1789, *Gazette of the State of Georgia*; and notice of Peter Henry Morel, May 21, 1789, *Gazette of the State of Georgia*, both in Windley, *Runaway Slave Advertisements*, 4:165–66; Notices of Bryan Morel and William Bryan, July 30, 1789, *Georgia Gazette*, in Windley, *Runaway Slave Advertisements*, 4:168–69; Notice of John Morel, *Gazette of the State of Georgia*, January 12, 1795; affidavits submitted by the Morel brothers and five other families related to the Morel family, October 1, 1791, EFP, reel 174.

7. For the revolutionary period, see Cassandra Pybus, *Epic Journeys of Freedom: Runaway Slaves of the American Revolution and Their Global Quest for Liberty* (Boston: Beacon Press, 2006); Maya Jasanoff, *Liberty's Exiles: American Loyalists in the Revolutionary World* (New York: Vintage Books, 2011); and Alexander X. Byrd, *Captives and Voyagers: Black Migrants across the Eighteenth-Century British Atlantic World* (Baton Rouge: Louisiana State University Press, 2008). For the antebellum period, see Damian Alan Pargas, *Freedom Seekers: Fugitive Slaves in North America, 1800–1860* (Cambridge: Cambridge University Press, 2022); Damian Alan Pargas, ed., *Fugitive Slaves and Spaces of Freedom in North America* (Gainesville: University Press of Florida, 2018); R. J. M. Blackett, *Making Freedom: The Underground Railroad and the Politics of Slavery* (Chapel Hill: University of North Carolina Press, 2013); Alice L. Baumgartner, *South to Freedom: Runaway Slaves to Mexico and the Road to the Civil War* (New York: Basic Books, 2020); and Eric Foner, *Gateway to Freedom: The Hidden History of the Underground Railroad* (New York: W. W. Norton, 2015).

8. Pargas, *Freedom Seekers*, 1–14.

9. Foner, *Gateway to Freedom*, 4.

10. "List of destinations, Commissioner for Evacuations, 1785," NAUK; Wilbur Henry Siebert, "East Florida as a Refuge of Southern Loyalists, 1774–1785," *Proceedings of the American Antiquarian Society* 37, pt. 2 (October 1927): 244. Commissioner for the Evacuation John Winniett and his successor William Brown produced multiple lists found in the Colonial Office records in the National Archives United Kingdom.

11. Charles Joyner, *Down by the Riverside: A South Carolina Slave Community* (Urbana: University of Illinois, 1985); Margaret Washington Creel, *"A Peculiar People": Slave Religion and Community-Culture among the Gullah*s (New York: New York University Press,

1988); Jacqueline Jones, *Saving Savannah: The City and the Civil War* (New York: Alfred A. Knopf, 2008), 17–20. For a divergent view, Melissa L. Cooper, *Making Gullah: A History of Sapelo Islanders, Race, and the American Imagination* (Chapel Hill: University of North Carolina Press, 2017).

12. Important articles on Black fugitives include Jane G. Landers, "Spanish Sanctuary: Fugitives in Florida, 1687–1790," *FHQ* 62 (January 1984), 296–313; Landers, "Gracia Real de Santa Teresa de Mose: A Free Black Town in Spanish Colonial Florida," *American Historical Review* 95 (February 1990), 9–30; Patrick Riordan, "Finding Freedom in Florida: Native Peoples, African Americans, and Colonists, 1670–1816," *FHQ* 75 (Summer 1996), 24–43; Richard K. Murdoch, "The Return of Runaway Slaves: 1790–1794," *FHQ* 38 (October 1959), 96–113; Richard K. Murdoch and Juan de Pierra, "The Seagrove-White Stolen Property Agreement of 1797," *GHQ* 42 (September 1958), 258–276; J. Leitch Wright Jr., "Blacks in British East Florida," *FHQ* 54 (April 1976), 425–42. Books include Jane Landers, *Atlantic Creoles in the Age of Revolutions* (Cambridge: Harvard University Press, 2010); Sylviane A. Diouf, *Slavery's Exiles: The Story of the American Maroons* (New York: New York University Press, 2014); Timothy James Lockley, ed., *Maroon Communities in South Carolina: A Documentary Record* (Columbia: University of South Carolina Press, 2009); John Hope Franklin and Loren Schweninger, *Runaway Slaves: Rebels on the Plantation* (Oxford, 1999); Kevin Mulroy, *Freedom on the Border: The Seminole Maroons in Florida, the Indian Territory, Coahuila and Texas* (Lubbock: Texas Tech University Pres, 1993); Frank Marotti, *Heaven's Soldiers: Free People of Color and the Spanish Legacy in Antebellum Florida* (Tuscaloosa: University of Alabama Press, 2013).

13. Elijah H. Gould, "Entangled Histories, Entangled Worlds: The English-Speaking Atlantic as a Spanish Periphery," *American Historical Review*, 112, no. 3 (January 2007): 764–86.

14. Jane Landers, *Black Society in Spanish Florida* (Urbana: University of Illinois Press, 1999); Jane Landers, *Atlantic Creoles in the Age of Revolutions* (Cambridge: Harvard University Press, 2010); and Jane Landers, 'Acquisition and Loss on a Spanish Frontier: The Free Black Homesteaders of Florida, 1784–1821," *Slavery and Abolition: A Journal of Slave and Post-Slave Studies*, 17, no. 1 (1996): 85–101.

15. "Our Southern Frontier," Major General John Floyd, *National Intelligencer*, October 29, 1817, cited in Cusick, *The Other War of 1812*, 298.

16. Kenneth W. Porter, *The Black Seminoles: History of a Freedom-Seeking People* (Gainesville: University Press of Florida, 1996); Jane G. Landers, "A Nation Divided: Blood Seminoles and Black Seminoles on the Florida Frontier," in *Coastal Encounters: The Transformation of the Gulf South in the Eighteenth Century*, edited by Richard F. Brown, 99–116 (Lincoln: University of Nebraska Press, 2007); C. Snyder, *Slavery in Indian Country*, 213–43; Andrew K. Frank, "Taking the State Out: Seminoles and Creeks in Late Eighteenth-Century Florida," *FHQ* 84, no. 1 (Summer 2005): 10–27; Andrew K. Frank, "Red, Black, and Seminole Community Convergence on the Florida Borderlands, 1780–1840," in *Borderland Narratives: Negotiation and Accommodation in North America's Contested Spaces, 1500–1850*, edited by Andrew K. Frank and A. Glenn Crothers, 46–67 (Gainesville: University Press of Florida, 2017); Watson W. Jennison, *Cultivating Race: The Expansion of Slavery in Georgia, 1750–1860* (Lexington: University Press of Kentucky, 2012), 127–56; Kevin Kokomoor, "A Re-assessment of Seminoles, Africans, and Slavery on the Florida Frontier," *FHQ*, 88, no. 2 (Fall 2009): 209–36; Brent Richards Weisman, *Like Beads on a String: A Culture History of the Seminole Indians in North Peninsular Florida* (Tuscaloosa: University of Alabama Press, 1989); Covington, *The Seminoles of*

Florida, 1–49; Claudio Saunt, *A New Order of Things: Property, Power, and the Transformation of the Creek Indians, 1733–1816* (Cambridge: Cambridge University Press, 1999), 233–47; Larry Eugene Rivers, *Slavery in Florida: Territorial Days to Emancipation* (Gainesville: University Press of Florida, 2000), 1–16; John K. Mahon and Brent R. Weisman, "Florida's Seminole and Miccosukee Peoples," in *The New History of Florida*, ed. Michael Gannon (Gainesville: University Press of Florida, 1996), 183–206.

17. Saunt, *A New Order of Things*; C. Snyder, *Slavery in Indian Country*; Daniel F. Littlefield Jr. *Africans and Creeks: From the Colonial Period to the Civil War* (Westport, Conn.: Greenwood Press, 1979); Kevin Kokomoor, *Of One Mind and of One Government: The Rise and Fall of the Creek Nation in the Early Republic* (Lincoln: University of Nebraska, 2018); Robbie Ethridge, *Creek Country: The Creek Indians and Their World* (Chapel Hill: University of North Carolina Press, 2003); Tiya Miles, *Ties that Bind: The Story of an Afro-Cherokee Family in Slavery and Freedom* (Oakland: University of California Press, 2015).

18. See Pargas, *Freedom Seekers*, a major contribution to the historical literature on fugitive slaves that uses a continental perspective.

Chapter 1. Black Sailors, Oglethorpe's Georgia, and Spanish Florida

1. Harold E. Davis, *The Fledgling Province: Social and Cultural Life in Colonial Georgia, 1733–1776* (Chapel Hill: University of North Carolina Press, 1976), 35.

2. Among the many works considering Savannah during the Trusteeship period are Walter J. Fraser, *Savannah in the Old South* (Athens: University of Georgia Press, 2003); Kenneth Coleman, *Colonial Georgia: A History* (Millwood, N.Y.: kto press, 1976); Betty Wood, *Slavery in Colonial Georgia, 1730–1775* (Athens: University of Georgia Press, 1984); Noeleen McIlvenna, *The Short Life of Free Georgia: Class and Slavery in the Colonial South* (Chapel Hill: University of North Carolina Press, 2015); Ben Marsh, *Georgia's Frontier Women: Female Fortunes in a Southern Colony* (Athens: University of Georgia Press, 2007); Julie Anne Sweet, *William Stephens: Georgia's Forgotten Founder* (Baton Rouge: Louisiana State University Press, 2010); Mart Stewart, *"What Nature Suffers to Groe": Life, Labor, and Landscape on the Georgia Coast, 1680–1920* (Athens: University of Georgia Press, 1996; Paul M. Pressly, *On the Rim of the Caribbean: Colonial Georgia and the British Atlantic* (Athens: University of Georgia Press, 2013); Mills Lane, *The People of Georgia: An Illustrated History* (Savannah: Beehive Press, 1992); Milton L. Ready, *The Castle Builders: Georgia's Economy under the Trustees, 1732–1754* (New York: Arno Press, 1978); Sarah Gober Temple and Kenneth Coleman, *Georgia's Journeys, 1732–1754* (Athens: University of Georgia Press, 1961); T. D. Wilson, *The Oglethorpe Plan: Enlightenment Design and Beyond* (Charlottesville: University of Virginia Press, 2015).

3. For a profile of slavery in South Carolina, see Philip D. Morgan, *Slave Counterpoint, Black Culture in the Eighteenth-Century Chesapeake and Lowcountry* (Chapel Hill: University of North Carolina Press, 1998); Max E. Edelson, *Plantation Enterprise in Colonial South Carolina* (Cambridge, Mass.: Harvard University Press, 2006); Peter H. Wood, *Black Majority: Negroes in Colonial South Carolina from 1670 through the Stono Rebellion* (New York: W. W. Norton, 1974); B. Wood, *Slavery in Colonial Georgia*, 1–23; Fraser, *Savannah in the Old South*, 33–41.

4. Temple and Coleman, *Georgia's Journeys*, 38–39.

5. Philip Morgan, "Lowcountry Georgia and the Early Modern Atlantic World, 1733–ca. 1820," in *African American Life in the Georgia Lowcountry: The Atlantic World and the*

Gullah Geechee, edited by Philip Morgan (Athens: University of Georgia Press, 2010), 15–19.

6. Ready, *The Castle Builders*, 263–68. By the 1740s, select farmers and "adventurers" played a game of cat-and-mouse with the magistrates over the use of enslaved labor. In 1749, there were 350 adults of African descent as well as their children. Deerskin merchants in and around the newly created town of Augusta relied on slave labor, while residents of the military outpost at Frederica occasionally feigned that Black people who appeared in their households were indentured servants.

7. See a case study of how Savannah's architecture developed its own style under New World conditions: Carl R. Louisbury, "Savannah: Loopholes in Metropolitan Design on the Frontier," in *Material Culture in Anglo-America: Regional Identity and Urbanity in the Tidewater, Lowcountry, and Caribbean*, ed. David S. Shields (Columbia: University of South Carolina Press, 2009): 58–73.

8. Elizabeth B. Cooksey, "Judaism and Jews," *New Georgia Encyclopedia*, https://www .georgiaencyclopedia.org/articles/arts-culture/judaism-and-jews.

9. B. Wood, *Slavery in Colonial Georgia*, 24–29; McIlvenna, *The Short Life of Free Georgia*, 23–39; Ready, *The Castle Builders*, 37; Fraser, *Savannah in the Old South*, 12–21; H. Davis, *The Fledgling Province*, 95–124; Pressly, *On the Rim of the Caribbean*, 11–24.

10. W. Jeffrey Bolster, *Black Jacks: African American Seamen in the Age of Sail* (Cambridge, Mass.: Harvard University Press, 1997); Marcus Rediker, *Between the Devil and the Deep Blue Sea: Merchant Seamen, Pirates, and the Anglo-Maritime World, 1700–1750* (Cambridge: Cambridge University Press, 2006); David S. Cecelski, *The Waterman's Song: Slavery and Freedom in Maritime North Carolina* (Chapel Hill: University of North Carolina Press, 2001); Lynn B. Harris, *Patroons and Periaguas: Enslaved Watermen and Watercraft of the Lowcountry* (Colombia: University of South Carolina Press, 2014); Werner Sollors, ed., *The Interesting Narrative of the Life of Olaudah Equiano, or Gustavus Vassa, The African, Written by Himself* (New York: W. W. Norton, 2001).

11. Ready, *The Castle Builders*, 268.

12. For an insightful comment on watermen, see Philip D. Morgan, *Slave Counterpoint*, 236–44. On Carolina slave watermen, see the study by Lynn Harris, *Patroons and Periaguas*.

13. William Stephens, Entry for March 10, 1741, *CRG*, vol. 4 suppl., 102; Robert Paulett, *An Empire of Small Places*, 72–75; Sweet, *William Stephens*, 149–50.

14. William Stephens, Entry for March 10, 1741, *CRG*, vol. 4 suppl., 102–3.

15. William Stephens, Entry for February 29, 1739, *A Journal of the Proceedings in Georgia* ([New York]: Readex Microprint, 1966), 2:298. This passage is not found in volume 4 of *CRG*.

16. Paulett, *An Empire of Small Places*, 49–52, 72–74.

17. The career of Captain Caleb Davis offers special insight into this world. See "The Most Astonishing Journal of Captain Caleb Davis, Eminent Merchant," September 20, 1763, box 6, Keith Read Collection, HAR; William Stephens, entries for December 15, 1738, May 28, 29, and 30, 1739, *CRG*, vol. 4, 247–48, 343–37; Diana Reigelsperger, "Early Eighteenth Century Contraband Trade and Slave Smuggling between Spanish Florida and the British Colonies," paper presented at the Southern Historical Association, St. Petersburg, Florida, November 2016; Landers, *Black Society in Spanish Florida*, 33; P. Wood, *Black Majority*, 306–7.

18. *CRG*, vol. 4, 247–48, 308–9, 343–47. For an analysis of frontier marriage patterns, see Marsh, *Georgia's Frontier Women*, 70–79, 89.

19. Marsh, *Georgia's Frontier Women*, 67–92.

20. *CRG*, vol. 4, 343–47.

21. *CRG*, vol. 4, 345–48; Marsh, *Georgia's Frontier Women*, 48–49.

22. *CRG*, vol. 4, 247–48.

23. Reigelsperger, "Early Eighteenth-Century Contraband Trade," 6–7. For the type of smuggling and illicit trade that existed in the Spanish Empire in the Americas, see Casey Schmitt, "Virtue in Corruption: Privateers, Smugglers, and the Shape of Empire in the Eighteenth-Century Caribbean," *Early American Studies: An Interdisciplinary Journal* 13, no. 1 (2015): 80–110.

24. Davis, "The Most Astonishing Journal of Captain Caleb Davis, Eminent Merchant," 1763, p. 2, HAR; Pressly, *On the Rim of the Caribbean*, 14, 21, 29; Joyce Elizabeth Harmon, *Trade and Privateering in Spanish Florida, 1732–1763* (Tuscaloosa: University of Alabama Press, 1969), 14–15, 40–43.

25. Susan Richbourg Parker, "St. Augustine in the Seventeenth-Century: Capital of La Florida," *FHQ* 92, no. 3 (Winter 2014): 554–576; Sherry Johnson, "The Historiography of Eighteenth-Century Florida," *FHQ* 93, no. 3 (Winter 2015): 296–326.

26. Amy Turner Bushnell, "Republic of Spaniards, Republic of Indians," in *The New History of Florida*, ed. Michael Gannon (Gainesville: University Press of Florida, 1996), 64–66; Saunt, "'The English Has Now a Mind to Make Slaves of Them All': Creeks, Seminoles, and the Problem of Slavery," *American Indian Quarterly* 22 (nos. 1–2), 1998, 157; Jane G. Landers, "Gracia Real de Santa Teresa de Mose: A Free Black Town in Spanish Colonial Florida," *American Historical Review* 95 (February 1990): 13.

27. William L Ramsey, *The Yamassee War: A Study of Culture, Economy, and Conflict in the Colonial South* (Lincoln: University of Nebraska Press, 2008).

28. Paul E. Hoffman, *Florida's Frontiers* (Indianapolis: Indiana University Press, 2002), 174–88; Max E. Edelson, "Visualizing the Southern Frontier: Cartography and Colonization in Eighteenth-Century Georgia," in *Coastal Nature, Coastal Culture: Environmental Histories of the Georgia Coast*, ed. Paul Sutter and Paul Pressly (Athens: University of Georgia Press, 2018), 91–121; Herbert E. Bolton and Mary Ross, *The Debatable Land: A Sketch of the Anglo-Spanish Contest for the Georgia Country* (Berkeley: University of California Press, 1925.

29. No other colony in British North America received such large subsidies. Over the life of the charter, Parliament disbursed £124,000 in grants in addition to the expenditures of the War Office for the regiment stationed on St. Simons Island. See Pressly, *On the Rim*, 25–26.

30. "An Act for Rendering the Colony of Georgia More Defencible by Prohibiting the Importation and Use of Black Slaves or Negroes into the Same," *CRG*, vol. 1, 53–56.

31. Morgan, "Lowcountry Georgia and the Early Modern Atlantic World," 13–47.

32. The Darien Petition of 1739 can be found in Christopher C. Meyers, *The Empire State of the South: Georgia History in Documents* (Macon, Ga.: Mercer University Press, 2008), 111–12; and "Petition against the Introduction of Slavery," *Wikisource*, https://en .wikisource.org/wiki/Petition_against_the_Introduction_of_Slavery, viewed July 17, 2021.

33. Matthew Mulcahy, *Hubs of Empire: The Southeastern Lowcountry and British Caribbean*. Baltimore: Johns Hopkins University Press, 2014, 70–73; Harmon, *Trade and Privateering in Spanish Florida*, 40–43.

34. Report of Acting Governor Arthur Middleton, June 13, 1728, British Public Record Office Transcript, 8:61–67, cited in P. Wood, *Black Majority*, 305.

35. Jane Landers, "Gracia Real de Santa Teresa de Mose: A Free Black Town in Spanish Colonial Florida," *American Historical Review* 95 (February 1990): 19

36. Montiano to captain-general of Cuba, January 3, 1739, *CGHS* 7, pt. 1:28. Governor Manuel de Montiano boasted to the captain-general of Cuba that he now possessed a true account of the situation in Georgia and South Carolina "for having had an intimate conversation with Mr. Davis and earned from him the present condition of those colonies."

37. Landers, "Gracia Real de Santa Teresa de Mose," 17n39.

38. J. H. Easterby, ed., *The Journal of the Commons House of Assembly: Assembly, September 12, 1739–March 26, 1740*, vol. 3 (Columbia: Historical Commission of South Carolina, 1952), 83 (July 1, 1741).

39. Testimony of an unnamed sea captain from Beaufort, April 21, 1738, Records in the British Public Record Office relating to South Carolina Transcripts, 19:76, cited in P. Wood, *Black Majority*, 306.

40. Landers, "Spanish Sanctuary," 298; "the men as well as the women": Jane Landers, ed., *Against the Odds: Free Blacks in the Slave Societies of the Americas* (Portland, Ore.: Frank Cass, 1996), 87.

41. Landers, "Gracia Real de Santa Teresa de Mose," 13–17.

42. Memorandum of Acting Lieutenant Governor Arthur Middleton, June 13, 1728, Records in the British Public Record Office Relating to South Carolina, 1663–1782, Sainsbury Transcripts, XIII, 61–67, cited in P. Wood, *Black Majority*, 305.

43. Robert Olwell, *Masters, Slaves, and Subjects: The Culture of Power in the South Carolina Low Country, 1740–1790* (Ithaca: Cornell University Press, 1998), 27–28.

44. Paul Lokken, "Useful Enemies: Seventeenth-Century Piracy and the Rise of Pardo Militias in Spanish Central America," *Journal of Colonialism and Colonial History* 5, no. 2 (2004), https://muse.jhu.edu/issue/9289.

45. For a summary of Fort Mose's impact, see Ira Berlin, *Many Thousands Gone: The First Two Centuries of Slavery in North America* (Cambridge: Belknap Press of Harvard University Press, 1998), 74–76.

46. Berlin, *Many Thousands Gone*, 38–45; Jane Landers, *Atlantic Creoles*, 1–14.

47. Landers, "Gracia Real de Santa Teresa de Mose," 17–19 (p. 18 for phrase "the most cruel").

48. Montiano to Governor General of Cuba, January 3, 1738, *Letters of Montiano*, in *CHGS* 3:28. The governor noted that only eight were laborers.

49. Easterby, *The Journal of the Commons House of Assembly*, 1:596 (January 19, 1739). However, the governor of Florida noted twenty-eight runaways coming in this wave, which suggests that one other vessel with a small number of people joined the escape.

50. Claim of Captain Caleb Davis, September 17, 1751, SD 2584, Archivo General de Indias, cited in Landers, "Gracia Real de Santa Teresa de Mose," 19.

51. Marcus Rediker, *Between the Devil and the Deep Blue Sea: Merchant Seamen, Pirates, and the Anglo-Maritime World, 1700–1750* (Cambridge: Cambridge University Press, 2006); Alfred F. Young and Gregory H. Nobles, *Whose American Revolution Was It? Historians Interpret the Founding* (New York: New York University Press, 2011), 202–3.

52. Reigelsperger, "Early Eighteenth Century Contraband Trade," 7.

53. Claim of Captain Caleb Davis, September 17, 1751, SD 2584, Archivo General de Indias, cited in Landers, *Black Society in Spanish Florida*, 33, 296n22.

54. William Stephens, December 11, 1738, *CRG*, vol. 4, 247–48.

55. Governor Manuel de Montiano to Captain General of Cuba, January 3, 1739, *CGHS* 7, pt. 1:28.

56. "An Account of the Negro Insurrection in South Carolina," *CRG*, vol. 22, pt. 2, 232–36; William Stephens, *A Journal of the Proceedings in Georgia* (Readex Microprint), 1:357–58; Montiano to captain-general of Cuba, April 2, 1739, *CGHS* 7, pt. 1:29–30. The officer was politely received but told that the "Court of Spain" had set the policy and there could be no deviation.

57. Jane Landers, "The Atlantic Transformations of Francisco Menendez," in *Biography and the Black Atlantic*, eds. John Wood Sweet and Lisa A. Lindsay (Philadelphia: University of Pennsylvania Press, 2014), 209–23; Landers, "Gracia Real de Santa Teresa de Mose," 9–30.

58. P. Wood, *Black Majority*, 308; Mark M. Smith, "Time Religion, Rebellion," in *Stono: Documenting and Interpreting a Southern Slave Revolt*, ed., Mark M. Smith (Columbia: University of South Carolina Press, 2005), 108–23; Peter Charles Hoffer, *Cry Liberty: The Stono River Slave Rebellion of 1739* (Oxford: Oxford University Press, 2012), vii; John R. Thornton, "African Dimensions of the Stono Rebellion", *American Historical Review* 96 (October 1991): 1101–13.

59. "An Account of the Negroe Insurrection in South Carolina," *CRG*, vol. 22, pt. 2, 232–36; P. Wood, *Black Majority*, 314–23.

60. "An Account of the Negroe Insurrection in South Carolina," *CRG*, 22, pt. 2, 232–36. The author of this detailed account is not known but thought to be either Oglethorpe or William Stevens.

61. Larry E. Ivers, *British Drums on the Southern Frontier: The Military Colonization of Georgia, 1733–1749* (Chapel Hill: University of North Carolina Press, 1974), 90–91; Reigelsperger, "Early Eighteenth-Century Contraband Trade," 7–8.

62. Landers, "Gracia Real de Santa Teresa de Mose," 19–20; Ivers, *British Drums Drums on the Southern Frontier*, 113–24; Julie Anne Sweet, *Negotiating for Georgia: British-Creek Relations in the Trustee Era, 1733–1752* (Athens: University of Georgia Press, 2005).

63. Julie A. Sweet, "Battle of Bloody Marsh," *New Georgia Encyclopedia*, accessed July 30, 2023, https://www.georgiaencyclopedia.org/articles/history-archaeology/battle-of-bloody-marsh; Ivers, *British Drums on the Southern Frontier*, 151–53; John Jay TePaske, *The Governorship of Spanish Florida, 1700–1763* (Durham: Duke University Press, 1964).

64. Ivers, *British Drums on the Southern Frontier*, 168–84. In 1743, Oglethorpe returned to England. A grateful Parliament reimbursed him £66,000 for the amounts he had spent on the war effort out of his own estate.

65. Trevor R. Reese, ed., *The Clamorous Malcontents: Criticisms and Defenses of the Colony of Georgia, 1741–1743* (Savannah: Beehive Press, 1973).

66. Dobell to Trustees, June 11, 1746, *CRG*, vol. 25, 72.

67. Betty Wood, *Slavery in Colonial Georgia*, 77–78.

68. Trevor Reese, *Frederica: Colonial Fort and Town* (St. Simons Island, Ga.: Fort Frederica Association, 1969); Francis Moore, *A Voyage to Georgia Begun in the Year 1735* (Jacksonville, Fla.: Fort Frederica Association, 1992), 44–89; J. T. Scott, *The First Families of Frederica: Their Lives and Locations* (Athens: J. T. Scott, 1985).

69. Entry of January 7, 1743, E. Merton Coulter, ed., *The Journal of William Stephens: 1741–1743* (Athens: University of Georgia Press, 1958), 1:157–58.

70. "Extract of a Letter from General Oglethorpe's Secretary," in Reese, *The Clamorous Malcontents*, 333–35.

71. Andrew C. Lannen, "James Oglethorpe and the Civil-Military Contest for Authority in Colonial Georgia, 1732–1749," *GHQ* 95 (Summer 2011): 203–31; Ready, *The Castle Builders*, 268; Pressly, *On the Rim of the Caribbean*, 25; Ivers, *British Drums on the Southern Frontier*, 204–7.

72. Benjamin Martyn to John Dobell, March 14, 1746/7, *CRG*, vol. 31, 56. "The Trustees are extreamly surpris'd at seeing in the Journal of August 21st, 1746, that the Rev. Mr. Thomas Bosomworth had sent to South Carolina for six Negroes, and had employed them on his plantation."

73. Ready, *The Castle Builders*, 268.

74. "The Most Astonishing Journal of Captain Caleb Davis, Eminent Merchant," p. 19, Hargrett Library.

75. William Logan, "William Logan's Journal of a Trip to Georgia, 1745," *Pennsylvania Magazine of History and Biography* 36, no. 2 (1912): 178.

76. Ivers, *British Drums on the Southern Frontier*, 206–7.

77. John Dobell to the Trustees, May 17, 1746, *CRG*, vol. 25, 42–54.

78. Linda M. Rupert, *Creolization and Contraband: Curaçao in the Early Modern Atlantic World* (Athens: University of Georgia Press, 2012), 1–13; Linda M. Rupert, "Marronage, Manumission, and Maritime Trade in the Early Modern Atlantic," *Slavery and Abolition* 30, no. 3 (September 2009), 361–32.

79. Dobell to the Trustees, May 17, 1746, *CRG*, vol. 25, 42–54; "John Mullryne," in *Biographical Directory of the South Carolina House of Representatives*, vol. 2, *The Commons House of Assembly, 1692–1775*, ed. Walter B. Edgar and N. Louis Bailey (Columbia: University of South Carolina Press, 1977), 488–89.

80. *Boston Weekly Magazine*, March 9, 1743, 16, cited in Landers, *Black Society in Spanish Florida*, 39.

81. Dobell to the Trustees, May 17, 1746, *CRG*, vol. 25, 45.

82. John Dobell to the Trustees, May 17, 1746, *CRG*, vol. 25, 42–54; Edgar and Bailey, *Biographical Directory of South Carolina*, 488.

83. Dobell to the Trustees, May 17, 1746, *CRG*, vol. 25, 44–45.

84. Dobell to the Trustees, *CRG*, vol. 25, 45.

85. Dobell to the Trustees, *CRG*, vol. 25, 45–47; Kenneth Coleman, "Henry Parker," in *Dictionary of Georgia Biography*, ed. Kenneth Coleman and Charles Stevens Gurr (Athens: University of Georgia Press, 1983), 2:777–78.

86. For an analysis of Horton's policies, see Lannen, "James Oglethorpe and the Civil-Military Contest," 214. To persuade the chief magistrate, three Savannahians, including the merchant James Habersham, offered to stand as guarantors of whatever decision would come from Curaçao. If John Peter could not prove he was a free man, the three would pay for the cost of maintaining him during that time, indemnify Mullryne for the lost labor, and cover the cost of the legal proceedings.

87. Frank Lambert, *James Habersham: Loyalty, Politics, and Commerce in Colonial Georgia* (Athens: University of Georgia Press, 2005).

88. Dobell to the Trustees, May 17, 1746, *CRG*, vol. 25, 46–47.

89. Kaye Kole, *The Minis Family of Georgia, 1733–1992* (Savannah: Georgia Historical Society, 1992), 3–4.

90. Noeleen McIlvenna, *The Short Life of Free Georgia: Class and Slavery in the Colonial South* (Chapel Hill: University of North Carolina Press, 2015).

91. B. Wood, *Slavery in Colonial Georgia*, 50–52.

92. William Stephens and the Assistants to Benjamin Martyn, July 19, 1750, *CRG*, vol. 26:22. In 1750, the governing magistrates estimated the Black population at 349 working adults (202 men, 147 women) and their children.

93. Ira Berlin, *Generations of Captivity: A History of African American Slaves* (Cambridge, Mass.: Harvard University Press, 2003), 15–92.

94. Bolster, *Black Jacks*, 31–40; Rhae Lynn Barnes, "Sailors and Slaves: Maritime History of the Long Eighteenth Century," U.S. History Scene. Accessed July 28, 2023. https://ushistoryscene.com/article/sailors-and-slaves.

Chapter 2. The Journeys of Mahomet

1. B. Wood, *Slavery in Colonial Georgia*, 74–87; David R. Chestnutt, *South Carolina's Expansion into Colonial Georgia, 1720–1765* (New York: Garland, 1989).

2. Pressly, *On the Rim of the Caribbean*, 76–80.

3. Louis De Vorsey Jr., ed., *De Brahm's Report of the General Survey in the Southern District of North America* (Columbia: University of South Carolina Press, 1971), 163–65; Jennison, *Cultivating Race*, 11–40; Edward J. Cashin, "Sowing the Wind: Governor Wright and the Georgia Backcountry on the Eve of the Revolution" in *Forty Years of Diversity: Essays on Colonial Georgia*, ed. Harvey H. Jackson and Phinizy Spalding, 233–50 (Athens: University of Georgia Press, 1984); Fraser, *Savannah in the Old South*, 42–80; Pressly, *On the Rim of the Caribbean*, 69–70.

4. Vincent Carretta, *Equiano the African: Biography of a Self-Made Man* (Athens: University of Georgia Press, 2005), 119–34.

5. Pressly, *On the Rim of the Caribbean*, 67–68, 79–80, 88, 90. Equiano earned his freedom from a Quaker merchant on Montserrat. His brutal encounters in Savannah did not change.

6. Fred Anderson, *Crucible of War: The Seven Years' War and the Fate of Empire in British North America, 1754–1766* (New York: Vintage Books, 2001), 505–6; Kathleen DuVal, *Independence Lost: Lives on the Edge of the American Revolution* (New York: Random House, 2016), 229–38.

7. James A. McMillin, "The Transatlantic Slave Trade Comes to Georgia" in *Slavery and Freedom in Savannah*, ed. Leslie M. Harris and Daina Ramey Berry (Athens: University of Georgia Press, 2014), 1–25; Pressly, *On the Rim of the Caribbean*, 114 (table 9); Karen B. Bell, "Rice, Resistance, and Forced Transatlantic Communities: (Re)Envisioning the African Diaspora in Low Country Georgia, 1750–1800," *Journal of African American History* 95, no. 2 (Spring 2010): 157–82.

8. *Georgia Gazette*, September 7, 1774, in Windley, *Runaway Slave Advertisements*, 4:56.

9. Governor's Council, March 6, 1769, *CRG*, vol. 10, 699–700; Gerald Lee Cates, "A Medical History of Georgia: The First Hundred Years, 1733–1833," PhD diss., University of Georgia, 1976: 56–58. The governor's council noted that Captain Dean arrived with "Negroes from the coast of Africa . . . infected with the small Pox." The council required him to quarantine his human cargo at the Lazaretto on Tybee Island.

10. On the controversy over the extent of the African contribution to rice technology in the Lowcountry, see Judith A. Carney, *Black Rice: The African Origins of Rice Cultivation in the Americas* (Cambridge, Mass.: Harvard University Press, 2001); David Eltis, Philip Morgan, and David Richardson, "Agency and Diaspora in Atlantic History: Reassessing the African Contribution to Rice Cultivation in the Americas," *American Histori-*

cal Review 112, no. 5 (December 2007): 1329–58; David Eltis, Philip D. Morgan, and David Richardson, "Black, Brown, or White? Color-Coding American Commercial Rice Cultivation with Slave Labor," *American Historical Review* 115, no. 1 (February 2010), 164–71.

11. Bell, "Rice, Resistance, and Forced Transatlantic Communities." See 166–68 for her assessment of the contribution of African enslaved people to rice cultivation.

12. Lillian Ashcraft-Eason, "'She Voluntarily Hath Come': A Gambian Woman Trader in Colonial Georgia in the Eighteenth Century" in *Identity in the Shadow of Slavery*, ed. Paul E. Lovejoy (London: Continuum, 2000), 202. The town of Kau-Ur was connected with the Muslim commercial network in the interior of western Sudan.

13. Memorandum signed by James Wright, John Graham, Joseph Clay, Lachlan McGillivray, William McGillivray, Williams Struthers, and John Deane, April 1775, box 29, Sir James Wright file, Keith Read Collection, HAR; Frank Lambert, *James Habersham: Loyalty, Politics, and Commerce in Colonial Georgia* (Athens: University of Georgia, 2005), 59–80.

14. Trans-Atlantic Slave Trade Database, accessed June 15, 2021, https://www.slavevoyages.org. The 1768 voyage was Deane's first appearance off the Georgia coast in the *New Britannia*. He returned with another shipment the following year and then again for a third time in 1770, bringing 490 enslaved people to Georgia, almost one-quarter of the total during that time. A fifth voyage brought additional Africans for a total of 610. See Robert Scott Davis, "Free but Not Freed: Stephen Deane's African Family in Early Georgia," *GHQ* 97, no. 1 (Spring 2013), 62.

15. Henry Laurens to Richard Oswald, May 17, 1756, in Henry Laurens, *The Papers of Henry Laurens*, vol. 2, ed. Philip M. Hamer and George C. Rogers Jr. (Columbia: University of South Carolina Press, 1970), 186; Daniel C. Littlefield, *Rice and Slaves: Ethnicity and the Slave Trade in Colonial South Carolina* (Urbana: University of Illinois Press, 1981), 8.

16. Joseph Clay to Scott, Mackie & Dover, December 10, 1772, Joseph Clay & Company letter book, Dec. 19, 1772–March 31, 1774, GHS.

17. Ashcraft-Eason, "She Voluntarily Hath Come," 202–21.

18. Barry Boubacar, *Senegambia and the Atlantic Slave Trade* (Cambridge: Cambridge University Press, 1998), 80–81.

19. Ashcraft-Eason, "She Voluntarily Hath Come," 207–9.

20. Sylviane A. Diouf, *Servants of Allah: African Muslims Enslaved in the Americas* (New York: New York University Press, 1998, 2013), 20–99.

21. Morgan, *Slave Counterpoint*, 78 (table 18). Of two shiploads for whom records exist, a total of 54 whites bought 172 Africans. About half went singly or in pairs. Pressly, *On the Rim of the Caribbean*, 128.

22. Mary Granger, ed., *Savannah River Plantations* (repr.; Savannah, Ga.: Oglethorpe Press, 1997). Merchants owned fourteen of twenty-one plantations whose ownership can be identified. These included John Graham, James Graham, Lachlan McGillivray, William McGillivray, Nathaniel Hall, "Greenwood & Higginson," John Rae, George Kincaid, Samuel Douglass, Edward Telfair, Basil Cowper, John Jamieson, Lewis Johnston, and Miles Brewton. The non-merchant owners were Jonathan Bryan, Governor James Wright, his son Alexander Wright, James Deveaux, William Knox, Dr. James Cuthbert, and James Hume.

23. Pressly, *On the Rim of the Caribbean*, 103–4.

24. "An account of land, Negroes and other effects the property of John Graham late

of Georgia," AO 13/35, Audit Office records, 1764–1835, series 13, box 35, 157–60, NAUK; minutes of interview of John Graham before the Commission of Claims, December 20, 1783, AO 12: Georgia, 57–98, Audit Office records, 1764–1835, NAUK; "A List of Slaves the Property of John Graham, Esq.," January 9, 1781, Colonial Book of Miscellaneous Bonds KK-2, 294–96, GA.

25. William Knox to James Habersham, March 2, 1768, Habersham Papers, GHS. James Habersham and John Graham served jointly as managers of Knox's estate.

26. "An account of land, Negroes and other effects," 157–60; minutes of interview of John Graham, 57–98.

27. "A List of Slaves the Property of John Graham Esq.," 294–97.

28. Judith A. Carney, *Black Rice: The African Origins of Rice Cultivation in the Americas* (Cambridge, Mass.: Harvard University Press, 2001); Joyce E. Chaplin, *An Anxious Pursuit: Agricultural Innovation and Modernity in the Lower South, 1730–1815* (Chapel Hill: University of North Carolina Press, 1993); "huge hydraulic machine": Mart A. Stewart, *"What Nature Suffers to Groe": Life, Labor, and Landscape on the Georgia Coast, 1620–1920* (Athens: University of Georgia Press, 1996), 98.

29. B. Wood, *Slavery in Colonial Georgia*, 133.

30. "Evidence on the Memorial of Sir James Wright, Baronet, Sir James Wright Sworn," October 22, 1783, AO 13/35, Audit Office records, 1764–1835, NAUK. Seventh page of the testimony: "He thinks 3 in 100 might die in a year on an average per year." See also "An account of lands, Negroes and other effects the property of John Graham," October 3, 1783, 132, AO 13/35, Audit Office records, 1764–1835, NAUK; and DeVorsey, *De Brahm's Report*, 162. In his estimate of the cost of a rice plantation, he calculated the purchase of forty working hands at £1,800 and the cost of their deaths on an annual basis, £100 (two slaves per year).

31. Mulcahy, *Hubs of Empire*, 131–38; P. Morgan, *Slave Counterpoint*, 443–66; Ira Berlin, *Many Thousands Gone*, 151–54.

32. Diouf, *Servants of Allah*, 71–158.

33. *Georgia Gazette*, September 7, 1774, in Windley, *Runaway Slave Advertisements*, 4:56.

34. B. Wood, *Slavery in Colonial Georgia*, 169–87; Philip Morgan, "Colonial South Carolina Runaways: Their Significance for Slave Culture," in *Out of the House of Bondage: Runaways, Resistance and Marronage in Africa and the New World*, ed. Gad Heuman ((London: Routledge, 2016), 57–78; John Hope Franklin and Loren Schweninger, *Runaway Slaves: Rebels on the Plantation* (Oxford: Oxford University Press, 1999).

35. B. Wood, *Slavery in Colonial Georgia*, 180.

36. *Georgia Gazette*, June 15, 1774, in Windley, *Runaway Slave Advertisements*, 4:51.

37. *Georgia Gazette*, March 22, 1775, in Windley, *Runaway Slave Advertisements*, 4:61.

38. *Georgia Gazette*, November 1, 1769, in Windley, *Runaway Slave Advertisements*, 4:40.

39. Betty Wood, "Some Aspects of Female Resistance to Chattel Slavery in Low Country Georgia, 1763–1815," *Historical Journal* 30 (September 1987), 612–13.

40. Kathryn Holland Braund, "The Creek Indians, Blacks, and Slavery," *JSH* 57, no. 4 (November 1981), 611; P. Wood, *Black Majority*, 260.

41. Ethridge, *Creek Country*, 22–31; E. Kathryn Holland Braund, *Deerskins and Duffels: Creek Indian Trade with Anglo-America, 1685–1815* (Lincoln: University of Nebraska Press, 1993), 3–25; Saunt, *A New Order of Things*, 11–37.

42. Braund, "The Creek Indians, Blacks, and Slavery," 617; Anthony Gene Carey, *Sold Down the River: Slavery in the Lower Chattahoochee Valley of Alabama and Georgia* (Tuscaloosa: University of Alabama Press, 2011), 28.

43. C. Snyder, *Slavery in Indian Country*, 127–51; Saunt, *A New Order of Things*, 111–35.

44. Lachlan McIntosh to George Houstoun, July 26, 1775 in Lilla Mills Hawes, ed., *Lachlan McIntosh Papers in the University of Georgia Library*, University of Georgia Miscellanea Publications, no. 7 (Athens: University of Georgia Press, 1968), 14.

45. Michael Craton, *Testing the Chains: Resistance to Slavery in the British West Indies* (Ithaca: Cornell University Press, 1982); Orlando Patterson, "Slavery and Slave Revolts: A Sociohistorical Analysis of the First Maroon War, 1665–1740," in *Maroon Societies: Rebel Slave Communities in the Americas*, ed. Richard Price (Baltimore: Johns Hopkins University Press, 1996), 246–92; Vincent Brown, *Tacky's Revolt: The Story of an Atlantic Slave War* (Cambridge, Mass.: Harvard University Press, 2020), 1–2.

46. Diouf, *Slavery's Exiles*, 1–4.

47. Commons House of Assembly, November 15, 1765, *CRG* 14:292–93.

48. Roderick McIntosh to Isaac Young, November 18, 1765, enclosed in Governor Wright to Lt. Gov. of South Carolina, Nov. 25, 1765, Council Journal, no. 32, 674–75, South Carolina Department of Archives and History, cited in Philip D. Morgan, *Slave Counterpoint*, 450.

49. Council meeting, December 4, 1771, *CRG*, vol. 12, 146–47.

50. Presentations of the presentments of the grand jury to the governor's council, July 7, 1772, *CRG*, vol. 12: 325–26. They robbed a boat, shot at a white man, and torched a house in which a white child was burned to death.

51. Michael Mullins, *Africa in America: Slave Acculturation and Resistance in the American South and the British Caribbean, 1736–1831* (Champaign: University of Illinois Press, 1995), 34–61 (p. 61 for the statement of the absence of a maroon dimension in the South). In discussing slave resistance, Mullins expressed the prevailing view at the end of the twentieth century when he spoke of the absence of a maroon dimension in the South and observed that it represented a serious loss for southern slaves.

52. Richard Price, "Maroons," in *The Princeton Companion to Atlantic History*, ed. Joseph C. Miller, Vincent Brown, Jorge Canizares-Esguerra, Laurent Dubois, and Karen Ordahl Kupperman (Princeton: Princeton University Press, 2015), 326–29; Brown, *Tacky's Revolt*, 105–10.

53. Diouf, *Slavery's Exiles*, 4–5, 72–96.

54. Diouf, *Slavery's Exiles*, 1–11, Rhys L. Isaac, *The Transformation of Virginia, 1740–1790* (Chapel Hill: University of North Carolina Press, 1982), 52–53.

55. B. Wood, *Slavery in Colonial Georgia*, 169–82. Matthew Mulcahy states that some 30 percent of South Carolina runaways whose intentions were known left home to reconnect with a relative, sometimes a parent, a child, or a sibling. Mulcahy, *Hubs of Empire*, 130.

56. "An account of land, Negroes and other effects the property of John Graham late of Georgia . . . the account being stated agreeable to an appraisement made of the said property in April 1776," John Graham, November 6, 1785, AO 13/35, NAUK, 132–40.

57. Jim Piecuch, *Three Peoples, One King: Loyalists, Indians, and Slaves in the Revolutionary South, 1775–1782* (Columbia: University of South Carolina Press, 2008), 158–63; Fraser, *Savannah in the Old South*, 104–18.

58. Rita Folse Elliott and Dan T. Elliott, *Savannah under Fire, 1779: Expanding the Boundaries* (Savannah, Ga.: Coastal Heritage Society, 2011), 53–55 (table 1).

59. An account of land, Negroes and other effects the property of John Graham late of Georgia . . . April 1776," John Graham, November 6, 1785, AO 13/35, NAUK, 132–40.

60. Memorial of James Graham, March 24, 1785, AO 13/35, NAUK, 124–31.

61. Marshall's Sales, John Nutt vs. James Habersham, *Royal Georgia Gazette*, May 17, 1781; Diouf, *Slavery's Exiles*, 188.

62. "A Return of Refugees, with their Negroes, who came to the Province of East Florida in consequence of the evacuation of Georgia. July 1783," CO 5:580, NAUK, cited in Lawrence H. Feldman, ed., *Colonization and Conquest: British Florida in the Eighteenth Century* (Baltimore: Clearfield, 2007), 60–77.

63. "The Memorial of Lieut. Col. Graham," in Wilbur Henry Siebert, *Loyalists in East Florida, 1774 to 1785* (DeLand: Florida State Historical Society, 1929), 2:76–81. The manager of the estate, Colonel Douglass, stated that there were 102 men, 67 women, and 56 children at work on five tracts of land. Crops of indigo and rice were planted as late as May 1784.

64. J. Leitch Wright Jr., *Florida in the American Revolution* (Gainesville: University Presses of Florida, 1975), 117–23; J. Leitch Wright Jr., *Anglo-Spanish Rivalry in North America* (Athens: University of Georgia Press, 1971), 136–37; Carole Watterson Troxler, "Loyalist Refugees and the British Evacuation of East Florida, 183–85," *FHQ*, 60, no. 1 (July 1981): 3. In Paris, diplomats from Spain, France, and Great Britain considered a variety of transfers that involved swapping territory in the Caribbean, North America, and the Mediterranean before deciding on the exchange of the two Floridas for Havana.

65. "The Memorial of Lieut. Col. Graham," in Siebert, *Loyalists in East Florida*, 2:80, 82. Graham wanted to sell his slaves in Jamaica, but Douglass thought the better price was in Beaufort even though government transport would not carry them there.

66. The Petition of Godin Guerard and Sworn Oath of Samuel Bostick, December 3, 1793, Records of the General Assembly, South Carolina Department of Archives and History", cited in Diouf, *Slavery's Exiles*, 189.

67. *Gazette of the State of Georgia*, May 12, 1785, in Windley, *Runaway Slave Advertisements*, 4:126–27. Fatima's name is not on the list of the sixteen who escaped. She made her break for freedom with a subsequent group. When captured, she identified herself as a slave of John Graham, not Godin Guerard.

68. The Petition of Godin Guerard, December 3, 1793, Records of the General Assembly, South Carolina Department of Archives and History, cited in Diouf, *Slavery's Exiles*, 189n12, 339.

69. Lockley, *Maroon Communities in South Carolina*, 40. According to his analysis, nearly 85 percent of colonial runaways were male, while more than a third of Revolutionary War runaways were women and children.

70. Trial Record of Lewis forwarded to governor by Savannah magistrates, May 21, 1787, Telamon Cuyler Collection, HAR, cited in Lockley, *Maroon Communities in South Carolina*, 62–65. At his trial, Lewis testified that, when he arrived at the Belleisle site in 1785, there were eleven men, including the leader Sharper, and a number of women.

71. Timothy Lockley, "'The King of England's Soldiers': Armed Blacks in Savannah and Its Hinterlands during the Revolutionary War Era, 1778–1787," in *Slavery and Freedom in Savannah*, ed. Leslie M. Harris and Daina Ramey Berry (Athens: University of Georgia Press, 2014), 26–41; "the very fellows": General James Jackson to Governor

George Matthews, 1786, Joseph Vallence Bevan Papers, GHS, cited in Lockley, *Maroon Communities in South Carolina*, 47.

72. *Charleston Morning Post*, May 8, 1787, reprinted in Lockley, *Maroon Communities*, 59–61 ("In this country": 60).

73. For Sharper's background, see the notice of William Woodward, *Gazette of the State of Georgia*, July 24, 1783, cited in Lockley, "The King of England Soldiers," 38n9, 219. In Diouf, *Slavery's Exiles*, 189, the trial documents list Sharper as a slave of Alexander Wright, son of the royal governor and owner of the Richmond and Kew Plantation on the Savannah River.

74. Landers, *Atlantic Creoles*, 97; Lockley, "The King of England's Soldiers," 37–39; Diouf, *Slavery's Exiles*, 189–90.

75. *Gazette of the State of Georgia*, October 19, 1786, reprinted in *Charleston Morning Post*, October 26, 1786; and *Georgia State Gazette*, October 28, 1786, cited in Lockley, *Maroon Communities in South Carolina*, 44–45. Planters posted notices for runaways believed to be "harbored by the Abercorn negroes," a reference to a creek thought to be nearby, while the grand jury of Chatham County complained about the "large gangs of runaway Negroes that are allowed to remain with a short distance of town."

76. Frey, *Water from the Rock*, 226–28; Betty Wood, "'High Notions of their Liberty': Women of Color and the American Revolution in Lowcountry Georgia and South Carolina, 1765–1785," in *African American Life in the Georgia Lowcountry: The Atlantic World and the Gullah Geechee*, ed. Philip Morgan (Athens: University of Georgia Press, 2010): 68. In *Maroon Communities*, Lockley emphasizes how great a threat the white community saw in a maroon community that would serve as an example for Black communities.

77. Alan Gilbert, *Black Patriots and Loyalists: Fighting for Emancipation in the War for Independence* (Chicago: University of Chicago Press, 2012), 160.

78. Diouf, *Slavery's Exiles*, 208.

79. Diouf, *Slavery's Exiles*, 190; Jackson to Matthews, 1786, Bevan Papers, GHS, cited in Lockley, ed., *Maroon Communities*, 47. The one time they went on the attack was to take the life of a Mr. Wolmar, "whose Negroe, one of their leaders was killed & whose head was fixed on the western road, in revenge for his life." The attack to extract revenge failed; Wolmar was not at home.

80. *Gazette of the State of Georgia*, October 19, 1786, reprinted in *Charleston Morning Post*, October 26, 1786; Jackson to Thomas Pinckney, governor of South Carolina, December 2, 1786, and Jackson to George Matthews, governor of Georgia, December 1786, reprinted in Lockley, ed., *Maroon Communities*, 44–47; Diouf, *Slavery's Exiles*, 190–92.

81. Military Dispatch from Col. James Gunn to Brig. General James Jackson, May 6, 1787, folder 10, item 84, Joseph Vallence Bevan Papers GHS, cited in Lockley, ed., *Maroon Communities*, 58–59.

82. Diouf, *Slavery's Exiles*, 198–201.

83. *Georgia State Gazette*, April 26, 1787, in Lockley, *Maroon Communities*, 57; Diouf, *Slavery's Exiles*, 201–3.

84. *Charleston (S.C.) Morning Post*, May 8, 1787, in Lockley, *Maroon Communities*, 59–61; trial record of Lewis, May 21, 1787, Georgia Slavery Trials, Telamon Cuyler Collection, HAR, reprinted in Lockley, ed., *Maroon Communities*, 62–65; Lockley, "The King of England Soldiers," 39–41.

85. "Trial Record of Lewis forwarded to the governor of Georgia by Savannah magistrates," box 71, folder 12, Georgia Slavery Trials, Telamon Cuyler Collection, HAR.

86. Landers, *Atlantic Creoles*, 97.

87. "Petitions for Compensation from the Owners of Slaves Killed in 1787," Lockley, *Maroon Communities*, 67.

88. Diouf, *Slavery's Exiles*, 205.

Chapter 3. Hercules, Revolution, and British Florida

1. The three delegates chosen by the Second Provincial Council in January 1775 elected not to go to Philadelphia for fear of setting off a riot in the streets of Savannah. Noble Wimberly Jones, Archibald Bulloch, John Houstoun to the President of the Continental Congress, Savannah, April 6, 1771, *Revolutionary Records of the State of Georgia*, comp. Allen D. Candler (Atlanta: Franklin-Turner, 1908) 1:63–66.

2. Pressly, *On the Rim of the Caribbean*, 213–28 Leslie Hall; *Land and Allegiance in Revolutionary Georgia* (Athens: University of Georgia Press, 2001), 31–53; Fraser, *Savannah in the Old South*, 102–23; Piecuch, *Three Peoples, One King*, 19–22; Sylvia R. Frey, *Water from the Rock: Black Resistance in a Revolutionary Age* (Princeton: Princeton University Press, 1991); Kenneth Coleman, *American Revolution in Georgia, 1763–1789* (Athens: University of Georgia Press, 1958), 55–75. Piecuch and Frey offer critical insights into the role of African Americans in revolutionary Georgia.

3. Notice of John Morel, *Royal Georgia Gazette*, October 11, 1781, in Windley, *Runaway Slave Advertisements*, 4:100; Inventory and appraisement of the personal estate of John Morel, deceased, June 27, 1777, book FF: 70–76, GA; Morel files, Walter Hartridge Collection, GHS; Indenture between William Stephens, Josiah Tattnall, and John Morel, January 25, 1772, 4000–04, conveyances. X-1, GHS; Will of John Morel, Morel Family Documents, mss 1326, box 28, GHS; Daniel T. Elliott, *Archaeological Investigations at Tabbies 1 and 2, North End Plantation, Ossabaw Island, Georgia*, LAMAR Institute publication series, report number 108 (Savannah: LAMAR Institute, 2005), 29–44.

4. Notice of John Morel, *Royal Georgia Gazette*, October 11, 1781, in Windley, *Runaway Slave Advertisements*, 100. Morel identified Hercules as being from Angola.

5. D. Elliott, *Archaeological Investigations at Tabbies 1 and 2*, 15–16; Indenture between Grey Elliott and Henry Bourquin, May 17, 1760, Conveyance Book C-1, and Indenture between Henry Bourquin and John Morel, October 10, 1760, Conveyance Book C-1, 597, both in GA. Grey Elliott, a lawyer-merchant with close ties to the governor, submitted the winning bid for Ossabaw Island at public auction. Two months later, he in turn sold the island to Bourquin for a handsome profit. In October that year, Bourquin sold an undivided half-interest to his son-in-law, John Morel.

6. Morel Family files, Walter Charlton Hartridge Jr. Collection, series XIV, 1349, GHS; D. Elliott, *Archaeological Investigations at Tabbies 1 and 2*; Pressly, *On the Rim of the Caribbean*, 260n18; Granger, *Savannah River Plantations*, 180. When Patrick Brown died, his brother, Alexander Brown, a gilder in Dublin, Ireland, moved the men, women, and children to a tract of land along the Savannah River that his brother had purchased but never developed. Brown attempted a rice plantation, but little rice was ever produced, and the enterprise failed. John Morel moved these people to Ossabaw Island.

7. Indenture between John Morel, merchant of Savannah and Alexander Brown, recorded June 20, 1763, Colonial Bond Book O, 71, GA.

8. Indenture between Morel and Brown.

9. Inventory and appraisement of the personal estate of John Morel, deceased, June 27, 1777, book FF, 70–76, GA.

10. Comparison of names in the indenture of 1763 with the inventory and appraisement of the personal estate of John Morel in 1777. Since most names appeared only once on both lists and the age of the person in question fits the given information, it is possible to have reasonable confidence in this picture. Diana's sister, Jenny, was married to Jack. Her other sister, Betty, was married to either Hercules, a leader on the plantation with whom she escaped in 1781, or Mingo, with whom she had five children.

11. There were two Bettys in the 1763 list. In the 1777 list, there are two Bettys, one married to Hercules, the other to Mingo.

12. John Martin, "Official Letters of Governor John Martin, 1782–1783," *Georgia Historical Quarterly* 1, no. 4: 334–35 (letter to Governor Patrick Tonyn, October 19 and 22, 1782); S. Max Edelson, "The Characters of Commodities: The Reputations of South Carolina Rice and Indigo in the Atlantic World," in *The Atlantic Economy during the Seventeenth and Eighteenth Centuries: Organization, Operation, Practice, and Personnel*, ed. Peter A. Coclanis, 350–52 (Columbia: University of South Carolina Press, 2005). The productivity of the Morel estate was confirmed by a raid by British loyalists, who took twenty-three hundred pounds of indigo in 1782. D. Elliott, *Archaeological Investigations at Tabbies 1 and 2*, 39.

13. R. C. Nash, "South Carolina Indigo, European Textiles, and the British Atlantic Economy in the Eighteenth Century," *English Economic History*, 63, no. 2 (May 2010), 362–92; Andrea Feeser, *Red, White, and Black Make Blue: Indigo in the Fabric of Colonial South Carolina Life* (Athens: University of Georgia, 2013); Robert M. Weir, *Colonial South Carolina: A History* (Columbia: University of South Carolina Press, 1997), 151.

14. John Wand Papers, 1771–1772, GHS. Legal documents and letters concerning the *Elizabeth*. The vessel carried rice from Savannah to Cowes and then northern Europe. It ended in the timber trade between St. Petersburg and England and was eventually scrapped. Wand lost a considerable amount on this venture.

15. D. Elliott, *Archaeological Investigations at Tabbies 1 and 2*, 46–49, 52–56.

16. Testimony in a postrevolutionary court case indicates that there were three plantations on the island before the Revolution. In addition, the total number of enslaved people—155—fits this profile. Deposition of John Morel, the son, March 1797, box 45, Nutt v. estate of John Morel, NARA, Atlanta.

17. For a general description of life on a plantation in Georgia, see Stewart, *What Nature Suffers to Groe*, 87–116; and Pressly, *On the Rim of the Caribbean*, 134–52.

18. James Corbett David, *Dunmore's New World: The Extraordinary Life of a Royal Governor in Revolutionary America* (Charlottesville: University of Virginia Press, 2013), 103–10 (107 for "Ethiopian Regiment"); Jasanoff, *Liberty's Exiles*, 48–49; Cassandra Pybus, *Epic Journeys of Freedom: Runaway Slaves of the American Revolution and Their Global Quest for Liberty* (Boston: Beacon Press, 2006), 11–12; Alan Gilbert, *Black Patriots and Loyalists*, 15–45; Parkinson, *The Common Cause*, 155–63;.

19. Diary entry, September 24, 1775, John Adams, *The Works of John Adams*, ed. by Charles Francis Adams (Boston: Little Brown, 1850–1856), 2:428.

20. Memorial of Sir James Wright and several other gentlemen to Lord George Germain, January 6, 1779 in *CGHS*, vol. 3, 249.

21. Joseph Clay to Mr. Brown, September 1, 1778, in *CGHS*, vol. 8:99.

22. Wright to Germain, March 10, 1776, *CRG*, vol. 38, pt. 2:80–81; Wright to My Lord (Germain), March 20/26, 1776, *CRG*, vol. 38, pt. 2, 80; Stephen Bull to Henry Laurens, March 13 and March 14, 1776, in Henry Laurens, *The Papers of Henry Laurens*, vol. 11, ed. David R. Chestnutt and C. James Taylor (Columbia: University of South Carolina

Press, 1988), 155, 163–64; James Johnson, *Militiamen, Rangers, and Redcoats: The Military in Georgia, 1754–1776* (Macon, Ga.: Mercer University Press, 1992), 154–55; Cassandra Pybus, "Jefferson's Faulty Math: The Question of Slave Defections in the American Revolution," *WMQ* 62, no. 2 (April 2005): 251. For a different view of the incident, see Olwell, *Masters, Slaves, and Subjects*, 242; and Jane Landers, *Atlantic Creoles*, 26–27. Despite a raid by patriots who captured twelve fugitives on Tybee and killed two marines, the new government failed to halt the leakage of slaves from a porous system.

23. Martha Condray Searcy, *The Georgia-Florida Contest in the American Revolution, 1776–1778* (Tuscaloosa: University of Alabama Press, 1985), 61. In September 1776, a British vessel took forty runaways to St. Augustine, an indication that there was a continual flight to Tybee Island. No great encampment ever emerged because the Royal Navy carried small groups from there to East Florida as needed.

24. Harvey H. Jackson, "The Battle of the Rice Boats: Georgia Joins the Revolution," *GHQ*, 58 (June 1974): 229–43; Hall, *Land and Allegiance*, 54–75.

25. William Drayton, 1732–1790, Force Papers, series 8D, item 37, Library of Congress, cited in Frey, *Water from the Rock*, 83.

26. Searcy, *The Georgia-Florida Contest*, 50, 51, 58.

27. Another planter had six of his thirty-three slaves die during their relocation to East Florida. Memorial of Martin Jolie, September 19, 1783, AO 13/36, pt. 2, Audit Office records, 1764–1835, NAUK.

28. Wright, *Florida in the American Revolution*, 22–23, 32–33, 40–44; Kevin J. Kokomoor, "Burning & Destroying all Before Them": Creeks and Seminoles on Georgia's Revolutionary Frontier," *GHQ* 98 no. 4 (Winter 2014): 300–340.

29. Clay to Laurens, September 9, 1778, *CGHS*, vol. 6, 106.

30. *Pennsylvania Journal*, September 1, 1779, cited in Parkinson, *The Common Cause*, 465–66; *South Carolina Gazette*, July 7, 1779, cited in Thomas J. Kirkland and Robert M. Kennedy, *Historic Camden: Colonial and Revolutionary* (Columbia, SC: State Company, 1905), 300.

31. Fraser, *Savannah in the Old South*, 118–24; Hall, *Land and Allegiance*, 50–53, 67–75; Coleman, *American Revolution in Georgia*, 100–109.

32. Hall, *Land and Allegiance*, 51–53, 71–75; Searcy, *Georgia-Florida Contest*, 134–47.

33. George McIntosh, *The Case of George M'Intosh, Esquire, a Member of the Late Council and Convention of the State of Georgia: With the Proceedings Thereon in the Hon. the Assembly and Council of That State* (Savannah: 1777); "An Account of the Losses sustained by Thomas Young late of Southampton in the Province of Georgia. Planter. December 23, 1783," AO 13/36, microfilm, 6015–5, 13–38, GHS.

34. R. Wylly and Wife v. Executors of Estate of J. Morel, Deceased, Superior Court Records, 5125 sp-45, box 6, 714, GHS.

35. Fraser, *Savannah in the Old South*, 124–28; Piecuch, *Three Peoples*, 132–33.

36. Gary Nash, "The African American's Revolution" in *The Oxford Handbook of the American Revolution*, ed. Edward C. Gray and Jane Kamensky (Oxford: Oxford University Press, 2013), 250; Gary Nash, *The Forgotten Fifth: African Americans in the Age of Revolution* (Cambridge: Harvard University Press, 200), 1–7.

37. Archibald Campbell to unknown, January 9, 1779, Prioleau Papers, South Carolina Historical Society, cited in Philip D. Morgan, "Black Society in the Lowcountry, 1760–1780," ed. Ira Berlin and Ronald Hoffman, *Slavery and Freedom in the Age of the American Revolution* (Charlottesville: University Press of Virginia, 1983), 109.

38. Lilla Mills Hawes, "Minute Book, Savannah Board of Police, 1779," *GHQ* 45 (1961): 245–57.

39. James Wright to Lord G. Germain, July 31, 1779, *CGHS*, vol. 3:256; minutes of governor's council, July 26, 1779, *CRG*, vol. 38, pt. 2:183. The great slave merchants of Georgia were particularly anxious to secure Wright's support in restoring a plantation economy and protecting their investments.

40. Frey, *Water from the Rock*, 94–99; Alexander A. Lawrence, *Storm over Savannah, The Story of Count d'Estaing and the Siege of the Town in 1779* (Athens: University of Georgia Press, 1951).

41. Meeting of governor's council, September 6, 1779, *CGHS*, vol. 10:49–50; Frey, *Water from the Rock*, 96. Mary Morel was one of nine slaveholders who failed to respond to a previous directive to send "Negroes" equipped with hoes, axes, and spades for six working days.

42. John D. Garrigus, "Catalyst or Catastrophe? Saint-Domingue's Free Men of Color and the Battle of Savannah, 1779–1782," *Review/Revista Interamericana* 22 (1992): 109–25; George P. Clark, "The Role of the Haitian Volunteers of Savannah in 1779: An Attempt at an Objective View," *Phylon* 41, no. 4 (Fall 1980): 356–66. In 2007, Savannah erected a statue in honor of these Haitian troops.

43. Petition of William Hanscomb to Augustine Prevost, March 30, 1780, cited in Piecuch, *Three Peoples*, 169, 371n317; Edward McCrady, *South Carolina in the Revolution* (New York: Macmillan, 1901), 342–44.

44. John J. Zubly to unnamed, November 30, 1779, Zubly Papers, GHS, cited in Piecuch, *Three Peoples*, 169.

45. *Plan of Siege of Savannah*, William Faden, Library of Congress, accessed February 8, 2022, https://www.loc.gov/resource/g3701sm.gar00004/?sp=6&r=-0.161,-0.234,1.274,0.784,0. Troop disposition is indicated by numbers. Number 7 is "Picket of the Line and Armed Negroes."

46. Petition of C. M. Handley of South Carolina, 1784, On-Line Institute for Advanced Loyalist Studies, accessed November 11, 2021, http://www.royalprovincial.com/military/mems/sc/clmhandley.htm.

47. John Jones to Polly Jones, October 3, 1779, Seaborn Jones Papers, cited in Piecuch, *Three Peoples*, 168.

48. Gilbert, *Black Patriots and Loyalists*, 124–25.

49. "Table 1. Negroes enumerated by the commissary General's Store at Savannah, October 11–20, 1779 (William L. Clements Library, 1779)," R. Elliott and D. Elliott, *Savannah under Fire, 1779*, 53–55.

50. Cashin, *The King's Ranger*, 83.

51. Piecuch, *Three Peoples, One King*, 148. Patriots arrested eight men stealing horses around Midway, former members of the Florida Rangers. Five were white; three were Black.

52. *Plan of Siege of Savannah*. The location of Brown's troops is at numbers 13 and 14.

53. "Account of the Siege of Savannah from a British Source," *CGHS*, vol. 5, pt. 1:138.

54. "An English Journal of the Siege of Savannah in 1779," in *Muskets, Cannon Balls and Bombs: Nine Narratives of the Siege of Savannah in 1779*, ed. Benjamin Kennedy (Savannah, Ga.: Beehive Press, 1974), 88.

55. *Gazette of the State of Georgia*, October 20, 1785, cited in Elizabeth Evans Kilbourne, comp., *Savannah, Georgia, Newspaper Clippings ("Georgia Gazette")* vol. 2, 1774–1785 (Sa-

vannah: E. E. Kilbourne, 1999), 444; D. Elliott, *Archaeological Investigations at Tabbies 1 and 2*, 32.

56. Deposition of M. King, King Papers, 1782, GHS.

57. *Royal Georgia Gazette*, January 18, 1781 in Windley, *Runaway Slave Advertisements*, vol. 4, 84.

58. R. Elliott and D. Elliott, *Savannah under Fire, 1779*, 52.

59. Meeting of Governor's Council, October 25, 1779, *CGHS*, vol. 10, 53–54.

60. Presentments of the Grand Jury of Chatham County, presented to the governor's council, December 28, 1779, *CGHS*, vol. 10, 75.

61. Presentments of the Grand Jury of Chatham County, *CGHS*, vol. 10, 75, 125–26.

62. R. Elliott and D. Elliott, *Savannah under Fire, 1779*, 52.

63. Frey, *Water from the Rock*, 99–104.

64. *Royal Georgia Gazette*, September 6, 1781, notice of John Morel, in Windley, *Runaway Slave Advertisements*, vol. 4, 97–98. Abraham and Billy escaped from the Beaulieu plantation on the mainland, not Ossabaw.

65. Notice by Peter Henry Morel, January 18, 1781, *Royal Georgia Gazette* in Windley, *Runaway Slave Advertisements*, vol. 4, 84. He was described as wearing "an old blue coat of the Hessian uniform" and having "several front teeth missing," and his wife, "country-born," was said to be wearing a blue coat and a petticoat.

66. Notice by John Morel, September 4, 1781, *Royal Georgia Gazette*, in Windley, *Runaway Slave Advertisements*, vol. 4, 93. Joe had been the "property" of Peter Tondee, a deceased taverner in Savannah. He refused to accept his forcible uprooting when sold to the Morels.

67. Notice by Thomas Gibbons, September 7, 1780, *Royal Georgia Gazette*, in Windley, *Runaway Slave Advertisements*, vol. 4, 78–79.

68. Notice by John Morel, January 4, 1781, *Royal Georgia Gazette*, in Windley, *Runaway Slave Advertisements*, vol. 4, 82–83.

69. Notice by John Morel, October 11, 1781, *Royal Georgia Gazette* in Windley, *Runaway Slave Advertisements*, 4:100.

70. Gloria Whiting, paper presented at the Omohundro Institute Coffeehouse, University of Wisconsin-Madison, March 12, 2021.

71. Notice by John Morel, October 11, 1781, *Royal Georgia Gazette*, in Windley, *Runaway Slave Advertisements*, vol. 4, 100.

72. William C. Fleetwood Jr., *Tidecraft: The Boats of South Carolina, Georgia, and Northeastern Florida, 1550–1950* (Tybee Island, Ga: WBG Marine Press, 1995), 36–43; Harris, *Patroons and Periaguas* (Columbia: University of South Carolina Press, 2014).

73. "Observations on East Florida," Lord Hawke in response to a request from Bernardo del Campo, June 8, 1783, in *East Florida, 1783–1785: A File of Documents Assembled, and Many of Them Translated*, comp. Joseph Byrne Lockey (Berkeley: University of California Press, 1949), 120–21.

74. William Drayton, 1732–1790, Force Papers, ser. 8D, item 37, cited in Frey, *Water from the Rock*, 83.

75. *East Florida Gazette*, May 3, 1783, cited in Riordan, "Seminole Genesis: Native Americans, African Americans, and Colonists on the Southern Frontier from Prehistory through the Colonial Era," PhD diss., University of Florida, 1996, 250. The commissioner of sequestered estates in South Carolina reported that many of the enslaved on estates for which he was responsible had headed for East Florida.

76. "The Memorial of Capt. Robert Bissett," in Wilbur Henry Siebert, *Loyalists in East Florida*, 2:250.

77. Robert Baillie to his mother, March 3, 1778, Florida, "Camp Necessity on St. John's River in East Florida," Robert Baillie Papers, GD 1/1155/72, NRS.

78. Frey, *Water from the Rock*, 102–3.

79. Report of the Board of Police to Gov. Wright, May 20, 1780, *CGHS*, vol. 3, 289–93.

80. Report of the Commissioners of Claims, April 24, 1780, *CGHS*, vol. 3, 294.

81. Robert Baillie to his mother, March 3, 1778"; Wright to Germain, December 20, 1780, *CGHS*, vol. 3, 328.

82. *Gazette of the State of Georgia*, October 20, 1785, cited in Kilbourne, comp., *Savannah, Georgia, Newspaper Clippings, 444*; D. Elliott, *Archaeological Investigations at Tabbies 1 and 2, 32*.

83. Cashin, *The King's Ranger*, 162–71.

84. *Gazette of the State of Georgia*, October 20, 1785, in Kilbourne, *Savannah, Georgia, Newspaper Clippings*, 444.

85. Landers, *Black Society in Spanish Florida*, 67–68.

86. Weisman, *Like Beads on a String*; Covington, *The Seminoles of Florida*; Porter, *The Black Seminoles*.

87. Winniett's report in Siebert, *Loyalists in East Florida*, 1:130–31; Siebert, "East Florida as a Refuge"; Maya Jasanoff, *Liberty's Exiles*, 70–73; Pybus, "Jefferson's Faulty Math," 262.

Chapter 4. Entangled Borders

1. The figures are taken from three censuses conducted by John Winniett, a military officer, between July 1782 and April 20, 1783, CO/5:560, 805, Library of Congress transcripts, NAUK. See also Siebert, *Loyalists in East Florida*, 1:130–131, 2:239, 244; Carole Watterson Troxler, "Loyalist Refugees and the British Evacuation of East Florida, 1783–85," *FHQ* 60, no. 1 (July 1981): 1–28. Winniett listed 1,659 African Americans from Georgia arriving between July and November 14, 1782, 1,786 between November 14 and December 31, and 1,336 arriving from Georgia and South Carolina from January 1 to April 20, 1783. It is assumed that 400 of those arriving in 1783 were Georgians, the rest Carolinians, given the late start for the evacuation in South Carolina.

2. Daniel L. Schafer, *St. Augustine's British Years, 1763–1784* (St. Augustine: St. Augustine Historical Society, 2001), 48–58; Landers, *Black Society in Spanish Florida*, 69–70; Helen Hornbeck Tanner, *Zespedes in East Florida, 1784–1790* (Jacksonville: University of North Florida Press, 1989), 29–30.

3. Hoffman, *Florida's Frontiers*, 230; Helen Hornbeck Tanner, "The Second Spanish Period Begins" in *Clash between Cultures: Spanish East Florida, 1784–1827*, ed. Jacqueline K. Fretwell and Susan R. Parker (St. Augustine: St. Augustine Historical Society, 1988), 17–22. Hoffman calculates 17,375 people, of whom 11,285 were Black, 3,000 of whom were present before the war.

4. J. Leitch Wright Jr., *Anglo-Spanish Rivalry in North America* (Athens: University of Georgia Press, 1971), 137; Troxler, "Loyalist Refugees and the British Evacuation," 3; Tanner, "The Second Spanish Period Begins," 18–19.

5. Troxler, "Loyalist Refugees and the British Evacuation," 2–8.

6. Diane Boucher, "Mayhem and Murder in the East Florida Frontier 1783 to 1789."

FHQ 93, no. 3 (Winter 2015): 446–71; Patrick Tonyn to Vicente Manuel de Zespedes, July 29, 1785, in Joseph Byrne Lockey, *East Florida, 1783–1785: A Collection of Documents Assembled and Many of Them Translated* (Berkeley: University of California Press, 1949), 214, 217, 607, 634; Troxler, "Loyalist Refugees and the British Evacuation," 1.

7. Jane G. Landers, "Francisco Zavier Sanchez, Floridano Planter and Merchant," in *Colonial Plantations and Economy in Florida* (Gainesville: University Press of Florida, 2000), 83–97 (esp. 87); Tanner, "The Second Spanish Period Begins," 27. McGirt sold Sanchez forty-six slaves in one transaction.

8. Boucher, "Mayhem and Murder in the East Florida Frontier," 457.

9. Nicolas Grenier, "Brief Description of the Coasts of East Florida," in Lockey, *East Florida*, 309.

10. Tanner, "The Second Spanish Period Begins," 15–43; Siebert, "East Florida as a Refuge," 239; Hoffman, *Florida's Frontiers*, 230–42; Susan R. Parker, "Men without God or King: Rural Settlers of East Florida, 1784–1790," *FHQ* 69 (October 1990), 135–55.

11. Schafer, *St. Augustine's British Years*, 252–72; Parker, "St. Augustine in the Seventeenth-Century," 554–76; Wright, *Florida in the American Revolution*, 125–43.

12. James Penman to Anthony Wayne, October 1, 1783, Anthony Wayne Family Papers, William L. Clements Library, University of Michigan, Ann Arbor; Daniel L. Schafer, *Governor James Grant's Villa: A British East Florida Indigo Plantation* (St. Augustine: St. Augustine Historical Society, 2000), 77–81. Grant finally sold his labor force to a consortium of South Carolina planters for £5,071.

13. Claim of Alexander Patterson, in Wilbur Henry Siebert, *Loyalists in East Florida, 1783–1785*, 2:126–128.

14. Siebert, "Loyalists in East Florida," 1:208.

15. Siebert, "Loyalists in East Florida," 1:208. The "missing" category reflects estimates by Tonyn and others that several thousand Black people and white people fled to the north and west in early 1784 before the formal evacuation. This unusually large number is suspect. It may have been calculated by subtracting all those who migrated to known destinations from a total of all refugees in the British records.

16. James A. McMillin, *The Final Victims: Foreign Slave Trade to North America, 1783–1810* (Columbia: University of South Carolina Press, 2004), 65–66.

17. Granger, *Savannah River Plantations*, 71–77, 120–26.

18. Gilbert, *Black Patriots and Loyalists*, 161.

19. Theodore Thayer, *Nathanael Greene: Strategist of the American Revolution* (New York: Twayne, 1960), 437.

20. James Penman to Anthony Wayne, Charleston, October 1, 1783, Anthony Wayne Family Papers, William L. Clements Library, University of Michigan; Memorandum Book, 1786, box 2, Anthony Wayne Family Papers; Paul David Nelson, *Anthony Wayne: Soldier of the Early Republic* (Bloomington: Indiana University Press, 1985). A former loyalist in East Florida, James Penman, acted as their broker.

21. Memorandum Book, 1786, box 2, Anthony Wayne Family Papers.

22. Census for Effingham, Chatham, Liberty, McIntosh, Glynn and Camden Counties, 1790, June 25, 1791; Robert Forsyth, Marshal, District of Georgia, Census 1790.

23. Landers, "Spanish Sanctuary," 304; Landers, *Black Society in Spanish Florida*, 76–77.

24. James Hume to Patrick Tonyn, St. Augustine, July 26, 1784, in Lockey, *East Florida*, 328–30.

25. The petition of John Milligan, October 26, 1784, EFP, reel 82, LOC.

26. Census Returns, 1784–1814, EFP, reel 148, LOC; Landers, *Black Society in Spanish Florida*, 77.

27. The petition of John Milligan, October 26, 1784, reel 82, EFP ("So many people from Georgia and South Carolina were in this province in quest of Negroes since the War"); Governor Samuel Elbert to governor of Florida, January 20, 1785, reel 41, EFP; Wright, *Florida in the American Revolution*, 133.

28. Zespedes to Houstoun, November 28, 1784, reel 41, EFP.

29. Julius S. Scott, *The Common Wind: Afro-American Currents in the Age of the Haitian Revolution* (London: Verso, 2018), 62–68.

30. *Revolutionary Records of the State of Georgia*, comp. Allen D. Candler (Atlanta: Franklin-Turner, 1908), 2:608–9; Landers, "Spanish Sanctuary," 303–13.

31. Jane Landers, "African Choices in the Revolutionary South," chap. 1 in *Atlantic Creoles*. A remarkable account of the life of Prince Whitten.

32. Landers, *Atlantic Creoles*, 34, 44, 45.

33. Alexander Temple to Mr. Pernan, December 16, 1786, reel 174, EFP; Landers, *Atlantic Creoles*, 30–35.

34. Alexander Temple to Mr. Penman, Amelia Island, December 16, 1786, reel 174, EFP. Temple wrote the letter in the absence of Weed, who was in Augusta.

35. Buddy Sullivan, *Sapelo: People and Place on a Georgia Sea Island* (Athens: University of Georgia Press, 2017), 94; Merton Coulter, *Thomas Spalding of Sapelo Island* (Baton Rouge: Louisiana State University Press: 1940), 7; Lewis Cecil Gray, *History of Agriculture in the Southern United States to 1860* (Gloucester, Mass.: Peter Smith, 1958) 2:676–78; Richard Dwight Porcher and Sarah Fick, *The Story of Sea Island Cotton* (Charleston, S.C.: Wyrick, 2005), 94.

36. Alexander Bissett to Governor Zespedes, September 30, 1788, reel 174, EFP.

37. Paul M. Pressly, "The Many Worlds of Titus: Marronage, Freedom, and the Entangled Borders of Lowcountry Georgia and Spanish Florida, *JSH* 84, no. 1 (August 2018): 545–78.

38. Zespedes to Domingo Cavello, October 17, 1789, reel 8, EFP; Zespedes to Gonzalo Zamorano, October 29, reel 8, EFP. The fugitives were sent on the ship *Rosa* instead of the *Diana*.

39. Presentments of the Grand Jury, *Gazette of the State of Georgia* (Savannah), October 23, 1788 (first and second quotation).

40. James Jackson to Governor Handley, June 2, 1788, DLG, accessed March 30, 2021, http://dlg.usg.edu/record/dlg_zlna_tcc930#item.

41. Amanda D. Roberts Thompson, "People, Place, and Taskscapes of Enslavement: African American life on the South End Plantation, Ossabaw Island, Georgia 1849–1861" (PhD diss., University of York, 2020), 16.

42. Most reports of intercepted fugitives included mention of a "canoe" and often of weapons. Blas de Bouchet to Governor Zespedes, St. Augustine, September 24; Governor Zespedes to Bias de Bouchet, September 28, 1788, reel 45, EFP. The governor announced that nineteen of twenty-one fugitive Georgia slaves had arrived in St. Augustine and approved of Bouchet's disposition of the "canoes and arms brought by the Negroes."

43. Harris, *Patroons and Periaguas*, 63.

44. W. John Davies Affidavit, Chatham County, July 31, 1789, document in possession of the author.

45. Fleetwood, *Tidecraft*, 31–44. "Pettyaguas": another local name for periaguas, a type of small craft used for bringing produce from plantations to coastal towns (p. 29).

46. Lieutenant Pedro Carne to Governor Zespedes, July 1, July 9, 1789, reel 46, EFP.

47. Onofre Gutierrez de Rosas to Governor Henrique White, Amelia Island, September 18, 1796, reel 53, EFP.

48. James Seagrove to governor of Florida, December 17, 1790, reel 41, EFP. The fugitives were Dick, Fortune, Prince, and March.

49. Truxillo to Zespedes, July 5 and July 8, 1788, reel 45, EFP.

50. James Spalding to Vicente Manuel de Zespedes, October 2, 1788, reel 174, EFP.

51. Blas de Bouchet to Zespedes, September 6, September 24, 1788, reel 45, EFP; Manuel Otero to Zespedes, September 25, 1788, reel 45, EFP.

52. Susan Richbourg Parker, "So in Fear of Both the Indians and the Americans," in *America's Hundred Years' War: American Expansion to the Gulf Coast and the Fate of the Seminoles, 1763–1858*, ed. William S. Belko (Gainesville: University Press of Florida, 2015), 36. In one notable case, frustrated Georgians attempted to kidnap the enslaved people of Florida resident George Aaron.

53. Gardoqui to Zespedes, September 24, 1788, reel 38, EFP.

54. Pierce Butler to Roger Saunders, August 26, 1790, in Terry W. Lipscomb, ed., *The Letters of Pierce Butler: Nation Building and Enterprise in the New American Republic* (Columbia: University of South Carolina Press, 2007), 60.

55. "Table 105: White and Colored Population of Each County Reported in 1790, Compared with That of the Same Area in 1900, Together with the Number of Colored per 1000 Whites: Georgia, A Century of Population Growth in the United States: From the First Census to the Twelfth: 1790–1900," U.S. Census Bureau, 1909, 207.

56. There were over 1,000 Africans in the area before 1775 compared to the 304 recorded in the census of 1790.

57. Seagrove to governor of Florida, August 6, 1791, reel 41, EFP.

58. Boucher, *East Florida Frontier*, 461–68.

59. Madeleine Hirsiger Carr, *Last Betrayal on the Wakulla: Florida's Forgotten Spanish Frontier* ([Morrisville, N.C.]: Lulu Publishing Services, 2019), 10–15.

60. William S. Coker and Thomas D. Watson, *Indian Traders of the Southeastern Spanish Borderlands: Panton, Leslie & Company and John Forbes & Company, 1783–1847* (Pensacola: University of West Florida Press, 1986), 32–33.

61. Deposition of James Moore, Camden County, August 30, 1802, GA, viewed October 5, 2022, https://vault.georgiaarchives.org/digital/collection/FileIINames/id/78099/rec/5.

62. Henry O'Neil to Carlos Howard, June 9, 1786, reel 45, EFP.

63. Deposition of John Hornsby, Glynn County, August 29, 1789, reel 46, EFP.

64. William Pengree to Carlos Howard, July 10, 1787, reel 82, EFP.

65. Thomas Sterling to Carlos Howad, March 3, 1793, reel 48, EFP.

66. Henry O'Neil to Carlos Howard, September 10, 1787, reel 45, EFP.

67. Henry O'Neil to Carlos Howard, April 17, 1785, reel 44, EFP. O'Neill noted that the Natives had stolen eight horses on the south side of the St. Marys River.

68. Quesada to Jefferson, August 28, 1790, quoted in annotations to George Washing-

ton, "[Diary Entry: 20 May 1791]," Founders Online, National Archives, https://founders
.archives.gov/documents/Washington/01-06-02-0002-0004-0020.

69. Scott, *The Common Wind*, 60–68; *Augusta Chronicle and Gazette of the State*, April 7,
1792; accessed April 9, 2021, Georgia Historic Newspapers, https://gahistoricnewspapers
-files.galileo.usg.edu/lccn/sn82015220/1792-04-07/ed-1/seq-1.pdf.

70. Robert W. Smith, *Amid a Warring World: American Foreign Relations, 1775–1815*
(Washington, D.C.: Potomac World, 2012), 58–59.

71. George Washington to Seagrove, 20 May 1791, quoted in annotations to George
Washington, "[Diary Entry: 20 May 1791]," Founders Online, National Archives, https://
founders.archives.gov/documents/Washington/01-06-02-0002-0004-0020.

72. James Seagrove to governor of East Florida, August 2, 1791, reel 174, EFP.

73. James Seagrove to governor of East Florida, August 9, 1791, reel 174, EFP.

Chapter 5. A Maroon in the
Postrevolutionary Southeast

1. This chapter is partially based on Paul M. Pressly, "The Many Worlds of Titus: Marronage, Freedom, and the Entangled Borders of Lowcountry Georgia and Spanish Florida," *Journal of Southern History* 84, no. 3 (August 2018): 545–78.

2. Richard Price, *Maroon Societies*, xi.

3. Sherry Johnson, "The Spanish St. Augustine Community, 1784–1795: A Reevaluation,"
FHQ 68 (July 1989): 27–54. Using Father Thomas Hassert's census of the town's population
in 1786, Johnson counts 772 free people, plus the Spanish troops, who after 1789 were the
Third Battalion of Cuba, "the dregs of Spanish and Cuban society" (38, 39). The free people included 216 residents who were of Spanish, Cuban, and Floridano extraction, 469 Majorcans, and 87 white foreigners. The number of free Blacks comes from a 1788 census. See
also Sherry Johnson, "The Historiography of Eighteenth-Century Florida." *FHQ* 93, no. 3
(Winter 2015): 296–326; Patricia C. Griffin, "The Spanish Return: The People-Mix Period,"
in *The Oldest City: St. Augustine, Saga of Survival*, ed. George E. Buker and Jean Parker Waterbury (St. Augustine: St. Augustine Historical Society, 1983), 125–50.

4. Landers, *Black Society in Spanish Florida*, 107 ("brothers in Christ"); Landers, *Atlantic Creoles*, 39–42.

5. "Investigation of reports concerning free 'Black Alicke' and several slaves planning
to flee to North Carolina," Judge and Commissioner Don Bartolome Morales, commandant of the battalion, November 22, 1791, reel 123, EFP.

6. Landers, *Black Society in Spanish Florida*, 183.

7. "African American Heritage and Ethnography," Park Ethnography Program, National Park Service, accessed August 30, 2020https://www.nps.gov/ethnography/aah/aa-
heritage/histContextsE.htm; Jane Landers, "Africans in the Spanish Colonies," *Historical
Archaeology* 31, no. 1 (1997): 94.

8. Landers, "A Nation Divided," 106–7; Landers, *Atlantic Creoles*, 167–68; Landers,
Black Society in Spanish Florida, 88, 96–97, 121, 122, 128, 163–64.

9. Susan Parker, "Men without God or King: Rural Settlers of East Florida, 1784–
1790," *FHQ* 69 (October 1990): 144–49.

10. Zespedes to Luis de las Casas, June 20, 1790, cited in James A. Lewis, "*Cracker*—
Spanish Florida Style," *FHQ* 63 (October 1984): 194.

11. Governor Zespedes to Josef de Espeleta, February 4, 1789, reel 174, EFP.

12. Proclamation by Quesada, September 2, 1790, reel 118, EFP (first quotation); Miguel Ysnardy, Jorge Fleming, and Bernardo Sequi to Quesada, February 12, 1792, reel 83, EFP (second quotation).

13. Governor Quesada to Zomorano, July 4, 1791, reel 25, EFP.

14. Carlos Howard to Governor Quesada, February 28, 1795, reel 51, EFP (first quotation); James Seagrove to Governor Quesada, August 9, 1791, reel 41, EFP (second quotation).

15. Carlos Howard to Acting Governor Bartolome Morales, May 13, 1795, reel 51, EFP.

16. Price, "Maroons."

17. Lockley, "The King of England's Soldiers"; Diouf, *Slavery's Exiles*, 187–208.

18. Marcus P. Nevius, *City of Refuge: Slavery and Petit Marronage in the Great Dismal Swamp, 1765–1856* (Athens: University of Georgia Press, 2020); Diouf, *Slavery's Exiles*, 209–29.

19. Historian Nathaniel Millett argues that the largest maroon community to appear in the United States was a fortification created by the British army on the Apalachicola River during the War of 1812, an encampment of several hundred African Americans armed with British weapons who were defiantly independent until destroyed by the American military during the summer of 1816. Nathaniel Millett, *The Maroons of Prospect Bluff and Their Quest for Freedom in the Atlantic World* (Gainesville: University Press of Florida, 2013); Nathaniel Millett, "Defining Freedom in the Atlantic Borderlands of the Revolutionary Southeast," *Early American Studies* 5, no. 2 (Fall 2007), 367–94.

20. Alvin O. Thompson, *Flight to Freedom: African Runaways and Maroons in the Americas* (Kingston, Jamaica: University of West Indies Press, 2006), 7; Diouf, *Slavery's Exiles*, 1–16.

21. Agreement between John Morel and Alexander Brown, April 1, 1763, Book of Bonds O, 71, GA; "Inventory and appraisement of the personal estate of John Morel, deceased, June 27, 1777," Book FF, 70–76, GA; Betty Wood, "Some Aspects of Female Resistance to Chattel Slavery in Lowcountry Georgia, 1763–1815," *Historical Journal* 30 (September 1987): 606–7. The prominence of Tom and Nelly flowed from their origin as one of the founding families on Ossabaw.

22. Paul M. Pressly, "The Many Worlds of Titus: Marronage, Freedom, and Entangled Borders of Lowcountry Georgia and Spanish Florida," *JSH* 84, no. 1 (August 2018): 545–78.

23. Granger, *Savannah River Plantations*, 215–18; "Titus," *Georgia Gazette*, July 7, 1785, in Windley, *Runaway Slave Advertisements* 4:130.

24. Notice of John Morel, *Georgia Gazette*, July 7, September 8, 1785, in Windley, *Runaway Slave Advertisements*, 4:130, 133; Wood, "Some Aspects of Female Resistance to Slavery," 614. Titus may have escaped twice that summer, first with Jesse and then with Ismael, a fourteen-year-old with whom he had grown up on Ossabaw. For a description of Yamacraw, see Pressly, *On the Rim of the Caribbean*, 80.

25. Notices placed in the *Georgia Gazette* between 1783 and 1795 record the names of 538 fugitives. Only 3 percent of the given destinations were Florida: masters knew that advertising in these cases was a waste of money. See Wood, "Some Aspects of Female Resistance," 614.

26. Governor John Martin, Georgia to Governor Patrick Tonyn, British East Florida, October 19 and 22, 1782, *GHQ* 1 (December 1917): 334–35. For an account of the raid,

see D. Elliott, *Archaeological Investigations at Tabbies 1 and 2*, 39. For the return of the enslaved people, see Wylly and wife vs. Executors of J. Morel, deceased, folder 714, box 6, Superior Court Records #5125, sp-45, GHS.

27. Black Georgians remembered the 1776 escape to Tybee Island of several hundred of their peers, most of whom were taken to St. Augustine. Border warfare between Georgia and British Florida was constant for the first three years of war, and even after the British invasion of Georgia there were raids along the coast by privateers sailing out of St. Augustine.

28. Notice for Hector by John Morel, and notice for Patty and Daniel by Peter Henry Morel, both in *Georgia Gazette*, May 21, 1789; notice for Tony by William Bryan, *Gazette of the State of Georgia*, July 30, 1789 ("a stout negro man, much pitted with the small pox"); notice for Abraham, Jacob, and Ishmael by Bryan Morel, *Georgia Gazette*, July 30, 1789, all in Windley, *Runaway Slave Advertisements*, 4:165–69. John Morel thought they were hiding in a tract of land opposite Ossabaw called Kilkenny but suspected they might head to Florida.

29. Carlos Howard to Governor Quesada, February 28, 1795, reel 51, EFP. Howard informed the governor, "Let it be known to the public that for three years, Titus has roamed about committing thefts in Savannah and its surroundings. He was already a maroon for about four years in this province and he is one of a gang that the aforementioned Mr. J. Brian Morel returned prior to now." Howard overstates the length of his marronage.

30. Diouf, *Slavery's Exiles*, 2.

31. Sebastian Creagh to Governor Quesada, September 12, 1791, reel 47, EFP; Bryan Morel to Quesada, October 17, 1791, reel 174, EFP. Creagh reported that eleven fugitive slaves were taken into custody; Bryan Morel requested the return of fifteen Morel-related fugitives, including Titus (it is assumed that three others were living as maroons in addition to Titus; all were returned as a group).

32. On the death of his first wife, the elder John Morel married Mary Bryan, daughter of Jonathan Bryan, a leading planter and political figure. Alan Gallay, *The Formation of a Planter Elite: Jonathan Bryan and the Southern Colonial Frontier* (Athens: University of Georgia Press, 1989), 108.

33. Landers, "Spanish Sanctuary," 310–13.

34. James Seagrove to Governor Quesada, August 2, 1791, 41, EFP; James Seagrove to Governor Quesada, August 9, 1791, reel 174, EFP; Richard K. Murdoch and Juan de Pierra, "The Seagrove-White Property Agreement of 1797," *GHQ* 42, no. 3 (September 1958): 263–64; Landers, *Black Society in Spanish Florida*, 79–81; Landers, "Spanish Sanctuary," 311–13.

35. Bryan Morel to governor, October 17, 1791, reel 174, EFP. Six affidavits with descriptions accompany his petition.

36. Notice by John Morel, *Gazette of the State of Georgia*, January 22, 1795; notice by Bryan Morel, *Gazette of the State of Georgia*, February 26, 1795.

37. Notice by John Morel, *Gazette of the State of Georgia*, January 22, 1795; notice by Bryan Morel, *Gazette of the State of Georgia*, February 26, 1795.

38. Diouf, *Slavery's Exiles*, 132–34.

39. John Nutt v. William Telfair, Peter H. Morel, John Morel, and Bryan Morel, Esq., of John Morel deceased, A-18, box 22, mixed cases "In Equity," 1790–1860, Southern Circuit Court, District of Georgia, NARA. Because all three Morels failed to pay property

taxes, the sheriff of Chatham County ordered the sale of "all the valuable land known by the name of Ossabaw, 8,000 acres in the County of Chatham." If the sale took place, it was a deftly played sleight-of-hand. The brothers retained ownership. Advertisements for the sale of Ossabaw Island: *Georgia Gazette*, January 9, 1794; July 3, 1794; September 3, 1794; December 4, 1794; January 28, 1795.

40. Sale of slaves by Peter Henry Morel, John Morel, and Bryan Morel to Thomas Netherclift and Peter Deveaux, February 5, 1794, Deed Book M, 309–12, Chatham County Courthouse, Georgia.

41. *Georgia Gazette*, February 26, 1795. Bryan Morel advertised for Lester and Simon on February 13 and speculated that they had fled to neighboring St. Catherines Island.

42. "List of fugitive Negroes fled from Georgia," February 22, 1795, reel 51, EFP; notice of John Morel, *Georgia Gazette*, January 22, 1795.

43. Governor Juan Nepomuceno de Quesada to Governor George Matthews, June 19, 1794, in "Georgia-East Florida-West Florida and Yazoo Land Sales, 1764–1850," WPA Project no. 5993, GA; James Spalding, planter, to Governor Juan Nepomuceno de Quesada, May 28, 1794, reel 41, EFP. Quesada lays out his frustrations; Spalding details why he thinks three slaves stolen from Florida planters and now on the Georgia coast cannot be returned. See also Richard K. Murdoch, *The Georgia-Florida Frontier, 1793–1796: Spanish Reactions to French Intrigue and American Designs* (Berkeley: University of California Press, 1951), 1–10.

44. Joseph de Jaudenes and Josef Ignacio de Viar, Spanish diplomats in Philadelphia, to Governor Quesada, July 26, 1794, reel 39, EFP; Governor Quesada to Luis de las Casas, October 9, 1794, reel 9, EFP; Governor Quesada to Governor George Matthews, January 31, 1795, reel 41, EFP.

45. Howard to Quesada, March 5, 1795, reel 51, EFP.

46. Howard to Quesada, March 5, 1795, reel 51, EFP.

47. Covington, *The Seminoles of Florida*, 15–16; Mulroy, *Freedom on the Border*, 6–7; Patrick Riordan, "Seminole Genesis: Native Americans, African Americans, and Colonists on the Southern Frontier from Prehistory through the Colonial Era" (PhD diss., University of Florida, 1996).

48. Carlos Howard to Bartolome Morales, May 25, 1795, reel 51, EFP; C. Snyder, *Slavery in Indian Country*, 213–17; Saunt, *A New Order of Things*, 129–35.

49. Howard to Quesada, April 6, 1795, "Account of principal events," reel 51, EFP. Howard said, based on what he had heard from Cohiti, "The rebels had kicked the Indians out of their lands; consequently, they didn't fear any others as long as they could hunt the lands of this province, which they always considered their own, but . . . nevertheless they would not do any evil, nor rob anything or anybody," Howard wrote to Quesada, "I stopped to show him the evil consequences of his Negro [named Pedro] wandering around, bribing renegade slaves to the Nation." Saunt, *A New Order of Things*, 128–29. For background, see James G. Cusick, "King Payne and His Policies: A Framework for Understanding the Diplomacy of the Seminoles of La Chua, 1784–1812," in *America's Hundred Years' War: American Expansion to the Gulf Coast and the Fate of the Seminoles, 1763–1858*, ed. William S. Belko (Gainesville: University Press of Florida, 2015), 41–53.

50. Landers, "A Nation Divided: Blood Seminoles and Black Seminoles on the Florida Frontier," 99–116; C. Snyder, *Slavery in Indian Country*, 213–43; Frank, "Taking the State Out," 10–27.

51. "Account of Principal Events," Carlos Howard to Governor Quesada, April 26, 1795, reel 51, EFP.

52. John McQueen to Carlos Howard, April 24, 1795, reel 51, EFP. The letter was included with the "Account of principal events" by Howard. See Walter C. Hartridge, *The Letters of Don Juan McQueen to His Wife, Written from Spanish East Florida, 1791–1807* (Columbia, S.C.: Boswick & Thornley, 1943).

53. Carlos Howard to Governor Quesada, April 6, 1795, reel 51, EFP.

54. John McQueen to Carlos Howard, April 24, 1795, reel 51, EFP.

55. Governor Juan Nepomuceno de Quesada to Governor George Matthews, St. Augustine, October 8, 1795, in "Georgia–East Florida–West Florida," GA; Janice Borton Miller, "The Rebellion in East Florida in 1795," *FHQ* 57 (October 1978): 173–86; James G. Cusick, "Some Thoughts on Spanish East and West Florida as Borderlands," *FHQ*, no. 2 (Fall 2011): 146–49.

56. Acting Governor Bartolomé Morales to Gonzalo Zamoranao, August 8, 1796, reel 26, EFP.

57. Robert W. Smith, *Amid a Warring World: American Foreign Relations, 1775–1815* (Washington, D.C.: Potomac World, 2012), 74–75. In late 1795, Spain and the United States finalized the Treaty of San Lorenzo, which accorded the United States the right of free navigation of the Mississippi River and duty-free transport through the port of New Orleans while resolving the vexing question of the territorial boundary between Spanish West Florida and its northern neighbor.

58. Robert K. Murdoch and Juan de Pierra, "The Seagrove-White Stolen Property Agreement of 1797," *GHQ* 42 (September 1958): 268–76. The Treaty for the Mutual Return of Fugitive Slaves between East Florida and Georgia negotiated by Governor Henrique White and U.S. Commissioner James Seagrove, May 19, 1797, can be found at reel 174, EFP. The treaty was apparently never ratified by the United States and remained a working document rather than a formal agreement.

59. *Colombian Museum and Savannah Advertiser,* May 26, 1797, 2. The article noted that the group "had become so great a nuisance to that country, that most of them were chained, and at work among the convicts." For the compensation agreement, see Enrique White to Thomas King, representative of the state of Georgia, August 25, 1797, in "Georgia–East Florida–West Florida Papers," GA.

60. Thomas Maxey for his father Robert Maxey to James Seagrove. May 12, 1797, reel 42, EFP.

61. James Seagrove to Governor Henrique White, July 4, 1797, reel 42, EFP.

62. Seagrove to White, July 4, 1797, reel 42, EFP (quotations); Landers, *Atlantic Creoles,* 98–100; Diouf, *Slavery's Exiles,* 132–34.

63. Manuel Rengil to Governor Enrique White, August 10, 1797, Savannah, reel 51, EFP.

64. For example: in 1807, James Seagrove, now a planter, asked for Governor White's help in capturing Robert Ross for "negroe stealing & taking them into Florida" and other related crimes. In Camden County, Ross claimed to be a Spanish or French citizen as the occasion demanded, and in Florida he was an American. James Seagrove to Governor Enrique White, January 12, 1807, box 9, Telamon Cuyler Collection, HAR.

65. Deposition of Israel Barber, Camden County, June 12, 1817, File II, Virtual Vault, GA, accessed November 22, 2021, http://vault.georgiaarchives.org/cdm/compoundobject /collection/FileIINames/id/4800/rec/1.

66. Diouf, *Slavery's Exiles*, 130–56.

67. Manuel Rengil to Governor Enrique White, August 10, 1797, Savannah, reel 51, EFP.

Chapter 6. The Florida of Don Juan McQueen

1. Hoffman, *Florida's Frontiers*, 244–46.

2. Andrew McMichael, *Atlantic Loyalties: Americans in Spanish West Florida, 1785–1810* (Athens: University Of Georgia Press, 2008), 17–34.

3. Zespedes to Luis de las Casas, June 20, 1790, cited in Lewis, "*Cracker*—Spanish Florida Style," 191.

4. Hoffman, *Florida's Frontiers*, 245; Landers, *Black Society in Spanish Florida*, 74–75.

5. Calculations made from James C. Cusick, transcriber, "Oaths of Allegiance, East Florida Papers, 1793–1804," unpublished manuscript based on Oaths of Allegiance, 1790–1821," F.04 E13c, George A. Smathers Libraries, University of Florida. The number includes 738 in 1791, 102 in 1792, and 81 in 1793. In *Black Society in Spanish Florida*, Jane Landers gives approximate numbers—300 whites and 1,000 slaves—on page 75.

6. Hartridge, *The Letters of Don Juan McQueen to His Wife*, xvi–xxxv.

7. Forrester to Quesada, December 7, 1792, reel 47, EFP, cited in Cormac A. O'Riordan, "The 1795 Rebellion in East Florida" (Master's thesis, University of North Florida, 1995), 38. Francis Goodwin came to East Florida to avoid facing claims on his property by a Mr. Armstrong of South Carolina while a member of the elite McIntosh family, heavily in debt, needed "to do justice with his creditors without immediate injury to his family." See Charles E. Bennett, *Florida's "French" Revolution, 1793–95* (Gainesville: University Presses of Florida, 1981), 140.

8. Cusick, "Oaths of Allegiance, East Florida Papers," PKY.

9. Anne Smith McQueen was the daughter of John Smith, a wealthy Scottish immigrant who owned multiple plantations in South Carolina. Of her two sisters, one married the son of Sir James Wright, royal governor of Georgia, and the other, Basil Cowper, one of the wealthiest merchants in Savannah. Both men were loyalists. John Smith was a leading patriot.

10. Hartridge, *The Letters of Don Juan McQueen*, xxxi; Cusick, "Oaths of Allegiance, East Florida Papers."

11. Hoffman, *Florida's Frontiers*, 238–39, table 9.5; Landers *Black Society in Spanish Florida*, 82, table 2.2. The censuses in Spanish Florida may be questionable in terms of accuracy but provide a serviceable sense of scale.

12. Hartridge, *Letters of Don Juan McQueen*, xxi–xxiv; Mackay-McQueen Family Papers, National Society of the Colonial Dames of America in the State of Georgia historical collection, GHS; McQueen Papers, Walter Hartridge Collection, GHS; Landers, *Black Society in Spanish Florida*, 164–67. The East Florida Papers contain numerous letters from John McQueen, primarily to the governor about state business.

13. George Washington to Captain John McQueen, March 10, 1779, and McQueen to General Nathanael Greene, April 18, 1782, folder 2302, box 126, Hartridge Collection, GHS. The folder contains other notes and letters describing McQueen's work during the Revolution. Hartridge, *Letters of Don Juan McQueen*, xxiii–xxiv.

14. Martha L. Keber, *Seas of Gold, Seas of Cotton: Christophe Poulain DuBignon of Jekyll Island* (Athens: University of Georgia Press, 2002), 147, 151–52, 158; Mary Bray Wheeler,

Eugenia Price's South: A Guide to the People and Places of Her Beloved Region (Franklin, Tenn.: Providence House Publishers, 2005), 84.

15. Nathanael Greene to Thomas Jefferson, Charleston, June 11, 1785, McQueen Papers, Hartridge Collection, GHS; Lafayette to McQueen, November 20, 1786, in Hartridge, *The Letters of Don Juan McQueen*, 10–11. "This letter will be handed to you by my friend Mr. John McQueen whose principal errand to Paris is to form a contract for live oak on which I wrote you some time since. I beg leave to recommend him to your good offices on the business which he comes."

16. For another account of why the proposed sale fell through, see Virginia Steele Wood, *Live Oaking: Southern Timber for Tall Ships* (Annapolis: Naval Institute Press, 1981), 18–19.

17. At his father's death many years before, the inventory for the estate listed 154 enslaved people. It is not clear how many came to him or how many of these survived the revolutionary upheaval.

18. Landers, *Black Society in Spanish Florida*, 166–167.

19. McQueen to Quesada, August 11, 1792, reel 42, EFP.

20. Thomas Shoolbred to Quesada, November 13, 1792, reel 41, EFP; James Shoolbred to Quesada, March 22, 1794, reel 39, EFP; detailed proceedings in suit by Mario de Lasagna and Jose Antonio Igquiniz, agents for James Shoolbred, against John McQueen, March 4, 1796, reel 153, EFP.

21. Keber, *Seas of Gold, Seas of Cotton*, 145–57.

22. Report by Don Vicente Zespedes, June 20, 1790, reproduced in Lewis, "*Cracker—Spanish Florida Style*," 194–95.

23. Sheet on John McQueen, in Cusick, "Oaths of Allegiance, East Florida Papers,", PKY; Hoffman, *Florida's Frontiers*, 238–39; Landers, *Black Society in Spanish Florida*, 82, table 1.

24. Juan Nepomuceno de Quesada to Luis de Las Casas, June 26, 1791, reel 46, EFP. John McQueen was baptized on June 22, 1791. The event was all the more remarkable because all those officials were keenly aware that less than one hundred English-speaking Catholics were in East Florida, and they had grown up in or been married into the faith. Quesada mentions the three hundred slaves that he is thought to have brought with him.

25. Fernando Medina to Juan Nepomuceno de Quesada, May 7, 1791, reel 46, EFP; Quesada to Fernando Medina, May 10, 1791, reel 46, EFP; Landers, *Black Society in Spanish Florida*, 117. Georgia authorities took into custody the five fugitive slaves and turned them over to a custodian on Amelia Island.

26. J. Leitch Wright Jr., *William Augustus Bowles, Director-General of the Creek Nation* (Athens: University of Georgia Press, 1967); DuVal, *Independence Lost*, 326–31; Gilbert C. Din, "William Augustus Bowles on the Gulf Coast, 1787–1803: Unraveling a Labyrinthine Conundrum," *FHQ* 89, no. 1 (Summer 2010): 1–25.

27. Quesada to Las Casas, October 15, 1791, reel 8, EFP. The governor provides a brief account of McQueen's expedition. See also Wright, *William Augustus Bowles, Director-General*, 61; extract from McQueen's diary, 1791, in Hartridge, ed., *The Letters of Don Juan McQueen*, 13–14.

28. "Memorandum, Lands granted by the Spanish Government of East Florida to John McQueen, B. A. Putnam to E. A. Mackay, October 2, 1830," folder 61, item 27, box 7-a, Mackay Family Papers, GHS.

29. Wheeler, *Eugenia Price's South*, 85, 86.

30. Landers, *Black Society in Spanish Florida*, 164–65.

31. Los Molinos, Testamentary Proceedings of Don Juan McQueen, October 27, 1807, Records of Testamentary Proceedings, 1756–1821, reel 141, EFP.

32. Las Casas to the Conde del Campo de Alange, October 27, 1791, cited in Hartridge, *Letters of Don Juan McQueen*, 14.

33. "Memorandum, Lands Granted by the Spanish Government of East Florida to John McQueen, B. A. Putnam to E. A. Mackay, October 2, 1830," folder 61, item 27, box 7-A, Mackay Family Papers, GHS. Putnam was a lawyer in St. Augustine.

34. Testamentary Proceedings of Don Juan McQueen, October 1807, Records of Testamentary Proceedings, 1756–1821, reel 141, EFP; Landers, *Black Society in Spanish Florida*, 166.

35. Hartridge, *Letters of Don Juan McQueen*, 32; San Pablo Plantation, inventory of John McQueen's estate, 1807, reel 141, EFP.

36. Landers, *Black Society in Spanish Florida*, 164–65.

37. John McQueen to Eliza Anne McQueen, April 24, 1792, and John McQueen to Liza Anne McQueen, January 20, 1801, in Hartridge, *Letters of Don Juan McQueen*, 18, 56.

38. John McQueen to Liza Anne McQueen, January 20, 1801, in Hartridge, *Letters of Don Juan McQueen*, 56.

39. Landers, *Black Society in Spanish Florida*, 117.

40. Baptisms of the McQueen slaves, April 27, 1793, Black Baptisms, vol. 1, CPR, reel 284, PKY, cited in Landers, *Black Society in Spanish Florida*, 120, 326n58 .

41. For the English hunting dogs, see the story of Titus in the preceding chapter. For other examples of returning enslaved people to their enslavers, see Governor White to Governor Telfair on the return of stolen slaves, April 26, 1797, reel 42, EFP.

42. A succession of letters and documents highlights the process: governor of Florida to Manuel Rengil, August 28, 1798, reel 40, section 26, EFP (the governor informs Rengil that John McQueen does not have permission to conduct duty-free slave sales off Amelia Island); McQueen to governor, September 15, 1798, reel 167, EFP (McQueen requests a passport to send seventy-seven slaves to his mother in Savannah for her support as a way of covering sales to Americans); McQueen receives a license to admit slaves, October 14, 1798, Papers on Negro Titles, Runaways, etc., 1787–1805, reel 167, EFP; Bartolome de Castro y Ferrer, agent for McQueen, requested a license to import between three hundred and four hundred slaves free of duties, December 24, 1798, reel 133, EFP; notice of Marshall, August 2, 1798, *Georgia Gazette* (notice was given that two families of Blacks, thirteen people in number, had been seized as the property of John McQueen at the suit of Andrew McCredie and Co., a slave trading firm.

43. Manuel Rengil to Enrique White, June 16, 1798, reel 40, EFP.

44. Robert Mackay to Eliza Anne Mackay, March 12, 1801, in Walter Charlton Hartridge, ed., *The Letters of Robert Mackay to His Wife* (Athens: University of Georgia Press, 1949), 21.

45. Civil Petition of Nancy, September 19, 1792, reel 151, EFP; Jane Landers, "African-American Women and Their Pursuit of Rights through Eighteenth-Century Spanish Texts," in *Haunted Bodies: Gender and Southern Texts*, ed. Anne Goodwyn Jones and Susan V. Donaldson (Charlottesville: University Press of Virginia, 1997), 66–68.

46. McMichael, *Atlantic Loyalties*, 35–40; Cusick, *The Other War of 1812*, 44; Keila Grinberg, "Manumission," in *The Princeton Companion to Atlantic History*, ed. Joseph C.

Miller, Vincent Brown, Jorge Canizares-Esguerra, Laurent Dubois, Karen Ordahl Kupperman (Princeton: Princeton University Press, 2015), 319–21. The Siete Partidas recognized the slave as a human being, offered protection against an abusive master, permitted the slave to testify in court, and provided a system whereby an enslaved person could obtain his or her manumission by earning the equivalent of her value through the hiring of her labor.

47. Civil Petition of Nancy, September 19, 1792, reel 151, EFP; Landers, "African-American Women and Their Pursuit of Rights," 66–68.

48. John McQueen to Juan Nepomuceno de Quesada, August 11, 1792, reel 47, EFP.

49. Civil Petition of Nancy, September 19, 1792, reel 151, EFP; Landers, "African-American Women and Their Pursuit of Rights," 68; Landers, *Black Society in Spanish Florida*, 143–44; John McQueen to Juan Nepomuceno de Quesada, August 11, 1792, reel 47, EFP. Landers provides a dramatic account of the closing moments of the trial in "African-American Women and Their Pursuit of Rights," 66–68.

50. John McQueen to Colonel Bartolome Morales, August 28, 1795, reel 51, EFP.

51. Cusick, "Some Thoughts on Spanish East and West Florida," 133–56.

52. Harry Ammon, *The Genet Mission* (New York: W. W. Norton, 1973); Richard K. Murdoch, *The Georgia–Florida Frontier 1793–1796: Spanish Reactions to French Intrigue and American Designs* (Berkeley: University of California Press, 1951); Robert J. Alderson, *This Bright Era of Happy Revolutions: French Consul Michel-Ange-Bernard Mangourit and International Republicanism in Charleston, 1792–1794* (Columbia: University of South Carolina Press, 2008).

53. Alderson, *This Bright Era of Happy Revolutions*, 127–28, 131–33, 170–71.

54. Janice B. Miller, "The Rebellion in East Florida in 1795," *FHQ* 57 (October 1978): 173–86; Robert J. Alderson, "Entangled Borderlands: The 1794 Projected French Invasion of Spanish East Florida and Atlantic History," *FHQ* 88, no. 1 (Summer 2009): 54–82. Samuel Hammond, a Savannah merchant, became the organizing force in hopes that his firm would displace Panton, Leslie & Company as the chief supplier of trading goods to the Seminoles and Creeks.

55. Deliberations of the Council of War, January 21, 1794, cited in Charles E. Bennett, *Florida's "French" Revolution, 1793–95* (Gainesville: University Presses of Florida, 1981), 75–78.

56. Alderson, *This Bright Era of Happy Revolutions*, 110–44; Michael Morris, "Dreams of Glory, Schemes of Empire: The Plan to Liberate Spanish Florida," *GHQ* 87 (Spring 2003): 1–21; O'Riordan, "The 1795 Rebellion in East Florida," 87.

57. O'Riordan, "The 1795 Rebellion in East Florida," 33–35. The leader, Richard Lang, had immigrated years earlier to Florida to escape a felony conviction in South Carolina and, once south of the border, became associated with a loosely structured network of horse thieves and cattle rustlers with family conveniently on both sides of the border.

58. Miller, "The Rebellion in East Florida in 1795," 177–79.

59. Landers, *Atlantic Creoles*, 51–54.

60. John McQueen to Colonel Bartolome Morales, August 28, 1795, reel 51, EFP.

61. Andrew Atkinson to Manual Rengil, September 20, 1795, reel 52, EFP; petition of Daniel Plummer, September 30, 1795, reel 124, EFP; Cusick, *The Other War of 1812*, 51. The men who attacked the farmer, Plummer, were former Florida residents who suspected he had informed on them.

62. "Report on what Corp. Dan McGirt learned in conversation with Coleraine party

concerning enemy activity," Nathaniel Hall to Andrew Atkinson, September 26, 1795, reel 52, EFP.

63. Wright, *William Augustus Bowles*; DuVal, *Independence Lost*, 326–31; Landers, "A Nation Divided," 104–6; Jennison, *Cultivating Race*, 127–55; Gilbert C. Din, "William Augustus Bowles on the Gulf Coast, 1787–1803: Unraveling a Labyrinthine Conundrum," *FHQ* 89, no. 1 (Summer 2010): 14.

64. McQueen to White, September 7, October 3, 1801, reel 56, EFP.

65. Cusick, *The Other War of 1812*, 45–46.

66. Daniel L. Schafer, *Zephaniah Kingsley Jr. and the Atlantic World: Slave Trader, Plantation Owner, Emancipator* (Gainesville: University Press of Florida, 2013), 70; calculations made from Cusick, "Oaths of Allegiance."

67. Rivers, *Slavery in Florida*, 6. The most reliable censuses are those of 1793, when 1,527 slaves were recorded, and of 1814, when 1,540 were counted. Hoffman, *Florida Frontiers*, 238–39 (table 9.5); Landers, *Black Society in Spanish Florida*, 82 (table 1); Cusick, "Oaths of Allegiance."

68. John McQueen to John McQueen Jr., January 5, 1804, in Hartridge, e*Letters of Don Juan McQueen*, 62–63.

69. John McQueen to Robert Mackay, March 4, 1804, in Hartridge, *Letters of Don McQueen*, 64; governor of Florida to Shoolbred, January 7, 1794, reel 39, EFP. Governor Quesada mentions McQueen's intention to sell all but twenty of his slaves.

70. Governor of Florida to James Shoolbred, January 7, 1794, reel 39, EFP.

71. Testamentary Proceedings of Don Juan McQueen, October 27, October 29, and November 1, 1807, Records of Testamentary Proceedings, 1756–1821, reel 141, EFP.

72. John McQueen to John McQueen Jr., January. 5, 1804, in Hartridge, *Letters of Don Juan McQueen*, 62–63.

73. Testimony of Harry McQueen, Testamentary Proceedings of Don Juan McQueen, October 14, 1807, cited in \Landers, *Black Society in Florida*, 166.

74. His closest friend in St. Augustine was John Leslie, partner in Panton, Leslie, who was in a relationship with successive Black women. Leslie recognized the children as his own.

75. Mark A. McDonough, *The Francis Richard Family: From French Nobility to Florida Pioneers, 1300–1900* (Lulu.com, 2010), 1–51.

76. Testamentary Proceedings of Don Juan McQueen, October 1807, Records of Testamentary Proceedings, 1756–1821, reel 141, EFP.

77. Landers, *Atlantic Creoles*, 49; Landers *Black Society in Spanish Florida*, 150, 242.

78. Jose Martinez to Enrique White, January 26, 1802, reel 56, EFP, cited in McDonough, *The Francis Richard Family*, 47.

79. "Complaint against William Dell for flogging the Negro Dominico belonging to Luis Jose Francois Richard," January 16, 1810, reel 125, EFP; depositions of the Negros Dominic and Lycurgus before Justice of the Peace William Craig, January 10, 1810, reel 125, EFP; deposition of Francis Richard before Justice of the Peace William Craig, January 11, 1810, reel 125, EFP.

80. Deposition of David Sweeney before Justice of the Peace, William Craig, February 19, 1810, reel 125, EFP.

81. Deposition of Captain Andrew Atkinson before Justice of the Peace William Craig, February 19, 1810, reel 125, EFP.

82. Cusick, *The Other War of 1812*, 175.

83. Robert Mackay to Eliza Anne Mackay, Amelia Island, March 21, 1810, in Hartridge, *The Letters of Robert Mackay*, 225–29, quotation from 226.

84. Robert Mackay to Eliza Anne Mackay, Amelia Island, March 20, 1810, in Hartridge, ed., *The Letters of Robert Mackay*, 223–25; quotation from 225.

85. Robert Mackay to Eliza Anne Mackay, March 21, 1810, in Hartridge, *The Letters of Robert Mackay*, 223–24.

86. J. Hall to "Dear Sir," June 30, 1800, reel 55, EFP; A. Atkinson to "Your Excellency," June 30, 1800, reel 42, EFP; Wiley Thompson to governor of Florida, April 20, 1803, reel 57, EFP. Six Indians from the "Black Creek settlement" had been in the settlement hunting when they snatched three field hands and rode off. One prisoner managed to escape on the first night of captivity.

87. Creek war parties were typically careful to stay along the outer edges of settlements but in a notable exception the town of Greensboro, Georgia, was sacked in 1787.

Chapter 7. War Captives of the Creek People

1. James Spalding to Vicente Manuel de Zespedes, October 2, 1788, reel 174, EFP; Alexander Bissett to Governor Zespedes, September 30, 1788, reel 174, EFP. In 1788, the two planters lost thirteen enslaved people who originally came from East Florida.

2. Saunt, *A New Order of Things*; C. Snyder, *Slavery in Indian Country*; Ethridge, *Creek Country*; Braund, *Deerskins and Duffels*; Kokomoor, *Of One Mind and of One Government*; James L. Hill, *Creek Internationalism in an Age of Revolution, 1763–1818* (Lincoln: University of Nebraska Press, 2022).

3. Peter H. Wood, "The Changing Population of the Colonial South: An Overview by Race and Region, 1685–1790," in *Powhatan's Mantle: Indians in the Colonial Southeast*, ed. Gregory A. Waselkov, Peter H. Wood, and Tom Hartley (Lincoln: University of Nebraska Press, 1989), 86. The figures come from a report to the governor of Spanish West Florida. The actual number of Creeks at the end of the eighteenth century remains an unknown. Estimates are typically based on the number of gunmen or male warriors. Scholars multiply the number of gunman by an estimate of how many people are in the typical household of a warrior, including women, children, and the aged and infirm. Best estimates for the Lower and Upper Towns are around 18,000 individuals by 1790.

4. Braund, "The Creek Indians, Blacks, and Slavery," 622–24; Christina Snyder, "Conquered Enemies, Adopted Kin, and Owned People: The Creek Indians and Their Captives," *Journal of Southern History* 73, no. 2 (May 2007): 255–88; Ethridge, *Creek Country*, 115–19; Littlefield, *Africans and Creeks*, 26–28; Landers, *Black Society in Spanish Florida*, 78.

5. Kokomoor, *Of One Mind and of One Government*, 168–70; Carr, *Last Betrayal on the Wakulla*, 10–15. "Mother Town" was the term used for the two leading towns among the Lower Creek settlements.

6. See map 5 for the trading path from Jack Kinnard's settlement.

7. Andrew K. Frank and A. Glenn Crothers, introduction to *Borderland Narratives: Negotiation and Accommodation in North America's Contested Spaces, 1500–1850* (Gainesville: University Press of Florida, 2017). Kokomoor, *Of One Mind and of One Government*, 269–71; Megan Kate Nelson, *Trembling Earth: A Cultural History of the Okefenokee Swamp* (Athens: University of Georgia Press, 2005), 11–39. The term "frontier" in this study means a territory that lay beyond the control of an often weak imperial or national power. Given the debate over frontier and borderland, "frontier" refers to a zone where

Europeans and Natives met and interacted for sustained periods. "Borderland" is understood as a region where two imperial powers share a border around which a vacuum of power exists.

8. Braund, "The Creek Indians, Blacks, and Slavery," 622–24; Littlefield, *Africans and Creeks*, 26–28.

9. Claudio Saunt, "'The English Has Now a Mind to Make Slaves of Them All': Creeks, Seminoles, and the Problem of Slavery," *American Indian Quarterly* 22 (Winter-Spring 1998): 165–67; Saunt, *A New Order of Things*, 111.

10. Snyder, *Slavery in Indian Country: The Changing Face of Captivity in Early America*, 1–12, 101–26, 182–212. The subtitle expresses the central theme.

11. Lee W. Formwalt, "Violence and Diplomacy in the Creek Country: Jack Kinnard, the Chehaw, and the United States government in Late Eighteenth-Century Southwest Georgia," *Journal of Southwest Georgia History* 7 (1989), 1–19.

12. Caleb Swan, "Position and State of Manners and Arts," 261–62; Carr, *Last Betrayal on the Wakulla*, 13–20, 28; Minutes of the Board of the President and Assistants, July 26, August 31, 1749, *CGR*, vol. 6:256, 287.

13. Kevin Kokomoor, "The Importance of the Oconee War in the Early Republic," *GHQ* 105, no. 1 (2021): 26–62.

14. "Treaty with the Creeks, 1790," Lillian Goldman Law Library, Yale Law School, accessed February 14, 2021, https://avalon.law.yale.edu/18th_century/cre1790.asp.

15. Swan, "Position and State of Manners and Arts in the Creeks, or Muscogee Nation in 1791," in *Information Respecting the History, Condition, and Prospects of the Indian tribes of the United States*, ed. Henry R. Schoolcraft (Philadelphia: Lippincott and Grambo, 1855), 261. The spelling of the surname is variously given as "Kennard" or "Kinnard," with considerably more variations in the correspondence of Spanish authorities. "Kennard is the spelling in local and family histories; "Kinnard" is the spelling by American authorities and most commonly used by historians. Kinnard was called John and Jack.

16. Swan, "Position and State of Manners and Arts," 261.

17. Kokomoor, *Of One Mind and of One Government*, 51–55.

18. "A Sketch of the Creek Country in the years 1798 and 1799," *LBH* 1:316; Hawkins to Daniel Steward, October 13, 1810, *LBH* 2:571–73. In "A Sketch," Hawkins remarked: "Several of the Indians have negroes taken during the revolutionary war. . . . These negroes were given, many of them, by the agents of Great Britain to the Indians in payment for their services and they generally call themselves "King's gifts."

19. Kokomoor, "The Importance of the Oconee War"; Haynes, *Patrolling the Border*, 88–90; 102–4, 124–29; Kokomoor, *Of One Mind and of One Government*, 75–110; Jennison, *Cultivating Race*, 93–95; Kenneth Coleman, *American Revolution in Georgia*, 238–43; Braund, *Deerskins and Duffels*, 170–75.

20. Haynes, *Patrolling the Border*, 1–16.

21. Kokomoor, "The Importance of the Oconee War," 44–47; Haynes, *Patrolling the Border*, 137.

22. "Returns of Depredations committed by the Creek Indians," ASPIA 1:77; Saunt, *New Order of Things*, 117.

23. Petition of Grand Jury of Glynn County, signed by James Spalding, *Georgia Gazette*, July 29, 1790, 2.

24. Roger Parker Saunders to General James Jackson, September 29, (1788), File II

Names, Virtual Vault, GA, accessed November 20, 2021, https://vault.georgiaarchives.org
/digital/collection/FileIINames/id/59976/rec/2.

25. Deposition of Winney Akin, August 15, 1800, File II Names, Virtual Vault, GA,
accessed November 20, 2021, https://vault.georgiaarchives.org/digital/collection
/FileIINames/id/705/rec/12.

26. Deposition of July 2, 1821, James Smith, Virtual Vault, File II Names, GA, accessed
January 18, 2021, https://vault.georgiaarchives.org/digital/collection/FileIINames
/id/81753/rec/19.

27. James Jackson to Governor Handley, June 2, 1788, HAR, accessed March 30, 2021,
https://dlg.usg.edu/record/dlg_zlna_tcc930#item.

28. "[Correspondence] 1788 Apr. 20 - 1788 May 27, [Georgia to] General James Jackson
/ Colonel Jacob Weed, Colonel James Maxwell, James Dunwoody . . . [et al.]," HAR, accessed March 8, 2021, https://dlg.usg.edu/record/dlg_zlna_tcc929#item.

29. Affidavit of Winny Akin, widow of James Allen. Camden County. August 5, 1800,
File II Counties, Virtual Vault, GA, accessed February 14, 2021, https://vault.georgia
archives.org/digital/collection/FileIINames/id/702/rec/12; Deposition of Corker, December 25, 1820, File II Names, Virtual Vault, GA, accessed February 14, 2021, https://vault
.georgiaarchives.org/digital/collection/FileIINames/id/19881/rec/6.

30. James Maxwell to "Dear Sir," Midway, May 28, 1789, File II Names, Virtual Vault,
GA, accessed February 14, 2021, https://vault.georgiaarchives.org/digital/collection
/FileIINames/id/84504/rec/3.

31. John Berrien to James Jackson, September 30, 1788, File II. Names, Virtual Vault,
GA, accessed February 14, 2021, https://vault.georgiaarchives.org/digital/collection
/FileIINames/id/75266/rec/4.

32. Deposition of Andrew Walthour, August 1789, File II Names, Virtual Vault, GA,
accessed February 14, 2021, https://vault.georgiaarchives.org/digital/collection
/FileIINames/id/69506/rec/2; Andrew Walthour to Governor Irwin, December 31, 1806,
File II Names, Virtual Vault, GA, accessed February 14, 2021, https://vault.georgia
archives.org/digital/collection/FileIINames/id/69505/rec/2; Daniel Stewart to Governor John Milledge, January 18, 1805, File II Names, Virtual Vault, GA, accessed March 4,
2021, https://vault.georgiaarchives.org/digital/collection/FileIINames/id/83908/rec/2.

33. Affidavit of Daniel Stewart, January 18 1805, File II Names, Virtual Vault, GA, accessed February 16, 2021, https://vault.georgiaarchives.org/digital/collection/FileIINames
/id/78729; "A return of sixteen prime field hands belonging to A. Maybank," October 27,1802, Andrew Maybank, File II Names, Virtual Vault, accessed February 14, 2021,
https://vault.georgiaarchives.org/digital/collection/FileIINames/id/44268; affidavit of
Andrew Maybank, October 27, 1802, File II Counties, Liberty County, GA, accessed
February 14, 2021, https://vault.georgiaarchives.org/digital/collection/FileIINames/
id/78729.

34. "Description of Negroes taken from Israel Bird," February 14, 1788," File II Names,
Virtual Vault, GA, accessed November 26, 2021, https://vault.georgiaarchives.org/digital
/collection/FileIINames/id/8450/rec/1.

35. Deposition of John LeConte, August 19, 1789, File II Names, Virtual Vault, GA,
accessed February 14, 2021, https://vault.georgiaarchives.org/digital/collection
/FileIINames/id/77741/rec/1.

36. Affidavit of William Girardeau, August 21, 1788, File II Names, Virtual Vault, GA,

accessed February 14, 2021, https://vault.georgiaarchives.org/digital/collection /FileIINames/id/77366/rec/5; inventory of losses of Wm. Girardeau to Creek Indians, August 5, 1791, File II Names, Virtual Vault, GA, accessed February 14, 2021, https://vault .georgiaarchives.org/digital/collection/FileIINames/id/77371/rec/5.

37. Affidavit of John B. Girardeau on behalf of Andrew Maybank, October 27, 1802, File II Names, Virtual Vault, GA, accessed March 5, 2021, https://vault.georgiaarchives .org/digital/collection/FileIINames/id/44268; "A return of negroes taken from Andrew Maybank by the Creek Indians," May 30, 1821, File II Names, Virtual Vault, GA, accessed March 5, 2021, https://vault.georgiaarchives.org/digital/collection/FileIINames/id/44271.

38. "A memorandum of property lost by John B. Girardeau, about August 10, 1788," John B. Girardeau, October 4, 1802, File II Names, Virtual Vault, GA, accessed February 14, 2021, https://vault.georgiaarchives.org/digital/collection/FileIINames/id/77343; affidavit of Andrew Maybank on behalf of John B. Girardeau, August 27, 1788, File II Names, Virtual Vault, GA, accessed March 5, 2021, https://vault.georgiaarchives.org/digital /collection/FileIINames/id/77336/rec/2; affidavit of William Girardeau, Liberty County, August 21, 1789, File II Names, Virtual Vault, GA, accessed March 5, 2021, https://vault .georgiaarchives.org/digital/collection/FileIINames/id/77366; deposition of John Bohrum Girardeau, of Newport, Liberty County, in Chatham County, July 30, 1791, File II Names, Virtual Vault, GA, accessed March 5, 2021, https://vault.georgiaarchives.org /digital/collection/FileIINames/id/77338/rec/2.

39. Deposition of Stephen Corker, December 25, 1820, Glynn County, File II, Virtual Vault, GA, accessed March 5, 2021, https://vault.georgiaarchives.org/digital/collection /FileIINames/id/19881/rec/2. Those taken include Charlotte, 36; her son Andrew, 20; Bess, 18; Bess's child Judy, 2; Sam, 15; and Sarah, 12.

40. Kokomoor, "The Oconee War," 51–53.

41. Saunt, *A New Order of Things*, 67–73.

42. Swan, "Position and State of Manners and Arts," 261.

43. For example, John Kinnard to Governor Enrique White, May 8, 1802, reel 56, EFP; and John Cannard to governor of Florida, October 2, 1801, reel 43, EFP.

44. Kinnard to Seagrove, August 28, 1792, File II Names, Virtual Vault, GA, accessed January 20, 2023. https://vault.georgiaarchives.org/digital/collection/FileIINames/id /40390/rec/1.

45. James Karnard to James Seagrove, June 5, 1803, File II Names, Virtual Vault, GA, accessed January 20, 2023, https://vault.georgiaarchives.org/digital/collection /FileIINames/id/41089/rec/1.

46. James Aiken Deposition, May 3, 1793, ASPIA 1:389–90; Talk from Kennard and Other Chiefs, May 16, 1793, ASPIA 1:388–89; Barnard to Seagrove, May 10, 1792, ASPIA 1:297. Kokomoor, *Of One Mind and of One Government*, 150–61; Wright, *William Augustus Bowles*, 72–74.

47. Affidavit of Ann Gray, Camden County, ASPIA 1:374; affidavit of Robert Brown, Camden County, March 14, 1793, File II Names, Virtual Vault, GA, accessed March 5, 2021, https://vault.georgiaarchives.org/digital/collection/FileIINames/id/75563/rec/4; James Seagrove to Governor Edward Telfair, March 17, 1793, File II Names, Virtual Vault, GA, accessed March 8, 2021, https://vault.georgiaarchives.org/digital/collection /FileIINames/id/81509/rec/3.

48. Deposition of James Akin, Camden County, March 18, 1800, File II, Virtual Vault, GA, accessed October 27, 2022, https://vault.georgiaarchives.org/digital/collection

/FileIINames/id/74970/rec/57; affidavit of Nathan Atkinson, Camden County, October 31, 1802, File II Names, Virtual Vault, GA, accessed February 15, 2021, https://vault.georgiaarchives.org/digital/collection/FileIINames/id/74977/rec/57; affidavit of Richard Carnes, March 18, 1800, affidavit of Amos Cheek, October 19, 1802, File II Names, Virtual Vault, GA, accessed February 15, 2021, https://vault.georgiaarchives.org/digital/collection/FileIINames/id/74977/rec/57.

49. Juan Forrester to Quesada, October 1, 1792, reel 47, EFP. For a statement of Galphin's griefs, see John Galphin to Henry Osborne, May 23, 1789, ASPIA 1:35–36; and Kokomoor, *Of One Mind and of One Government*, 194–95.

50. J. Leitch Wright Jr., *Creeks and Seminoles* (Lincoln: University of Nebraska Press, 1986), 75–77, 85; Richard Lang to governor of East Florida, April 19, 1793, reel 48, EFP.

51. Title of head warrior granted by George III to Philatouche, February 9, 1793, signed by Governor Dunmore of the Bahamas, February 1793, reel 55, EFP: "Whereas you have been faithful and loyal to us and friendly to our subjects in East Florida . . ., particularly your extraordinary valor and conduct at the late battle at Savannah with the Rebels."

52. John Forrester to Quesada, April 23, 1793, reel 48, EFP; John Cannard to headmen of Lower Creeks, May 25, 1793, reel 43, EFP; Saunt, *A New Order of Things*, 130.

53. Julian Carballo to Arturo O'Neill, n.d., PC, reel 162, EFP, cited in Saunt, *New Order of Things*, 124; Saunt, "The English Has Now a Mind," 167.

54. Affidavit of Isaac Green for the estate of James Green, June 12, 1835, Indian Depredations, File II Names, Virtual Vault, GA, accessed February 15, 2021, https://vault.georgiaarchives.org/digital/collection/FileIINames/id/29713/rec/31.

55. Richard Lang to governor of East Florida, April 19, 1793, reel 48, EFP; Seagrove to Timothy Barnard, April 19, 1793, ASPIA 1:378–79.

56. John Cannard to Juan Nepomuceno de Quesada, May 25, 1793, and John Cannard to the principal headmen of the Lower Creeks, May 25, 1793, reel 25, EFP; Saunt, "The English Has Now a Mind," 167–68; Saunt, *A New Order of Things*, 130–31.

57. John Hambly to Carlos Howard, May 8, 1793, reel 43, EFP.

58. Richard Lang to governor of East Florida, April 19, 1793, reel 48, EFP; John Forrester to Quesada, April 20, 1793, reel 43, EFP.

59. In May 1793, Creeks carried off thirteen slaves from the plantation of William Smith. Affidavit of William Smith, June 4, 1821, File II Names, Virtual Vault, GA, accessed February 14, 2021, https://vault.georgiaarchives.org/digital/collection/FileIINames/id/81694/rec/14. John Kinnard reported that the Chiaja people "brought large gangs of cattle and horses in with them with some negroes." See John Cannard to William Panton, May 27, 1793, PC, reel 286, PKY, cited in Saunt, *A New Order of Things*, 126; Kokomoor, *Of One Mind and of One Government*, 170.

60. Seagrove to secretary of war, October 31, 1793, Fort Fidius, ASPIA 1:468–69.

61. James Jackson to governor, October 25, 1795, File II Names, Virtual Vault, GA, accessed February 17, 2022, https://vault.georgiaarchives.org/digital/collection/FileIINames/id/37130/rec/13.

62. James Jackson to the governor of Georgia, July 21, 1793, File II, Camden County, Virtual Vault, GA, accessed October 27, 2022, https://vault.georgiaarchives.org/digital/collection/p17154coll2/id/1225/rec/152.

63. Kokomoor, *Of One Mind and of One Government*, 173–74.

64. James Jackson to Lt. Col. Stewart, October 16, 1795, Savannah, in *CGHS*, vol. II, 87–88.

65. Kokomoor, *Of One Mind and of One Government*, 74.

66. Kokomoor, *Of One Mind and of One Government*, 215. Haynes, *Patrolling the Border*, 180–85; Littlefield, *Africans and Creeks*, 35–36; Correspondence concerning the Treaty of Coleraine, 1795, ASPIA, 1:587–620.

67. Hawkins to Daniel Steward, October 13, 1810, *LBH* 2:571–73. Hawkins pointed out the unfairness of the negotiations at Colerain. Virtually all the headmen were illiterate; they depended on translators provided by the Americans for their understanding of each clause.

68. "The Talk of the Commissioners of Georgia to the Kings, Headmen, and Warriors of the Creek Nation," June 18, 1796, ASPIA 1:614–15. Among a list of griefs, they pointed out, "Very few Negroes have been returned."

69. Swan, "Position and State of Manners," 261; Kokomoor, "Burning and Destroying All Before Them," *GHQ* 98, no. 4 (Winter 2014), 300–340.

70. Representatives of the Creek Land, Negotiations for the Treaty of Colerain, June 24, 1795, ASPIA 1:603.

71. Affidavit of David Garvin, February 4, 1803, File II Names, Virtual Vault, GA, https://vault.georgiaarchives.org/digital/collection/FileIINames/id/30441/rec/88; affidavit of John Whitehead, Liberty County, September 5, 1791, File II Names, Virtual Vault, GA, accessed November 28, 2021, https://vault.georgiaarchives.org/digital/collection /FileIINames/id/71828.

72. Snyder, *Slavery in Indian Country*, 194.

73. Affidavit of Daniel Stewart, January 18 1805, File II Names, Virtual Vault, GA, accessed February 16, 2021, https://vault.georgiaarchives.org/digital/collection /FileIINames/id/78729.

74. Morris, *George Galphin and the Transformation of the Georgia–South Carolina Backcountry*, 161–62.

75. Deposition of Andrew Walthour for the estate of David Anderson, April 29, 1796, accessed September 28, 2021, https://vault.georgiaarchives.org/digital/collection /FileIINames/id/2009/rec/1.

76. "The Creek Nation to the estate of James Smith," May 3, 1793; affidavit of James Smith, July 2, 1821, related financial documents, File II Names, Virtual Vault, GA, accessed November 28, 2021, https://vault.georgiaarchives.org/digital/collection /FileIINames/id/81743/rec/19.

77. Affidavit of John B. Girardeau, July 30, 1791, File II Names, Virtual Vault, GA, accessed March 7, 2021, https://vault.georgiaarchives.org/digital/collection/FileIINames /id/77338/rec/2.

78. Affidavit of John B. Girardeau, October 26, 1802, Liberty County, File II Names, Virtual Vault, GA, accessed November 29, 2021, https://vault.georgiaarchives.org/digital /collection/FileIINames/id/56395/rec/2. The affidavit is followed by affidavits by William Ball and others. The affidavits appear under a case involving Thomas Quarterman.

79. Saunt, *A New Order of Things*, 122.

80. Swan, "Position and State of Manners and Arts," 254.

81. Ethridge, *Creek Country*, 160, 169, 170.

82. Synder, *Slavery in Indian Country*, 188–90; Saunt, "The English Has Now a Mind," 169–70; Carr, *Last Betrayal on the Wakulla*, 51–52.

83. Snyder, *Slavery in Indian Country*, 201.

84. Deposition of James Akin, Camden County, March 18, 1800, File II, Virtual Vault, GA, accessed October 27, 2022, https://vault.georgiaarchives.org/digital/collection /FileIINames/id/74970/rec/57

85. Affidavit of Nathan Atkinson, Camden County, October 31, 1802; affidavit of Richard Carnes, March 18, 1800; and affidavit of Amos Cheek, October 19, 1802, all in File II Names, Virtual Vault, GA, accessed February 15, 2021, https://vault.georgiaarchives.org /digital/collection/FileIINames/id/74977/rec/57.

86. Governor James Jackson to the Chehaw King, March 5, 1799, File II Names, Virtual Vault, GA, accessed November 29, 2021, https://vault.georgiaarchives.org/digital /collection/FileIINames/id/80148/rec/11.

87. James Jackson to Chehaw King, March 5, 1799, File II Names, Virtual Vault, GA, accessed November 29, 2021, https://vault.georgiaarchives.org/digital/collection /FileIINames/id/80148/rec/11.

88. James Jackson to (the governor of Georgia), July 21, 1793, File II Counties, Indians, Virtual Vault, GA, accessed December 30, 2022, https://vault.georgiaarchives.org/digital /collection/p17154coll2/id/1225/rec/3 . An investigation suggested that these people were responsible for the killing of a Dr. St. Johns in South Carolina.

89. Snyder, *Slavery in Indian Country*, 194.

90. Snyder, *Slavery in Indian Country*, 187.

91. William Laurence to William Panton, August 15, 1798, Cruzat Papers, PKY.

92. Hargrett, ms2599, July 3, Aug. 26, 1801, box 1, folder 1, (Affidavits, 1801), Cuyler Collection

93. John Karnard (Kinnard) to James Seagrove, June 5, 1803, File II Names, Virtual Vault, Ga, accessed March 8, 2021, https://vault.georgiaarchives.org/digital/collection /FileIINames/id/41089/rec/1.

94. John Karnard (Kinnard) to James Seagrove, June 5, 1803, File II Names, Virtual Vault, Ga, accessed March 8, 2021, https://vault.georgiaarchives.org/digital/collection /FileIINames/id/41089/rec/1.

95. John Galphin to governor of East Florida, November 12, 1795, reel 43, EFP.

96. Frank, "Red, Black, and Seminole," 49–56.

97. Swan, "Position and State of Manners and Arts," 260–61.

Chapter 8. Flight to the Seminoles

1. Landers, "A Nation Divided," 99–116; Snyder, *Slavery in Indian Country*, 213–43; Frank, "Taking the State Out"; Frank, "Red, Black, and Seminole," 46–67; Jennison, *Cultivating Race*, 127–56; Kokomoor, "A Re-assessment of Seminoles, Africans, and Slavery"; Weisman, *Like Beads on a String*; Covington, *The Seminoles of Florida*, 1–49; Saunt, *A New Order of Things*, 233–47; Rivers, *Slavery in Florida*, 1–16; Mahon and Weisman, "Florida's Seminole and Miccosukee Peoples"; Patrick Riordan, "Seminole Genesis: Native Americans, African Americans, and Colonists on the Southern Frontier from Prehistory through the Colonial Era" (PhD diss., University of Florida, 1996); Porter, *The Black Seminoles*, 3–24.

2. Jason Herbert, "Alachua Seminole Identity and Autonomy, 1750–1776," *FHQ* 100, no. 1 (summer 2021): 52–75.

3. Saunt, *New Order of Things*, 206; Richard Winn, Andrew Pickens, and George Mat-

thews to Henry Knox, Secretary of War, Nov. 28, 1788, ASPIA 1:30 (the commissioners stated that they did not know "whether the Seminoles belong[ed] to any part of the Creeks"); Weisman, *Like Beads on a String.*

4. William Hayne Simmons, *Notices of East Florida with an Account of the Seminole Nation of Indians* (Charleston, S.C.: N.p., 1822), 54.

5. Swan, "Position and State of Manners and Arts," 261.

6. Covington, *The Seminoles of Florida,* 5–13; Simmons, *Notices of East Florida,* 54–55; Colin G. Callaway, "Cuscowilla: Seminole Loyalism and Seminole Genesis," in *The American Revolution in Indian Country: Crisis and Diversity in Native American Communities,* ed. Colin G. Callaway (Cambridge: Cambridge University Press, 1995), 244–47.

7. Herbert, "Alachua Seminole Identity and Autonomy, 1750–1776," 55–56.

8. Callaway, "Cuscowilla: Seminole loyalism and Seminole genesis," 244–77; Weisman, *Like Beads on a String,* 1–13; Wright, *Creeks and Seminoles,* 113–16; Gregory A. Waselkov and Kathryn E. Holland Braund, eds., *William Bartram on the Southeastern Indians* (Lincoln: University of Nebraska Press, 1995), 50–52; Edward J. Cashin, *William Bartram and the American Revolution on the Southern Frontier* (Columbia: University of South Carolina Press, 2000), 97–99.

9. James L. Hill, *Creek Internationalism in an Age of Revolution, 1763–1818* (Lincoln: University of Nebraska Press, 2022), 9–11.

10. Simmons, *Notices of East Florida,* 75; Porter, *The Black Seminoles,* 5–7; Kenneth Wiggins Porter, "Negroes and the East Florida Annexation Plot, 1811–1813," *Journal of Negro History* 30, no. 1 (January 1945): 9–29.

11. Snyder, *Slavery in Indian Country,* 227–31; "At liberty," 227; Jennison, *Cultivating Race,* 130–31; Brent Weisman, "The Plantation System of the Florida Seminole Indian and Black Seminoles during the Colonial Era," in *Colonial Plantations and Economy in Florida,* ed. Jane G. Landers (Gainesville: University of Florida Press, 2000), 136–49.

12. Testimony of Wiley Thompson, Seminole Agency, April 27, 1835, Doc. No. 271, Register of Debates, House of Representatives, 24th Congress, 183–84.

13. Simmons, *Notices of East Florida,* 76.

14. Snyder, *Slavery in Indian Country,* 213, 216, 232–33; Mulroy, *Freedom on the Border,* 1. Mulroy prefers the term "Seminole maroons" on the grounds that the communities that they established closely matched the classic definition of maroon societies formulated by others. The debate over proper terminology began in the earliest days as army officers, officials, and outside observers struggled to classify them.

15. Frank, "Taking the State Out," 10–27.

16. James L. Hill, "New Systems, Established Traditions: Governor James Grant's Indian Diplomacy and the Evolution of British Colonial Policy, 1760–1771," *FHQ* 93, no. 2 (Fall 2014), 157–66; Charles Loch Mowat, *East Florida as a British Province, 1763–1784* (Berkeley: University of California Press, 1943); Schafer, *St. Augustine's British Years,* 29, 36; David Hancock, *Citizens of the World: London Merchants and the Integration of the British Atlantic Community, 1735–1785* (New York: Cambridge University Press, 1997), 153–70.

17. Moultrie to Lord Hillsborough, June 29, 1771, cited by Riordan, "Seminole Genesis," 247.

18. Schafer, *St. Augustine's British Years,* 88.

19. "Copy of a Talk from the Seminollie Indians date Flint River 3rd September 1777," in James Stuart to Lord George Germain, cited in Riordan, "Seminole Genesis," 220.

20. Martha Condray Searcy, "The Introduction of African Slavery into the Creek In-

dian Nation," *GHQ* 66, no. 1 (Spring 1982): 29. Governor Tonyn referred to both Seminoles and Creeks as Creek Indians.

21. Covington, *The Seminoles of Florida*; Porter, *The Black Seminoles*; Saunt, *A New Order of Things* (Cambridge University Press, 1999); Weisman, *Like Beads on a String*.

22. Jane G. Landers, "Spanish Sanctuary: Fugitives in Florida, 1687–1790," *FHQ* 62 (September 1984): 296–313.

23. Jesse Dupont to Enrique White, January 24, 1802, reel 83, EFP.

24. Enrique White to Martinez de Yrujo, October 4, 1796, reel 29, EFP, cited in Saunt, *A New Order of Things*, 125.

25. "Account of the principal events with Indians in this Port of Saint Vincent Ferrer," sent by Carlos Howard to Governor Quesada, April [26], 1795, reel 51, EFP.

26. Howard to Quesada, April [26], 1795, reel 51, EFP.

27. Enrique White to Martinez de Yrujo, October 4, 1796, reel 29, EFP, cited in Saunt, *A New Order of Things*, 125.

28. Swan, "Position and State of Manners and Arts," 260–61.

29. Waselkov and Braund, *William Bartram on the Southeastern Indians*, 51–53.

30. Brent Richards Weisman, *Florida's Seminole and Miccosukee Indians: Unconquered People* (Gainesville: University Press of Florida, 1999), 22; Weisman, *Like Beads on a String*, 77.

31. Weisman, "The Plantation System of the Florida Seminole Indians," 141.

32. Brent W. Weisman, "Nativism, Resistance, and Ethnogenesis of the Florida Seminole Indian Identity," *Historical Archaeology* 41, no. 4 (2007), 198–212. Lake Miccosukee is a large swampy prairie lake in Jefferson County, Florida.

33. Wright, *Creeks and Seminoles*, 99, 126; Covington, *The Seminoles of Florida*, 21–36; Landers, "A Nation Divided," 104.

34. Swan, "Position and State of Manners and Arts," 260–61.

35. Cusick, "King Payne and His Policies," 44–45.

36. Covington, *The Seminoles of Florida*, 15–26; Saunt, *A New Order of Things*, 206. For a statement on how Georgians saw the Mikasukis, see Buckner Harris to Governor David Mitchell, November 8, 1810, File II, Virtual Vault, GA, accessed December 16, 2020, https://vault.georgiaarchives.org/digital/collection/FileIINames/id/84042.

37. Wright, *William Augustus Bowles*, 24, 29, 71–86.

38. Wright, *William Augustus Bowles*, 87–106; DuVal, *Independence Lost*, 326–31; Landers, "A Nation Divided," 99–116; Jennison, *Cultivating Race*, 139–42;

39. Cusick, "King Payne and His Policies," 44–46.

40. Andrew Ellicott, *Journal of Andrew Ellicott* (Philadelphia: William Fry, 1814), 230.

41. Gilbert C. Din, *War on the Gulf Coast: The Spanish Fight against William Augustus Bowles* (Gainesville: University of Florida, 2012), 143–73; Wright, *William Augustus Bowles*, 107–41.

42. Seagrove to McQueen, June 24, 1800, reel 24, EFP.

43. Nathaniel Hall to Enrique White, July 8, 1800, reel 55, EFP.

44. A. Atkinson to governor, July 10, 1800, reel 55, EFP.

45. Landers, "A Nation Divided," 105–6.

46. Marguerite Reddick, comp., *Camden's Challenge: A History of Camden County, Woodbine, Ga.* ([Woodbine, Ga.]: Camden Historical Commission, 1976), 5.

47. Depositions of Samuel Mercer, Robert and James Ross, and Lewis Levi, Camden County, February 7, 1807, reel 58, EFP.

48. Richard Lang to the governor, January 12, 1791, reel 82, EFP.

49. Col. Hannaford to governor, July 25, 1796, reel 83, EFP.

50. James Seagrove to John McQueen, June 25, 1800, reel 55, EFP; July 26, 1800, Andrew Atkinson to governor of Florida, July 26, 1800, reel 55, EFP.

51. Thomas King to governor, October 15, 1800, File II Names, Virtual Vault, GA, March 16, 2021, https://vault.georgiaarchives.org/digital/collection/FileIINames/id/40318/rec/4; John King to the governor of Georgia, July 12, 1800, File II Names, Virtual Vault, GA, accessed March 16, 2021, https://vault.georgiaarchives.org/digital/collection/FileIINames/id/40209/rec/5; William Jones to governor of Georgia, August 17, 1800, File II Names, Virtual Vault, GA, accessed March 16, 2021, https://vault.georgiaarchives.org/digital/collection/FileIINames/id/39675/rec/5.

52. Cormac A. O'Riordan, "The 1795 Rebellion in East Florida" (Master's thesis, University of North Florida, 1995), https://digitalcommons.unf.edu/etd/99.

53. Manuel de Castilla to Enrique White, November 10 1800, reel 55, EFP. An officer delegated by the governor, Manuel de Castilla accompanied McQueen on an expedition to capture Bowles.

54. John McQueen to Enrique White, November 10, 1800, reel 55, EFP.

55. Wright, *William Augustus Bowles*, 140–41; proclamation of Governor James Jackson, July 8, 1800, Executive Minutes, GA; proclamation of Governor James Jackson, July 8, 1800, reel 40, EFP.

56. Proclamation of Governor James Jackson, July 8, 1800, Executive Minutes, GA; Proclamation of Governor James Jackson, July 8, 1800, reel 40, EFP.

57. Parker, "So in Fear of Both the Indians and the Americans," 34–35. Robert Allen may have been a son of James Allen, a noted horse and cattle thief twenty years earlier.

58. Seagrove to McQueen, June 24, 1800, reel 42, EFP; letter from a planter, *Augusta Chronicle and Gazette of the State*, July 12, 1800.

59. John King to Governor James Jackson, July 12, 1800, File II Names, Virtual Vault, GA, accessed March 16, 2021, https://vault.georgiaarchives.org/digital/collection/FileIINames/id/40209/rec/5.

60. Governor of East Florida to Andrew Atkinson, March 18, 1800, reel 55, EFP.

61. John King to Governor James Jackson, July 10, 1800, File II Names, Virtual Vault, GA, accessed March 16, 2021, https://vault.georgiaarchives.org/digital/collection/FileIINames/id/80618/rec/26; Saunt, *A New Order of Things*, 208. One of the Black men was "a certain man named Cudjo, an inhabitant of the Creek nation."

62. William Floyd to William Augustus Bowles, November 31, 1801, Cruzat Papers, PKY.

63. Benjamin Hawkins to Daniel Stewart, October 13, 1810, *LBH* 2:571–73.

64. Jennison, *Cultivating Race*, 127, 143. According to Jennison, building a hybrid society in racial terms was a high priority for Bowles.

65. Hawkins to Efau Haojo and chiefs, June 2, 1802, ASPIA 1:677. Some fled for crimes, others for curiosity (see Saunt, *A New Order of Things*, 207.)

66. Francis Philip Fatio to Mrs. Fatio, October 18, 1800, cited in William Scott Willis, "A Swiss Settler in East Florida: A Letter of Francis Philip Fatio," *FHQ* 64, no. 2 (October 1985): 180.

67. McQueen to White, April 18, 1801, reel 55, EFP; Kinnard to White, October 2, 1802, reel 43, EFP; Snyder, *Slavery in Indian Country*, 127–28. Snyder gives the name as "Macloggy."

68. John Cannard to governor of Florida, October 2, 1801, reel 43, EFP.

69. "The Following Trifling Observations Made during a Journey through the Indian Country," Fatio Jr., November 12, 1801, reel 83, EFP.

70. Francis Philip Fatio Jr. to father, October 2, 1801, reel 83, EFP.

71. "The Following Trifling Observations made during a Journey through the Indian Country," Francis Philip Fatio Jr., reel 83, EFP.

72. Jesse Dupont to Enrique White, January 24, 1802, reel 83, EFP.

73. Frank, "Red, Black, and Seminole," 49–51.

74. Wiley Thompson to governor of Florida, April 20, 1803, reel 57, EFP.

75. Wiley Thompson to governor of Florida, April 20, 1803, reel 57, EFP.

76. Wright, *William Augustus Bowles*, 163–71; Jennison, *Cultivating Race*, 151–154.

77. Landers, *Atlantic Creoles*, 182–83.

78. Simmons, *Notices of East Florida*, 76.

79. Kevin Kokomoor, "A Re-assessment of Seminoles, Africans, and Slavery"; Weisman, Nativism, Resistance, and Ethnogenesis," 198–212; Frank, "Red, Black, and Seminole," 49–51; Simmons, *Notices of East Florida*, 76–77.

80. James Cashen to John Hampton, November 27, 1806, reel 83, EFP, https://www.loc.gov/resource/mss19398.mss19398-083_0540_1092/?sp=518.

81. Kokomoor, "A Re-assessment of Seminoles, Africans, and Slavery."

82. Snyder, *Captivity in Indian Country*, 217, 229.

83. Snyder, *Captivity in Indian Country*, 1–16, 213, 216, 232–33.

84. Frank, "Red, Black, and Seminole."

85. Kokomoor, "A Re-assessment of Seminoles, Africans, and Slavery."

86. Schafer, *Zephaniah Kingsley Jr. and the Atlantic World*, 101–6.

87. Cusick, *The Other War of 1812*, 41, 104.

88. Landers, *Atlantic Creoles*, 178–85.

89. "Our Southern Frontier," *National Intelligencer*, October 29, 1817, cited in Cusick, *The Other War of 1812*, 298.

90. Cusick, *The Other War of 1812*, 38–55; John K. Mahon, *History of the Second Seminole War, 1835–1842* (Gainesville, Fla.: Library Press, 1967, 128–31, 196–97.

91. Rembert W. Patrick, *Florida Fiasco: Rampant Rebels on the Georgia-Florida Border, 1810–1815* (Athens: University of Georgia Press, 1954), 83–98; Cusick, *The Other War of 1812*, 126.

92. Cusick, *The Other War of 1812*, 128–34; Patrick, *Florida Fiasco*, 99–127.

93. Patrick, *Florida Fiasco*, 128–43; Cusick, *The Other War of 1812*, 166–68.

94. Floyd to Senator William Henry Crawford, March 26, 1812, Misc. Let., Department of State, National Archives, cited in Cusick, *The Other War of 1812*, 130.

95. Lt. Col. Smith to Maj. Gen. Pinckney (copy) Point Petre 30 July, 1812," in T. Frederick Davis, ed., "United States Troops in Spanish East Florida, 1812–1813, II," *FHQ* 9, no. 2, (October 1930): 107.

96. Patrick, *Florida Fiasco*, 154, 184.

97. David Mitchell to James Monroe, September 19, 1812, Territorial Papers of the Department of State, National Archives, cited by Cusick, *The Other War of 1812*, 189.

98. A. H. Alexander, "The Ambush of Captain John Williams, U.S.M.C.: Failure of the East Florida Invasion, 1812–1813," *FHQ* 56, no. 3 (January 1978): 280–96.

99. "Newnan's Expeditions," *National Intelligencer*, December 5, 1812, https://ufdcimages.uflib.ufl.edu/UF/00/00/24/08/00001/UF00002408_00001_00001.pdf.

100. Patrick, *Florida Fiasco*, 231.

101. Between 1785 and 1810, Georgia took in as many as thirty-two thousand Africans according to an estimate by McMillin, *The Final Victims*, 48. Thousands more came from the Chesapeake and hundreds from Saint-Domingue.

Chapter 9. Erasing a Borderland

1. Mary Bullard, *Black Liberation on Cumberland Island in 1815* (De Leon Springs, Fla.: E. O. Painter Printing, 1983), 104–5; Jennison, *Cultivating Race*, 201. This estimate includes Georgia slaves thought to have fled to Spanish Florida, the Seminoles, and the Creeks between 1812 and 1816 or left with the British in the War of 1812. Bullard calculates at least seventeen hundred Black Georgians left with the British or attempted to leave. Jennison thinks that roughly one thousand Black Georgians escaped into the communities bordering the state during the War of 1812.

2. Justin Iverson, "Fugitives on the Front: Maroons in the Gulf Coast Borderlands War, 1812–1823," *FHQ* 92, no. 2 (Fall 2019): 105–29. Iverson highlights the importance of African Americans in the Gulf Coast wars and how European imperial rivalries both supported and threatened maroon communities in the Atlantic. His use of the term "maroon" includes virtually any Black who resisted enslavement no matter the circumstances. See Jane Landers, *Atlantic Creoles*, 120–37.

3. Colonel Smith to General Flournoy, February 24, 1813, in T. Frederick Davis, "United States Troops in Spanish East Florida, IV," *FHQ* 9, no. 4 (April 1931): 271–74; Patrick, *Florida Fiasco*, 232–34; Cusick, *The Other War of 1812*, 256–57.

4. Canter Brown Jr., "Tales of Angola: Free Blacks, Red Stick Creeks, and International Intrigue in Spanish Southwest Florida, 1812–1821," in *Go Sound the Trumpet! Selections in Florida's African American History*, ed. Canter Brown and David Jackson (Tampa: University of Tampa Press, 2005), 5–21; Canter Brown Jr., *African Americans on the Tampa Bay Frontier* (Tampa: Tampa Bay History Center, 1997), 7, 45; Canter Brown Jr., "The 'Sarrazota, or Runaway Negro Plantations': Tampa Bay's First Black Community, 1812–1814," *Tampa Bay History* 12 (Fall/Winter 1990): 5–6; Rosalyn Howard, "'Looking for Angola': An Archaeological and Ethnohistorical Search for a Nineteenth Century Florida Maroon Community and its Caribbean Connections," *FHQ* 92, no. 1 (Summer 2013): 32–68.

5. Benjamin Hawkins to D. B. Mitchell, May 31, 1813, in Louise Frederick Hayes, "Letters of Benjamin Hawkins, 1797–1815 (typescript, Atlanta, 1939), GA, cited in Jackson and Brown, eds., *Go Sound the Trumpets*, 7.

6. Howard, "Looking for Angola," 32–68; Brown, "Tales of Angola," 7–12.

7. John H. McIntosh to Governor Peter Early, September 11, 1813, File II Counties and Subjects, Virtual Vault, GA, accessed October 25, 2020, https://vault.georgiaarchives.org /digital/collection/p17154coll2/id/4066/rec/1.

8. Francis Philip Fatio to Governor Early, December 11, 1813, File II Names, Virtual Vault, GA, https://vault.georgiaarchives.org/digital/collection/FileIINames/id/25648, viewed October 25, 2020. Fatio gave a detailed assessment of the damage done to East Florida by the patriots.

9. Jose Hibberson to Charles Harris, November 19, 1813, File II Names, Virtual Vault, GA, accessed December 16, 2020, https://vault.georgiaarchives.org/digital/collection /FileIINames/id/44849; Patrick, *Florida Fiasco*, 275; T. Frederick Davis, "MacGregor's Invasion of Florida, 1817," *FHQ* 7, no. 1 (July 1928): 8–9.

10. Hibberson to Harris, November 19, 1813, File II Names, Virtual Vault, GA, accessed December 16, 2020, https://vault.georgiaarchives.org/digital/collection/FileIINames /id/44849; William Gibson to Governor Mitchell, July 31, 1816, File II Names, Virtual Vault, GA; accessed October 27, 2020, https://vault.georgiaarchives.org/digital/collection /FileIINames/id/28102/rec/18.

11. Deposition of Jacob Summelin before Buckner Harris, June 16, 1813, File II Names, Virtual Vault, GA, accessed December 16, 2020, https://vault.georgiaarchives.org/digital /collection/FileIINames/id/83963; Cusick, *The Other War*, 272–73.

12. Jose Hibberson to Charles Harris, November 19, 1813, in "East Florida Documents," *GHQ* 13, no. 2 (June 1929): 154–58.

13. Landers, *Black Society in Spanish Florida*, 238; notices in the *Savannah Republican*, February 27, 1812, March 28, 1812, April 9, 1812, May 23, 1812, June 2, 1812, cited in Jennison, *Cultivating Race*, 157.

14. Deposition of James Nephew and William Dunham, December 13, 1813, File II Names, Virtual Vault, GA, accessed December 16, 2020, https://vault.georgiaarchives. org/digital/collection/FileIINames/id/83582.

15. David Mitchell to James Monroe, October 13, 1812, State Department Territorial Papers, Florida Series, 1772–1824, 2:133, cited in Saunt, *A New Order of Things*, 245.

16. Jose Hibberson to Charles Harris, November 19, 1813, in "East Florida Documents," *GHQ* 13, no. 2 (June 1929), 154–58.

17. Deposition of James Black, June 11, 1813, File II Names, Virtual Vault, GA, accessed December 16, 2020, https://vault.georgiaarchives.org/digital/collection/FileIINames /id/3009; deposition of Jacob Summerlin before Buckner Harris, June 16, 1813, File II Names, Virtual Vault, GA, https://vault.georgiaarchives.org/digital/collection /FileIINames/id/83963, viewed December 16, 2020.

18. Gordon S. Wood, *Empire of Liberty: A History of the Early Republic, 1789–1815* (New York: Oxford University Press, 2009), 659–700; Alan Taylor, *The Civil War of 1812: American Citizens, British Subjects, Irish Rebels, and Indian Allies* (New York: Vintage Books, 2011), 110–13; Frank Lawrence Owsley, *Struggle for the Gulf Borderlands: The Creek War and the Battle of New Orleans, 1812–1815* (Tuscaloosa: University of Alabama Press, 1981), 1–5.

19. Taylor, *The Internal Enemy: Slavery and War in Virginia, 1772–1832* (New York: W. W. Norton, 2013), 179–93, 200–213; Gene Allen Smith, *The Slaves' Gamble: Choosing Sides in the War of 1812* (New York: Palgrave MacMillan, 2013).

20. Taylor, *The Internal Enemy*, 208–13; Millett, *The Maroons of Prospect Bluff*, 16–19.

21. Admiral Cochrane's position represented a creative reworking of the Somerset doctrine set forth by the chief justice, Lord Mansfield, over the fate of an escaped slave in Great Britain in 1772. Mansfield's decision promised freedom but only under certain well-defined circumstances that limited the practical import.

22. Alan Taylor, *The Internal Enemy: Slavery and War in Virginia, 1772–1832* (New York: W. W. Norton, 2013), 275–314; Millett, *The Maroons of Prospect Bluff*, 16–19.

23. Christopher Leslie Brown and Philip d. Morgan, eds., *Arming Slaves from Classical Times to the Modern Age* (New Haven: Yale University Press, 2006).

24. Bullard, *Black Liberation on Cumberland Island*, 55; Millett, *The Maroons of Prospect Bluff*, 43.

25. Millett, *The Maroons of Prospect Bluff*, 43.

26. Millett, *The Maroons of Prospect Bluff*, 40–43.

27. William Belko, "Epilogue to the War of 1812: The Monroe Administration, Amer-

ican Anglophobia, and the First Seminole War," in *America's Hundred Years' War: U.S. Expansion to the Gulf Coast and the Fate of the Seminole, 1763–1858*, ed. William Belko (Gainesville: University Press of Florida, 2011), 59–63.

28. Bullard, *Black Liberation on Cumberland Island*, 55; Millett, *The Maroons of Prospect Bluff*, 44.

29. Hawkins to John Houston McIntosh, District of Fort Hawkins, Nov. 26, 1814, *LBH* 2:706–7.

30. Millett, *The Maroons of Prospect Bluff*, 12–30, quotation from 77–78 ("encourage").

31. Hawkins to Andrew Jackson, November 11, 1814, *LBH* 2:704; Hawkins to Jackson, August 30, 1814, Enclosure to Tustunnuggee Hopole, Speaker for the Lower Creeks, *LBH* 2:694 ("negro-stealing").

32. "Narrative of the Operations of the British in the Floridas," 1815, Curzat Papers, PKY, cited in Millett, *The Maroons of Prospect Bluff*, 75.

33. Millett, *The Maroons of Prospect Bluff*, 45, 127. Robin escaped during the Patriot War and hid as a maroon until heading towards the fort.

34. Kathryn E. Holland Braund, ed., *Tohopeka: Rethinking the Creek War and the War of 1812* (Tuscaloosa: University of Alabama Press, 2012), 1–9; Saunt, *A New Order of Things*, 139–232; Kokomoor, *Of One Mind and of One Government*, 293–329.

35. Gregory A. Waselkov, *A Conquering Spirit: Fort Mims and the Redstick War of 1813–1814* (Tuscaloosa: University of Alabama Press, 2006); Braund, *Tohopeka*, 84–104; Saunt, *A New Order of Things*, 249–72; John Sugden, *Tecumseh: A Life* (New York: Henry Holt, 1999), 244–49.

36. Braund, *Tohopeka*, 1–9; Saunt, *A New Order of Things*, 139–232; Kokomoor, *Of One Mind and of One Government*, 293–329.

37. Waselkov, *A Conquering Spirit*, 167–71; Eve Jensen, "Horseshoe Bend: A Living Memorial," in Braund, *Tohopeka*, 146–57.

38. Hawkins to Andrew Jackson, Creek Agency, August 30, 1814 in *LBH* 2:694; Millett, *The Maroons at Prospect Bluff*, 78. James Perryman, another wealthy Creek, lost slaves as well.

39. Benjamin Hawkins to Peter Early, Fort Hawkins, Oct. 26, 1814, in *LBH*, 2:698.

40. Hawkins to Andrew Jackson, Creek Agency, Nov. 11, 1814, in *LBH* 2:704.

41. Hawkins to Jackson, Creek Agency, August 30, 1814, in *LBH*, 2:694.

42. Bullard, *Black Liberation on Cumberland Island*, 11, 54; *Republican* (Chatham County), December 27, 1814, accessed February 22, 2022, image 3, https://gahistoric newspapers.galileo.usg.edu/lccn/sn82014388/1814-12-27/ed-1/seq-3; and January 19, 1815, accessed February 22, 2022, image 3, https://gahistoricnewspapers .galileo.usg.edu/lccn/sn82014388/1815-01-19/ed-1/seq-3.

43. June Hall McCash, *Jekyll Island's Early Years: From Prehistory through Reconstruction* (Athens: University of Georgia Press, 2005), 119–22.

44. Smith, *The Slaves' Gamble*, 147–48; Taylor, *The Internal Enemy*, 327–32.

45. Bullard, *Black Liberation on Cumberland Island*, 54–59.

46. John McIlraith, *Life of Sir John Richardson* (London: N.p., 1868), 56–57.

47. Taylor, *The Internal Enemy*, 327–28; Bullard, *Black Liberation on Cumberland Island*, 56–57; Malcolm Bell, *Major Butler's Legacy*, 176. Butler's manager, Roswell King, reported that twenty-five hundred troops had landed, sixteen hundred were Black, and the Blacks had behaved better than the whites.

48. Mary R. Bullard, "Ned Simmons, American Slave: The Role of Imagination in

American History," *African Diaspora Newsletter*, 10, no. 2 (June 2007), article 7, accessed December 19, 2020, https://scholarworks.umass.edu/adan/vol10/iss2/7.

49. James A. Percoco, "The British Corps of Colonial Marines: African Americans Fight for their Freedom," American Battlefield Trust, accessed January 8, 2020, https://www.battlefields.org/learn/articles/british-corps-colonial-marines.

50. Zephaniah Kingsley Jr., *A Treatise on the Patriarchal System, or the Cooperative System of Society* (18929; repr., Freeport, N.Y.: Books for Libraries Press, 1970), 11.

51. Bullard, "Ned Simmons, American Slave," 18–26.

52. Interview printed in 1867 as part of a war miscellany called *Anecdotes, Poetry and Incidents of the Civil War: North and South, 1860–1865*, collected and arranged by Frank Moore, cited by Bullard, "Ned Simmons, American Slave," 6.

53. Granger, *Savannah River Plantations*, 78–80. The Millers switched from rice production that had encumbered the estate with massive debt to the more profitable cultivation of Sea Island cotton and cutting live oak timber.

54. Bullard, "Ned Simmons, American Slave," 44–50.

55. Bullard, "Ned Simmons, American Slave," 25, 35, 36. During the Civil War, Simmons managed to join in a flight of people from Cumberland Island to Union-controlled territory. One of his requests was to be taught how to read.

56. M. Bell, *Major Butler's Legacy*, 19–30. For a landmark environmental history of the Butler plantations, see Mart S. Stewart, *"What Nature Suffers to Groe": Life, Labor, and Landscape on the Georgia Coast, 1620–1920* (Athens: University of Georgia Press, 1996), 87–150. For a treatment of the Butler plantations during the Antebellum Period, see William Dusinberre, *Them Dark Days: Slavery in the American Rice Swamps* (Athens: University of Georgia Press, 2000), 213–84.

57. James M. Couper to Caroline Couper Lovell, August 12, 1912, Cate Collection, GHS, cited in Bell, *Major Butler's Legacy*, 127.

58. Bell, *Major Butler's Legacy*, 134.

59. Roswell King to Honored Sir [Butler], November 1, 1806, Butler Family Papers, HSP; see the correspondence about Sambo, the lead driver, in the first half of 1806. Butler refused to sell the man but finally acceded to having Sambo and his family traded for fourteen slaves from South Carolina.

60. Bell, *Major Butler's Legacy*, 170–91.

61. Roswell King to Pierce Butler, February 12, 1815, Butler Family Papers, HSP.

62. Affidavit by Roswell King, "A Narrative of the Conduct of the British Armed Forces from the 30th Jany to the 14th of Feb. 1815," February 14, 1815, Butler Family Papers, HSP.

63. Bell, *Major Butler's Legacy*, 182.

64. King to Butler, January 14, February 26, 1815, affidavit by Roswell King, February 14, 1815, Butler Family Papers, HSP. Molly and Old Betty appear in the list of fugitives.

65. Bell, *Major Butler's Legacy*, 172.

66. Smith, *The Slaves' Gamble*, 192.

67. John Miller to Thomas Miller, February 12, 1815, in *Examiner*, April 8, 1815, 493, accessed October 29, 2020, https://www.google.com/books/edition/The_Examiner_Containing_Political_Essays/vixIAQAAMAAJ?hl=en&gbpv=1&dq=Blackey,+on+the+impulse+of+the+moment,+left+the+ranks&pg=PA493&printsec=frontcover.

68. Taylor, *Internal Enemies*, 335–42.

69. Bell, *Major Butler's Legacy*, 182.

70. Bullard, *Black Liberation on Cumberland Island*, 104–6. For the subsequent history of these fugitives, see Bell, *Major Butler's Legacy*, 183–91.

71. Taylor, *The Internal Enemy*, 334; Smith, *The Slaves' Gamble*, 152–54. The official copy of the Treaty of Ghent did not reach Washington until February 16. Congress did not ratify it until the evening of February 17. That gave Cockburn a justification for returning only those fugitives who were still on Cumberland Island and not on British ships at that date and time. All others were declared free.

72. Bullard, "Ned Simmons, American Slave," 6–11; Wright, *Creeks and Seminoles*, 93–94. Years after his brief moment as a Colonial Marine, Simmons treasured his British regimental button, found by archaeologists in his cabin in the twentieth century.

73. King to Butler, February 12 and 26, 1815, Butler Family Papers, HSP.

74. Millett, *The Maroons of Prospect Bluff*, 147–213.

75. Nathaniel Millett, "The Radicalism of the First Seminole War and Its Consequences," in *Warring for America: Cultural Contests in the Era of 1812*, ed. Nicole Eustace and Fredrika J. Teute (Chapel Hill: University of North Carolina Press, 2017), 164–201; Millett, *The Maroons of Prospect Bluff*, 231–49.

76. Millett, *The Maroons of Prospect Bluff*, 69–70.

77. Quoted in Millett, *The Maroons at Prospect Bluff*, 150.

78. John Floyd to David Mitchell, April 12, 1816, DLG, accessed December 19, 2021, https://dlg.usg.edu/record/dlg_zlna_tcc859?canvas=0&x=1250&y=1410&w=5959.

79. John Paul Nuño, "'Republica de Bandidos': The Prospect Bluff Fort's Challenge to the Spanish Slave System," *FHQ* 94, no. 2 (Fall 2015): 192–221; Nathaniel Millett, "Defining Freedom in the Atlantic Borderlands of the Revolutionary Southeast," *Early American Studies* 5, no. 2 (Fall 2007): 383–86.

80. Gene Allen Smith, *The Slaves' Gamble*, 179; Millett, *The Maroons of Prospect Bluff*, 124–28; 205–7.

81. John Floyd to David Mitchell, April 12, 1816, DLG, accessed December 19, 2021, https://dlg.usg.edu/record/dlg_zlna_tcc859?canvas=0&x=1250&y=1410&w=5959.

82. Frank Lawrence Owsley and Gene A. Smith eds., *Filibusters and Expansionists: Jeffersonian Manifest Destiny, 1800–1821* (Tuscaloosa: University of Alabama Press, 1997), 111; Millett, "The Radicalism of the First Seminole War," 185.

83. Millett, *The Maroons of Prospect Bluff*, 214–30; Saunt, *A New Order of Things*, 273–90; Wright, *Creeks and Seminoles*, 198–200.

84. Brown, "Tales of Angola," 1–20; Brown, *African Americans on the Tampa Bay Frontier* (Tampa: Tampa Bay History Center, 1997), 7, 45; Brown, "The 'Sarrazota, or Runaway Negro Plantations,'" 5–6.

85. Millett, "The Radicalism of the First Seminole War," 186–88; John K. Mahon, "The First Seminole War: November 21, 1817–May 24, 1818," *FHQ* 77, no. 1 (Summer 1998): 62–67.

86. L. Kingsley to David Brydie Mitchell, September 13, 1816, Hargrett, DLG, accessed December 20, 2021, https://dlg.usg.edu/record/dlg_zlna_tcc442?canvas=1&x=1086&y=1857&w=9277.

87. Millett, "The Radicalism of the First Seminole War," 187–88.

88. Landers, *Atlantic Creoles*, 175–203; Covington, *The Seminoles*, 45.

89. Extract of a Letter from George Perryman to Lieutenant Sands, February 24, 1817, ASPIA 2: 681–82.

90. Thomas H. Miller to Dear Sir, April 12, 1817, File II Names, Virtual Vault, GA,

accessed October 24, 2020, https://vault.georgiaarchives.org/digital/collection/FileIINames/id/48413/rec/3.

91. Extract of a Letter from George Perryman to Lieutenant Sands, February 24, 1817, ASPIA 2:681–82.

92. B. Low to (governor), April 8, 1817, St. Marys, Camden County, File II Counties and Subjects, GA, accessed December 21, 2020, https://vault.georgiaarchives.org/digital/collection/p17154coll2/id/1238/rec/3.

93. Millett, "The Radicalism of the First Seminole War," 191–92.

94. General Gaines to "Sir," probably the governor of Georgia, November 21, 1817, File II Names, Virtual Vault, GA, accessed December 20, 2020, https://vault.georgiaarchives.org/digital/collection/FileIINames/id/27312/rec/4; Hoffman, *Florida's Frontiers*, 274–76.

95. Landers, *Atlantic Creoles*, 185–87; Covington, *The Seminoles*, 42.

96. Owsley and Smith, *Filibusters and Expansionists*, 141–63; David S. Hiedler and Jeanne T. Hiedler, *Old Hickory's War: Andrew Jackson and the Quest for Empire* (Baton Rouge: Louisiana University Press, 2003); Mahon, "The First Seminole War: November 21, 1817–May 24, 1818," 62–67.

97. Millett, "The Radicalism of the First Seminole War," 193–96 ("The main drift" on p. 194); Covington, *The Seminoles*, 43, 46; Wright, *Creeks and Seminoles*, 204–8. The young man was Chrystie Ambrister, later hung by Jackson. Wright, *Creeks and Seminoles*, 305–6.

98. James Gadsden, "The Defenses of the Floridas," *FHQ* 15, no. 4 (April 1937): 248. Captain James Gadsden, aide-de-camp to General Andrew Jackson, made a general report.

99. Landers, *Atlantic Creoles*, 192–93.

100. President James Monroe and his secretary of war, John C. Calhoun, initially thought to punish Jackson for his insubordination, but Adams took Jackson's side when the secretary of state sensed the opportunity for concluding the acquisition of Florida.

101. Brown, "Tales of Angola," 11–14. According to reports sent to the War Office, Coweta Indians took 120 "Negroes" at Angola, brought back 59, and returned about 20 to their masters (Brown, *African Americans on the Tampa Bay Frontier*, 13). According to a Charleston newspaper, about 300 prisoners were taken at Angola, while 250 escaped to the tip of the Florida Keys, where fishermen took them to the Bahamas. See Rosalyn Howard, "The 'Wild Indians' of Andros Island: Black Seminole Legacy in the Bahama Islands," *Journal of Black Studies* 37, no. 2 (November 2006): 275–98; Landers, *Black Society in Spanish Florida*, 237; and Landers, *Atlantic Creoles*, 194–95.

102. Owsley and Smith, *Filibusters and Expansionists*, 118–40; David Head, *Privateers of the Americas: Spanish American Privateers from the United States in the Early Republic* (Athens: University of Georgia Press, 2015), 92–121; Jennifer Heckard, "The Crossroads of Empires: The 1817 Liberation and Occupation of Amelia Island, East Florida" (PhD diss., University of Connecticut, 2006); Christopher Ward, "The Commerce of East Florida during the Embargo, 1806–1812: The Role of Amelia Island," *FHQ* 68, no. 2 (October 1989): 160–79; Landers, *Black Society in Spanish Florida*, 244–46.

103. Governor Coppinger, memo quoting a letter from Gregor MacGregor demanding the surrender of Florida, July 11, 1817, reel 117, EFP; Heckard, "The Crossroads of Empires"; Oswley and Smith, *Filibusters and Expansionists*, 122–32; T. Davis, "MacGregor's Invasion of Florida."

104. Heckard, "The Crossroads of Empires," 86–87, 92, 109–10.

105. John Henry McIntosh to William Crawford, October 30, 1817, in Crawford to

John Quincy Adams, November 21, 1817, H.R. Doc. 12, 15th Cong., 1st Sess., cited in Heckard, "The Crossroads of Empires," 137.

106. Head, *Privateers of the Americas*, 106–13; Owsley and Smith, *Filibusters and Expansionists*, 135–40; Heckard, "The Crossroads of Empires," 121–88.

107. Heckard, "The Crossroads of Empires," 137–39 ("St. Domingo Rovers" and "brigands" on p. 138).

108. Head, *Privateers of the Americas*, 108–14; Heckard, "The Crossroads of Empires," 156–58.

109. Ex Parte John Clark, Governor of Georgia vs. Sundry African Negroes, July 22, 1820, File II Names, Virtual Vault, GA, accessed January 4, 2021, https://vault.georgia archives.org/digital/collection/FileIINames/id/82379/rec/25; D. Mitchell, Creek Agency, to Governor William Rabun, February 13, 1818, File II Names, Virtual Vault, GA, accessed December 24, 2021, https://vault.georgiaarchives.org/digital/collection /FileIINames/id/48871/rec/26.

110. Landers, *Atlantic Creoles*, 243, 244, 253.

111. Landers, *Atlantic Creoles*, 243–53; Jane Landers, "An Eighteenth-Century Community in Exile: The 'Floridanos' in Cuba," *New West Indian Guide* 70, no. 1/2 (1996): 39–58.

112. Trevor Barnard, "Ending with a Whimper, Not a Bang: The Relationship between Atlantic History and the Study of the Nineteenth-Century South," in *The American South and the Atlantic World*, ed. Brian Ward, Martyn Bone, and William A. Link (Gainesville: University Press of Florida, 2013), 129–48.

Conclusion. Underground Railroad

1. Smith, *The Slaves' Gamble*.

2. Angela Pulley Hudson, *Creek Paths and Federal Roads: Indians, Settlers, and Slaves and the Making of the American South* (Chapel Hill: University of North Carolina Press, 2010), 121–24.

3. James W. Covington, *The Seminoles of Florida* (Gainesville: University Press of Florida, 1993), 50; Weisman, *Florida's Seminole and Miccosukee Indians*.

4. Schafer, *Zephaniah Kingsley Jr. and the Atlantic World*, 177–90; Rivers, *Slavery in Florida*, 1–15.

5. Millett, *The Maroons of Prospect Bluff*, 7–9, 34–35.

6. Alice L. Baumgartner, *South to Freedom: Runaway Slaves to Mexico and the Road to the Civil War* (New York: Basic Books, 2020); Matthew J. Clavin, *Aiming for Pensacola: Fugitives on the Atlantic and Southern Frontiers* (Cambridge, Mass.: University of Harvard Press, 2015; James F. Brooks, *Captives and Cousins: Slavery, Kinship, and Community in the Southwest Borderlands* (Chapel Hill: University of North Carolina Press, 2002); Timothy D. Walker, ed., *Sailing to Freedom: Maritime Dimensions of the Underground Railroad* (Boston: University of Massachusetts Press, 2021).

7. Pargas, *Freedom Seekers*; R. J. M. Blackett, *Making Freedom: The Underground Railroad and the Politics of Slavery* (Chapel Hill: University of North Carolina Press, 2013); Eric Foner, *Gateway to Freedom: The Hidden History of the Underground Railroad* (New York: W. W. Norton, 2015); Pargas, ed., *Fugitive Slaves and Spaces of Freedom*.

8. Jeffrey Ostler and Nancy Shoemaker, "Settler Colonialism in Early American History: Introduction," *WMQ* 76, no. 3 (July 2019): 361–68.

BIBLIOGRAPHY

Newspapers

Augusta (GA) Chronicle and Gazette of the State
Columbian Museum and Savannah (GA) Advertiser
Examiner (New York)
Gazette of the State of Georgia (Savannah)
Georgia Gazette (Savannah)
National Intelligencer (Washington, DC)
Royal Georgia Gazette (Savannah)
Savannah Republican

Manuscript Collections

Emory University, Stuart A. Rose Manuscript, Archives, and Rare Book Library, Atlanta

Thiot family papers

Georgia Archives

Chatham County Deed Books
Colonial Conveyances
Colonial Wills
Creek Indian Letters, Talks, and Treaties, 1705–1839
Georgia, East Florida, and West Florida Papers
Historic Maps
"Negroes," 1733–1800
Unpublished Letters of Timothy Barnard, 1784–1820
Virtual Vault—File II Counties and Subjects
Virtual Vault—File II Names

The Georgia Archives has placed online most correspondence of individual Georgians claiming compensation for damage caused by Creek raiding parties as well as for state militia officers and traders in Creek lands during the late eighteenth and early nineteenth centuries. The entry points are through Georgia Archives, the Virtual Vault, File

II Names. One need only type in a person's name to access the file. Accessed April 26, 2022, https://vault.georgiaarchives.org/digital/collection/FileIINames.

Georgia Historical Society

Bevan, Joseph Vallence. Papers.
Chatham County Court of Ordinary: Record of Wills.
Hartridge, Walter Charlton, Jr. Collection.
Graham, John. Letter and Claim.
Habersham, Joseph. Papers. 1769–1802.
Habersham Family Papers, 1712–1842.
Jackson, James. Papers.
Mackay, Robert. Papers. Walter Charlton Hartridge, Jr. Collection, Georgia Historical Society.
McQueen, John. Papers. Walter Charlton Hartridge, Jr. Collection, Georgia Historical Society.
Mackay-McQueen Family Papers, National Society Colonial Dames of America in the State of Georgia historical collection on deposit, Georgia Historical Society.
Superior Court Records.
Telfair, Edward. Papers.
Wand, John. Papers.

Historical Society of Pennsylvania

Butler, Pierce. Family Papers.

Library of Congress

East Florida Papers.

The Library of Congress placed online the invaluable East Florida Papers that the Spanish government left behind when it departed in 1821. The papers include some sixty-five thousand documents stretching from 1784 to 1821. The George A. Smathers Libraries at the University of Florida in Gainesville offer an online search function that permits the researcher to enter the name of a person and find the date, box number, and a summary of the contents of the document. https://web.uflib.ufl.edu/spec/pkyonge/eflapap.html.

National Archives, United Kingdom. London

Audit Office 12: Loyalist Claims Commission.
Audit Office 13 Loyalist Claims Commission.
Colonial Office 5: America and West Indies.

National Archives and Records Administration, Atlanta

U.S. Circuit Court, Southern District of Georgia, Savannah, Georgia, Mixed Cases, 1790–1860.

National Records of Scotland, Edinburgh

Baillie, Robert. Family Papers. 1745–1780.
Grant, James. Papers. Ballindalloch Muniments.

South Carolina Department of History and Archives, Columbia

South Carolina Commons House Journals, 1736–1739.

University of Florida, George Smathers Libraries, Gainesville

Cruzat, Heloise H. Papers.
Greenslade, Marie Taylor. Papers.

University of Georgia, Hargrett Rare Book and Manuscript Library, Athens

Cuyler, Telamon. Collection. Series 1, Historical Manuscripts.
Read, Keith M. Collection.

University of Michigan, William L. Clement Library, Ann Arbor

Wayne, Anthony. Family Papers.

Online Sources

On-Line Institute for Advanced Loyalist Studies, http://www.royalprovincial.com.
Trans-Atlantic Slave Trade Database, https://www.slavevoyages.org.

Books, Pamphlets, and Articles

Adams, John. *The Works of John Adams*. Edited by Charles Francis Adams. 10 vols. Boston: Little, Brown, 1850–56.
"African American Heritage and Ethnography." Park Ethnography Program, National Park Service, accessed April 29, 2022, https://www.nps.gov/ethnography/aah/aaheritage/histContextsE.htm.
Alderson, Robert J. "Entangled Borderlands: the 1794 Projected French Invasion of Spanish East Florida and Atlantic History." *Florida Historical Quarterly* 88, no. 1 (summer 2009): 54–82.
———. *This Bright Era of Happy Revolutions: French Consul Michel-Ange-Bernard Mangourit and International Republicanism in Charleston, 1792–1794*. Columbia: University of South Carolina Press, 2008.
Alexander, A. H. "The Ambush of Captain John Williams, U.S.M.C.: Failure of the East Florida Invasion, 1812–1813." *Florida Historical Quarterly* 56, no. 3 (Jan. 1978): 280–96.
American State Papers: Indian Affairs. 2 vols. Washington, D.C.: Gales and Seaton, 1832–61.
Ammon, Harry. *The Genet Mission*. New York: W. W. Norton, 1973.
Anderson, Fred. *Crucible of War: The Seven Years' War and the Fate of Empire in British North America, 1754–1766*. New York: Vintage Books, 2001.
Arnade, Charles W. "Raids, Sieges, and International Wars." In *The New History of Florida*, edited by Michael Gannon, 100–116. Gainesville: University Press of Florida, 1996.
Ashcraft-Eason, Lillian. "'She Voluntarily Hath Come': A Gambian Woman Trader in Colonial Georgia in the Eighteenth Century." In *Identity in the Shadow of Slavery*, edited by Paul E. Lovejoy, 202–21. London: Continuum, 2000.

Bagwell, James. *Rice Gold: James Hamilton Couper and Plantation Life on the Georgia Coast*. Macon: Mercer University Press, 2000.

Ball, Charles. *Slavery in the United States: A Narrative of the Life and Adventures of Charles Ball*. New York, 1837.

Barnard, Trevor. "Ending with a Whimper, Not a Bang: The Relationship between Atlantic History and the Study of the Nineteenth-Century South." In *The American South and the Atlantic World*, edited by Brian Ward, Martyn Bone, and William A. Link, 129–148. Gainesville: University Press of Florida, 2013.

Barnes, Rhae Lynn. "Sailors and Slaves: Maritime History of the Long Eighteenth Century." U.S. History Scene. Accessed July 28, 2023. https://ushistoryscene.com/article/sailors-and-slaves.

Baumgartner, Alice L. *South to Freedom: Runaway Slaves to Mexico and the Road to the Civil War*. New York: Basic Books, 2020.

Beckert, Sven. *Empire of Cotton: A Global History*. New York: Alfred A. Knopf, 2014.

Belko, William S. "Epilogue to the War of 1812: The Monroe Administration, American Anglophobia, and the First Seminole War." In *America's Hundred Years' War: U.S. Expansion to the Gulf Coast and the Fate of the Seminole, 1763–1858*, 54–102. Gainesville: University Press of Florida, 2011.

Bell, Karen B. "Rice, Resistance, and Forced Transatlantic Communities: (RE)Envisioning the African Diaspora in Low Country Georgia, 1750–1800," *Journal of African American History* 95, no. 2 (Spring 2010): 157–82.

Bell, Malcolm, Jr. *Major Butler's Legacy: Five Generations of a Slaveholding Family*. Athens: University of Georgia Press, 1987.

Bennett, Charles E. *Florida's "French" Revolution, 1793–95*. Gainesville: University Presses of Florida, 1981.

Berlin, Ira. *Generations of Captivity: A History of African American Slaves*. Cambridge, Mass.: Harvard University Press, 2003.

———. *Many Thousands Gone: The First Two Centuries of Slavery in North America*. Cambridge, Mass.: Belknap Press of Harvard University Press, 1998.

Berlin, Ira, and Ronald Hoffman. *Slavery and Freedom in the Age of the American Revolution*. Charlottesville: University Press of Virginia, 1983.

Berry, Daina Ramey. *Swing the Sickle for the Harvest Is Ripe: Gender and Slavery in Antebellum Georgia*. Urbana: University of Chicago Press, 2010.

Blackburn, Robin. "Haiti, Slavery, and the Age of the Democratic Revolution." *William and Mary Quarterly* 63, no. 4 (October 2006): 643–74.

Blackett, R. J. M. *Making Freedom: The Underground Railroad and the Politics of Slavery*. Chapel Hill: University of North Carolina Press, 2013.

Bolster, W. Jeffrey. *Black Jacks: African American Seamen in the Age of Sail*. Cambridge: Harvard University Press, 1997.

Bolton, Herbert E., and Mary Ross. *The Debatable Land: A Sketch of the Anglo-Spanish Contest for the Georgia Country*. Berkeley: University of California Press, 1925.

Boubacar, Barry. *Senegambia and the Atlantic Slave Trade*. Cambridge: Cambridge University Press, 1998.

Boucher, Diane. "Mayhem and Murder in the East Florida Frontier 1783 to 1789." *Florida Historical Quarterly* 93, no. 3 (Winter 2015): 446–71.

Braund, E. Kathryn Holland. "The Creek Indians, Blacks, and Slavery." *Journal of Southern History* 57, no. 4 (November 1991): 601–36.

————. *Deerskins and Duffels: Creek Indian Trade with Anglo-America, 1685–1815.* Lincoln: University of Nebraska Press, 1993.

————, ed. *Tohopeka: Rethinking the Creek War and the War of 1812.* Tuscaloosa: University of Alabama Press, 2012.

Brooks, James F. *Captives and Cousins: Slavery, Kinship, and Community in the Southwest Borderlands.* Chapel Hill: University of North Carolina Press, 2002.

Brown, Canter, Jr. *African Americans on the Tampa Bay Frontier.* Tampa: Tampa Bay History Society, 1997.

————. "The 'Sarrazota, or Runaway Negro Plantations': Tampa Bay's First Black Community, 1812–1821." *Tampa Bay History* 12, no. 2 (Fall/Winter 1990), article 3, https://digitalcommons.usf.edu/tampabayhistory/vol12/iss2/3.

————. "Tales of Angola: Free Blacks, Red Stick Creeks, and International Intrigue in Spanish Southwest Florida, 1812–1821." In *Go Sound the Trumpet! Selections in Florida's African American History,* edited by Canter Brown and David Jackson, 1–20. Tampa: University of Tampa Press, 2005.

Brown, Canter, Jr., and David Jackson, eds. *Go Sound the Trumpet! Selections in Florida's African American History.* Tampa: University of Tampa Press, 2005.

Brown, Christopher Leslie, and Philip D. Morgan. *Arming Slaves from Classical Times to the Modern Age.* New Haven: Yale University Press, 2006.

Brown, Vincent. *Tacky's Revolt: The Story of an Atlantic Slave War.* Cambridge, Mass.: Belknap Press of Harvard University Press, 2020.

Bullard, Mary R. *Black Liberation on Cumberland Island in 1815.* De Leon Springs, Fla.: E. O. Painter Printing, 1983.

————. *Cumberland Island: A History.* Athens: University of Georgia Press, 2003.

————. "Ned Simmons, American Slave: The Role of Imagination in American History." *African Diaspora Newsletter,* 10, no. 2 (June 2007), article 7, https://scholarworks.umass.edu/adan/vol10/iss2/7.

Burnard, Trevor. "Ending with a Whimper, Not a Bang: The Relationship between Atlantic History and the Study of the Nineteenth-Century South." In *The American South and the Atlantic World,* edited by Brian Ward, Martyn Bone, and William A. Link, 129–48. Gainesville, University Press of Florida, 2013.

Bushnell, Amy Turner. "Republic of Spaniards, Republic of Indians." In *The New History of Florida,* edited by Michael Gannon, 62–77. Gainesville: University Press of Florida, 1996.

Byrd, Alexander X. *Captives and Voyagers: Black Migrants across the Eighteenth-Century British Atlantic World.* Baton Rouge: Louisiana State University Press, 2008.

Callaway, Colin G. "Cuscowilla: Seminole Loyalism and Seminole Genesis." In *The American Revolution in Indian Country: Crisis and Diversity in Native American Communities,* 244–71. Cambridge: Cambridge University Press, 1995.

Campbell, Archibald. *Journal of an Expedition against the Rebels of Georgia in North America under the Orders of Archibald Campbell, Esquire, Lieut. Colol. of this Majesty's 71st Regimt., 1778.* Edited by Colin Campbell. Darien, Ga.: Ashantilly Press, 1981.

Canny, Nicholas, and Philip Morgan. *The Oxford Handbook of the Atlantic World, 1450–1850.* Oxford: Oxford University Press, 2011.

Carey, Anthony Gene. *Sold down the River: Slavery in the Lower Chattahoochee Valley of Alabama and Georgia.* Tuscaloosa: University of Alabama Press, 2011.

Carney, Judith A. *Black Rice: The African Origins of Rice Cultivation in the Americas.* Cambridge, Mass.: Harvard University Press, 2001.

Carr, Madeleine Hirsiger. *Last Betrayal on the Wakulla: Florida's Forgotten Spanish Period.* [Morrisville, N.C.]: Lulu Publishing Services, 2019.

Carretta, Vincent. *Equiano, the African: Biography of a Self-Made Man.* Athens: University of Georgia Press, 2005.

Carrington, Selwyn H. H. "The American Revolution and the British West Indies Economy." *Journal of Interdisciplinary History* 17, no. 4 (Spring 1987): 823–50.

Cashin, Edward J. *The King's Ranger: Thomas Brown and the American Revolution on the Southern Frontier.* New York: Fordham University Press, 1999.

———. *Lachlan McGillivray, Indian Trader: The Shaping of the Southern Colonial Frontier.* Athens: University of Georgia Press, 1992.

———. "Sowing the Wind: Governor Wright and the Georgia Backcountry on the Eve of the Revolution." In *Forty Years of Diversity: Essays on Colonial Georgia,* edited by Harvey H. Jackson and Phinizy Spalding, 233–50. Athens: University of Georgia Press, 1984.

———. *William Bartram and the American Revolution on the Southern Frontier.* Columbia: University of South Carolina Press, 2000.

Cates, Gerald Lee. "A Medical History of Georgia: The First Hundred Years, 1733–1833." PhD diss., University of Georgia, 1976.

Caughey, John Walton. *McGillivray of the Creeks.* Columbia: University of South Carolina Press, 2007. First published 1938.

Cecelski, David S. *The Waterman's Song: Slavery and Freedom in Maritime North Carolina.* Chapel Hill: University of North Carolina Press, 2001.

Chapin, Joyce E. *An Anxious Pursuit: Agricultural Innovation and Modernity in the Lower South, 1730–1815.* Chapel Hill: University of North Carolina Press, 1993.

———. "Expansion and Exceptionalism in Early American History." *Journal of American History* 89, no. 4 (March 2003): 1431–55.

Chestnutt, David R. *South Carolina's Expansion into Colonial Georgia, 1720–1765.* New York: Garland, 1989.

Clark, George P. "The Role of the Haitian Volunteers at Savannah in 1779: An Attempt at an Objective View." *Phylon* 41, no. 4 (1980): 356–66.

Clavin, Matthew J. *Aiming for Pensacola: Fugitives on the Atlantic and Southern Frontiers.* Cambridge, Mass.: University of Harvard Press, 2015.

Coker, William S., and Thomas D. Watson. *Indian Traders of the Southeastern Spanish Borderlands: Panton, Leslie & Company and John Forbes & Company, 1783–1847.* Pensacola: University of West Florida Press, 1986.

Coldham, Peter Wilson. *American Migrations, 1765–1799.* Baltimore: Genealogical Publishing, 2000.

Coleman, Kenneth. *American Revolution in Georgia, 1763–1789.* Athens: University of Georgia Press, 1958.

———. *Colonial Georgia: A History.* Millwood, N.Y.: kto press, 1976.

———. "Henry Parker." In *Dictionary of Georgia Biography,* edited by Kenneth Coleman and Charles Stevens Gurr, 2:777–78. Athens: University of Georgia Press, 1983.

Collections of the Georgia Historical Society, vol. 3. Savannah: Morning News Office, 1873.

Collections of the Georgia Historical Society, vol. 5, part 1, *Proceedings of the First Provincial Congress of Georgia, 1775; Proceedings of the Georgia Council of Safety, 1775–1777; Account of the Siege of Savannah, 1779, from a British Source.* Savannah: Savannah Chapter of the Daughters of the American Revolution, 1901.

Collections of the Georgia Historical Society, vol. 6, *The Letters of the Hon. James Habersham, 1756–1775.* Savannah: Savannah Morning News Print, 1904.

Collections of the Georgia Historical Society, vol. 8, *Letters of Joseph Clay, Merchant of Savannah, 1776–1793.* Savannah: Savannah Morning News, 1913.

Collections of the Georgia Historical Society, vol. 9, *Letters of Benjamin Hawkins, 1796–1806.* Savannah: Savannah Morning News, 1916.

Collections of the Georgia Historical Society, vol. 10, *The Proceedings and Minutes of the Governor and Council of Georgia, October 4, 1774, through November 7, 1775, and September 6, 1779, through September 20, 1780.* Edited by Lilla Mills Hawes. Savannah: Georgia Historical Society, 1952.

Collections of the Georgia Historical Society, vol. 11, *The Papers of James Jackson, 1781–1798.* Edited by Lilla M. Hawes. Savannah: Georgia Historical Society, 1955.

Collections of the Georgia Historical Society, vol. 12, *The Papers of Lachlan McIntosh, 1774–1779.* Edited by Lilla M. Hawes. Savannah: Georgia Historical Society, 1957.

Collections of the Georgia Historical Society, vol. 17, *The Jones Family Papers, 1760–1810.* Edited by John Eddins Simpson. Savannah: [Georgia Historical] Society, 1976.

Collections of the Georgia Historical Society, vol. 19, *Checklist of Eighteenth Century Manuscripts in the Georgia Historical Society.* Compiled by Lilla Mills Hawes and Karen Elizabeth Oswald. Savannah: [Georgia Historical] Society, 1976.

Colonial Records of the State of Georgia, vol. 1. *By-Laws and Journal, 1732–1752.* Compiled by Allen D. Chandler. Atlanta: Franklin Printing Press, 1904.

Colonial Records of the State of Georgia, vol. 4. *William Stephens' Journal, 1737–1740.* Compiled by Allen Chandler. Atlanta: Franklin Printing, 1906.

Colonial Records of the State of Georgia, vol. 4 suppl., *Journal of Colonel William Stephens, 1740–1741.* Compiled by Allen D. Candler. Atlanta: Franklin Printing, 1908.

Colonial Records of the State of Georgia, vol. 10, *Proceedings and Minutes of the Governor and Council (January 6, 1767 to December 6, 1769).* Compiled by Allen D. Chandler. Atlanta: Franklin-Turner, 1907.

Colonial Records of the State of Georgia, vol. 12, *Proceedings and Minutes of the Governor and Council (August 6, 1771–February 13, 1782).* Compiled by Allen D. Candler. Atlanta: Franklin-Turner, 1907.

Colonial Records of the State of Georgia, vol. 14, *Journal of the Commons House of Assembly, (1763–1768).* Compiled by Allen D. Candler. Atlanta: Franklin-Turner, 1907.

Colonial Records of the State of Georgia, vol. 22, *Original Papers: Correspondence, Trustees, General Oglethorpe, and Others, 1737–1739.* Compiled by Allen D. Candler. Atlanta: Chas. P. Byrd, 1910.

Colonial Records of the State of Georgia, vol. 25, *Original Papers: Correspondence, Trustees, General Oglethorpe, and Others, 1745–1750.* Compiled by Allen D. Candler. Atlanta: Chas. P. Byrd, 1915.

Colonial Records of the State of Georgia, vol. 26, *Original Papers: Correspondence, Trustees, President and Assistants, and Others, 1750–1752.* Compiled by Allen D. Candler. Atlanta: Chas. P. Byrd, 1916.

Colonial Records of the State of Georgia, vol. 38. Part 2. Typescript, Georgia Archives and Georgia Historical Society, Savannah.

Colonial Records of the State of Georgia, vol. 39. "Letters, etc., General Oglethorpe and

Trustees, Governors Reynolds, Ellis and Wright, 1733–1783." Typescript, Georgia Archives and Georgia Historical Society, Savannah.

Cooksey, Elizabeth B. "Judaism and Jews." *New Georgia Encyclopedia*, https://www.georgiaencyclopedia.org/articles/arts-culture/judaism-and-jews.

Cooper, Melissa L. *Making Gullah: A History of Sapelo Islanders, Race, and the American Imagination*. Chapel Hill: University of North Carolina Press, 2017.

Coulter, E. Merton *Thomas Spalding of Sapelo Island*. Baton Rouge: Louisiana State University Press: 1940.

Covington, James W. *The Seminoles of Florida*. Gainesville: University Press of Florida, 1993.

Craton, Michael, and Gail Saunders. *Islanders in the Stream: A History of the Bahamian People*, vol. 1, *From Aboriginal Times to the End of Slavery*. Athens: University of Georgia Press, 1992.

Creel, Margaret Washington. *"A Peculiar People": Slave Religion and Community-Culture among the Gullah*. New York: New York University Press, 1988.

Cusick, James G. "Across the Border: Commodity Flow and Merchants in Spanish St. Augustine." *Florida Historical Quarterly* 69, no. 3 (January 1991): 277–99.

———. "Creolization and the Borderlands." *Historical Archaeology*. 34, no. 3 (2000): 46–55.

———. "King Payne and His Policies: A Framework for Understanding the Diplomacy of the Seminoles of La Chua, 1784–1812." In *America's Hundred Years' War: American Expansion to the Gulf Coast and the Fate of the Seminoles, 1763–1858*, edited by William S. Belko, 41–53. Gainesville: University Press of Florida, 2015.

———, transcriber. "Oaths of Allegiance, East Florida Papers, 1793–1804." Unpublished manuscript based on Oaths of Allegiance, 1790–1821, F.04, E13c, P. K. Yonge Library of Florida History, University of Florida.

———. *The Other War of 1812: The Patriot War and the American Invasion of Spanish East Florida*. Athens: University of Georgia Press, 2007.

———. "Some Thoughts on Spanish East and West Florida as Borderlands." *Florida Historical Quarterly* 90, no. 2 (Fall 2011): 133–56.

David, James Corbett. *Dunmore's New World: The Extraordinary Life of a Royal Governor in Revolutionary America, with Jacobites, Counterfeiters, Land Schemes, Shipwrecks, Scalping, Indian Politics, Runaway Slaves, and Two Illegal Royal Weddings*. Charlottesville: University of Virginia Press, 2013.

Davis, Harold E. *The Fledgling Province: Social and Cultural Life in Colonial Georgia, 1733–1776*. Chapel Hill: University of North Carolina Press, 1976.

Davis, Robert Scott. "Free but Not Freed: Stephen Deane's African Family in Early Georgia." *Georgia Historical Quarterly*, 97, no. 1 (Spring 2013): 61–72.

Davis, T. Frederick. "MacGregor's Invasion of Florida, 1817." *Florida Historical Quarterly* 7, no. 1 (July 1928): 2–71.

———. "United States Troops in Spanish Florida, 1812–1813, II." *Florida Historical Quarterly* 9, no. 2 (October 1930): 96–116.

———. "United States Troops in Spanish Florida, 1812–1813, III." *Florida Historical Quarterly* 9, no. 3 (January 1931): 135–55.

———. "United States Troops in Spanish Florida, 1812–1813, IV." *Florida Historical Quarterly* 9, no. 4 (April 1931): 259–78.

———. "United States Troops in Spanish Florida, 1812–1813, V." *Florida Historical Quarterly* 10, no. 1 (July 1931): 24–34.

De Vorsey, Louis, Jr., ed. *De Brahm's Report of the General Survey in the Southern District of North America and the Atlantic Pilot*. Columbia: University of South Carolina Press, 1971.

Din, Gilbert C. ———. *War on the Gulf Coast: The Spanish Fight against William Augustus Bowles*. Gainesville: University of Florida, 2012.

———. "William Augustus Bowles on the Georgia Frontier: A Reexamination of the Surrender of Fort San Marcos de Apalache, 1800." *Georgia Historical Quarterly* 88 (Fall 2004): 304–37.

———. "William Augustus Bowles on the Gulf Coast, 1787–1803: Unraveling a Labyrinthine Conundrum." *Florida Historical Quarterly* 89, no. 1 (Summer 2010): 1–25.

Diouf, Sylviane A. *Servants of Allah: African Muslims Enslaved in the Americas*. New York: New York University Press, 1998.

———. *Slavery's Exiles: The Story of the American Maroons*. New York: New York University Press, 2014.

Dubois, Laurent. *Avengers of the New World: The Story of the Haitian Revolution*. Cambridge, Mass.: Belknap Press of Harvard University Press, 2004.

Dubois, Laurent, and Julius S. Scott, eds. *Origins of the Black Atlantic*. Hoboken: Routledge, 2010.

Dusinberre, William. *Them Dark Days: Slavery in the American Rice Swamps*. Athens: University of Georgia Press, 2000.

DuVal, Kathleen. *Independence Lost: Lives on the Edge of the American Revolution*. New York: Random House, 2015.

Easterby, J. H., ed., *The Journal of the Commons House of Assembly, September 12, 1739–March 26, 1740*, vol. 3. Columbia: South Carolina Historical Commission, 1952.

Edelson, S. Max. *Plantation Enterprise in Colonial South Carolina*. Cambridge, Mass.: Harvard University Press, 2006.

———. "Visualizing the Southern Frontier: Cartography and Colonization in Eighteenth-Century Georgia." In *Coastal Nature, Coastal Culture: Environmental Histories of the Georgia Coast*, edited by Paul S. Sutter and Paul M. Pressly, 91–122. Athens: University of Georgia Press, 2018.

Edgar, Walter B., and N. Louis Bailey, eds. *Biographical Directory of the South Carolina House of Representatives*, vol 2, *The Commons House of Assembly, 1692–1775*. Columbia: University of South Carolina Press, 1977.

Egerton, Douglas R. *Gabriel's Rebellion: The Virginia Slave Conspiracies of 1800 and 1802*. Chapel Hill: University of North Carolina Press, 1993.

Ellicott, Andrew. *Journal of Andrew Ellicott*. Philadelphia: William Fry, 1814. Kislak collection, Library of Congress. Accessed April 4, 2021. https://www.loc.gov/resource/rbc0001.2007kislak01311/?sp=10.

Elliott, Daniel T. *Archaeological Investigations at Tabbies 1 and 2, North End Plantation, Ossabaw Island, Georgia*. LAMAR Institute publication series, report number 108. Savannah: LAMAR Institute, 2005.

Elliott, J. H. *Empires and of the Atlantic World: Britain and Spain in America, 1402–1830*. New Haven: Yale University Press, 2006.

Elliott, Rita Folse, and Dan T. Elliott. *Savannah under Fire, 1779: Expanding the Boundaries*. Savannah: Coastal Heritage Society, 2011.

Eltis, David, Philip Morgan, and David Richardson, "Agency and Diaspora in Atlantic History: Reassessing the African Contribution to Rice Cultivation in the Americas." *American Historical Review* 112, no. 5 (December 2007): 1329–58.

———. "Black, Brown, or White? Color-Coding American Commercial Rice Cultivation with Slave Labor." *American Historical Review*, 115, no. 1 (February 2010): 164–71.

Ethridge, Robbie. *Creek Country: The Creek Indians and Their World*. Chapel Hill: University of North Carolina Press, 2003.

Feeser, Andrea. *Red, White, and Black Make Blue: Indigo in the Fabric of Colonial South Carolina Life*. Athens: University of Georgia, 2013.

Feldman, Lawrence H. *Colonization and Conquest: British Florida in the Eighteenth Century*. Baltimore: Clearfield, 2009.

Ferguson, T. Reed. *The John Couper Family at Cannon's Point*. Macon: Mercer University Press, 1995.

Fleetwood, William C., Jr. *Tidecraft: The Boats of South Carolina, Georgia, and Northeastern Florida, 1550–1950*. Tybee Island, Ga.: WBG Marine Press, 1995.

Fogelman, Aaron Spencer. "The Transformation of the Atlantic World, 1776–1867." *Atlantic Studies* 6 (April 2009): 5–28.

Foner, Eric. *Gateway to Freedom: The Hidden History of the Underground Railroad*. New York: W. W. Norton, 2015.

Ford, Lacy K., *Deliver Us from Evil: The Slavery Question in the Old South*. Oxford: Oxford University Press, 2009.

Formwalt, Lee W. "Violence and Diplomacy in the Creek Country: Jack Kinnard, the Chehaw, and the United States Government in Late Eighteenth-Century Southwest Georgia." *Journal of Southwest Georgia History* 7 (1989–1992): 1–19.

Frank, Andrew K. "Red, Black, and Seminole: Community Convergence on the Florida Borderlands, 1780–1840." In *Borderland Narratives: Negotiation and Accommodation in North America's Contested Spaces, 1500–1850*, edited by Andrew K. Frank and A. Glenn Crothers (Gainesville: University Press of Florida, 2017): 46–67.

———. "Taking the State Out: Seminoles and Creeks in Late Eighteenth-Century Florida." *Florida Historical Quarterly* 84, no. 1 (Summer 2005): 10–27.

Frank, Andrew K., and A. Glenn Crothers. Introduction to *Borderland Narratives: Negotiation and Accommodation in North America's Contested Spaces, 1500–1850*, 1–17. Gainesville: University Press of Florida, 2017.

Franklin, John Hope, and Loren Schweninger. *Runaway Slaves: Rebels on the Plantation*. Oxford: Oxford University Press, 1999.

Fraser, Jr., Walter J., Jr. *Savannah in the Old South*. Athens: University of Georgia Press, 2003.

Frey, Sylvia R. "The British and the Black: A New Perspective." *Historian* 38, no. 2 (February 1976): 225–38.

———. *Water from the Rock: Black Resistance in a Revolutionary Age*. Princeton: Princeton University Press, 1991.

Frey, Sylvia R., and Betty Wood. *Come Shouting to Zion: African American Protestantism in the American South and British Caribbean to 1830*. Chapel Hill: University of North Carolina Press, 1998.

Gabaccia, Donna. "A Long Atlantic in a Wider World." *Atlantic Studies* 1 (2004): 1–27.

Gadsden, James. "The Defences of the Floridas: A Report of Captain James Gadsden, Aide-de-camp to General Jackson." *Florida Historical Quarterly*. 15, no. 4 (April 1937): 242–48.

Gallay, Alan. *The Formation of a Planter Elite: Jonathan Bryan and the Southern Colonial Frontier*. Athens: University of Georgia Press, 1989.

———. *The Indian Slave Trade: The Rise of the English Empire in the American South, 1670–1717*. New Haven: Yale University Press, 2002.

Games, Alison. "Atlantic History: Definitions, Challenges, and Opportunities." *American Historical Review* III, no. 3, (2006): 741–57.

Gannon, Michael, ed. *The New History of Florida*. Gainesville: University Press of Florida, 1996.

Garrigus, John D. "Catalyst or Catastrophe? Saint-Domingue's Free Men of Color and the Battle of Savannah, 1779–1782." *Review/Revista Interamericana* 22 (1992): 109–25.

Geggus, David Patrick. *Slavery, War, and Revolution: The British Occupation of Saint Domingue, 1793–1798*. New York: Clarendon Press, 1982.

———. "Slavery, War, and Revolution in the Greater Caribbean, 1789–1815." In *A Turbulent Time: The French Revolution and the Greater Caribbean*, ed. David Barry Gaspar and David Patrick Geggus, 1–50. Bloomington: Indiana University Press, 1997.

George, David. "An Account of the Life of Mr. David George, from Sierra Leone in Africa Given by Himself in Conversation with Brother Rippon of London, and Brother Pierce of Birmingham." *Baptist Annual Register* (1790): 473–84.

Giddings, Joshua R. *The Exiles of Florida, or, the Crimes Committed by Our Government against the Maroons, Who Fled from South Carolina and Other Slave States, Seeking Protection under Spanish Law*. Columbus, Ohio: Follett, Foster, 1858.

Gilbert, Alan. *Black Patriots and Loyalists: Fighting for Emancipation in the War for Independence*. Chicago: University of Chicago Press, 2012.

Gomez, Michael A. *Exchanging Our Country Marks: The Transformation of African Identities in the Colonial and Antebellum South*. Chapel Hill: University of North Carolina Press, 1998.

Gould, Elijah. "Entangled Histories, Entangled Worlds: The English-Speaking Atlantic as a Spanish Periphery." *American Historical Review* 112, no. 3 (January 2007): 764–86.

Granger, Mary, ed. *Savannah River Plantations*. 1947. Repr., Savannah, Ga.: Oglethorpe Press, 1997.

Grant, C. L., ed., *Letters, Journals and Writings of Benjamin Hawkins*. 2 vols. Savannah, Ga.: Beehive Press, 1980.

Gray, Lewis Cecil. *History of Agriculture in the Southern United States to 1860*. 2 vols. Gloucester, Mass.: Peter Smith, 1958.

Griffin, Patricia C. "Blue Gold: Andrew Turnbull's New Smyrna Plantation." In *Colonial Plantations and Economy in Florida*, edited by Jane G. Landers, 39–68. Gainesville: University Press of Florida, 2000.

———. "The Spanish Return: The People-Mix Period." In *The Oldest City: St. Augustine, Saga of Survival*, edited by George E. Buker and Jean Parker Waterbury, 125–50. St. Augustine, Fla.: St. Augustine Historical Society, 1983.

Grinberg, Keila. "Manumission." In *The Princeton Companion to Atlantic History*, edited by Joseph C. Miller, Vincent Brown, Jorge Canizares-Esguerra, Laurent Dubois, and Karen Ordahl Kupperman, 319–321. Princeton: Princeton University Press, 2015.

Hahn, Steven C. *The Invention of the Creek Nation, 1670–1763*. Lincoln: University of Nebraska Press, 2004.

Hall, Leslie. *Land and Allegiance in Revolutionary Georgia*. Athens: University of Georgia Press, 2001.

Hancock, David. *Citizens of the World: London Merchants and the Integration of the British Atlantic Community, 1735–1785*. New York: Cambridge University Press, 1997.

Handley, Scipio. "Claims and Memorials: Petition of Scipio Handley of South Carolina, January 13, 1784." On-Line Institute for Advanced Loyalist Studies. Accessed April 26, 2022, http://www.royalprovincial.com/military/mems/sc/clmhandley.htm.

Harman, Joyce Elizabeth. *Trade and Privateering in Spanish Florida, 1732–1763*. Tuscaloosa: University of Alabama Press, 1969.

Harris, Lynn B., *Patroons and Periaguas: Enslaved Watermen and Watercraft of the Lowcountry*. Columbia: University of South Carolina Press, 2014.

Hartridge, Walter C., Jr., ed. *The Letters of Don Juan McQueen to His Wife, Written from Spanish East Florida, 1791–1807*. Columbia, S.C.: Bostwick & Thornley, 1943.

———, ed. *The Letters of Robert Mackay to His Wife*. Athens: University of Georgia Press, 1949.

Hawes, Lilla Mills, ed. *Lachlan McIntosh Papers in the University of Georgia Libraries*. University of Georgia Libraries Miscellanea Publications, no. 7. Athens: University of Georgia Press, 1968.

———, ed. "Minute Book, Savannah Board of Police, 1779." *Georgia Historical Quarterly* 45 (1961), 245–257.

Haynes, Joshua S. *Patrolling the Border: Theft and Violence on the Creek-Georgia Frontier, 1770–1796*. Athens: University of Georgia Press, 2018.

Head, David. *Privateers of the Americas: Spanish American Privateers from the United States in the Early Republic*. Athens: University of Georgia Press, 2015.

Heckard, Jennifer. "The Crossroads of Empires: The 1817 Liberation and Occupation of Amelia Island, East Florida." PhD diss., University of Connecticut, 2006.

Heidler, David S. "The Politics of National Aggression: Congress and the First Seminole War." *Journal of the Early Republic* 13, no. 4 (Winter 1993): 501–30.

Herbert, Jason. "Alachua Seminole Identity and Autonomy, 1750–1776." *Florida Historical Quarterly* 100, no. 1 (summer 2021): 52–75.

Hiedler, David S., and Jeanne T. Hiedler. "Mr. Rhea's Missing Letter and the First Seminole War." In *America's Hundred Years' War*, edited by William S. Belko, 103–27. Tallahassee: University Press of Florida, 2011.

———. *Old Hickory's War: Andrew Jackson and the Quest for Empire*. Baton Rouge: Louisiana State University Press, 2003.

Hill, James L. *Creek Internationalism in an Age of Revolution, 1763–1818*. Lincoln: University of Nebraska Press, 2022.

———. "New Systems, Established Traditions: Governor James Grant's Indian Diplomacy and the Evolution of British Colonial Policy, 1760–1771." *Florida Historical Quarterly* 93, no. 2 (Fall 2014): 133–66.

Hoffer, Peter Charles. *Cry Liberty: The Great Stono River Slave Rebellion of 1739*. Oxford: Oxford University Press, 2012.

Hoffman, Paul E. *Florida's Frontiers*. Bloomington: Indiana University Press, 2002.

Howard, Rosalyn. "'Looking for Angola': An Archaeological and Ethnohistorical Search for a Nineteenth Century Florida Maroon Community and Its Caribbean Connections." *Florida Historical Quarterly* 92, no. 1 (Summer 2013): 32–68.

———. "The 'Wild Indians' of Andros Island: Black Seminole Legacy in the Bahama Islands." *Journal of Black Studies* 37, no. 2 (November 2006): 275–98.

Hudson, Angela Pulley. *Creek Paths and Federal Roads: Indians, Settlers, and Slaves and the Making of the American South*. Chapel Hill: University of North Carolina Press, 2010.

Isaac, Rhys L. *The Transformation of Virginia, 1740–1790.* Chapel Hill: University of North Carolina Press, 1982.

Ivers, Larry E. *British Drums on the Southern Frontier: The Military Colonization of Georgia, 1733–1749.* Chapel Hill: University of North Carolina Press, 1974.

Iverson, Justin. "Fugitives on the Front: Maroons in the Gulf Coast Borderlands War, 1812–1823." *Florida Historical Quarterly,* no. 2 (Fall 2019): 105–29.

Jackson, Harvey H. "The Battle of the Rice Boats: Georgia Joins the Revolution." *Georgia Historical Quarterly* 58 (June 1974): 229–43.

Jasanoff, Maya. *Liberty's Exiles: American Loyalists in the Revolutionary World.* New York: Vintage Books, 2011.

Jennison, Watson W. *Cultivating Race: The Expansion of Slavery in Georgia, 1750–1860.* Lexington: University Press of Kentucky, 2012.

Johnson, James M. *Militiamen, Rangers, and Redcoats: The Military in Georgia, 1754–1776.* Macon, Ga.: Mercer University Press, 1992.

Johnson, Sara E. *The Fear of French Negroes: Transcolonial Collaboration in the Revolutionary Americas.* Berkeley: University of California Press, 2012.

Johnson, Sherry. "East Florida Papers, 1784–1821." *Florida Historical Quarterly* 71, no. 1 (July 1992): 63–69.

———. "The Historiography of Eighteenth-Century Florida." *Florida Historical Quarterly* 93, no. 3 (Winter 2015): 296–326.

———. "The Spanish St. Augustine Community, 1784–1795: A Reevaluation." *Florida Historical Quarterly* 68, no. 1 (July 1989): 27–54.

Johnson, Walter. *Rivers of Dark Dreams: Slavery and Empire in the Cotton Kingdom.* Cambridge, Mass.: Harvard University Press, 2013.

Johnson, Whittington. *Black Savannah, 1784–1864.* Fayetteville: University of Arkansas Press, 1996.

Jones, Charles C., Jr., ed. *The Siege of Savannah in 1779 as Described in Two Contemporaneous Journals of French Officers in the Fleet of Count d'Estaing.* Albany, N.Y.: Joel Munsell, 1874.

Jones, Jacqueline. *Saving Savannah: The City and the Civil War.* New York: Alfred A. Knopf, 2008.

Joyner, Charles. *Down by the Riverside: A South Carolina Slave Community.* Urbana: University of Illinois Press, 1985.

Juricek, John T. *Colonial Georgia and the Creeks: Anglo-Indian Diplomacy on the Southern Frontier, 1733–1763.* Gainesville: University Press of Florida: 2010.

———. *Endgame for Empire: British-Creek Relations in Georgia and Vicinity, 1763–1776.* Gainesville: University Press of Florida, 2015.

Keber, Martha L. *Seas of Gold, Seas of Cotton: Christophe Poulain DuBignon of Jekyll Island.* Athens: University of Georgia Press, 2002.

Kennedy, Benjamin, ed., *Muskets, Cannon Balls and Bombs: Nine Narratives of the Siege of Savannah in 1779.* Savannah, Ga.: Beehive Press, 1974.

Kennedy, Roger G. *Burr, Hamilton, and Jefferson: A Study in Character.* Oxford: Oxford University Press, 2000.

Kilbourne, Elizabeth Evans, comp. *Savannah, Georgia, Newspaper Clippings ("Georgia Gazette"),* vol. 2, *1774–1785.* Savannah: E. E. Kilbourne, 1999.

Kingsley, Zephaniah, Jr. *A Treatise on the Patriarchal System, or The Cooperative System of Society.* 1829; repr., Freeport, N.Y.: Books for Libraries Press, 1970.

Kirkland, Thomas J., and Robert M. Kennedy. *Historic Camden: Colonial and Revolutionary*. Columbia, SC: State Company, 1905.

Klos, George. "Blacks and the Seminole Removal Debate." In *The African American Heritage of Florida*, edited by David R. Colburn and Jane L. Landers, 128–56. Gainesville: University Press of Florida, 1995.

Kokomoor, Kevin. "'Burning & Destroying All before Them': Creeks and Seminoles on Georgia's Revolutionary Frontier." *Georgia Historical Quarterly* 98, no. 4 (Winter 2014): 300–340.

———. "Creeks, Federalists, and the Idea of Coexistence in the Early Republic." *Journal of Southern History* 81, no. 4 (November 2015): 803–42.

———. "The Importance of the Oconee War in the Early Republic," *Georgia Historical Quarterly* 105, no. 1 (2021): 26–61.

———. *Of One Mind and of One Government: The Rise and Fall of the Creek Nation in the Early Republic*. Lincoln: University of Nebraska Press, 2018.

———. "A Re-assessment of Seminoles, Africans, and Slavery on the Florida Frontier." *Florida Historical Quarterly* 88, no. 2 (Fall 2009): 209–36.

Kole, Kaye. *The Minis Family of Georgia, 1733–1992*. Savannah: Georgia Historical Society, 1992.

Kozy, Charlene. "Tories Transplanted: The Caribbean Exile and Plantation Settlement of Southern Loyalists." *Georgia Historical Quarterly* 75, no. 1 (Spring 1991): 18–42.

Kuethe, Allan J., and Kenneth J. Andrien. *The Spanish Atlantic World in the Eighteenth Century: War and the Bourbon Reforms, 1713–1796*. Cambridge: Cambridge University Press, 2014.

Lambert, Frank. *James Habersham: Loyalty, Politics, and Commerce in Colonial Georgia*. Athens: University of Georgia Press, 2005.

Lamplugh, George R. *Politics on the Periphery: Factions and Parties in Georgia, 1783–1806*. Newark: University of Delaware Press, 1986.

Landers, Jane G. "Acquisition and Loss on a Spanish Frontier: The Free Black Homesteaders of Florida, 1784–1821." In *Against the Odds: Free Blacks in the Slave Societies of the Americas*. Portland, Ore.: Frank Cass, 1996.

———. "African-American Women and Their Pursuit of Rights through Eighteenth-Century Spanish Texts." In *Haunted Bodies: Gender and Southern Texts*, edited by Anne Goodwyn Jones and Susan V. Donaldson, 56–78. Charlottesville: University Press of Virginia, 1997.

———. "Africans in the Spanish Colonies." *Historical Archaeology* 31, no. 1, (1997): 84–103.

———, ed.

———. *Atlantic Creoles in the Age of Revolutions*. Cambridge, Mass.: Harvard University Press, 2010.

———. "The Atlantic Transformations of Francisco Menendez." In *Biography and the Black Atlantic*, edited by Lisa A. Lindsay and John Wood Sweet, 209–23. Philadelphia: University of Pennsylvania Press, 2014.

———. *Black Society in Spanish Florida*. Urbana: University of Illinois, 1999.

———. "An Eighteenth-Century Community in Exile: The Floridanos in Cuba." *New West Indian Guide* 70, no. 1/2 (1996): 39–58.

———. "Francisco Zavier Sanchez, Floridano Planter and Merchant." In *Colonial Plantations and Economy in Florida*, edited by Jane G. Landers, 83–97. Gainesville: University Press of Florida, 2000.

————. "Gracia Real de Santa Teresa de Mose: A Free Black Town in Spanish Colonial Florida." *American Historical Review* 95, no. 1 (February 1990): 9–30.

————. "A Nation Divided? Blood Seminoles and Black Seminoles on the Florida Frontier." In *Coastal Encounters: The Transformation of the Gulf South in the Eighteenth Century*, edited by Richard F. Brown, 99–116. Lincoln: University of Nebraska Press, 2007.

————. "Rebellion and Royalism in Spanish Florida: The French Revolution on Spain's Northern Colonial Frontier." In *A Turbulent Time: The French Revolution and the Greater Caribbean*, edited by David Barry Gaspar and David Patrick Geggus, 156–77. Bloomington: Indiana University Press, 1997.

————. "Slavery in the Spanish Caribbean and the Failure of Abolition." *Review* (Fernand Braudel Center) 31, no. 3 (2008), 343–71.

————. "Spanish Sanctuary: Fugitives in Florida, 1687–1790." *Florida Historical Quarterly* 62, no. 3 (September 1984): 296–313.

————. "Traditions of African American Freedom and Community." In *The African American Heritage of Florida*, edited by David R. Colburn and Jane L. Landers, 17–41. Gainesville: University Press of Florida, 1995.

————. "Transforming Bondsmen into Vassals: Arming Slaves in Colonial Spanish America." In *Arming Slaves from Classical Times to the Modern Age, edited by* Christopher Leslie Brown and Philip D. Morgan, 120–45. New Haven: Yale University Press, 2006.

Lane, Mills. *General Oglethorpe's Georgia: Colonial Letters, 1738–1743*. 2 vols. Savannah: Beehive Press, 1975.

————. *The People of Georgia: An Illustrated History*. Savannah: Beehive Press, 1992.

Lannen, Andrew C. "James Oglethorpe and the Civil-Military Contest for Authority in Colonial Georgia, 1732–1749." *Georgia Historical Quarterly* 95 (Summer 2011): 203–31.

Laurens, Henry. *The Papers of Henry Laurens*, vol. 2. Edited by Philip M. Hamer and George C. Rogers Jr.. Columbia: University of South Carolina Press, 1970.

Laurens, Henry. *The Papers of Henry Laurens*, vol. 11. Edited by David R. Chestnutt and C. James Taylor. Columbia: University of South Carolina Press, 1988.

Lawrence, Alexander A. *Storm over Savannah: The Story of Count d'Estaing and the Siege of the Town in 1779*. Athens: University of Georgia Press, 1951.

Lewis, James A. "Cracker—Spanish Florida Style." *Florida Historical Quarterly* 63 (October 1984): 184–204.

Lipscomb, Terry W. *The Letters of Pierce Butler: 1790–1794: Nation Building and Enterprise in the New American Republic*. Columbia: University of South Carolina Press, 2007.

Littlefield, Daniel C., Jr. *Africans and Creeks: From the Colonial Period to the Civil War*. Westport, Conn.: Greenwood Press, 1979.

————. *Rice and Slaves: Ethnicity and the Slave Trade in Colonial South Carolina*. Urbana: University of Illinois Press, 1981.

Lockey, Joseph Byrne. *East Florida, 1783–1785: A Collection of Documents Assembled and Many of Them Translated*. Berkeley: University of California Press, 1949.

Lockley, Timothy James. "'The King of England's Soldiers': Armed Blacks in Savannah and Its Hinterlands during the Revolutionary War Era, 1778–1787." In *Slavery and Freedom in Savannah*, edited by Leslie M. Harris and Daina Ramey Berry, 26–41. Athens: University of Georgia Press, 2014.

———. *Maroon Communities in South Carolina: A Documentary Record.* Columbia: University of South Carolina Press, 2009.

Lockley, Timothy, and David Doddington. "Maroon and Slave Communities in South Carolina before 1865." *South Carolina Historical Magazine* 113, no. 2 (April 2012): 125–45.

Logan, William. "William Logan's Journal of a Trip to Georgia, 1745." *Pennsylvania Magazine of History and Biography* 36, no. 2 (1912): 162–86.

Lokken, Paul. "Useful Enemies: Seventeenth-Century Piracy and the Rise of Pardo Militias in Spanish Central America." *Journal of Colonialism and Colonial History* 5, no. 2 (2004). https://muse.jhu.edu/issue/9289.

Louisbury, Carl R. "Savannah: Loopholes in Metropolitan Design on the Frontier." In *Material Culture in Anglo-America: Regional Identity and Urbanity in the Tidewater, Lowcountry, and Caribbean,* edited by David S. Shields, 58–73. Columbia: University of South Carolina Press, 2009.

Lynch, John. *Bourbon Spain, 1700–1708.* Oxford: Oxford University Press, 1989.

Mahon, John K. "The First Seminole War: November 21, 1817–May 24, 1818." *Florida Historical Quarterly* 77, no. 1 (Summer 1998): 62–67.

———. *History of the Second Seminole War, 1835–1842.* Gainesville, Fla.: Library Press, 1967.

Mahon, John K., and Brent R. Weisman. "Florida's Seminole and Miccosukee Peoples." In *The New History of Florida,* edited by Michael Gannon. 183–206. Gainesville, Fla.: University Press of Florida, 1996.

Marotti, Frank. *Heaven's Soldiers: Free People of Color and the Spanish Legacy in Antebellum Florida.* Tuscaloosa: University of Alabama Press, 2013.

Marsh, Ben. *Georgia's Frontier Women: Female Fortunes in a Southern Colony.* Athens: University of Georgia Press, 2007.

Martin, John. "Official Letters of Governor John Martin, 1782–1783." *Georgia Historical Quarterly* 1, no. 4 (December 1917): 334–35.

McCash, June Hall. *Jekyll Island's Early Years: From Prehistory through Reconstruction.* Athens: University of Georgia Press, 2005.

McCrady, Edward. *South Carolina in the Revolution.* New York: Macmillan, 1901.

McDonough, Mark. *The Francis Richard Family: From French Nobility to Florida Pioneers, 1300–1900.* Lulu.com, 2010.

McIlraith, John. *Life of Sir John Richardson.* London: N.p., 1868.

McIlvenna, Noeleen. *The Short Life of Free Georgia: Class and Slavery in the Colonial South.* Chapel Hill: University of North Carolina Press, 2015.

McIntosh, George. *The Case of George M'Intosh, Esquire, a Member of the Late Council and Convention of the State of Georgia: With the Proceedings Thereon in the Hon. the Assembly and Council of That State.* Georgia Legislature, 1777.

McMillin, James A. *The Final Victims: Foreign Slave Trade to North America, 1783–1810.* Columbia: University of South Carolina Press, 2004.

———. "The Transatlantic Slave Trade Comes to Georgia." In *Slavery and Freedom in Savannah,* edited by Leslie M. Harris and Daina Ramey Berry, 1–25. Athens: University of Georgia Press, 2014.

McMichael, Andrew. *Atlantic Loyalties: Americans in Spanish West Florida, 1785–1810.* Athens: University of Georgia Press, 2008.

Meyers, Christopher C. *The Empire State of the South: Georgia History in Documents and Essays.* Macon, Ga.: Mercer University Press, 2008.

Miles, Tiya. "Haunted Waters: Stories of Slavery, Coastal Ghosts, and Environmental Consciousness." In *Coastal Nature, Coastal Culture: Environmental Histories of the Georgia Coast*, edited by Paul S. Sutter and Paul M. Pressly, 149–74. Athens: University of Georgia Press, 2018.

———. *Ties That Bind: The Story of an Afro-Cherokee Family in Slavery and Freedom*. Oakland: University of California Press, 2015.

Miller, Janice Borton *Juan Nepomuceno de Quesada, Governor of Spanish East Florida, 1790–1795*. Washington, D.C.: University Press of America, 1981.

———. "The Rebellion in East Florida in 1795." *Florida Historical Quarterly* 57 (October 1978): 173–86.

———. "The Struggle for Free Trade in East Florida and the Cedula of 1793." *Florida Historical Quarterly* 55, no. 1 (July 1976): 48–59.

Millett, Nathaniel. "Defining Freedom in the Atlantic Borderlands of the Revolutionary Southeast." *Early American Studies* 5, no. 2 (Fall 2007): 367–94.

———. *The Maroons of Prospect Bluff and Their Quest for Freedom in the Atlantic World*. Gainesville: University Press of Florida, 2013.

———. "The Radicalism of the First Seminole War and Its Consequences." In *Warring for America: Cultural Contests in the Era of 1812*, edited by Nicole Eustace and Fredrika J. Teute, 164–202. Chapel Hill: University of North Carolina Press, 2017.

Mitchell, Robert G. "Losses and Compensation of Georgia Loyalists." *Georgia Historical Quarterly* 68, no. 2 (Summer 1984): 233–43.

Monaco, Chris. "Fort Mitchell and the Settlement of the Alachua Country." *Florida Historical Quarterly* 79, no. 1 (Summer 2000): 1–25.

Moore, Francis. *A Voyage to Georgia Begun in the Year 1735*. Jacksonville, Fla.: Fort Frederica Association, 1992.

Morgan, Philip D. "Black Society in the Lowcountry, 1760–1780." In *Slavery and Freedom in the Age of the American Revolution*, edited by Ira Berlin and Ronald Hoffman, 83–142. Charlottesville: University Press of Virginia, 1983.

Morgan, Philip D. "Colonial South Carolina Runaways: Their Significance for Slave Culture." In *Out of the House of Bondage: Runaways, Resistance and Marronage in Africa and the New World*, edited by Gad Heuman, 57–78. London: Routledge, 2016.

———. "Lowcountry Georgia and the Early Modern Atlantic World, 1733–ca. 1820." In *African American Life in the Georgia Lowcountry: The Atlantic World and the Gullah Geechee*, edited by Philip Morgan, 13–47. Athens: University of Georgia Press, 2010.

———. *Slave Counterpoint: Black Culture in the Eighteenth-Century Chesapeake and Lowcountry*. Chapel Hill: University of North Carolina Press, 1998.

———. "Work and Culture: The Task System and the World of Lowcountry Blacks, 1700 to 1880." *William and Mary Quarterly* 39, no. 4 (October 1982): 563–99.

Morgan, Philip D., and Andrew Jackson O'Shaughnessy. "Arming Slaves in the American Revolution." In *Arming Slaves from Classical Times to the Modern Age*, edited by Christopher Leslie Brown and Philip D. Morgan, 180–208. New Haven: Yale University Press, 2006.

Morrill, Dan E. *Southern Campaigns of the American Revolution*. Mount Pleasant, S.C.: Nautical & Aviation Publishing, 1999.

Morris, Michael. "Dreams of Glory, Schemes of Empire: The Plan to Liberate Spanish East Florida." *Georgia Historical Quarterly* 87, no. 1 (Spring 2003): 1–21.

———. *George Galphin and the Transformation of the Georgia–South Carolina Backcountry*. New York: Lexington Books, 2015.

Mowat, Charles Loch. *East Florida as a British Province, 1763–1784*. Gainesville: University of Florida Press, 1964.

Mulcahy, Matthew. *Hubs of Empire: The Southeastern Lowcountry and British Caribbean*. Baltimore: Johns Hopkins University Press, 2014.

Mullins, Michael. *Africa in America: Slave Acculturation and Resistance in the American South and the British Caribbean, 1736–1831*. Champaign: University of Illinois Press, 1995.

Mulroy, Kevin. *Freedom on the Border: The Seminole Maroons in Florida, the Indian Territory, Coahuila, and Texas*. Lubbock: Texas Tech University Press, 1993.

Murdoch, Richard K. "The Case of the Spanish Deserters, 1791–1793." *Georgia Historical Quarterly* 44, no. 3 (Sept. 1960): 278–305.

———. *The Georgia-Florida Frontier, 1793–1796: Spanish Reactions to French Intrigue and American Designs*. Berkeley: University of California Press, 1951.

———. "Governor Cespedes and the Religious Problem in East Florida, 1786–1787." *Florida Historical Quarterly* 26, no. 4 (April 1948): 325–44.

———. "The Return of Runaway Slaves, 1790–1794." *Florida Historical Quarterly*, 38, no. 2 (October 1959): 96–113.

Murdoch, Richard K., and Juan de Pierra. "The Seagrove-White Stolen Property Agreement of 1797." *Georgia Historical Society* 42, no. 3 (September 1958): 258–76.

Narrative of a Voyage to the Spanish Main in the Ship "Two Friends": The Occupation of Amelia Island by M'Gregor, &c, Sketches of the Province of East Florida, and Anecdotes Illustrative of the Habits and Manners of the Seminoles. London: printed for John Miller, 1819.

Narrett, David. *Adventurism and Empire: The Struggle for Mastery in the Louisiana-Florida Borderlands, 1762–1803*. Chapel Hill: University of North Carolina Press, 2015.

Nash, Gary. "The African Americans' Revolution." *The Oxford Handbook of the American Revolution*, edited by Edward C. Gray and Jane Kamensky, 250–72. Oxford: Oxford University Press, 2013.

———. *The Forgotten Fifth: African Americans in the Age of Revolution*. Cambridge: Harvard University Press, 2006.

Nash, R. C. "South Carolina Indigo, European Textiles, and the British Atlantic Economy in the Eighteenth Century." *English Economic History*, 63, no. 2 (May 2010), 362–92.

Nelson, Megan Kate. *Trembling Earth: A Cultural History of the Okefenokee Swamp*. Athens: University of Georgia Press, 2005.

Nelson, Paul David. *Anthony Wayne: Soldier of the Early Republic*. Bloomington: Indiana University Press, 1985.

Nevius, Marcus P. *City of Refuge: Slavery and Petit Marronage in the Great Dismal Swamp, 1765–1856*. Athens: University of Georgia Press, 2020.

Nichols, David Andrew. *Red Gentlemen and White Savages: Indians, Federalists, and the Search for Order on the American Frontier*. Charlottesville: University of Virginia Press, 2008.

Norton, Mary Beth. *The British-Americans: The Loyalist Exiles in England, 1774–1789*. Boston: Little, Brown, 1972.

Nuño, John Paul. "'Republica de Bandidos': The Prospect Bluff Fort's Challenge to the Spanish Slave System." *Florida Historical Quarterly* 94, no. 2 (Fall 2015): 192–221

Oatis, Steven J. *A Colonial Complex: South Carolina's Frontiers in the Era of the Yamasee War.* Lincoln: University of Nebraska Press, 2004.

Olwell, Robert. *Masters, Slaves, and Subjects: The Culture of Power in the South Carolina Low Country, 1740–1790.* Ithaca: Cornell University Press, 1998.

O'Malley, Gregory E. *Final Passages: The Intercolonial Slave Trade of British North America, 1619–1807.* Chapel Hill: University of North Carolina Press, 2014.

———. "Beyond the Middle Passage: Slave Migration from the Caribbean to North America, 1619–1807." *William and Mary Quarterly* 3rd series, 66, no. 1 (January 2009): 125–72.

O'Riordan, Cormac A. "The 1795 Rebellion in East Florida." Master's thesis, University of North Florida, 1995. https://digitalcommons.unf.edu/etd/99.

Ostler, Jeffrey and Nancy Shoemaker. "Settler Colonialism in Early American History: Introduction." *William and Mary Quarterly* 76, No. 3 (July 2019), 361–68.

Owsley, Frank Lawrence. *Struggle for the Gulf Borderlands: The Creek War and the Battle of New Orleans, 1812–1815.* Tuscaloosa: University of Alabama Press, 1981, 2000.

Owsley, Frank Lawrence, Jr., and Gene A. Smith, eds. *Filibusters and Expansionists: Jeffersonian Manifest Destiny, 1800–1821.* Tuscaloosa: University of Alabama Press, 1997.

Panagopoulos, E. P. *New Smyrna: An Eighteenth Century Greek Odyssey.* Gainesville: University of Florida Press, 1966.

Pargas, Damian Alan. *Freedom Seekers: Fugitive Slaves in North America, 1800–1860.* Cambridge: Cambridge University Press, 2022.

———, ed. *Fugitive Slaves and Spaces of Freedom in North America.* Gainesville: University Press of Florida, 2018.

Parker, Susan R. "Men without God or King: Rural Settlers of East Florida, 1784–1790." *Florida Historical Quarterly* 69, no. 2 (October 1990): 135–55.

———. "St. Augustine in the Seventeenth-Century: Capital of La Florida," *Florida Historical Quarterly* 92, no. 3 (Winter 2014): 554–76.

———. "So in Fear of Both the Indians and the Americans." In *America's Hundred Years' War: American Expansion to the Gulf Coast and the Fate of the Seminoles, 1763–1858,* edited by William S. Belko, 25–40. Gainesville: University Press of Florida, 2015.

Parkinson, Robert G. *The Common Cause: Creating Race and Nation in the American Revolution.* Chapel Hill: University of North Carolina Press, 2016.

Patrick, Rembert W. *Florida Fiasco: Rampant Rebels on the Georgia-Florida Border, 1810–1815.* Athens: University of Georgia Press, 1954.

Patterson, Orlando. "Slavery and Slave Revolts: A Sociohistorical Analysis of the First Maroon War, 1665–1740." In *Maroon Societies: Rebel Slave Communities in the Americas,* edited by Richard Price, 246–92. Baltimore: Johns Hopkins University Press, 1996.

Paulett, Robert. *An Empire of Small Places: Mapping the Southeastern Anglo-Indian Trade, 1732–1795.* Athens: University of Georgia Press, 2012.

Percoco, James A. "The British Corps of Colonial Marines: African Americans Fight for their Freedom." American Battlefield Trust, 2022. n.d. https://www.battlefields.org/learn/articles/british-corps-colonial-marines.

Piecuch, Jim. *Three Peoples, One King: Loyalists, Indians, and Slaves in the American Revolution.* Columbia: University of South Carolina Press, 2008.

Porcher, Richard Dwight, and Sarah Fick. *The Story of Sea Island Cotton.* Charleston, S.C.: Wyrick, 2005.

Porter, Kenneth W. *The Black Seminoles: History of a Freedom-Seeking People*. Gainesville: University Press of Florida, 1996.

———. "Negroes and the East Florida Annexation Plot, 1811–1813." *Journal of Negro History*, 30, no. 1 (January 1945): 9–29.

Pressly, Paul M. "The Many Worlds of Titus: Marronage, Freedom, and the Entangled Borders of Lowcountry Georgia and Spanish Florida." *Journal of Southern History* 84, no. 1 (August 2018): 545–78.

———. *On the Rim of the Caribbean: Colonial Georgia and the British Atlantic World*. Athens: University of Georgia Press, 2013.

Price, Richard, ed. *Maroon Societies: Rebel Slave Communities in the Americas*. Baltimore: Johns Hopkins University Press, 1976.

———. "Maroons." In *The Princeton Companion to Atlantic History*, edited by Joseph C. Miller, Vincent Brown, Jorge Canizares-Esguerra, Laurent Dubois, and Karen Ordahl Kupperman, 326–29. Princeton: Princeton University Press, 2015.

Pybus, Cassandra. *Epic Journeys of Freedom: Runaway Slaves of the American Revolution and Their Global Quest for Liberty*. Boston: Beacon Press, 2006.

———. "Jefferson's Faulty Math: The Question of Slave Defections in the American Revolution." *William and Mary Quarterly* 3rd series, 62, no. 2, (April 2005): 243–64.

Raab, James W. *Spain, Britain, and the American Revolution in Florida, 1763–1783*. Jefferson, N.C., McFarland, 2008.

Ramsey, William L. *The Yamasee War: A Study of Culture, Economy, and Conflict in the Colonial South*. Lincoln: University of Nebraska Press, 2008.

Ready, Milton L. *The Castle Builders: Georgia's Economy under the Trustees, 1732–1754*. New York: Arno Press, 1978.

Reddick, Marguerite, comp. *Camden's Challenge: A History of Camden County, Georgia*. [Woodbine, Ga.]: Camden Historical Commission, 1976.

Rediker, Marcus. *Between the Devil and the Deep Blue Sea: Merchant Seamen, Pirates, and the Anglo-Maritime World, 1700–1750*. Cambridge: Cambridge University Press, 2006.

Reese, Trevor R., ed., *The Clamorous Malcontents: Criticisms and Defenses of the Colony of Georgia, 1741–1743*. Savannah: Beehive Press, 1973.

———. *Frederica: Colonial Fort and Town: Its Place in History*. St. Simons Island, Ga.: Fort Frederica Association, 1969.

Reigelsperger, Diana. "Early Eighteenth Century Contraband Trade and Slave Smuggling between Spanish Florida and the British Colonies." Paper presented at the Southern Historical Association, St. Petersburg, Florida, November 2016.

Revolutionary Records of the State of Georgia. 3 vols. Compiled by Allen D. Candler. Atlanta: Franklin-Turner, 1908.

Riley, Sandra. *Homeward Bound: A History of the Bahama Islands to 1850*. Miami: Island Research, 1983.

Rindfleisch, Bryan C. *George Galphin's Intimate Empire: the Creek Indians, Family, and Colonialism in Early America*. Tuscaloosa: University of Alabama Press, 2019.

Riordan, Patrick. "Finding Freedom in Florida: Native Peoples, African Americans, and Colonists, 1670–1816." *Florida Historical Quarterly* 75, n. 1 (Summer 1996): 24–43.

———. "Seminole Genesis: Native Americans, African Americans, and Colonists on the Southern Frontier from Prehistory through the Colonial Era." PhD diss., University of Florida, 1996.

Rivers, Larry Eugene. *Rebels and Runaways: Slave Resistance in Nineteenth-Century Florida*. Urbana: University of Illinois Press, 2013.

———. *Slavery in Florida: Territorial Days to Emancipation*. Gainesville: University Press of Florida, 2000.

Romans, Bernard. *A Concise Natural History of East and West Florida*. Edited by Kathryn E. Holland Braund. Tuscaloosa: University of Alabama Press, 1999.

Rowland, Lawrence S., Alexander Moore, and George C. Rogers Jr., eds. *The History of Beaufort County, South Carolina*. 2 vols. Columbia: University of South Carolina Press, 1996.

Rupert, Linda M. "Marronage, Manumission, and Maritime Trade in the Early Modern Atlantic." *Slavery and Abolition* 30, no. 3 (September 2009): 361–82.

Rupert, Linda M. *Creolization and Contraband: Curacao in the Early Modern Atlantic World*. Athens: University of Georgia Press, 2012.

Russell, David Lee. *Oglethorpe and Colonial Georgia: A History, 1733–1783*. Jefferson, NC: McFarland, 2006.

Saunt, Claudio. *Black, White, and Indian: Race and the Unmaking of an American Family*. New York: Oxford University Press, 2005.

———. "'The English Has Now a Mind to Make Slaves of Them All': Creeks, Seminoles, and the Problem of Slavery." *American Indian Quarterly* 22, nos. 1–2 (Winter/Spring 1998): 157–80.

———. *A New Order of Things: Property, Power, and the Transformation of the Creek Indians, 1733–1816*. Cambridge: Cambridge University Press, 1999.

Scarborough, Ruth. The *Opposition to Slavery in Georgia Prior to 1860*. Nashville: Georgia Peabody College for Teachers, 1933.

Schafer, Daniel L. "'A Class of People neither Freemen nor Slaves': From Spanish to American Race Relations in Florida, 1821–1861." *Journal of Social History* 26, no. 3 (Spring 1993): 587–609.

———. *Governor James Grant's Villa: A British East Florida Indigo Plantation*. Escribano 37. St. Augustine: St. Augustine Historical Society, 2000.

———. "'. . . not so gay a Town in America as this . . .': St. Augustine, 1763–1784." In *The Oldest City: St. Augustine, Saga of Survival*, edited by George E. Buker and Jean Parker Waterbury, 91–124. St. Augustine: St. Augustine Historical Society, 1983.

———. *St. Augustine's British Years, 1763–1784*. St. Augustine: St. Augustine Historical Society, 2001.

———. "'Yellow Silk Ferret Tied round Their Wrists': African Americans in British East Florida, 1763–1784." In *The African American Heritage of Florida*, edited by David R. Colburn and Jane L. Landers, 71–103. Gainesville: University Press of Florida, 1995.

———. *Zephaniah Kingsley Jr. and the Atlantic World: Slave Trader, Plantation Owner, Emancipator*. Gainesville: University Press of Florida, 2013.

Schmitt, Casey. "Virtue in Corruption: Privateers, Smugglers, and the Shape of Empire in the Eighteenth-Century Caribbean." *Early American Studies: An Interdisciplinary Journal* 13, no. 1 (2015): 80–110.

Scott, J. T. *The First Families of Frederica: Their Lives and Locations*. Athens, Ga.: J. T. Scott, 1985.

Scott, Julius S. *The Common Wind: Afro-American Currents in the Age of the Haitian Revolution*. London: Verso, 2018.

Searcy, Martha Condray. "The Introduction of African Slavery into the Creek Indian Nation." *Georgia Historical Quarterly* 66, no. 1 (Spring 1982): 21–32.

———. *The Georgia-Florida Contest in the American Revolution, 1776–1778.* Tuscaloosa: University of Alabama Press, 1985.

———. "1779: The First Year of the British Occupation of Georgia." *Georgia Historical Quarterly* 67 (Summer 1983): 168–88.

Siebert, Wilbur Henry. "East Florida as a Refuge for Southern Loyalists, 1774–1785." *Proceedings of the American Antiquarian Society* 37, pt. 2 (October 1927): 226–46.

———. *Loyalists in East Florida, 1774 to 1785.* 2 vols. DeLand: Florida State Historical Society, 1929.

———. "Slavery in East Florida, 1776 to 1785." *Florida Historical Quarterly* 10, no. 3 (1932): 139–61.

Simmons, William Hayne. *Notices of East Florida with an Account of the Seminole Nation of Indians.* Charleston, S.C.: J. D. Miller, 1822.

Smith, Gene Allen. *The Slaves' Gamble: Choosing Sides in the War of 1812.* New York: Palgrave MacMillan, 2013.

Smith, Mark M. "Time, Religion, Rebellion." In *Stono: Documenting and Interpreting a Southern Slave Revolt*, 108–23. Columbia: University of South Carolina Press, 2005.

Smith, Robert W. *Amid a Warring World: American Foreign Relations, 1775–1815.* Washington, D.C.: Potomac World, 2012.

Snyder, Christina. "Conquered Enemies, Adopted Kin, and Owned People: The Creek Indians and Their Captives." *Journal of Southern History* 73, no. 2 (May 2007): 255–88.

———. *Slavery in Indian Country: The Changing Face of Captivity in Early America.* Cambridge, Mass.: Harvard University Press, 2010.

Snyder, Jennifer K. "Revolutionary Refugees: Black Flight in the Age of Revolution." In *The American South and the Atlantic World*, edited by Brian Ward, Martyn Bone, and William A. Link, 81–103. Gainesville: University Press of Florida, 2013.

———. "Revolutionary Repercussions: Loyalist Slaves in St. Augustine and Beyond." In *The Loyal Atlantic: Remaking the British Atlantic in the Revolutionary Era*, edited by Jerry Bannister and Liam Riordan, 165–84. Toronto: University of Toronto Press, 2012.

Sollors, Werner, ed. *The Interesting Narrative of the Life of Olaudah Equiano, or Gustavus Vassa, the African, Written by Himself.* New York: W. W. Norton, 2001.

Spalding, Phinizy. "James Edward Oglethorpe's Quest for an American Zion." In *Forty Years of Diversity: Essays on Colonial Georgia*, edited by Harvey H. Jackson and Phinizy Spalding, 60–79. Athens: University of Georgia Press, 1984.

Sparks, Randy J. *Africans in the Old South: Mapping Exceptional Lives across the Atlantic World.* Cambridge, Mass.: Harvard University Press, 2016.

Stephens, William. *A Journal of the Proceedings in Georgia.* 2 vols. [New York]: Readex Microprint, 1966.

———. *The Journal of William Stephens: 1741–1745.* 2 vols. Edited by E. Merton Coulter. Athens: University of Georgia Press, 1958–1959.

Stewart, Mart A. *"What Nature Suffers to Groe": Life, Labor, and Landscape on the Georgia Coast, 1620–1920.* Athens: University of Georgia Press, 1996.

Sugden, John. *Tecumseh: A Life.* New York: Henry Holt, 1999.

Sullivan, Buddy. *Sapelo: People and Place on a Georgia Sea Island.* Athens: University of Georgia Press, 2017.

———. *Thomas Spalding: Antebellum Planter of Sapelo.* Cedar Point, Ga.: N.p., 2019.

Swan, Caleb. "Position and State of Manners and Arts in the Creeks, or Muscogee Nation in 1791." In *Information Respecting the History, Condition, and Prospects of the Indian tribes of the United States*, edited by Henry R. Schoolcraft and S. Eastman, 5:250–83. Philadelphia: Lippincott and Grambo, 1855.

Sweet, Julie Anne. "Battle of Bloody Marsh." In *New Georgia Encyclopedia*. Accessed July 30, 2023. https://www.georgiaencyclopedia.org/articles/history-archaeology/battle-of-bloody-marsh.

———. *Negotiating for Georgia: British-Creek Relations in the Trustee Era, 1733–1752*. Athens: University of Georgia Press, 2005.

———. *William Stephens: Georgia's Forgotten Founder*. Baton Rouge: Louisiana State University Press, 2010.

Tanner, Helen Hornbeck. "The Second Spanish Period Begins." In *Clash between Cultures: Spanish East Florida, 1784–1827*, edited by Jacqueline K. Fretwell and Susan R. Parker, 15–42. Escribano. St. Augustine, Fla.: St. Augustine Historical Society, 1988.

———. *Zespedes in East Florida, 1784–1790*. Jacksonville: University of North Florida Press, 1989.

Taylor, Alan. *American Revolutions: A Continental History, 1750–1804*. New York: W. W. Norton, 2016.

———. *The Civil War of 1812: American Citizens, British Subjects, Irish Rebels, and Indian Allies*. New York: Vintage Books, 2011.

———. *The Internal Enemy: Slavery and War in Virginia, 1772–1832*. New York: W. W. Norton, 2013.

Temple, Sarah Gober, and Kenneth Coleman. *Georgia's Journeys, 1732–1754*. Athens: University of Georgia Press, 1961.

TePaske, John J. "The Fugitive Slave: Intercolonial Rivalry and Spanish Slave Policy, 1687–1764." In *Eighteenth-Century Florida and Its Borderlands*, edited by Samuel Proctor, 1–22. Gainesville: University Press of Florida, 1975.

———. *The Governorship of Spanish Florida, 1700–1763*. Durham: Duke University Press, 1964.

Thayer, Theodore. *Nathanael Greene: Strategist of the American Revolution*. New York: Twayne, 1960.

Thompson, Amanda D. Roberts. "People, Place, and Taskscapes of Enslavement: African American Life on the South End Plantation, Ossabaw Island, Georgia 1849–1861." PhD diss. University of York, 2020.

Thompson, Alvin O. *Flight to Freedom: African Runaways and Maroons in the Americas*. Kingston, Jamaica: University of West Indies Press, 2006.

Thornton, John R. "African Dimensions of the Stono Rebellion." *American Historical Review* 96, n. 4 (October 1991): 1101–13.

Troxler, Carole Watterson. "Loyalist Refugees and the British Evacuation of East Florida, 1783–85." *Florida Historical Quarterly* 60, no. 1 (July 1981): 1–28.

———. "Refuge, Resistance, and Reward: The Southern Loyalists' Claim on East Florida." *Journal of Southern History* 55, no. 4 (November 1989): 563–96.

———. "The Uses of the Bahamas by Southern Loyalist Exiles." In *The Loyal Atlantic: Remaking the British Atlantic in the Revolutionary Era*, edited by Jerry Bannister, Liam Riordan, 185–207. Toronto: University of Toronto Press, 2012.

Walker, Timothy D., ed. *Sailing to Freedom: Maritime Dimensions of the Underground Railroad*. Amherst: University of Massachusetts Press, 2021.

Ward, Christopher. "The Commerce of East Florida during the Embargo, 1806–1812: The Role of Amelia Island." *Florida Historical Quarterly* 68, no. 2 (October 1989): 160–79.

Waselkov, Gregory A. *A Conquering Spirit: Fort Mims and the Redstick War of 1813–1914.* Tuscaloosa: University of Alabama Press, 2006.

Waselkov, Gregory A., and Kathryn E. Holland Braund, eds. *William Bartram on the Southeastern Indians.* Lincoln: University of Nebraska Press, 1995.

Waselkov, Gregory A., Peter H. Wood, and Tom Hartley, eds. *Powhatan's Mantle: Indians in the Colonial Southeast.* Lincoln: University of Nebraska, 1989.

Weber, David J. *The Spanish Frontier in North America.* New Haven: Yale University Press, 1992.

Weir, Robert M. *Colonial South Carolina: A History.* Columbia: University of South Carolina Press, 1997.

Weisman, Brent Richards. "The Background and Continued Cultural and Historical Importance of the Seminole Wars in Florida." *FIU Law Review* 9, no. 2 (Spring 2014): 391–404.

———. *Florida's Seminole and Miccosukee Indians: Unconquered People.* Gainesville: University Press of Florida, 1999.

———. *Like Beads on a String: A Culture History of the Seminole Indians in North Peninsular Florida.* Tuscaloosa: University of Alabama Press, 1989.

———. "Nativism, Resistance, and Ethnogenesis of the Florida Seminole Indian Identity." *Historical Archaeology* 41, no. 4 (2007): 198–212.

———. "The Plantation System of the Florida Seminole Indian and Black Seminoles during the Colonial Era." In *Colonial Plantations and Economy in Florida*, edited by Jane G. Landers, 136–49. Gainesville: University of Florida Press, 2000.

Wheeler, Mary Bray. *Eugenia Price's South: A Guide to the People and Places of Her Beloved Region.* Franklin, Tenn.: Providence House, 2005.

Williams, Linda K. "East Florida as a Loyalist Haven." *Florida Historical Quarterly* 54, no. 4 (April 1976): 465–78.

Willis, William Scott. "A Swiss Settler in East Florida: A Letter of Francis Philip Fatio." *Florida Historical Quarterly* 64, no. 2 (October 1985): 174–88.

Wilson, T. D. *The Oglethorpe Plan: Enlightenment Design and Beyond.* Charlottesville: University of Virginia Press, 2015.

Windley, Lathan, comp. *Runaway Slave Advertisements: A Documentary History from the 1730s to 1790.* 4 vols. Westport, Conn.: Greenwood Press, 1983.

Wood, Betty. "High Notions of their Liberty:' Women of Color and the American Revolution in Lowcountry Georgia and South Carolina, 1765–1785." In *African American Life in the Georgia Lowcountry: The Atlantic World and the Gullah Geechee*, edited by Philip Morgan, 48–76. Athens: University of Georgia Press, 2010.

———. *Slavery in Colonial Georgia: 1730–1775.* Athens: University of Georgia Press, 1984.

———. "Some Aspects of Female Resistance to Chattel Slavery in Low Country Georgia, 1763–1815." *Historical Journal* 30, n. 3 (September 1987): 603–22.

———. *Women's Work, Men's Work: The Informal Slave Economies of Lowcountry Georgia.* Athens: University of Georgia Press, 1995.

Wood, Gordon S. *Empire of Liberty: A History of the Early Republic, 1789–1815.* New York: Oxford University Press, 2009.

Wood, Peter H. *Black Majority: Negroes in Colonial South Carolina from 1670 through the Stono Rebellion.* New York: W. W. Norton, 1974.

———. "The Changing Population of the Colonial South: An Overview by Race and Region, 1685–1790." In *Powhatan's Mantle: Indians in the Colonial Southeast*, edited by Gregory A. Waselkow, Peter H. Wood, and Tom Hatley, 57–132. Lincoln: University of Nebraska Press, 2006.

Wood, Virginia Steele. *Live Oaking: Southern Timber for Tall Ships*. Annapolis: Naval Institute Press, 1981.

Woodward, Thomas Simpson. *Woodward's Reminiscences of the Creek, or Muscogee Indians, Contained in Letters to Friends in Georgia and Alabama*. Montgomery, Ala.: Harrett & Wimbish, 1859.

Wright, J. Leitch, Jr. *Anglo-Spanish Rivalry in North America*. Athens: University of Georgia Press, 1971.

———. "Blacks in British East Florida." *Florida Historical Quarterly* 54, no. 4 (April 1976): 425–42.

———. "British Designs on the Old Southwest: Foreign Intrigue on the Florida Frontier, 1783–1803." *Florida Historical Quarterly* 44, no. 4 (April 1966): 265–84.

———. "Creek-American Treaty of 1790: Alexander McGillivray and the Diplomacy of the Old Southwest." *Georgia Historical Quarterly* 51, no. 4 (December 1967): 379–400.

———. *Creeks and Seminoles*. Lincoln: University of Nebraska Press, 1986.

———. *Florida in the American Revolution*. Gainesville: University Presses of Florida, 1975.

———. "Lord Dunmore's Loyalist Asylum in the Floridas." *Florida Historical Quarterly* 49, no. 4 (April 1971): 370–79.

———. *William Augustus Bowles, Director-General of the Creek Nation*. Athens: University of Georgia Press, 1967.

Wylly, Charles Spalding. *Annals and Statistics of Glynn County, Georgia*. Brunswick, Ga.: H. A. Wrench and Sons, 1897.

Young, Alfred F. and Gregory H. Nobles. *Whose American Revolution Was It? Historians Interpret the Founding*. New York: New York University Press, 2011.

INDEX

Locators in italics indicate a figure. Enslaved individuals with identical names are differentiated by additional information in parentheses.

EARLY AMERICAN PLACES

Printed in the USA
CPSIA information can be obtained
at www.ICGtesting.com
CBHW022326020724
11059CB00002B/45